Shojo Beat

VAMPIRE KNIGHT

Story & Art by
Matsuri
Hino

Vol. 8

VAMPIRE KNIGHT

Contents

The Story of VAMPIRE KNIGHT

1 Cross Academy, a private boarding school, is where the Day Class and the Night Class coexist. The Night Class—a group of beautiful elite students—are all vampires!

2 Four years ago, when his twin brother Ichiru turned against him, Zero was turned into a vampire by Shizuka. Kaname kills Shizuka, but she hints there is another evil. Yuki tries to regain her memories, but mysterious powers prevent her from doing so.

3 Yuki questions Kaname about her past and he says he'll tell her about her past if she becomes his lover... Kaname treats Yuki as if he is protecting her from something. Shiki returns to the Academy with his body possessed by Rido. Rido claims to be the true head of the Kuran family. When Yuki tries to probe her memories, she hallucinates and sees blood. Then Kaname comes to her...

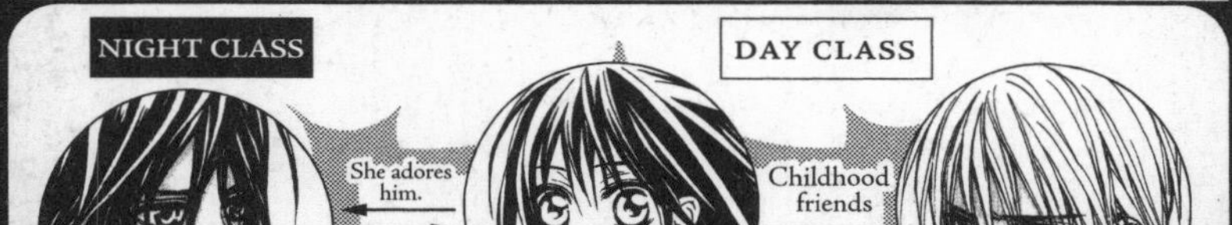
NIGHT CLASS
DAY CLASS
She adores him.
He saved her 10 years ago.
Childhood friends
Foster Father
KANAME KURAN
Night Class President and pureblood vampire. Yuki adores him.
TAKUMA ICHIJO
Night Class Vice President. He and Kaname are old friends.
YUKI CROSS
The heroine. The adopted daughter of the Headmaster, and a Guardian who protects Cross Academy. She has no memories of herself prior to 10 years ago.
ZERO KIRYU
Yuki's childhood friend, and a Guardian. Shizuka turned him into a vampire. He will eventually lose his sanity, falling to Level E.
HEADMASTER CROSS
NIGHT CLASS STUDENTS
COUSINS
HANABUSA AIDO
Nickname: Idol
AKATSUKI KAIN
Nickname: Wild
SENRI SHIKI
He does things at his own pace.
ICHIRU
Zero's younger twin brother. He transferred to the Academy after Shizuka's death.
❊Purebloods are vampires who do not have a single drop of human blood in their lineage. They are very powerful, and they can turn humans into vampires by drinking their blood.

Yuki suffers, searching for her lost memories

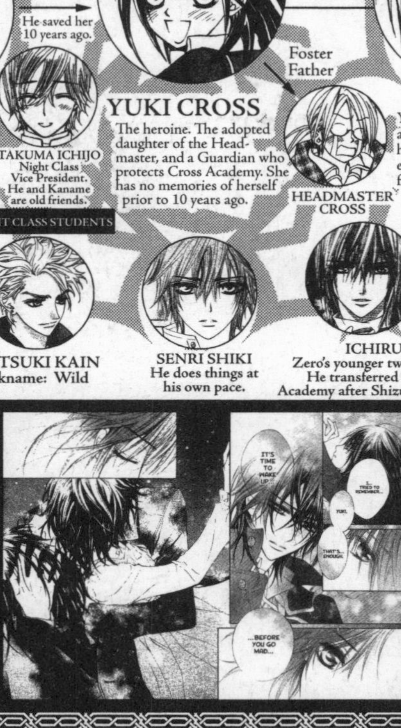
I... TRIED TO REMEMBER...
IT'S TIME TO WAKE UP...
YUKI.
THAT'S... ENOUGH.
...BEFORE YOU GO MAD...

Kaname's fangs sink into her neck!!

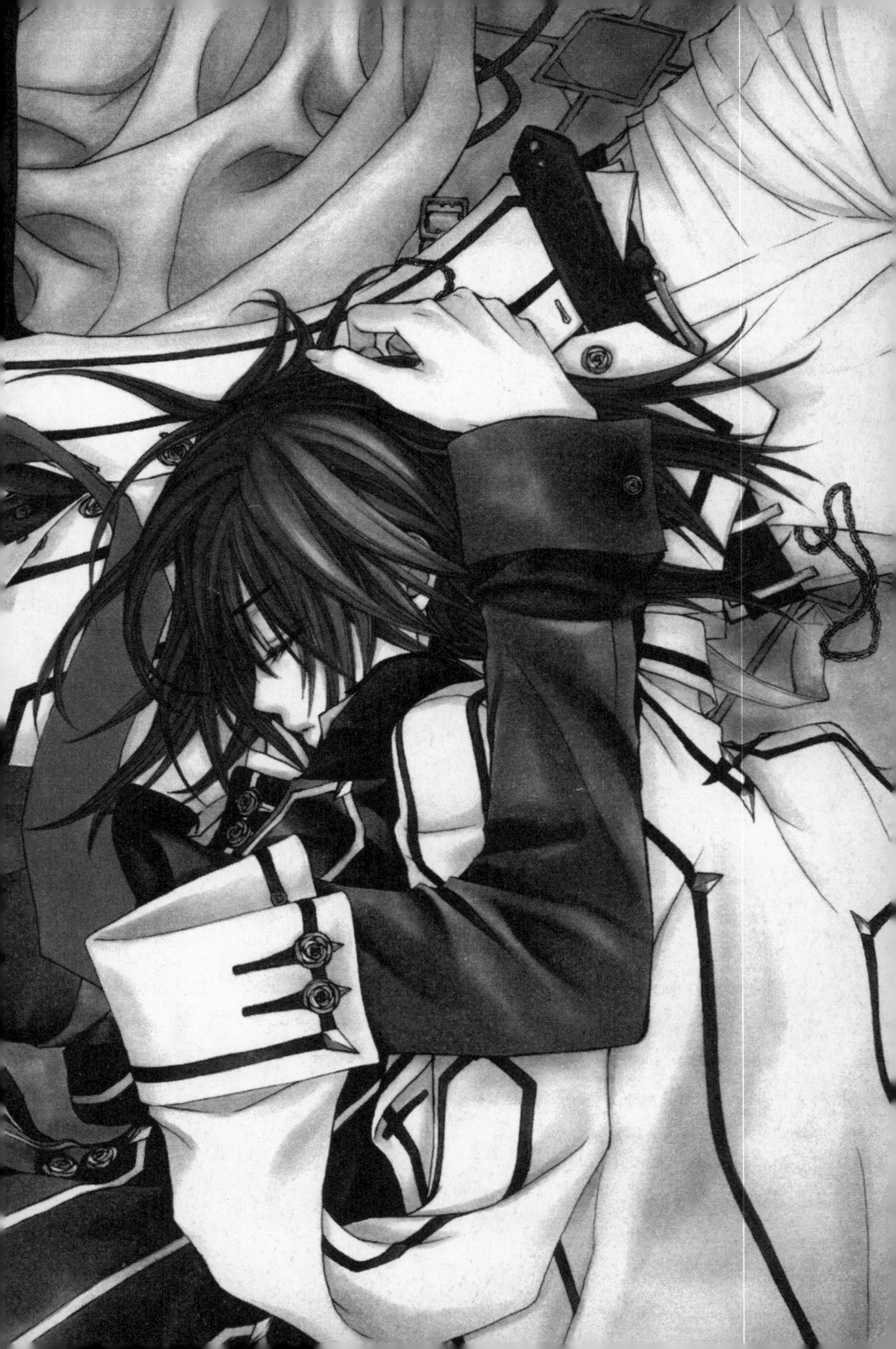

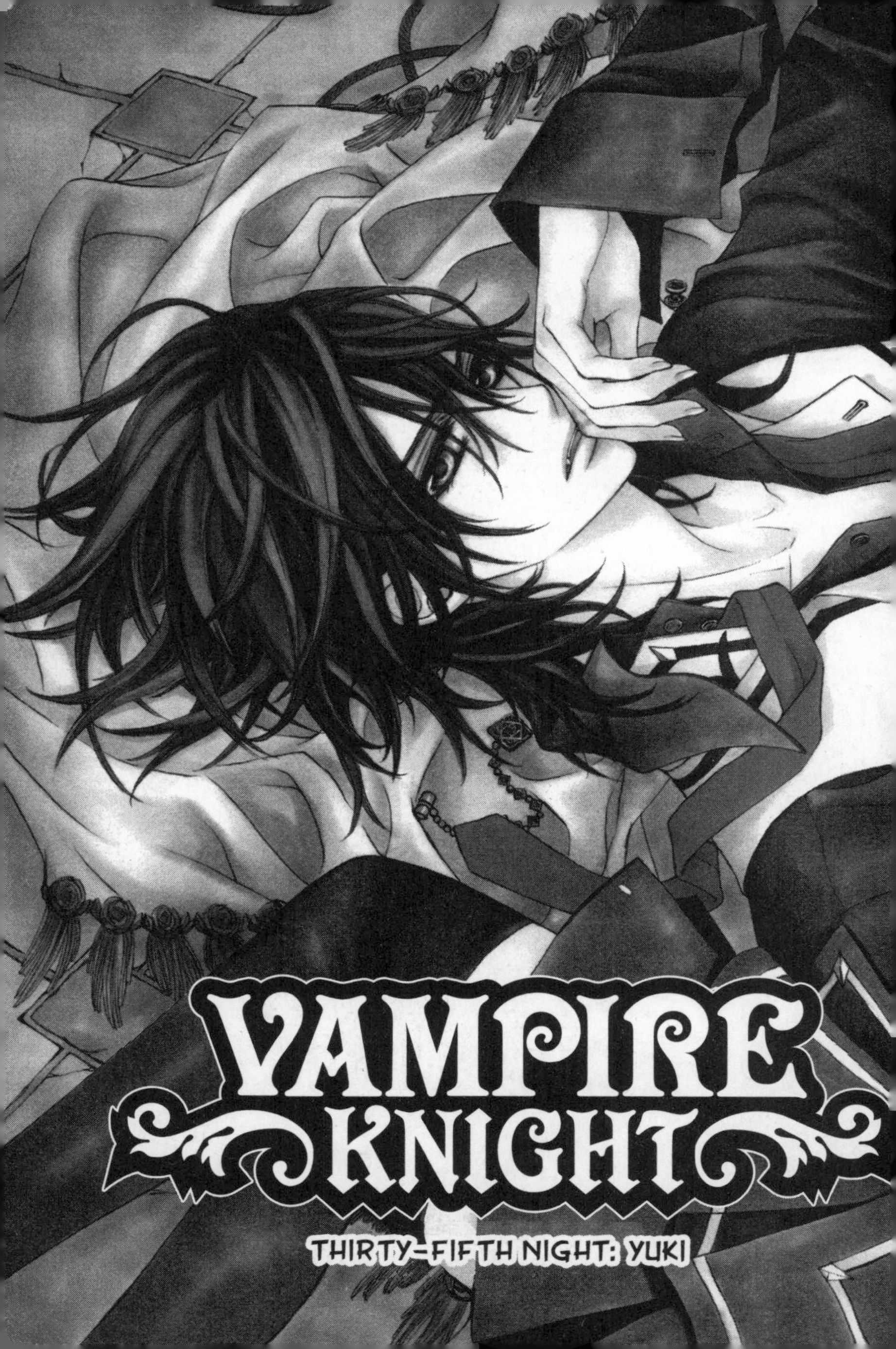
VAMPIRE
KNIGHT
THIRTY-FIFTH NIGHT: YUKI

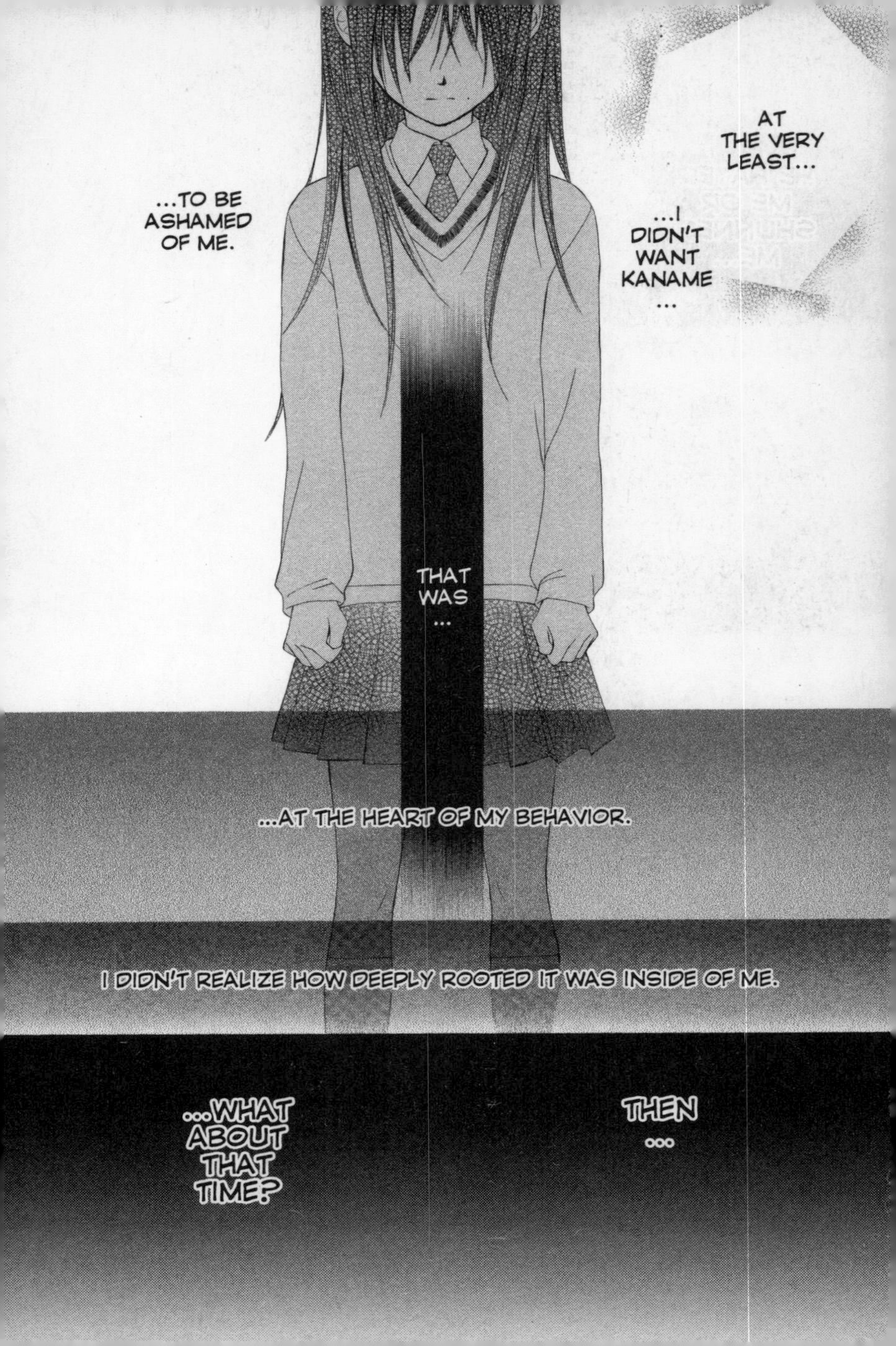
AT THE VERY LEAST...
...I DIDN'T WANT KANAME...
...TO BE ASHAMED OF ME.
THAT WAS...
...AT THE HEART OF MY BEHAVIOR.
I DIDN'T REALIZE HOW DEEPLY ROOTED IT WAS INSIDE OF ME.
THEN...
...WHAT ABOUT THAT TIME?

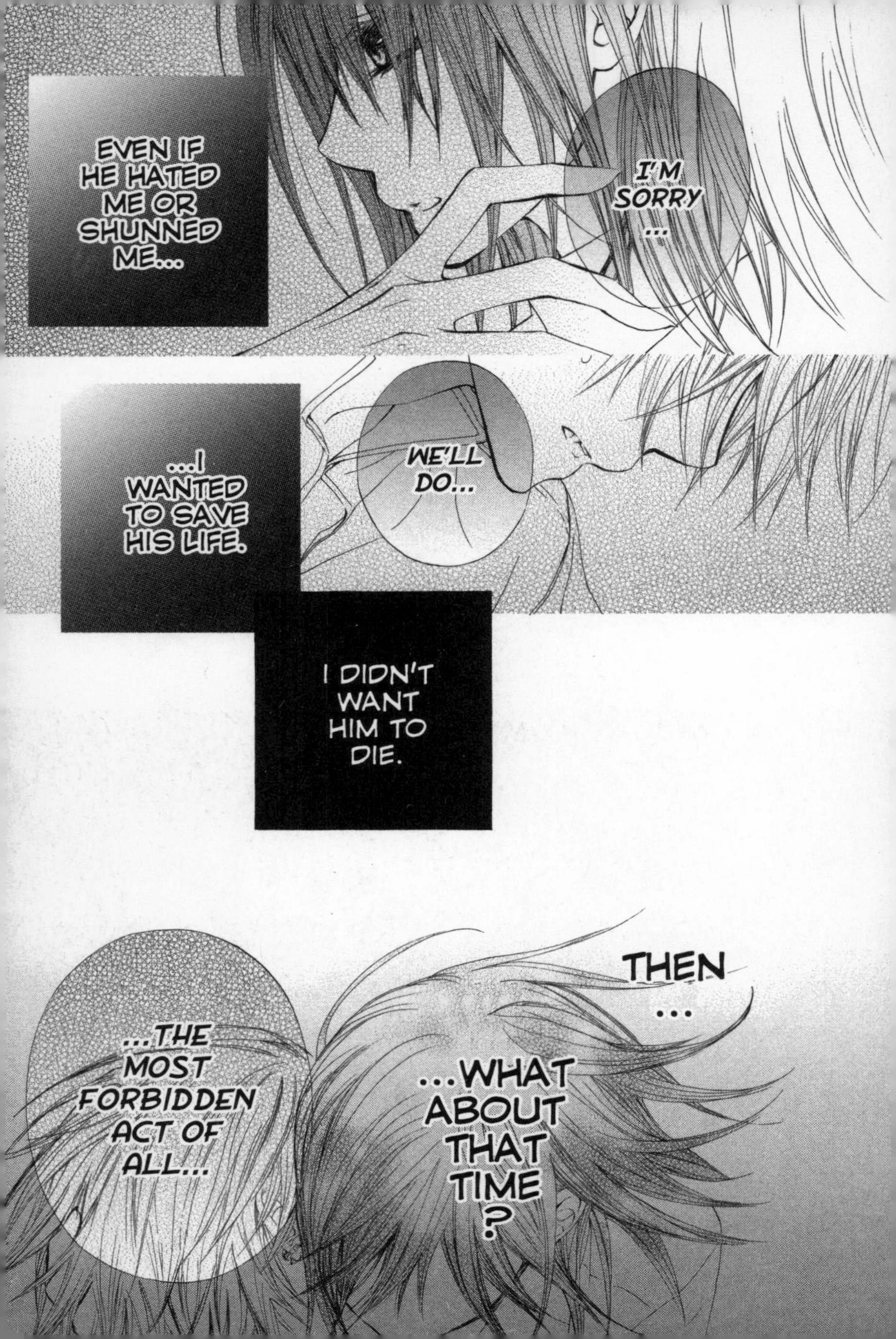
I'M SORRY ...
EVEN IF HE HATED ME OR SHUNNED ME...
WE'LL DO...
...I WANTED TO SAVE HIS LIFE.
I DIDN'T WANT HIM TO DIE.
THEN ...
...WHAT ABOUT THAT TIME ?
...THE MOST FORBIDDEN ACT OF ALL...

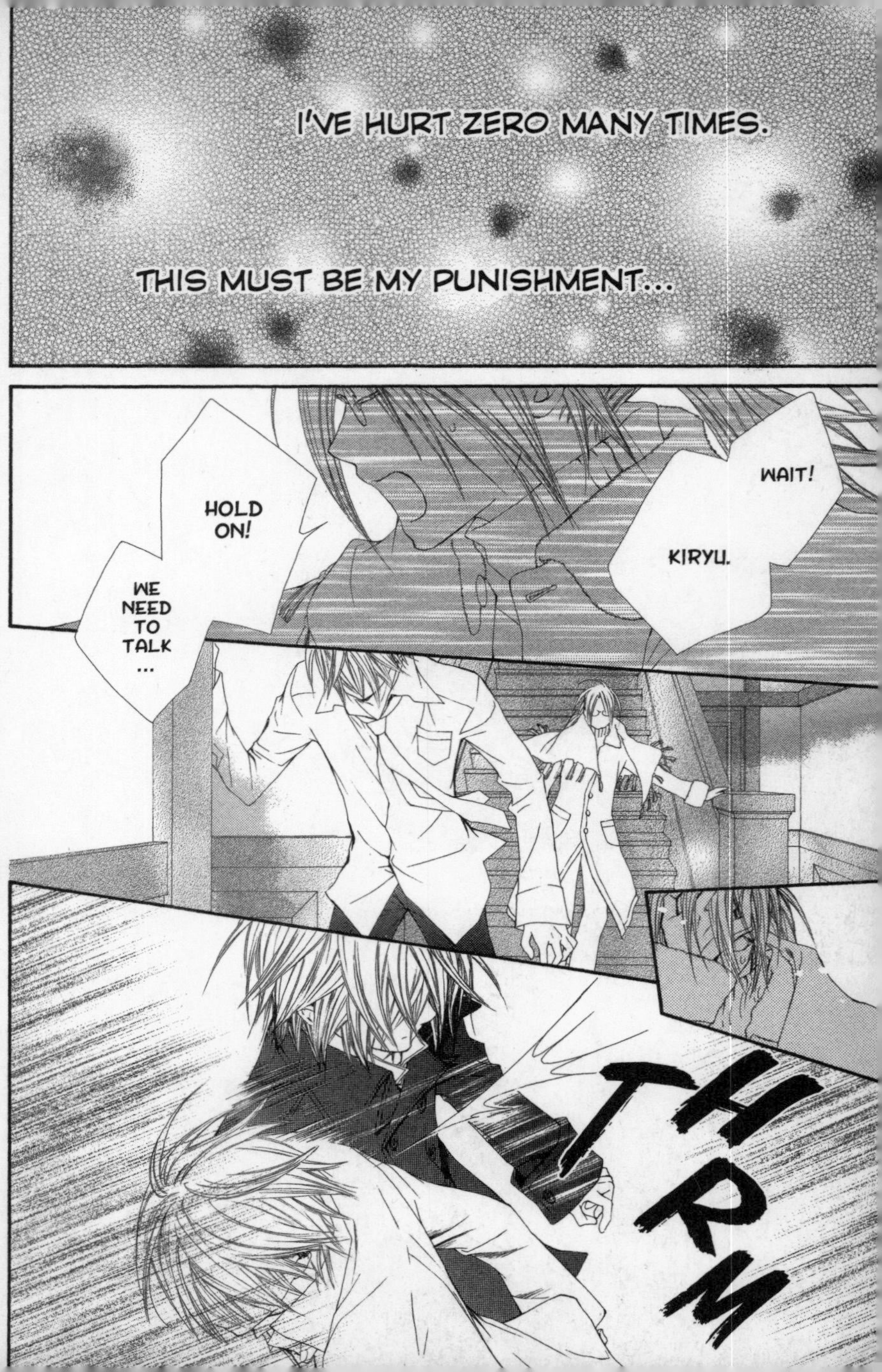
I'VE HURT ZERO MANY TIMES.
THIS MUST BE MY PUNISHMENT...
WAIT!
KIRYU.
HOLD ON!
WE NEED TO TALK...
THRM

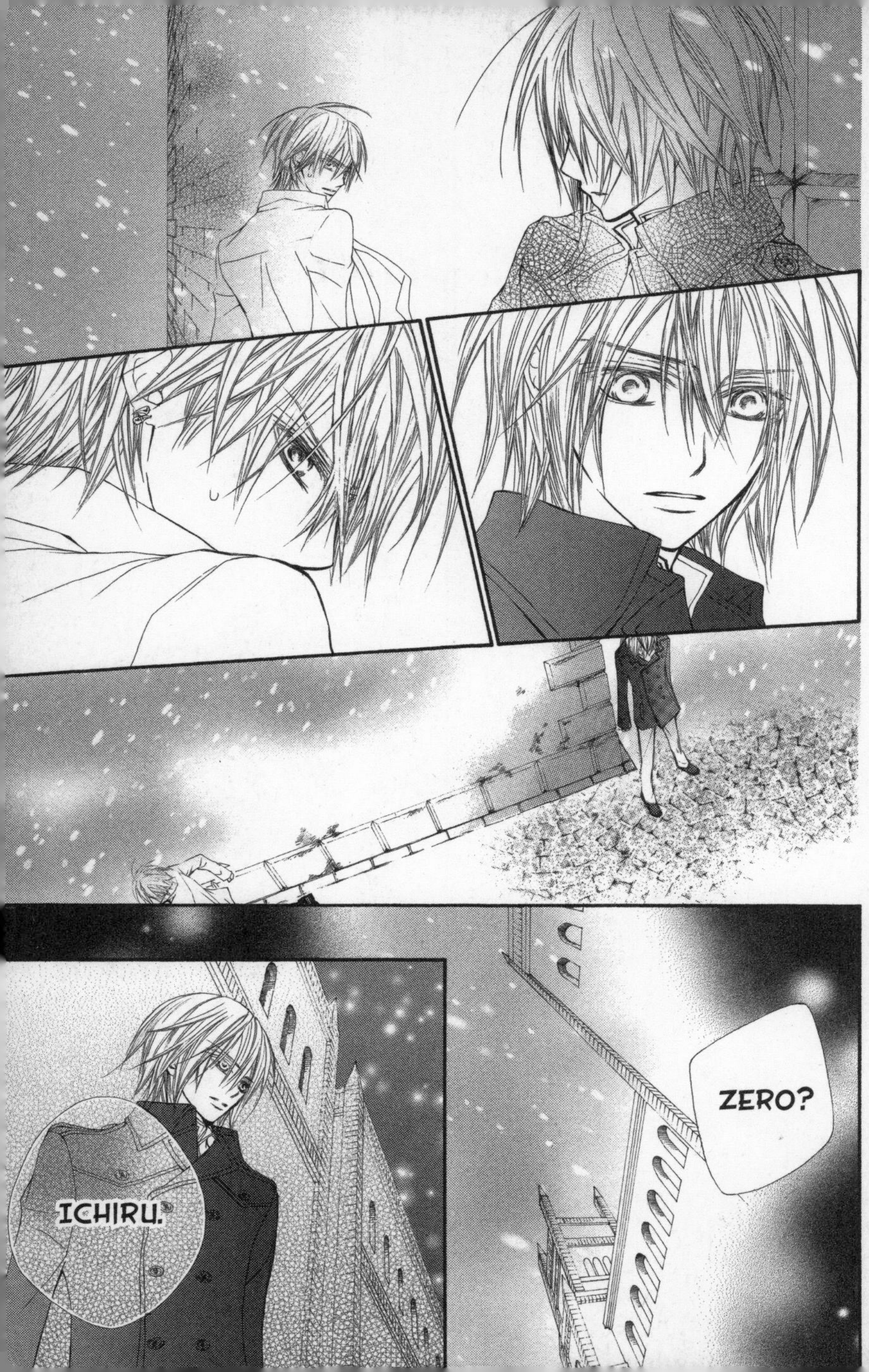
ZERO?
ICHIRU.

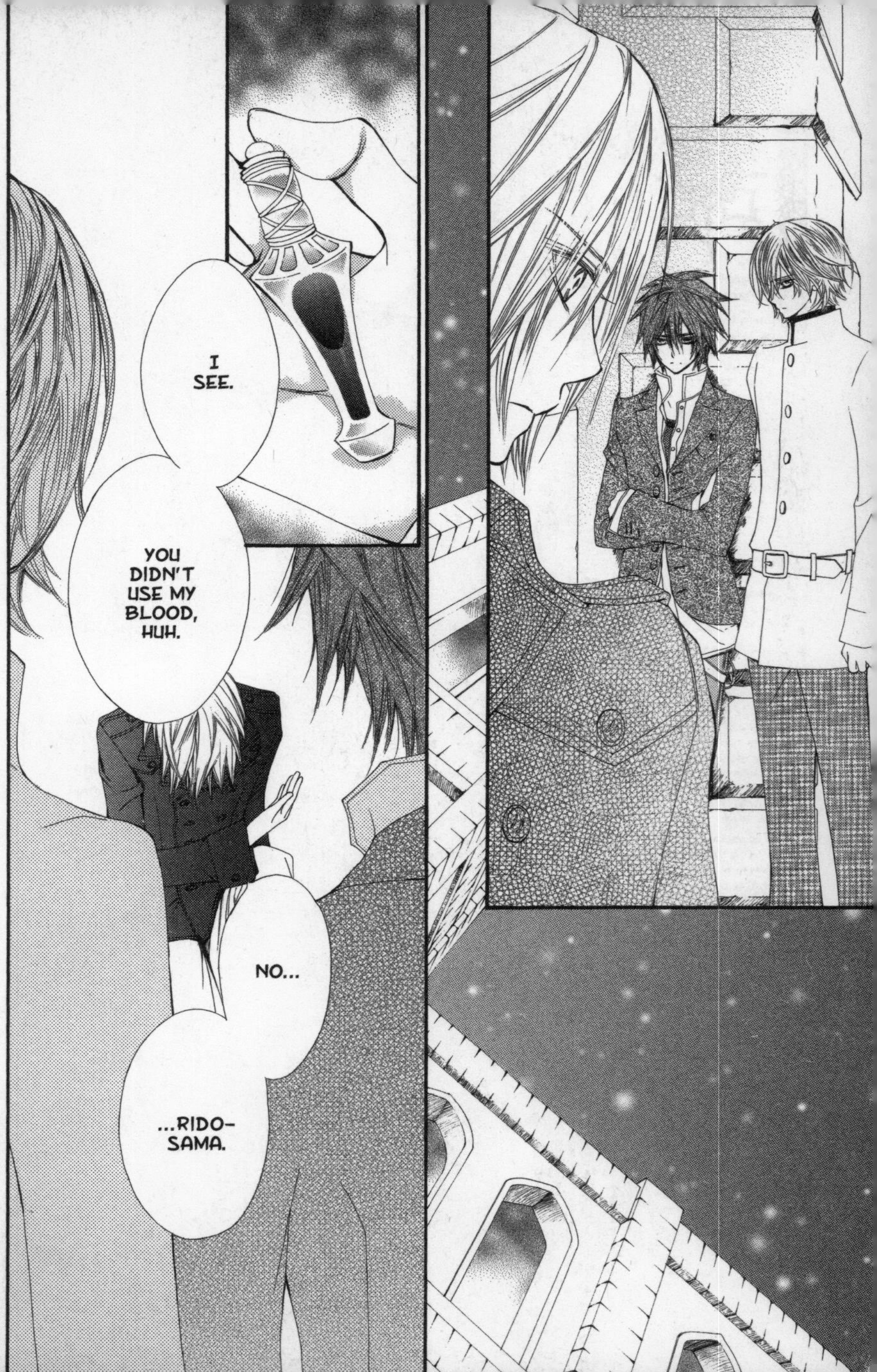
I SEE.
YOU DIDN'T USE MY BLOOD, HUH.
NO...
...RIDO-SAMA.

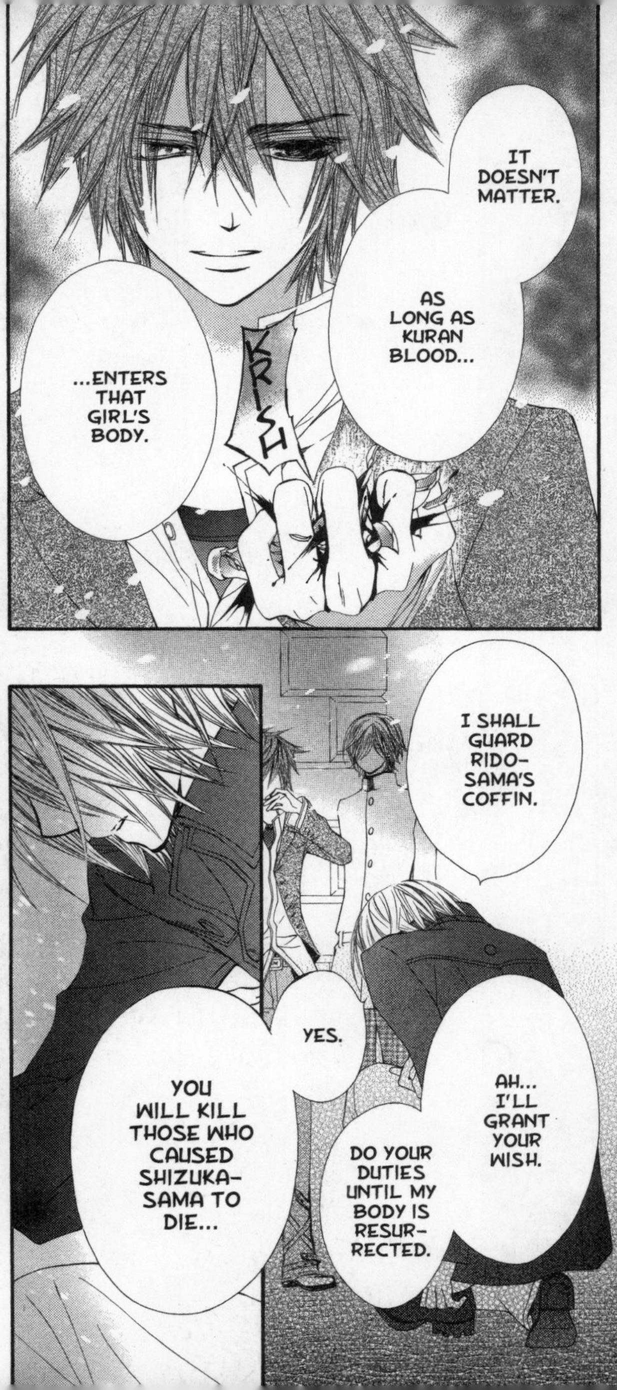
IT DOESN'T MATTER.
AS LONG AS KURAN BLOOD...
KRISH
...ENTERS THAT GIRL'S BODY.
I SHALL GUARD RIDO-SAMA'S COFFIN.
AH... I'LL GRANT YOUR WISH.
DO YOUR DUTIES UNTIL MY BODY IS RESURRECTED.
YES.
YOU WILL KILL THOSE WHO CAUSED SHIZUKA-SAMA TO DIE...

I

Hello!! This is Matsuri Hino!

Surprise, surprise. In Japan, the second novel goes on sale together with vol. 8...and next month, the Vampire Knight FAN BOOK will be on sale together with vol. 9. Hakusensha is being reckless... No. What a passionate appeal to all the readers this is... Thank you, Hakusensha-sama. I'm happy. I can't experience things like this too often.

This is all thanks to everyone who has been cheering on the manga, my editor, the editorial department, everyone related to the manga, and the people around me who do such great work. Thank you so much.

The second novel was written by Ayuna Fujisaki-san, just like the first novel! You can read about Shindo-san, who is in love with Zero, and the class rep who is in love with Ruka. There is also a story where everyone in the Night Class is involved! (Hino drew illustrations this time too! Sneaky!) I was involved with the fan book as much as I could, and it has material that is being made public for the first time: Q&A, bonus manga, etc., etc. So please do take a look!

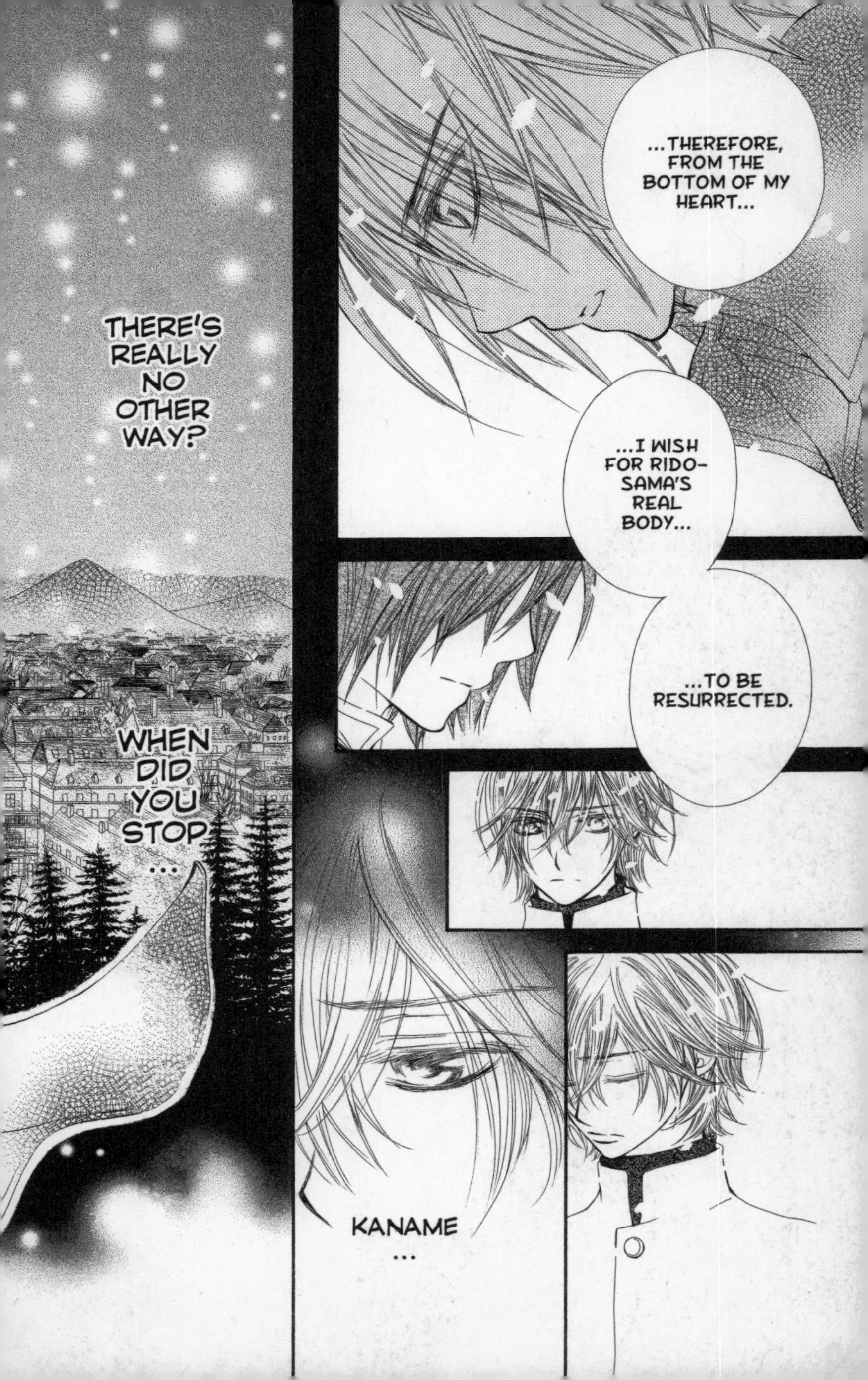
...THEREFORE, FROM THE BOTTOM OF MY HEART...
...I WISH FOR RIDO-SAMA'S REAL BODY...
...TO BE RESURRECTED.
KANAME ...
THERE'S REALLY NO OTHER WAY?
WHEN DID YOU STOP ...

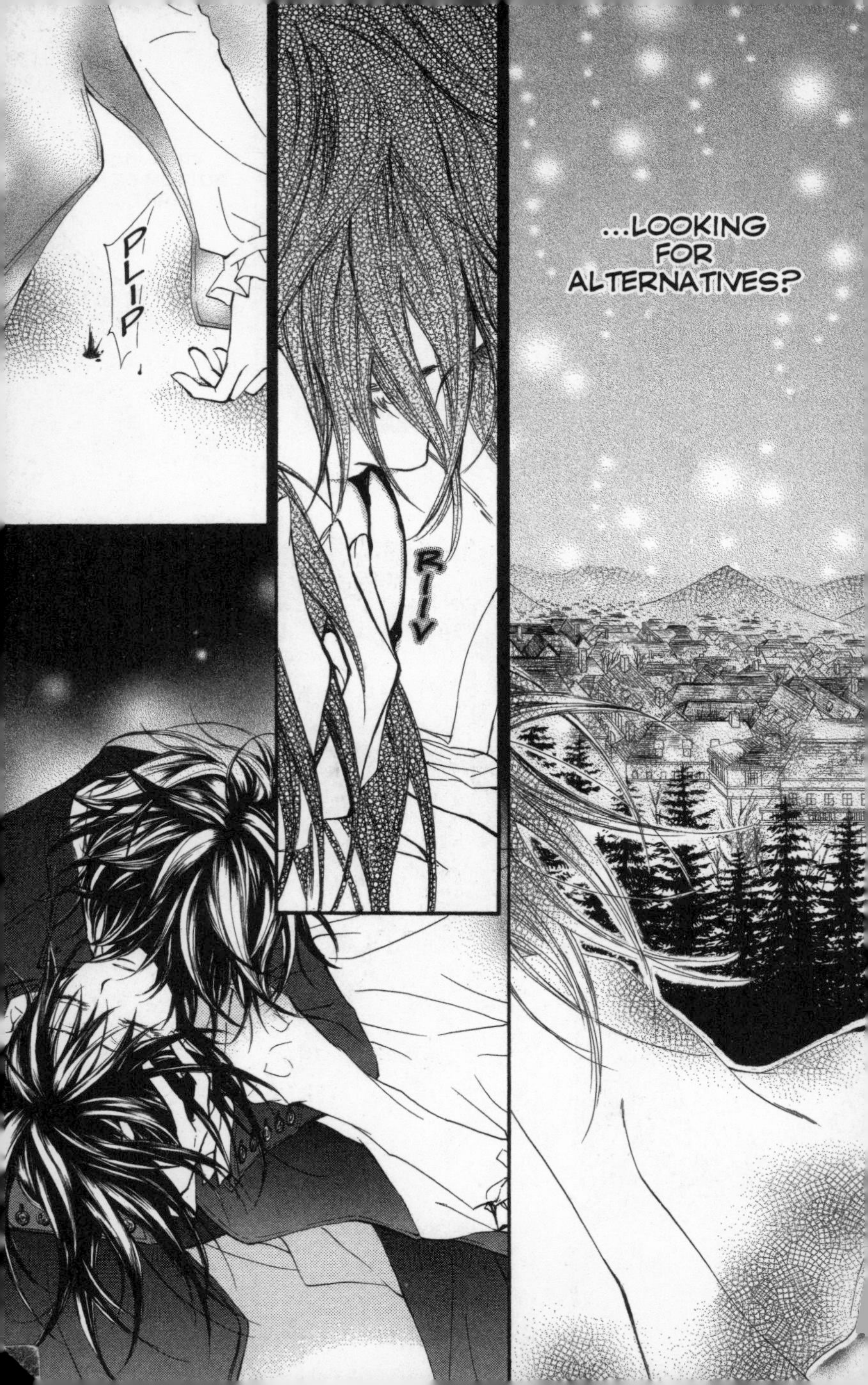
...LOOKING FOR ALTERNATIVES?
RIV
PLIP

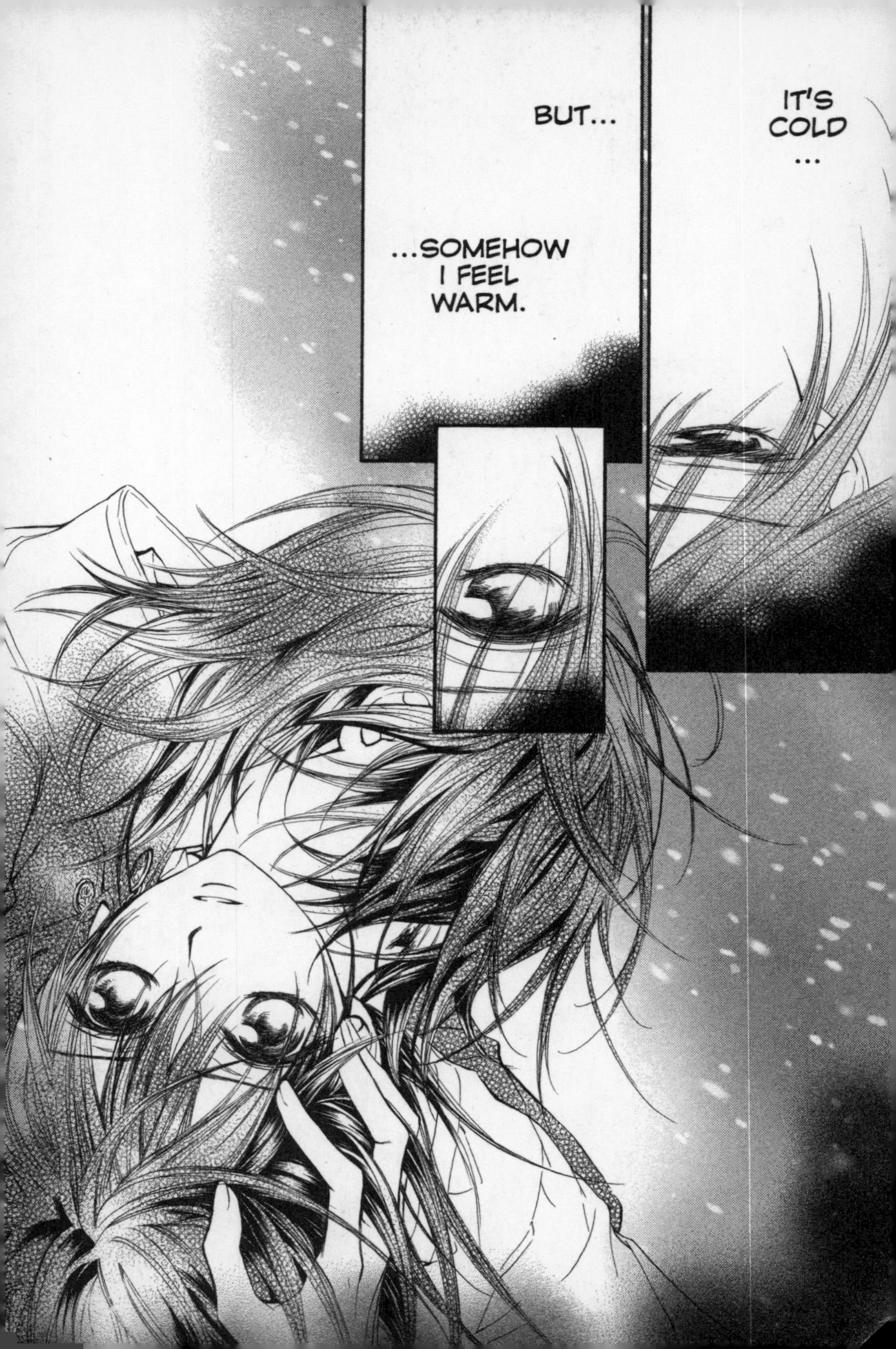
IT'S COLD ...
BUT...
...SOMEHOW I FEEL WARM.

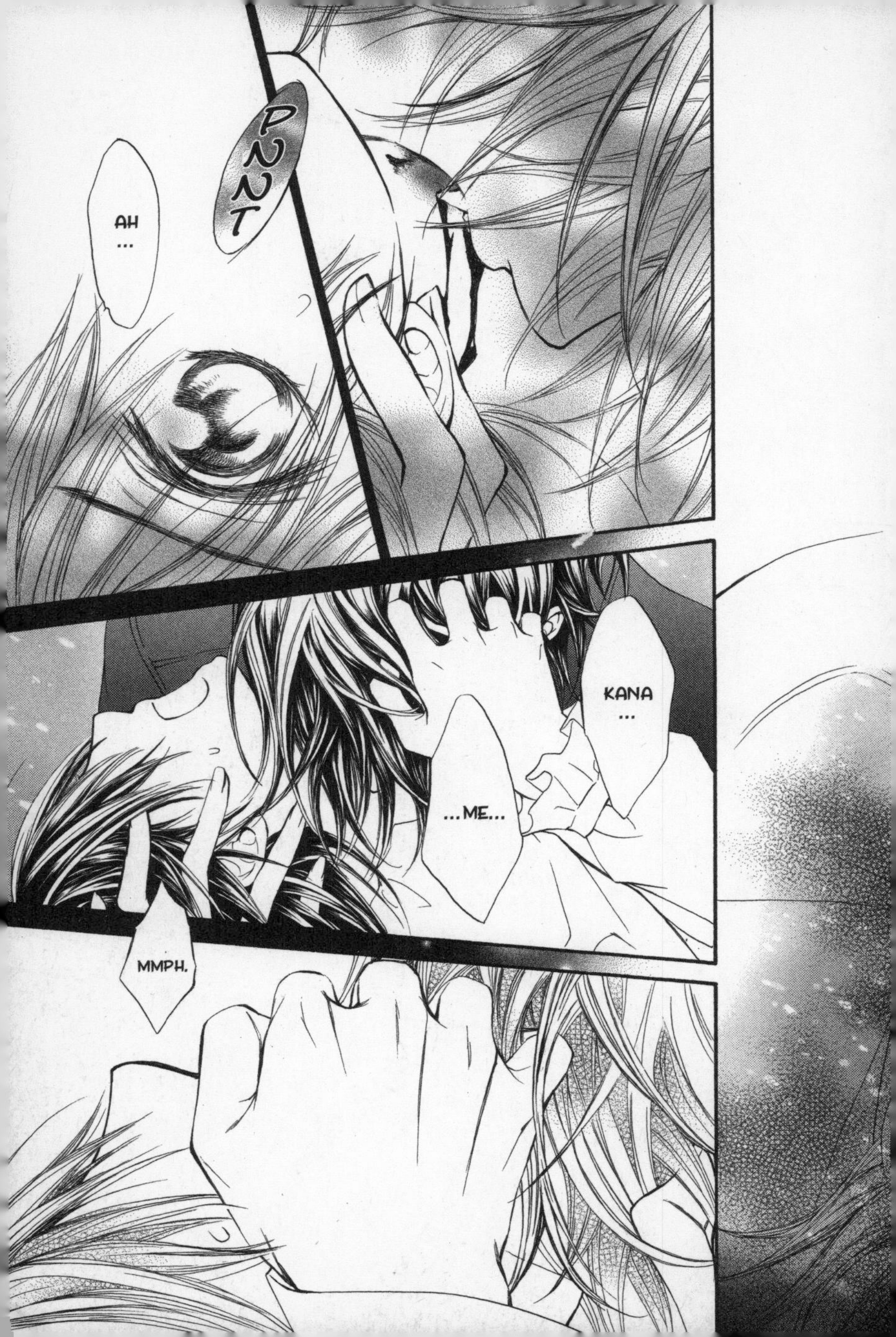
PNNT
AH ...
KANA ...
...ME...
MMPH.

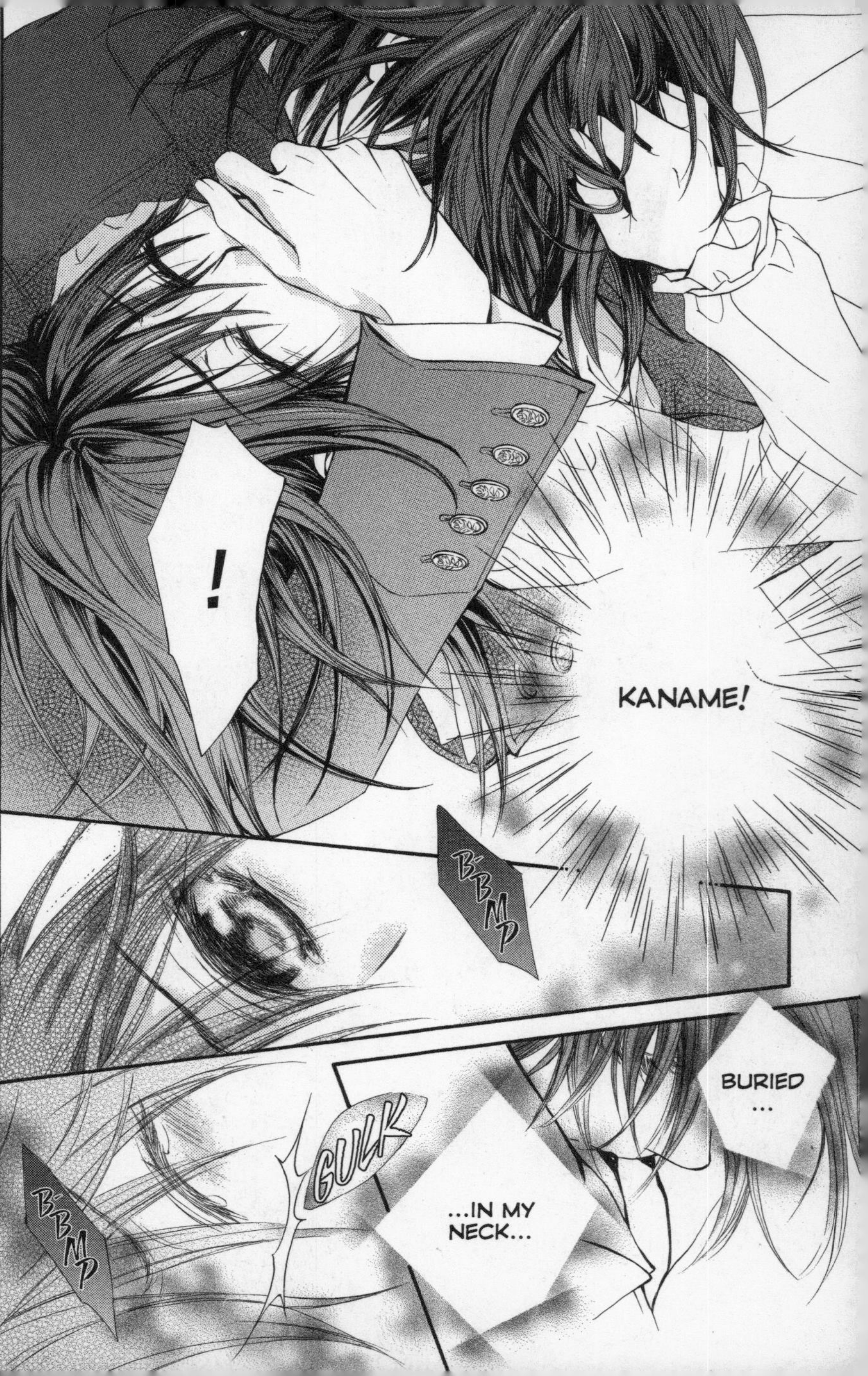
KANAME!
!
B-BMP
BURIED ...
...IN MY NECK...
GULK
B-BMP

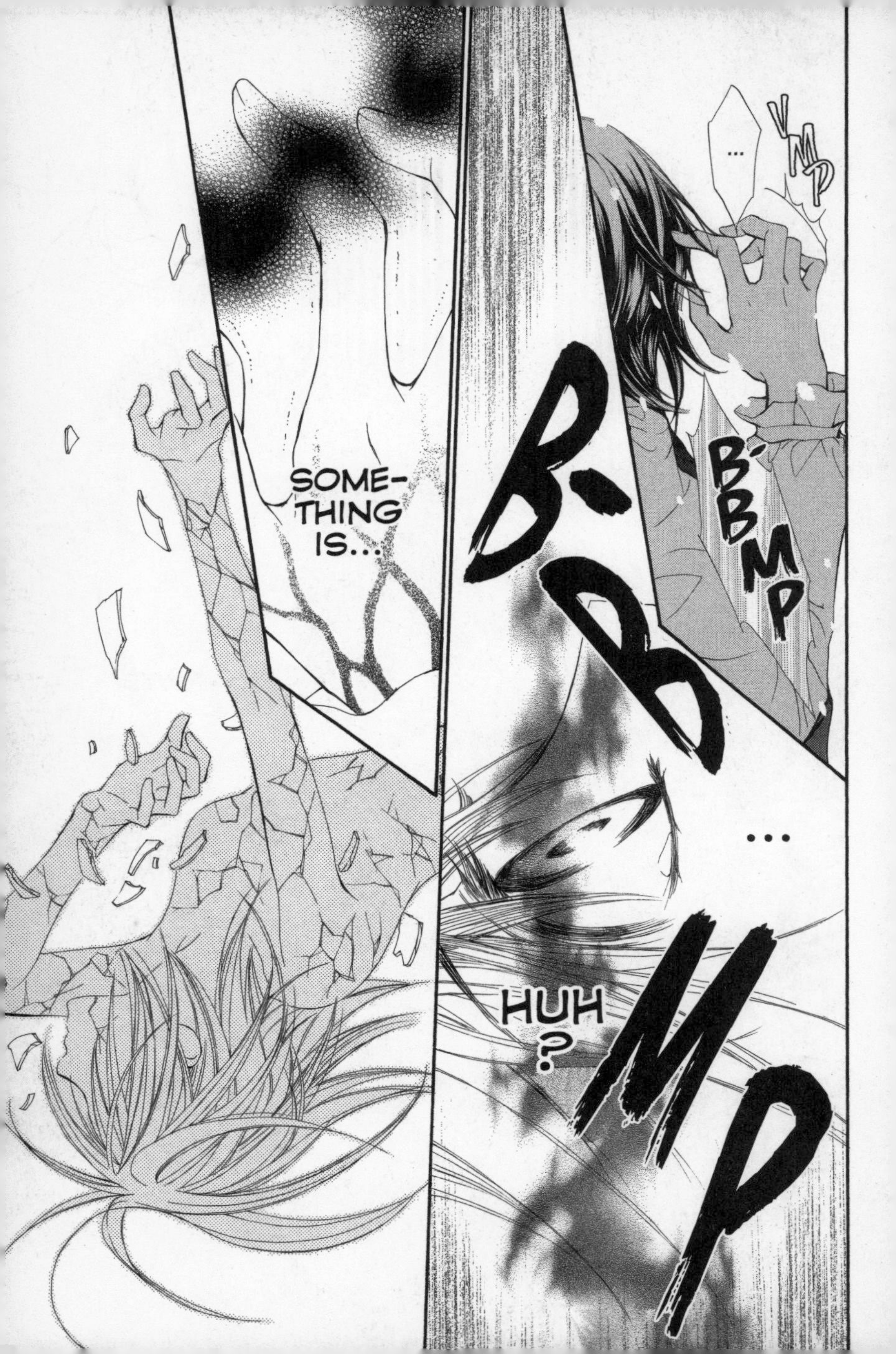
...
VMP
B-BMP
B-BMP
...
HUH?
SOME-THING IS...

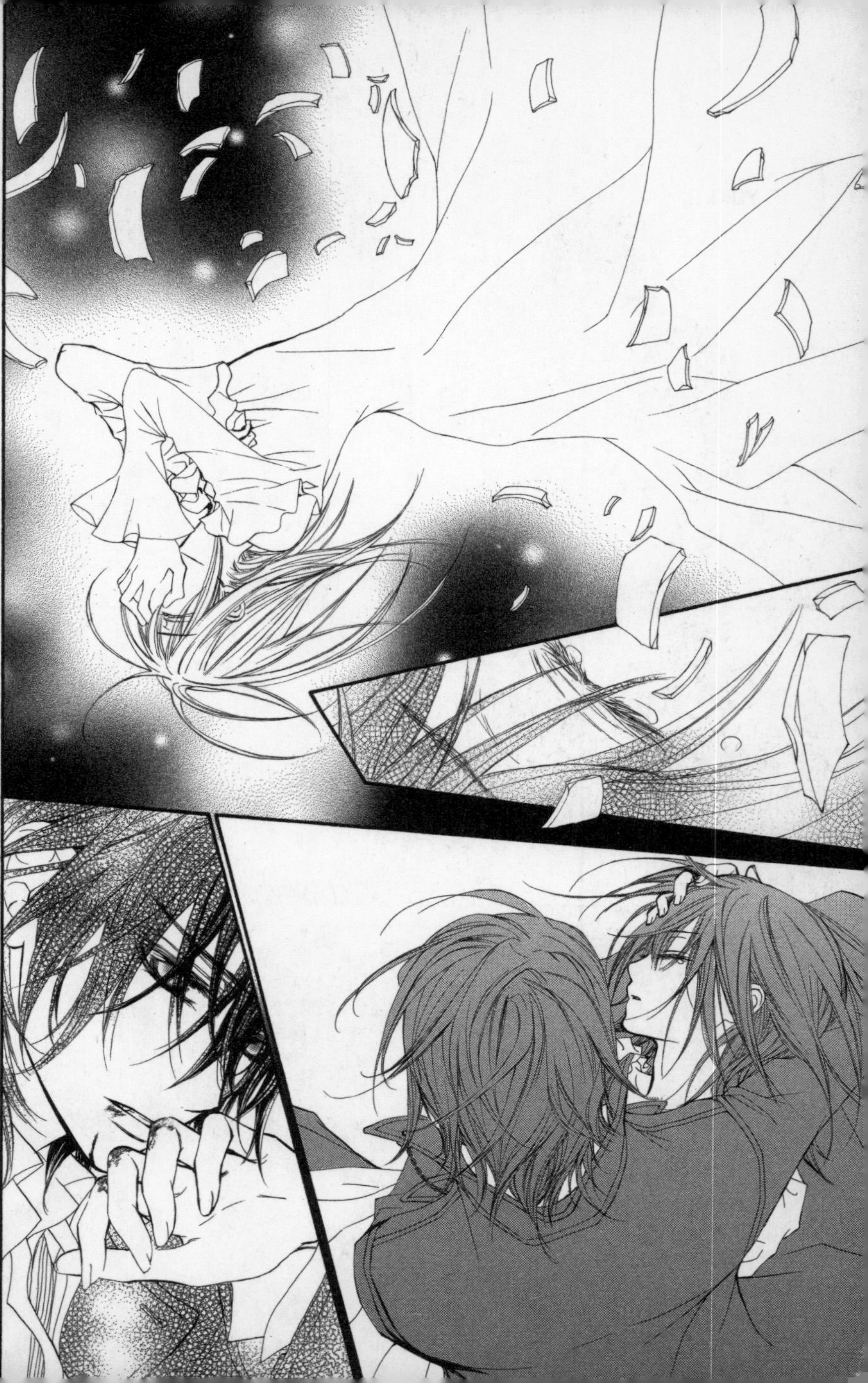

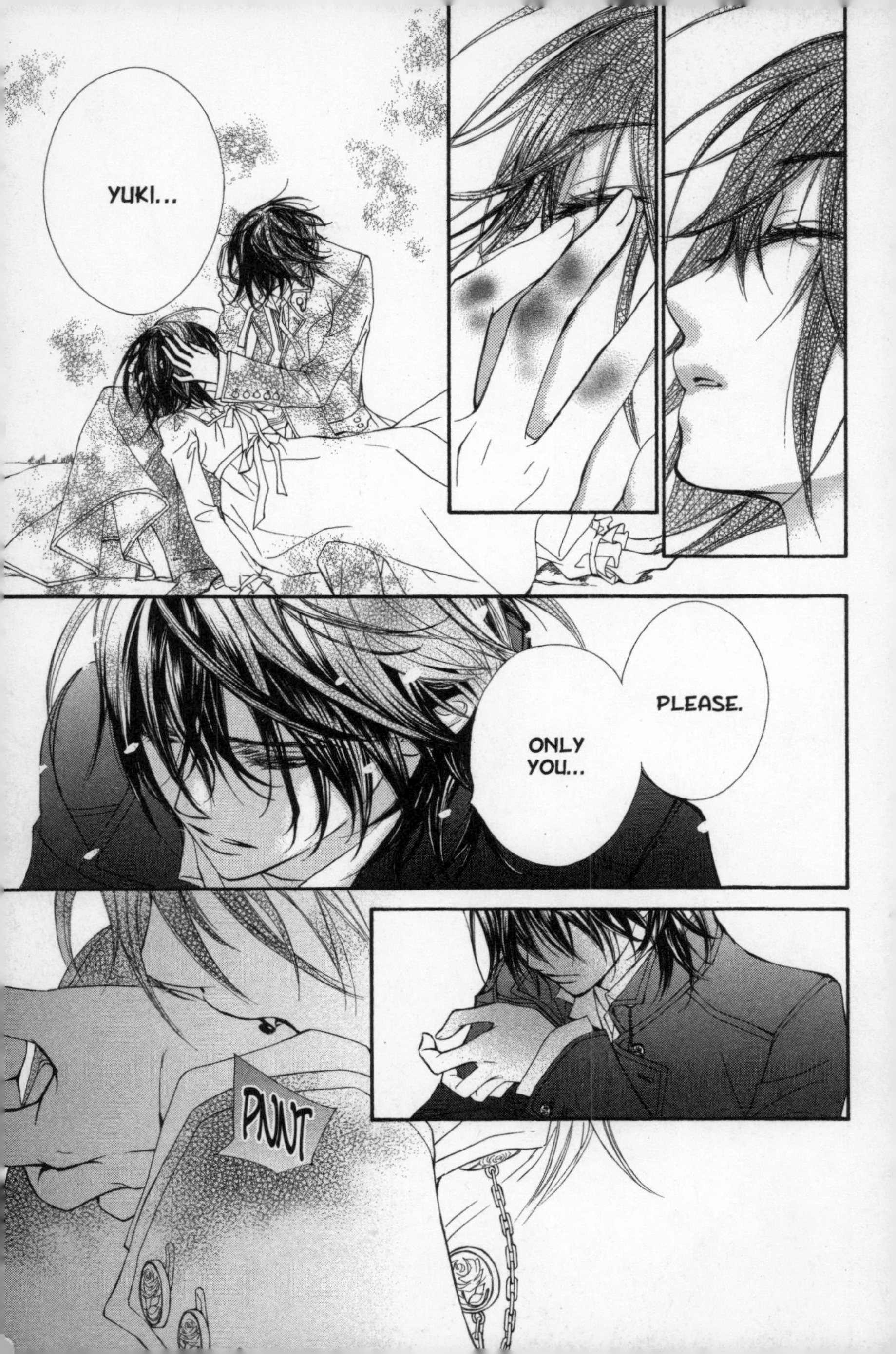
YUKI...
PLEASE.
ONLY YOU...
PNNT

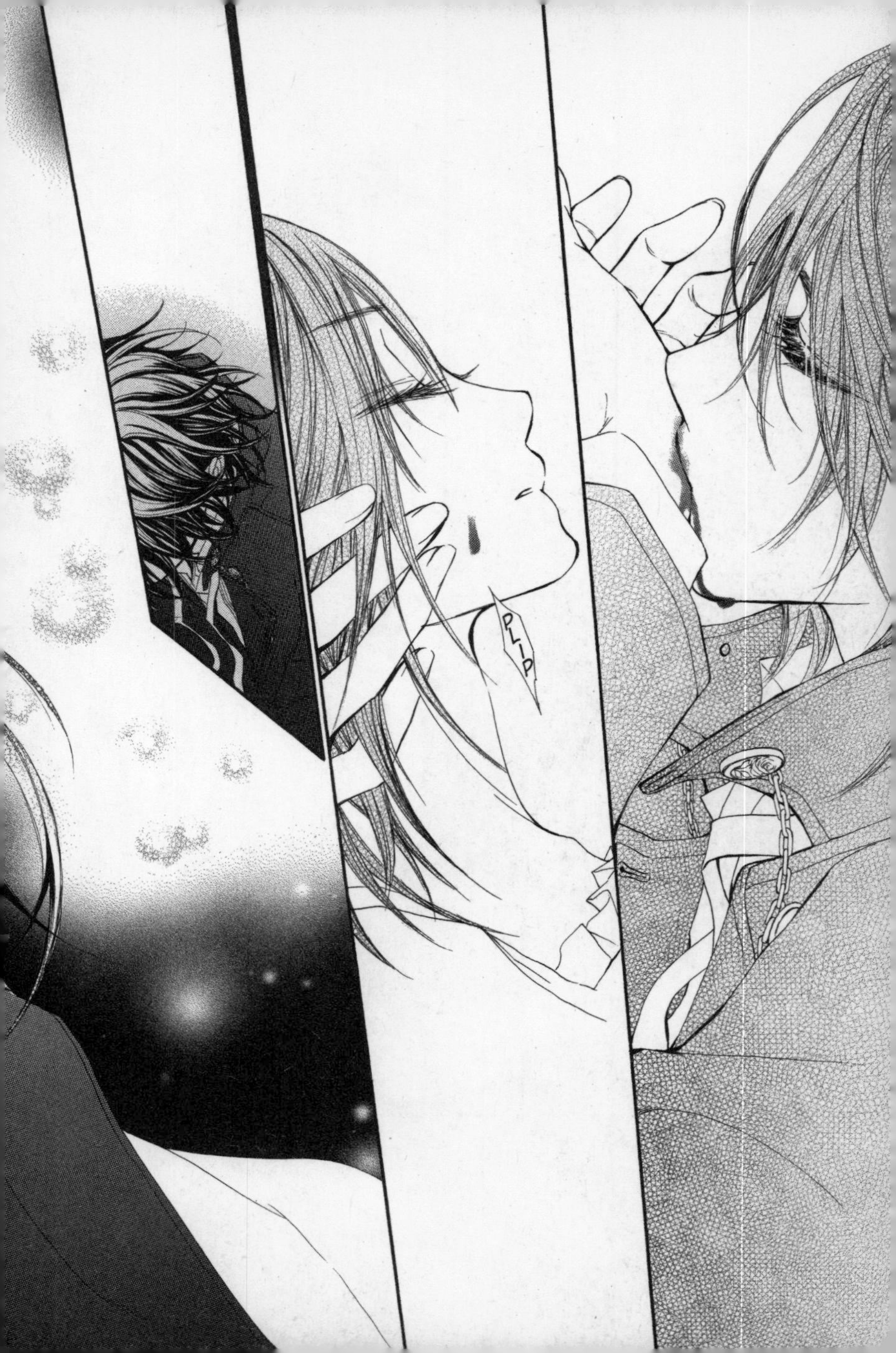
PLIP

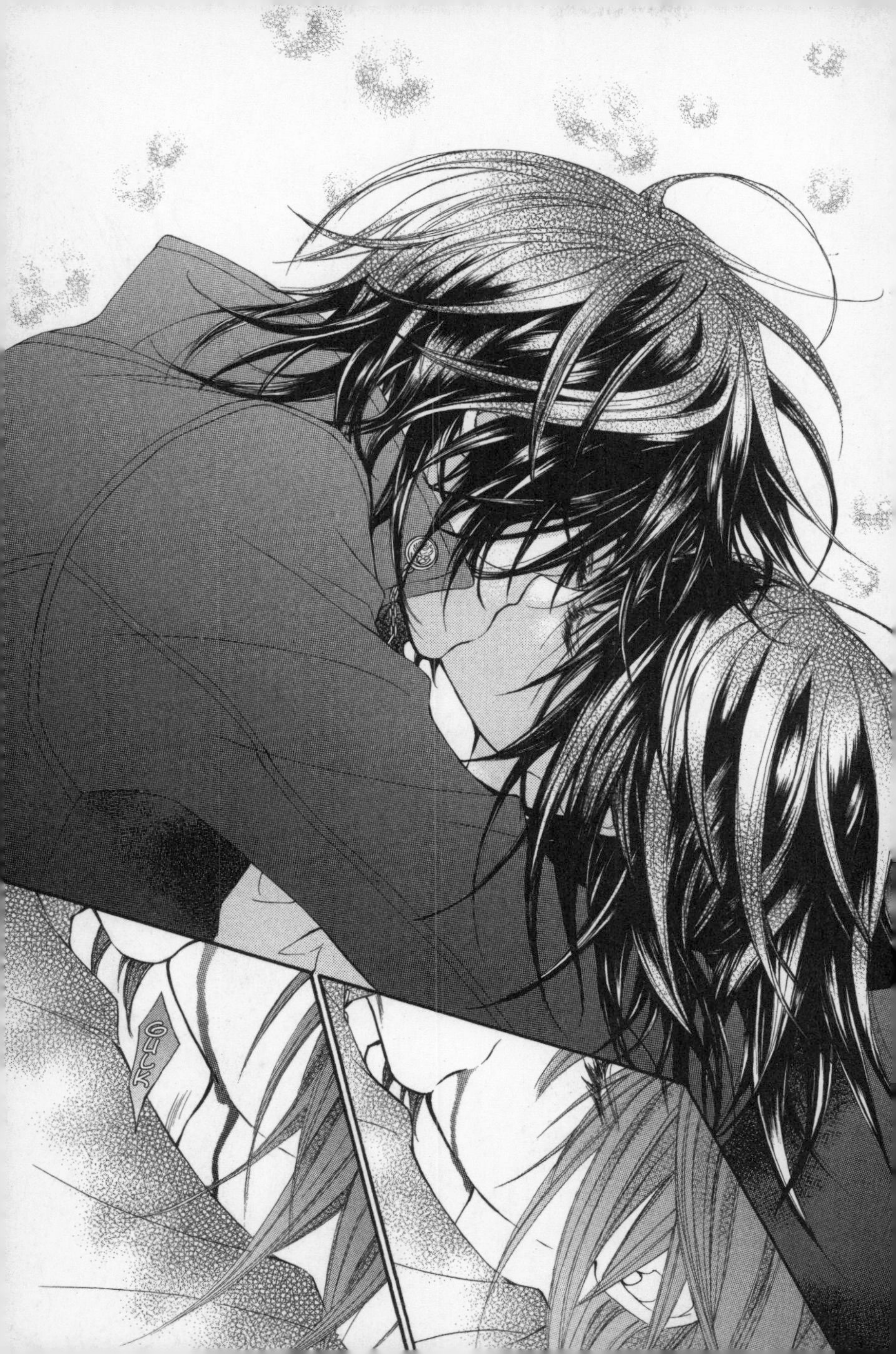
GULK

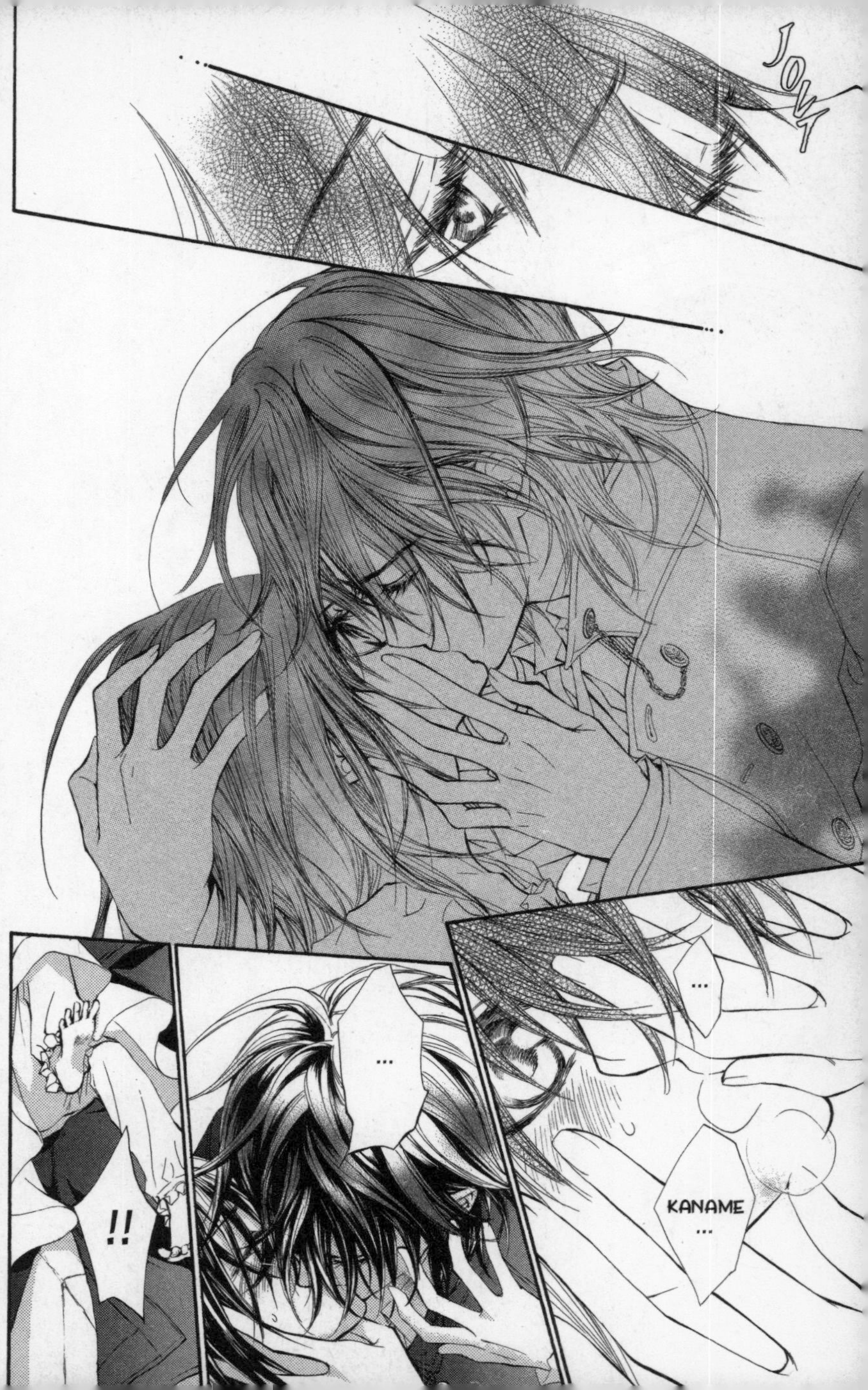
JOLT
...
...
...
KANAME ...
...
!!

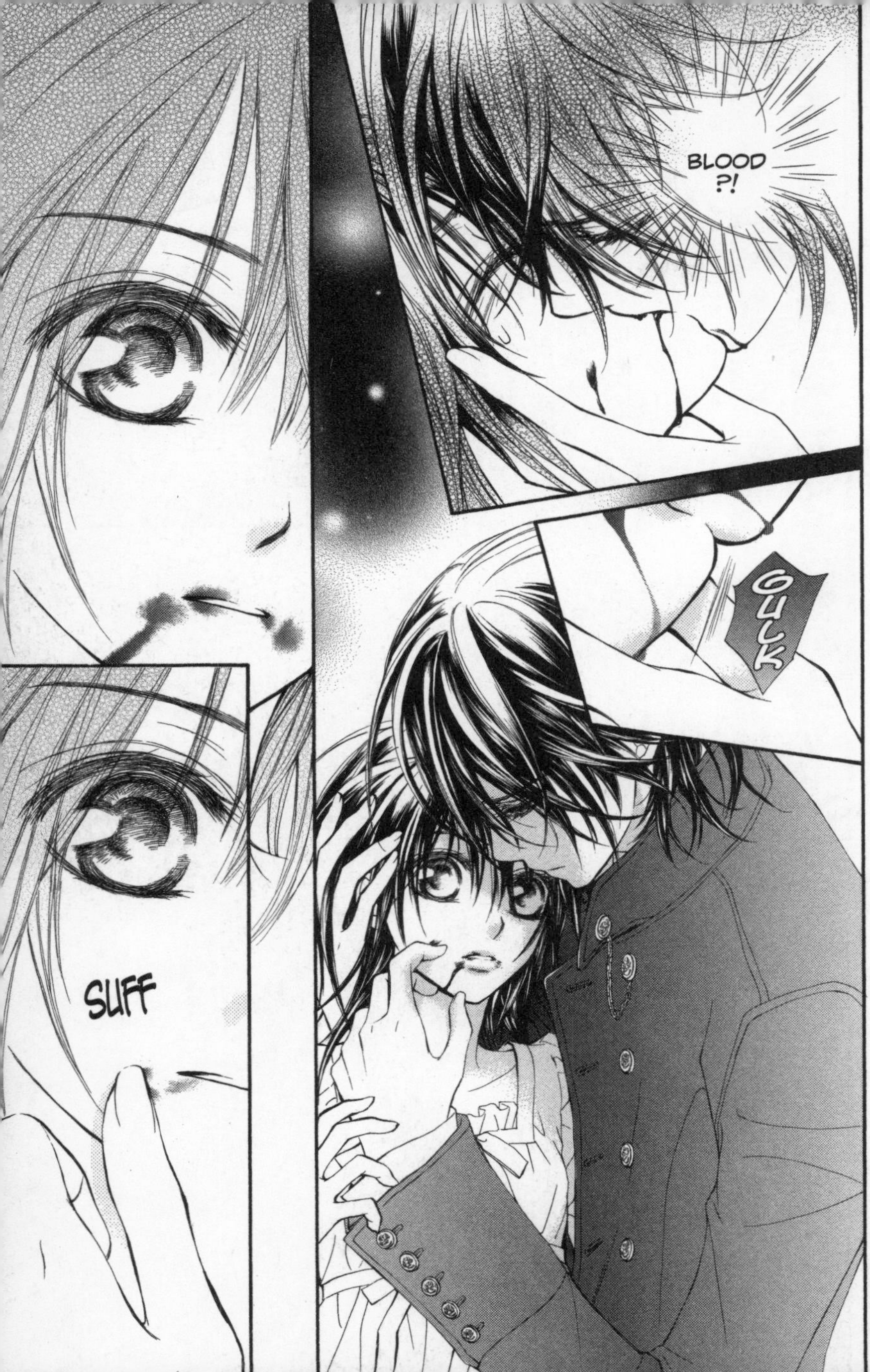
BLOOD ?!
GULK
SUFF

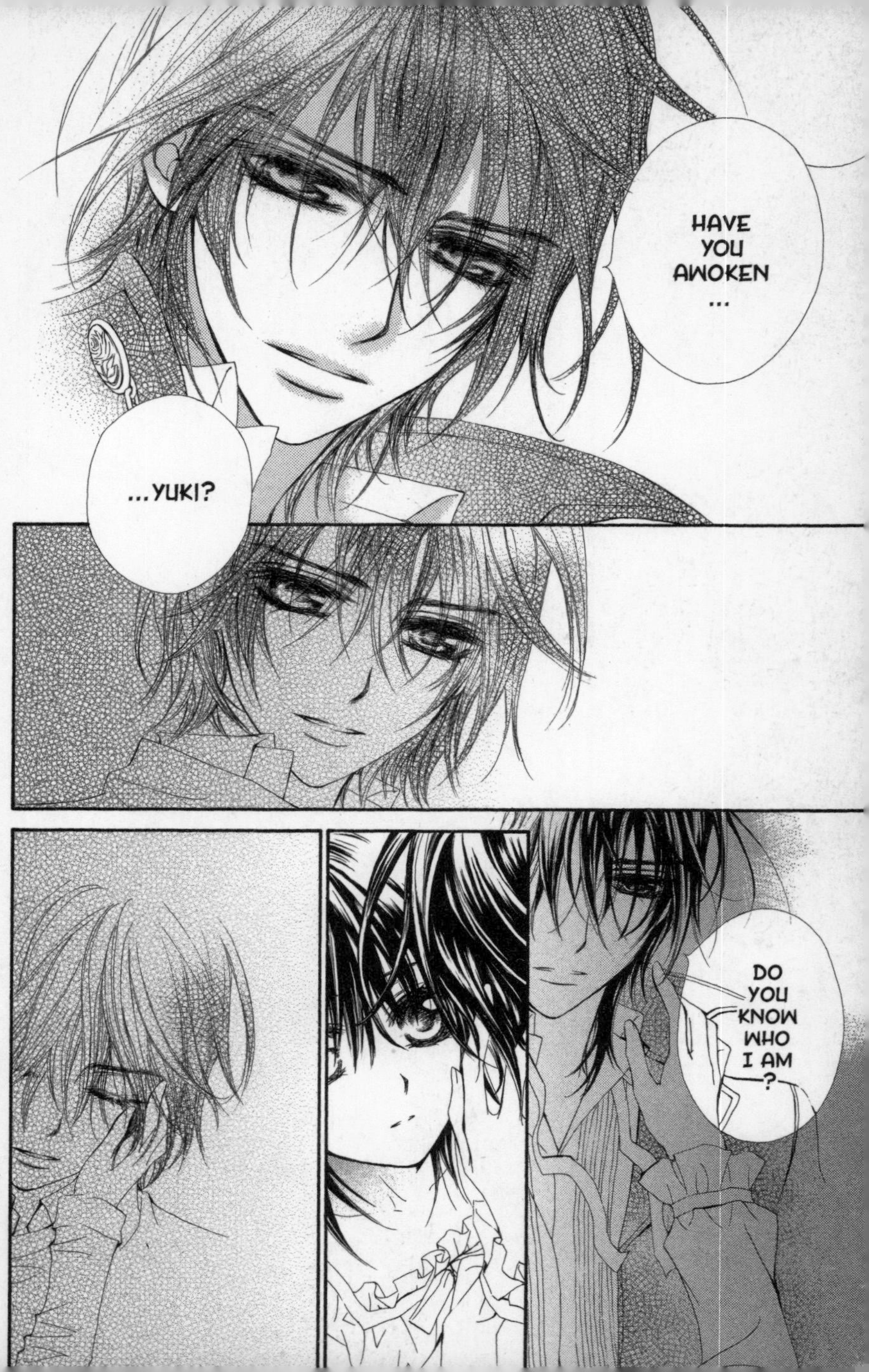
HAVE YOU AWOKEN ...
...YUKI?
DO YOU KNOW WHO I AM ?

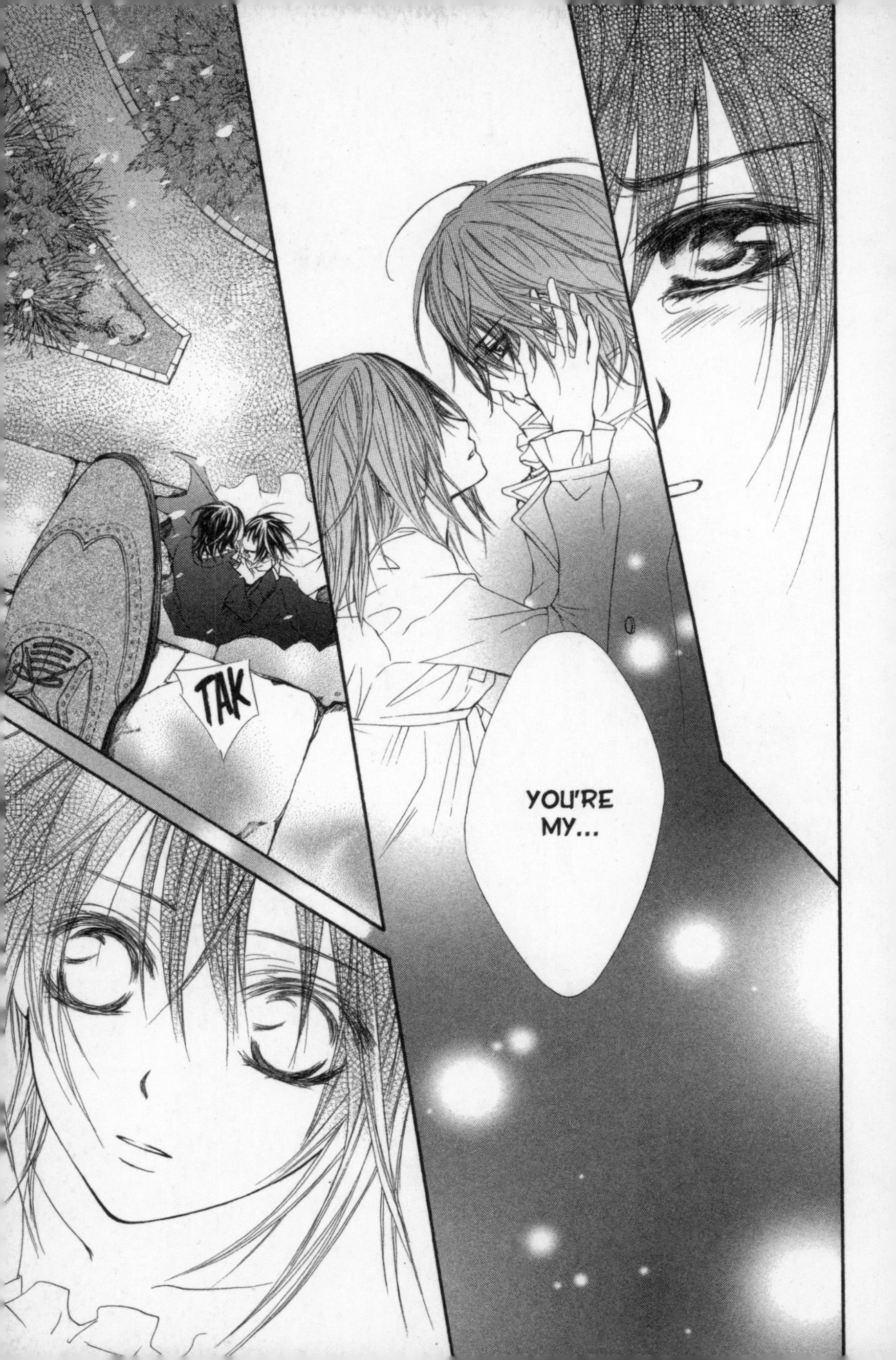
TAK
YOU'RE MY...

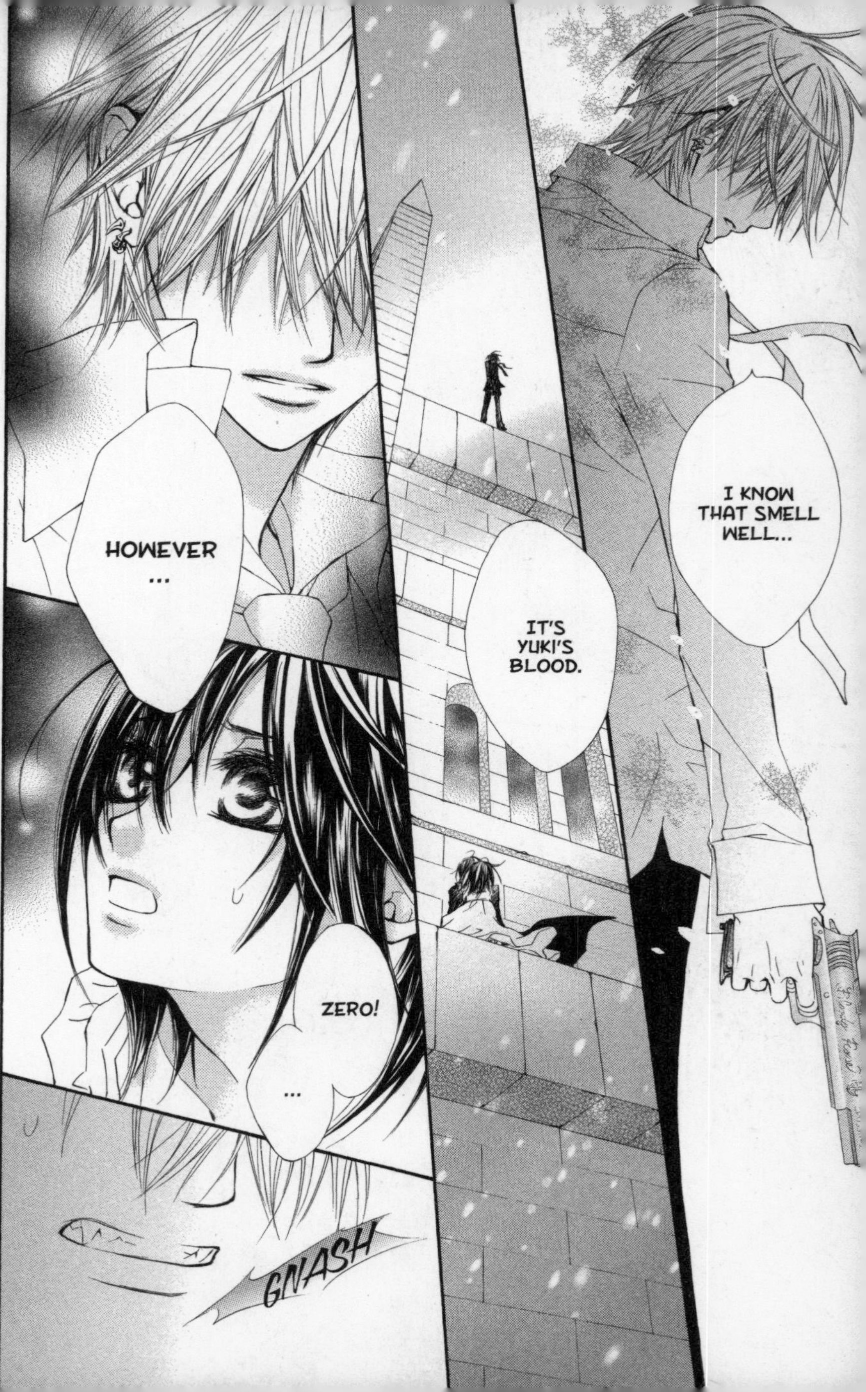
I KNOW THAT SMELL WELL...
IT'S YUKI'S BLOOD.
HOWEVER ...
ZERO! ...
GNASH

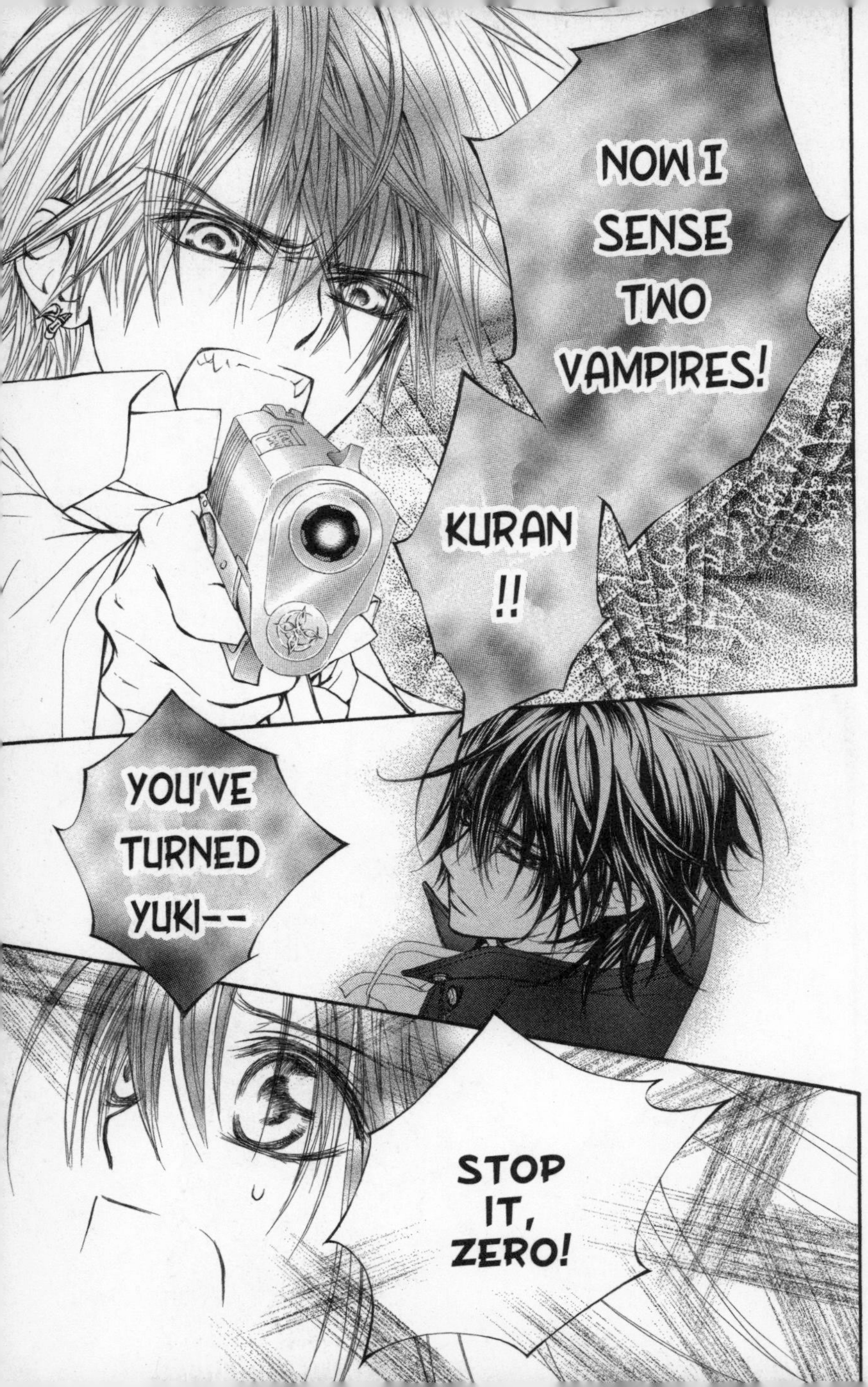
NOW I SENSE TWO VAMPIRES!
KURAN !!
YOU'VE TURNED YUKI--
STOP IT, ZERO!

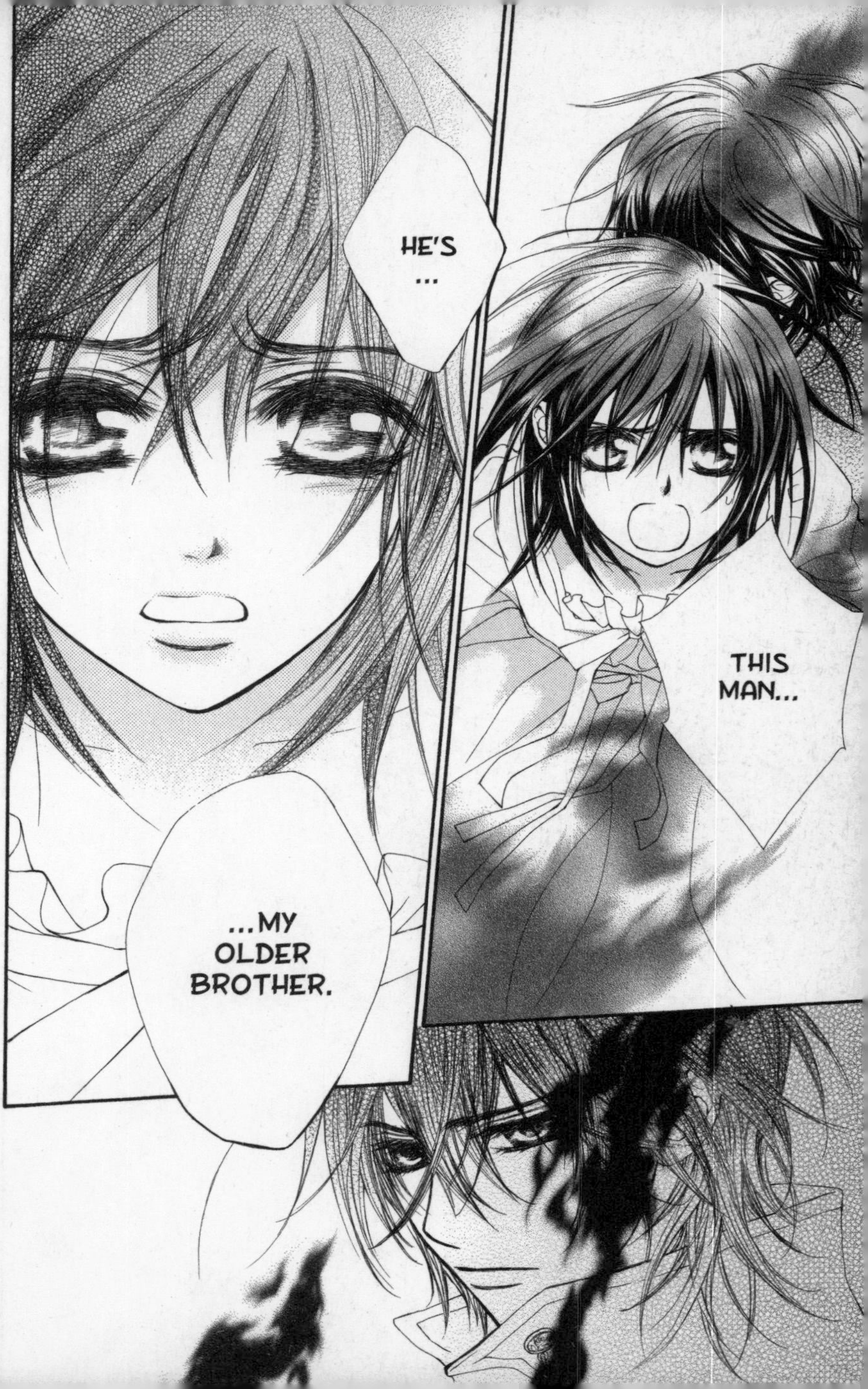
THIS MAN...
HE'S ...
...MY OLDER BROTHER.

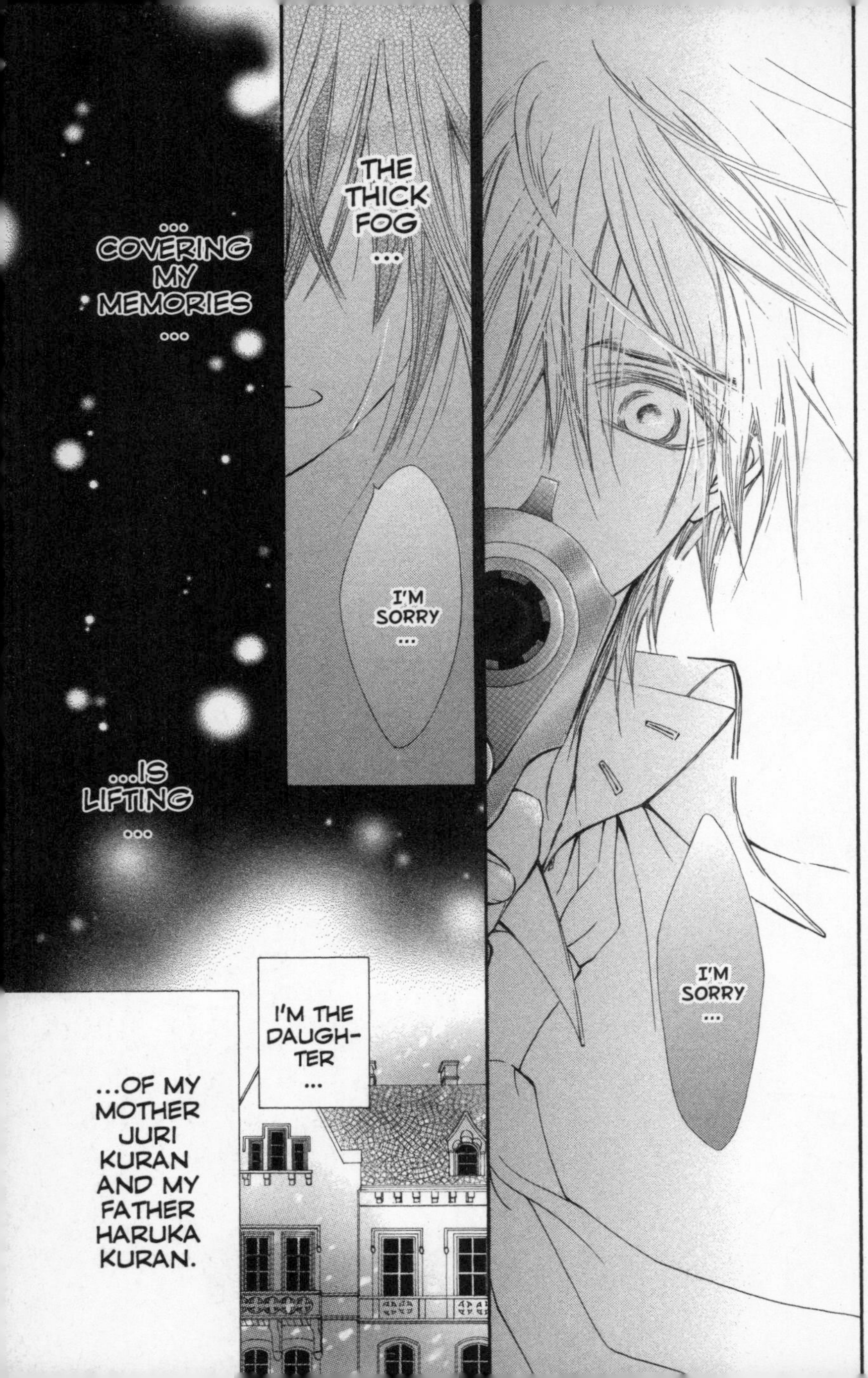
I'M SORRY ...
THE THICK FOG ...
I'M SORRY ...
... COVERING MY MEMORIES ...
...IS LIFTING ...
I'M THE DAUGHTER ...
...OF MY MOTHER JURI KURAN AND MY FATHER HARUKA KURAN.

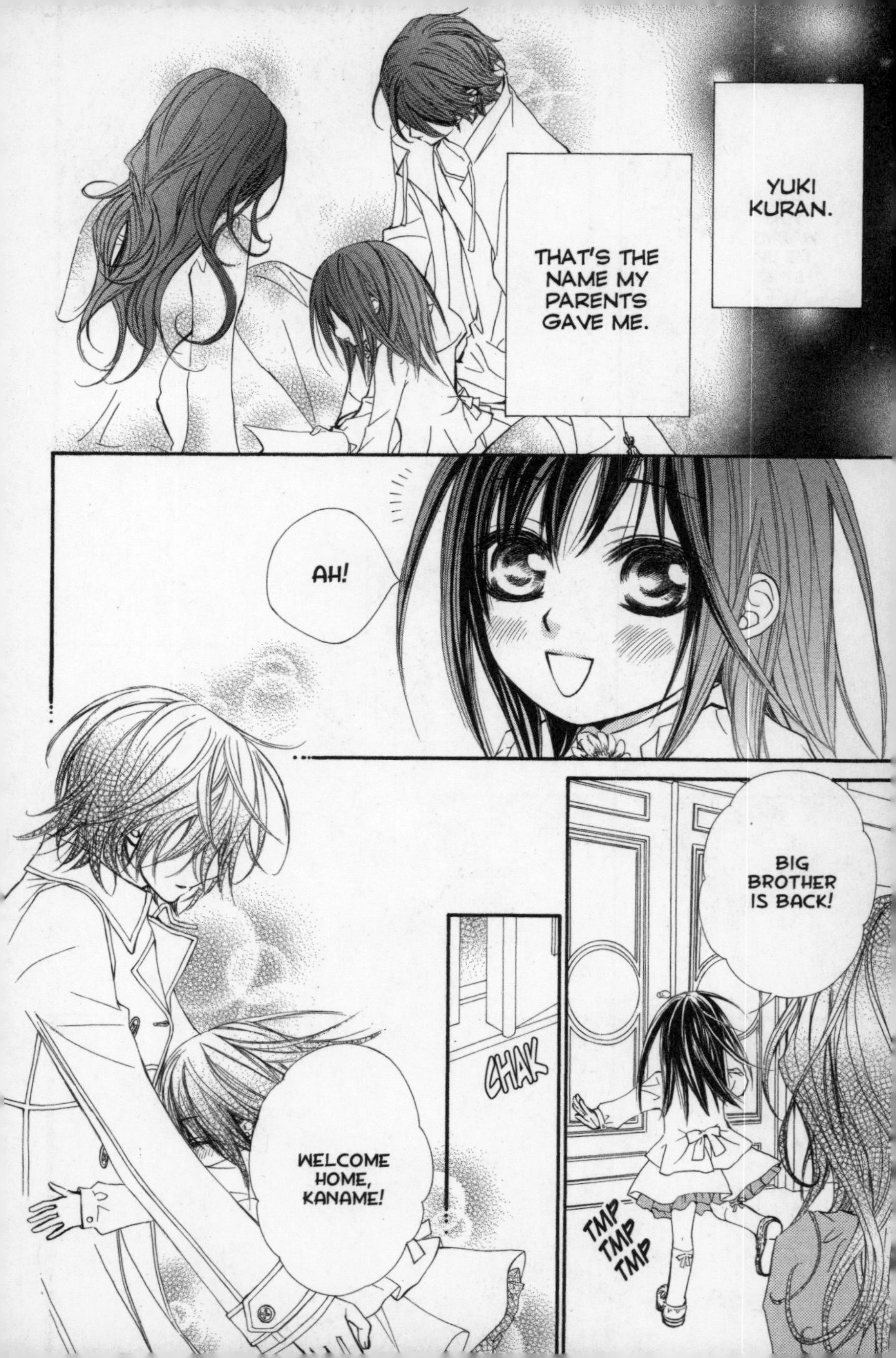
YUKI KURAN.
THAT'S THE NAME MY PARENTS GAVE ME.
AH!
BIG BROTHER IS BACK!
CHAK
TMP TMP TMP
WELCOME HOME, KANAME!

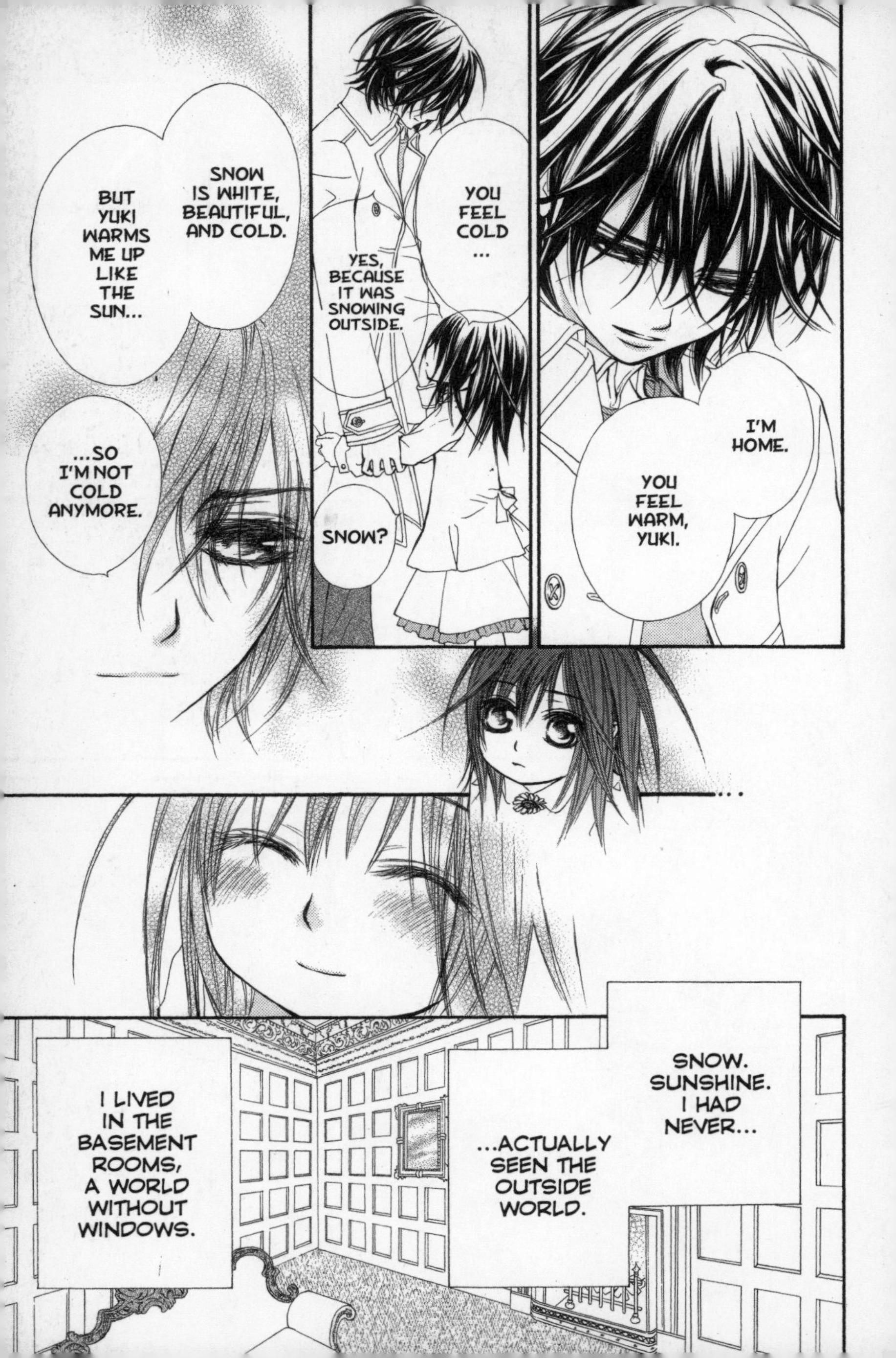
I'M HOME.
YOU FEEL WARM, YUKI.
YOU FEEL COLD ...
YES, BECAUSE IT WAS SNOWING OUTSIDE.
SNOW?
SNOW IS WHITE, BEAUTIFUL, AND COLD.
BUT YUKI WARMS ME UP LIKE THE SUN...
...SO I'M NOT COLD ANYMORE.
...
SNOW. SUNSHINE. I HAD NEVER...
...ACTUALLY SEEN THE OUTSIDE WORLD.
I LIVED IN THE BASEMENT ROOMS, A WORLD WITHOUT WINDOWS.

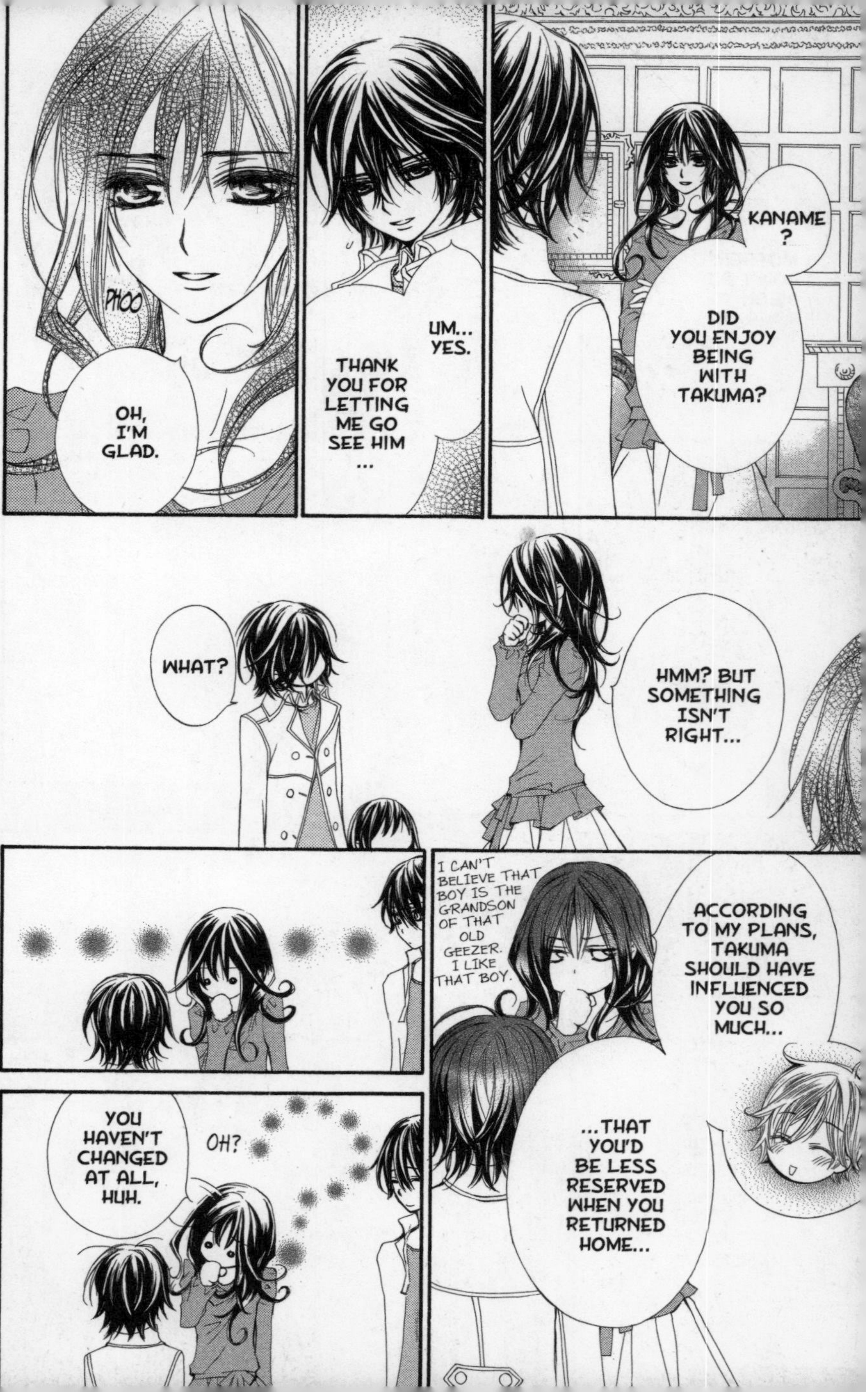
KANAME ?
DID YOU ENJOY BEING WITH TAKUMA?
UM... YES.
THANK YOU FOR LETTING ME GO SEE HIM ...
PHOO
OH, I'M GLAD.
HMM? BUT SOMETHING ISN'T RIGHT...
WHAT?
ACCORDING TO MY PLANS, TAKUMA SHOULD HAVE INFLUENCED YOU SO MUCH...
I CAN'T BELIEVE THAT BOY IS THE GRANDSON OF THAT OLD GEEZER. I LIKE THAT BOY.
...THAT YOU'D BE LESS RESERVED WHEN YOU RETURNED HOME...
OH?
YOU HAVEN'T CHANGED AT ALL, HUH.

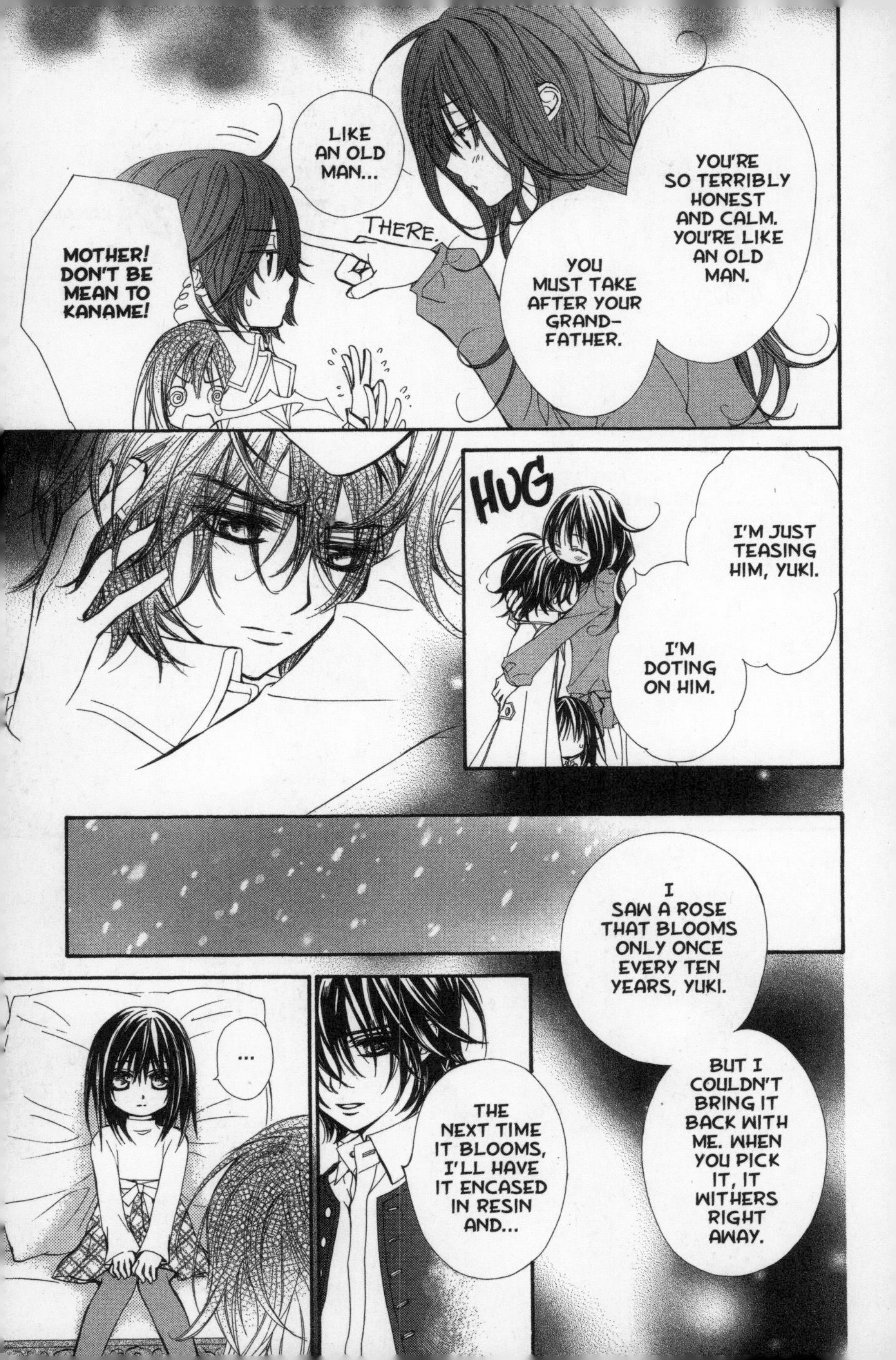
YOU'RE SO TERRIBLY HONEST AND CALM. YOU'RE LIKE AN OLD MAN.
YOU MUST TAKE AFTER YOUR GRAND-FATHER.
THERE.
LIKE AN OLD MAN...
MOTHER! DON'T BE MEAN TO KANAME!
HUG
I'M JUST TEASING HIM, YUKI.
I'M DOTING ON HIM.
I SAW A ROSE THAT BLOOMS ONLY ONCE EVERY TEN YEARS, YUKI.
BUT I COULDN'T BRING IT BACK WITH ME. WHEN YOU PICK IT, IT WITHERS RIGHT AWAY.
THE NEXT TIME IT BLOOMS, I'LL HAVE IT ENCASED IN RESIN AND...
...

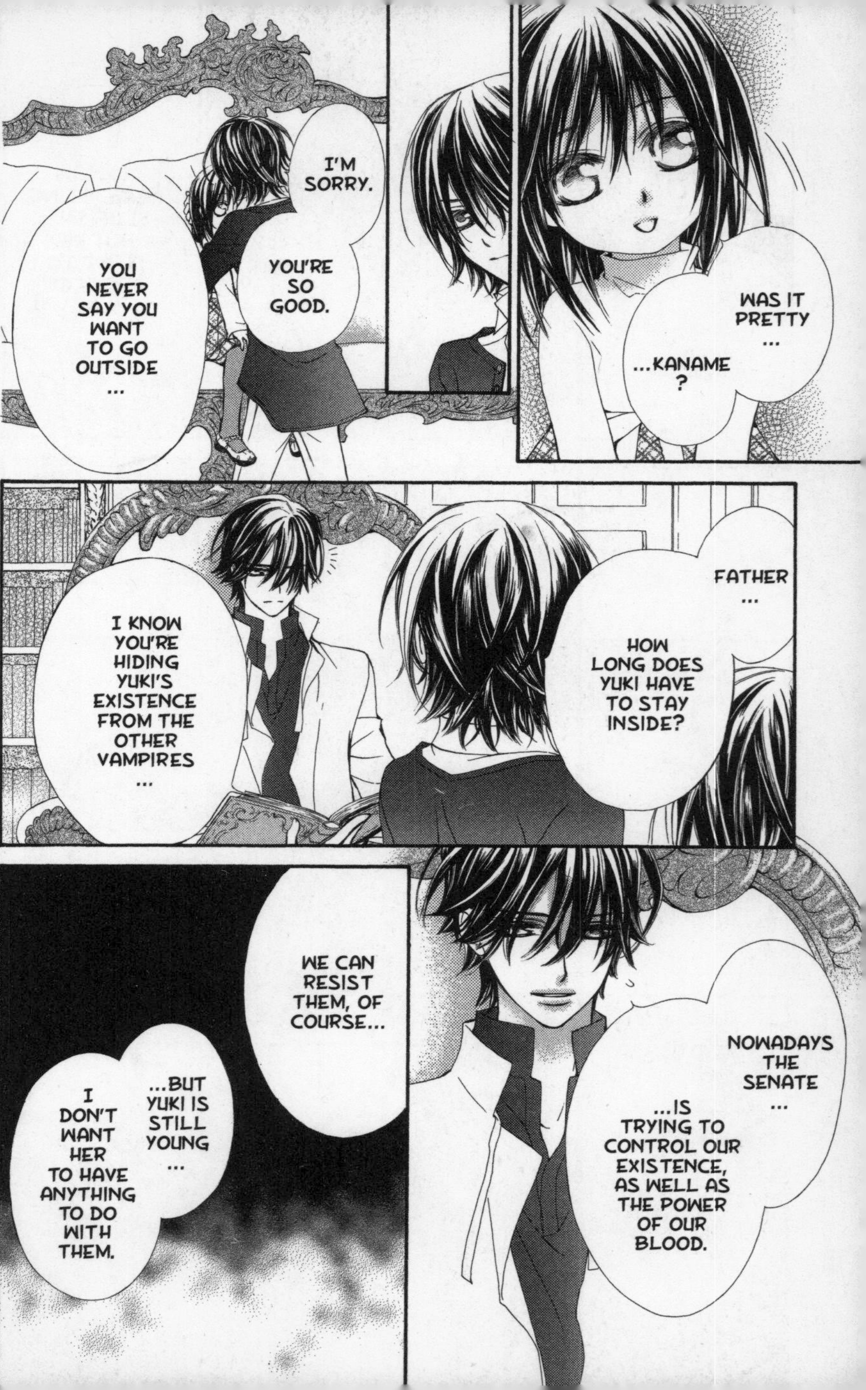
WAS IT PRETTY ...
...KANAME ?
I'M SORRY.
YOU'RE SO GOOD.
YOU NEVER SAY YOU WANT TO GO OUTSIDE ...
FATHER ...
HOW LONG DOES YUKI HAVE TO STAY INSIDE?
I KNOW YOU'RE HIDING YUKI'S EXISTENCE FROM THE OTHER VAMPIRES ...
NOWADAYS THE SENATE ...
...IS TRYING TO CONTROL OUR EXISTENCE, AS WELL AS THE POWER OF OUR BLOOD.
WE CAN RESIST THEM, OF COURSE...
...BUT YUKI IS STILL YOUNG ...
I DON'T WANT HER TO HAVE ANYTHING TO DO WITH THEM.

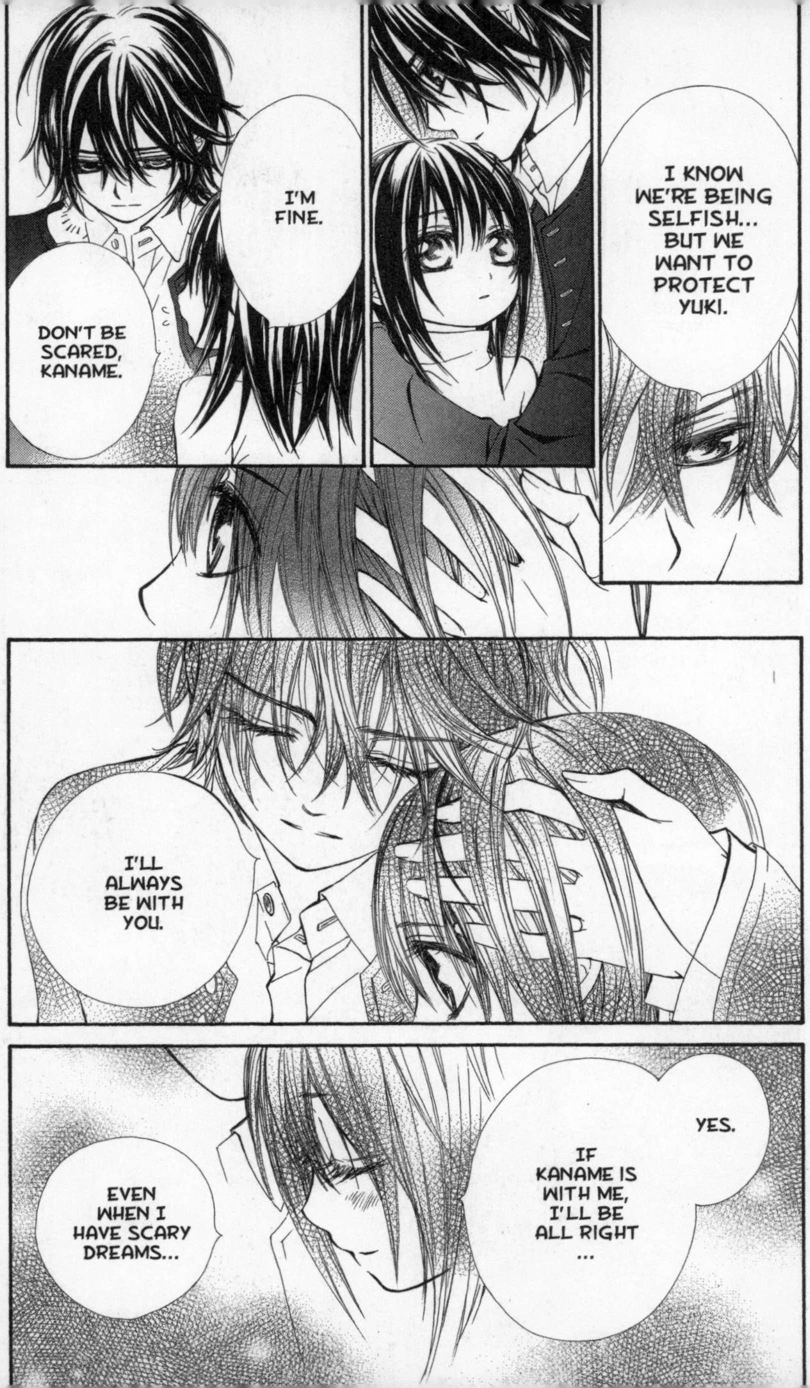
I KNOW WE'RE BEING SELFISH... BUT WE WANT TO PROTECT YUKI.
I'M FINE.
DON'T BE SCARED, KANAME.
I'LL ALWAYS BE WITH YOU.
YES.
IF KANAME IS WITH ME, I'LL BE ALL RIGHT ...
EVEN WHEN I HAVE SCARY DREAMS...

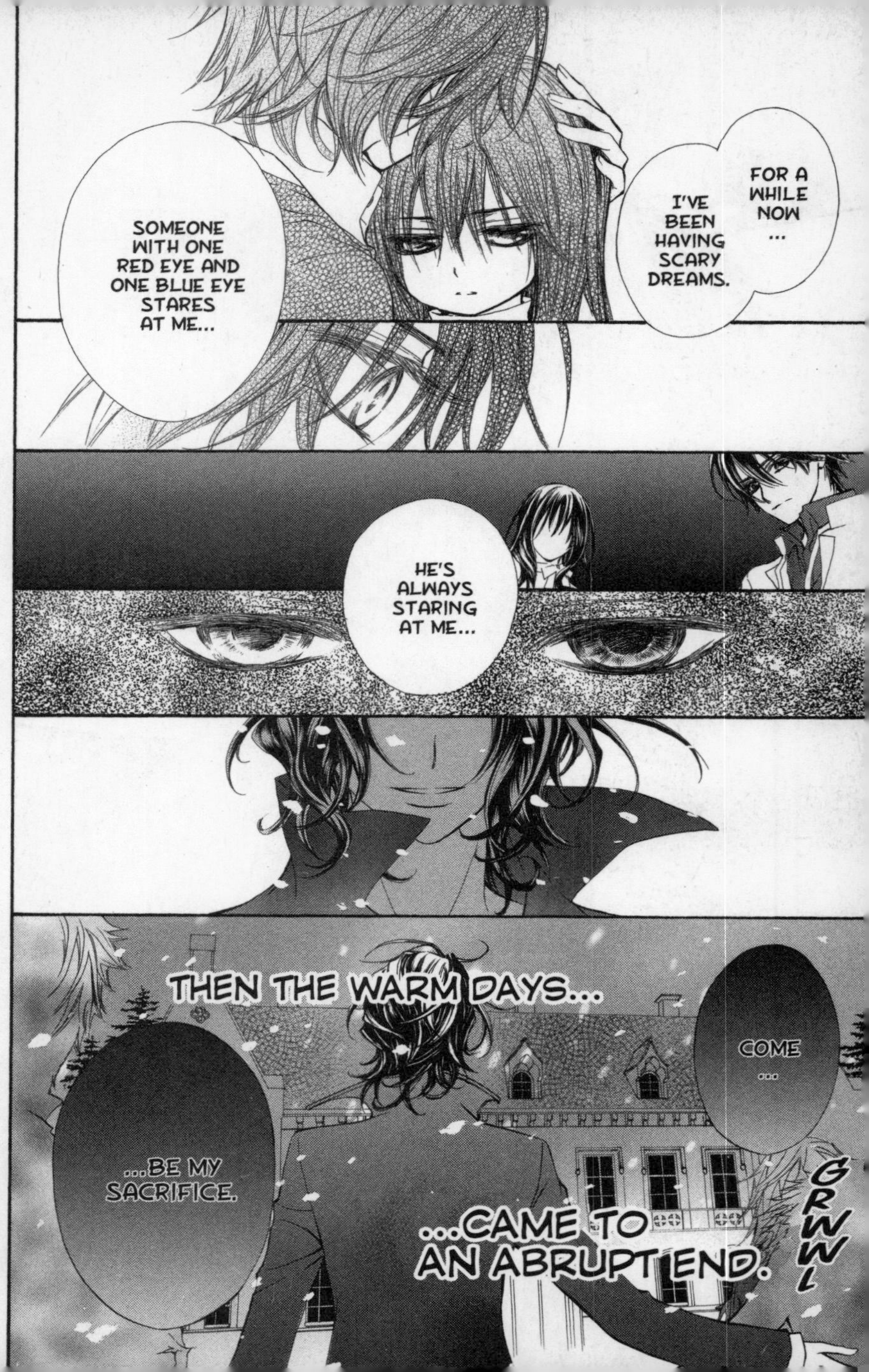
FOR A WHILE NOW ...
I'VE BEEN HAVING SCARY DREAMS.
SOMEONE WITH ONE RED EYE AND ONE BLUE EYE STARES AT ME...
HE'S ALWAYS STARING AT ME...
THEN THE WARM DAYS...
COME ...
...BE MY SACRIFICE.
...CAME TO AN ABRUPT END.
GRWWL

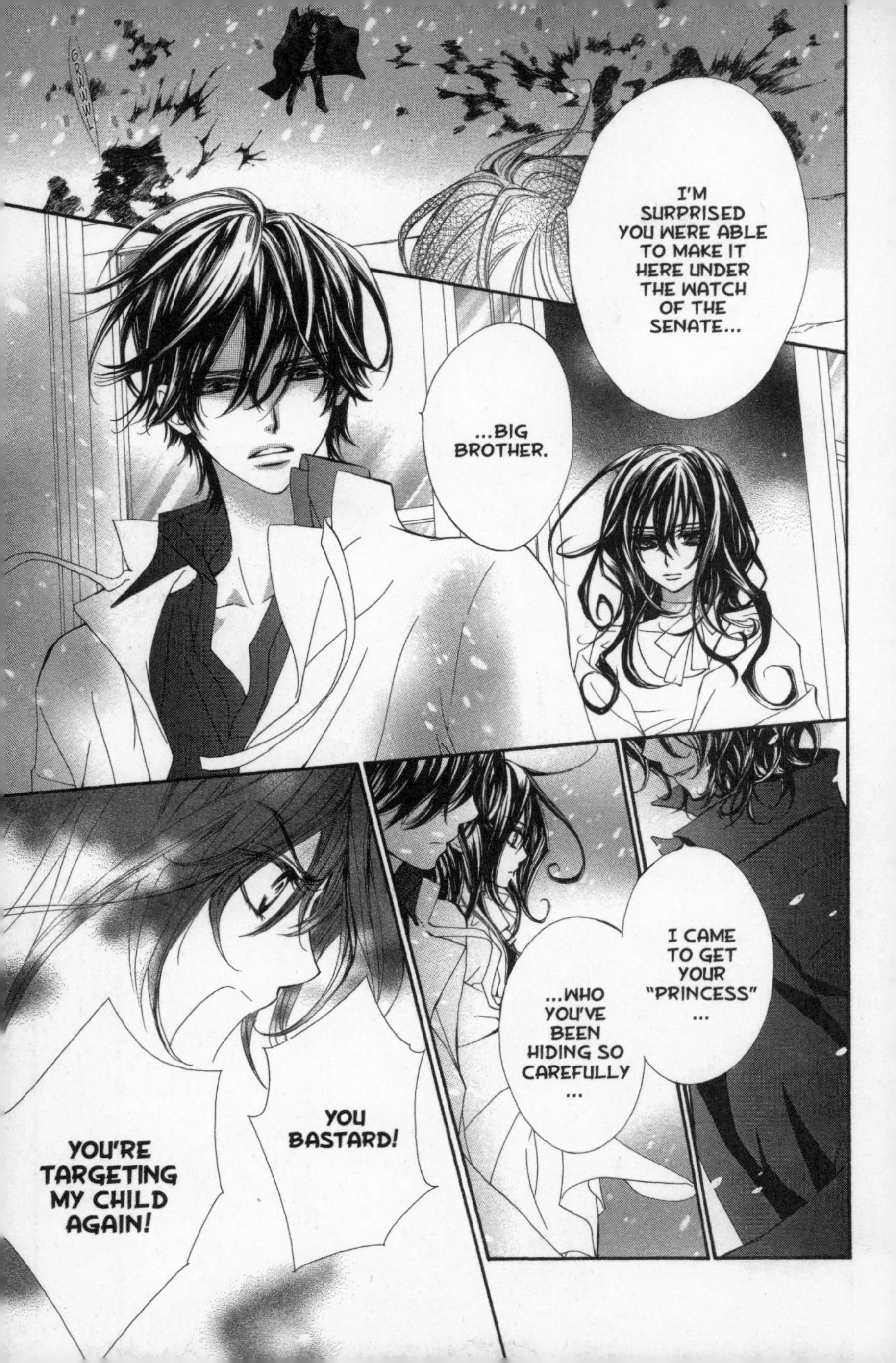
GRWWWL
I'M SURPRISED YOU WERE ABLE TO MAKE IT HERE UNDER THE WATCH OF THE SENATE...
...BIG BROTHER.
I CAME TO GET YOUR "PRINCESS"...
...WHO YOU'VE BEEN HIDING SO CAREFULLY...
YOU BASTARD!
YOU'RE TARGETING MY CHILD AGAIN!

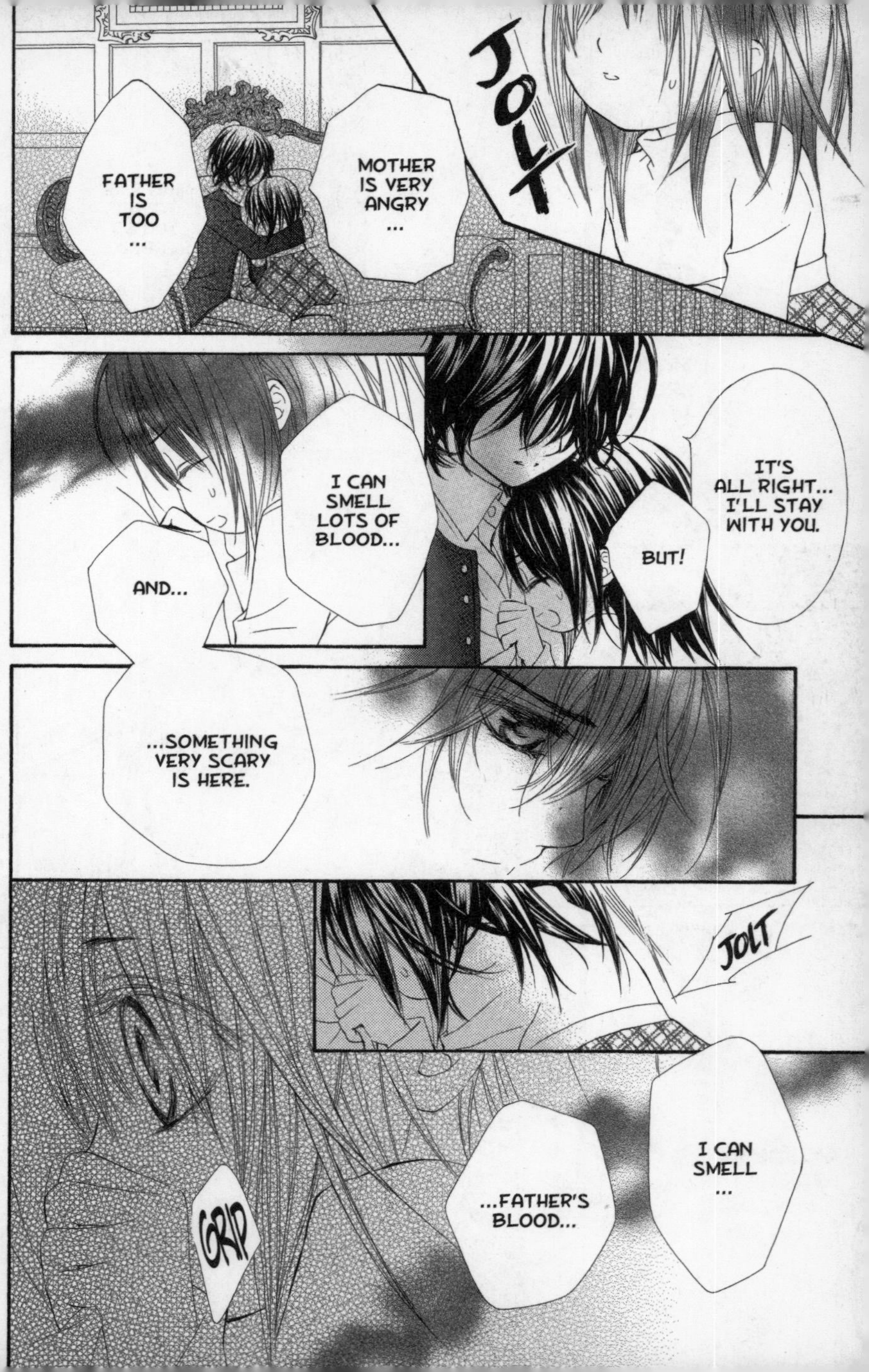
JOLT
MOTHER IS VERY ANGRY ...
FATHER IS TOO ...
IT'S ALL RIGHT... I'LL STAY WITH YOU.
BUT!
I CAN SMELL LOTS OF BLOOD...
AND...
...SOMETHING VERY SCARY IS HERE.
JOLT
I CAN SMELL ...
...FATHER'S BLOOD...
GRIP

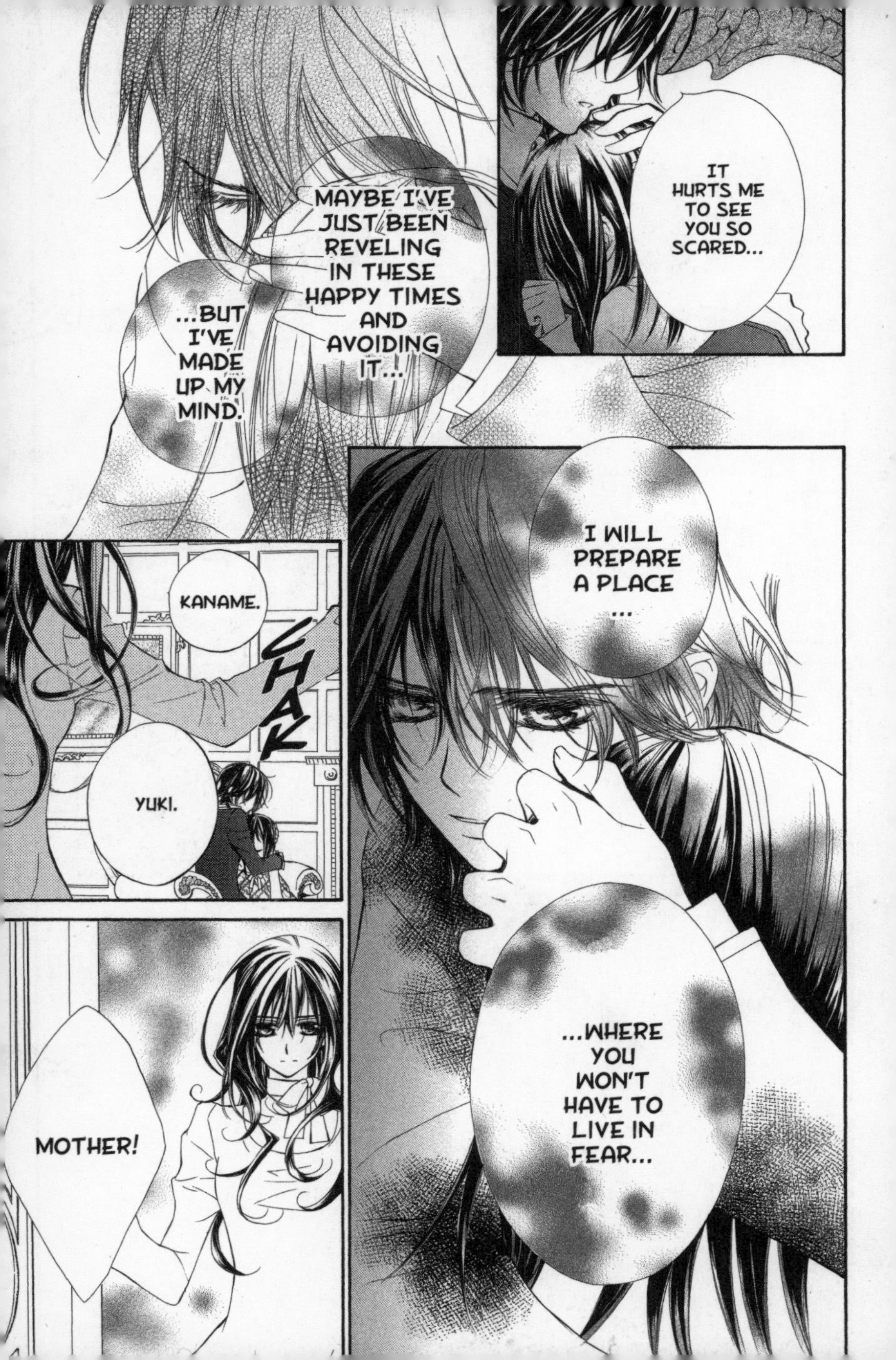
IT HURTS ME TO SEE YOU SO SCARED...
MAYBE I'VE JUST BEEN REVELING IN THESE HAPPY TIMES AND AVOIDING IT...
...BUT I'VE MADE UP MY MIND.
I WILL PREPARE A PLACE ...
...WHERE YOU WON'T HAVE TO LIVE IN FEAR...
KANAME.
CHAK
YUKI.
MOTHER!

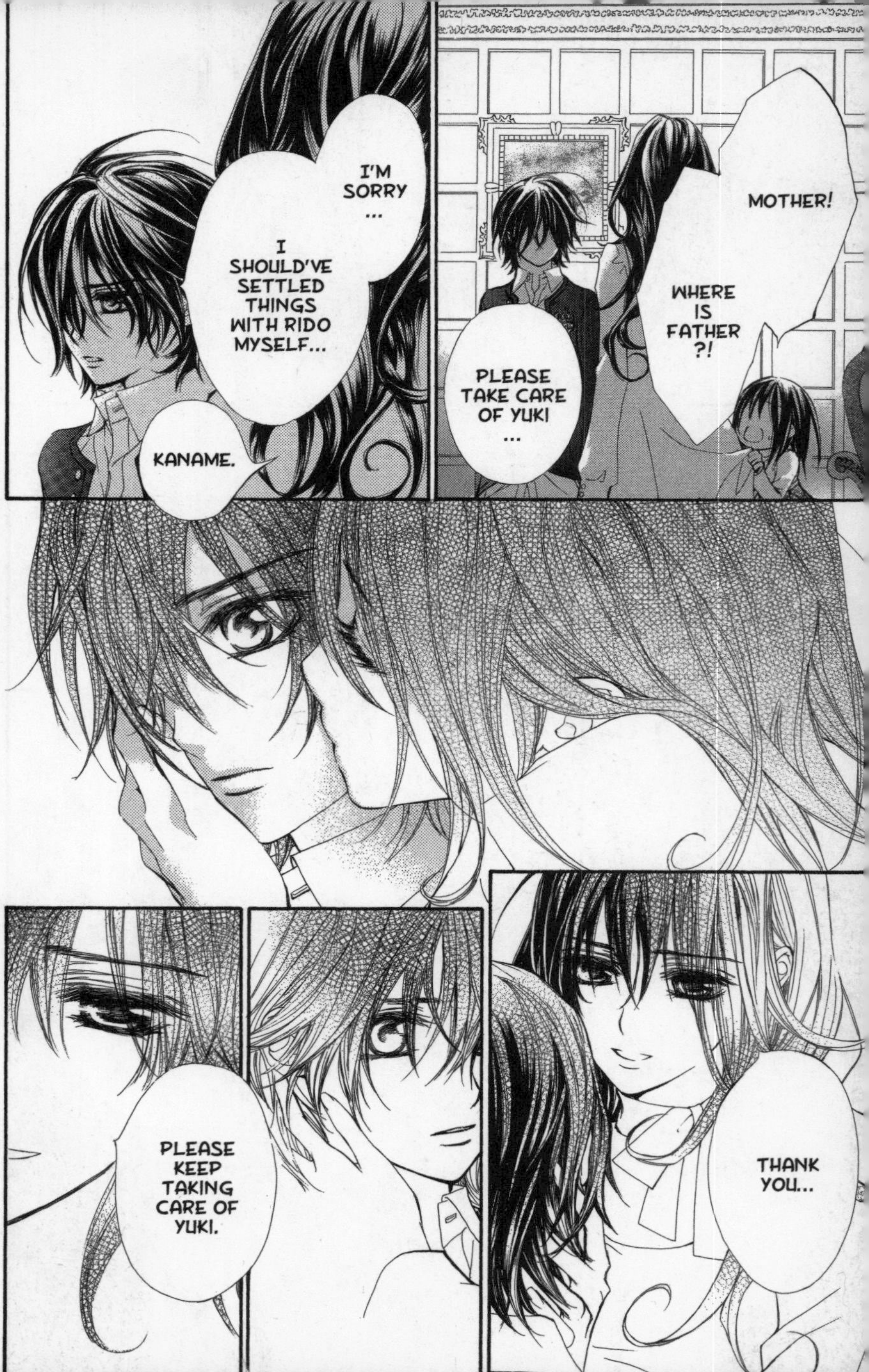
MOTHER!
WHERE IS FATHER ?!
PLEASE TAKE CARE OF YUKI ...
I'M SORRY ...
I SHOULD'VE SETTLED THINGS WITH RIDO MYSELF...
KANAME.
THANK YOU...
PLEASE KEEP TAKING CARE OF YUKI.

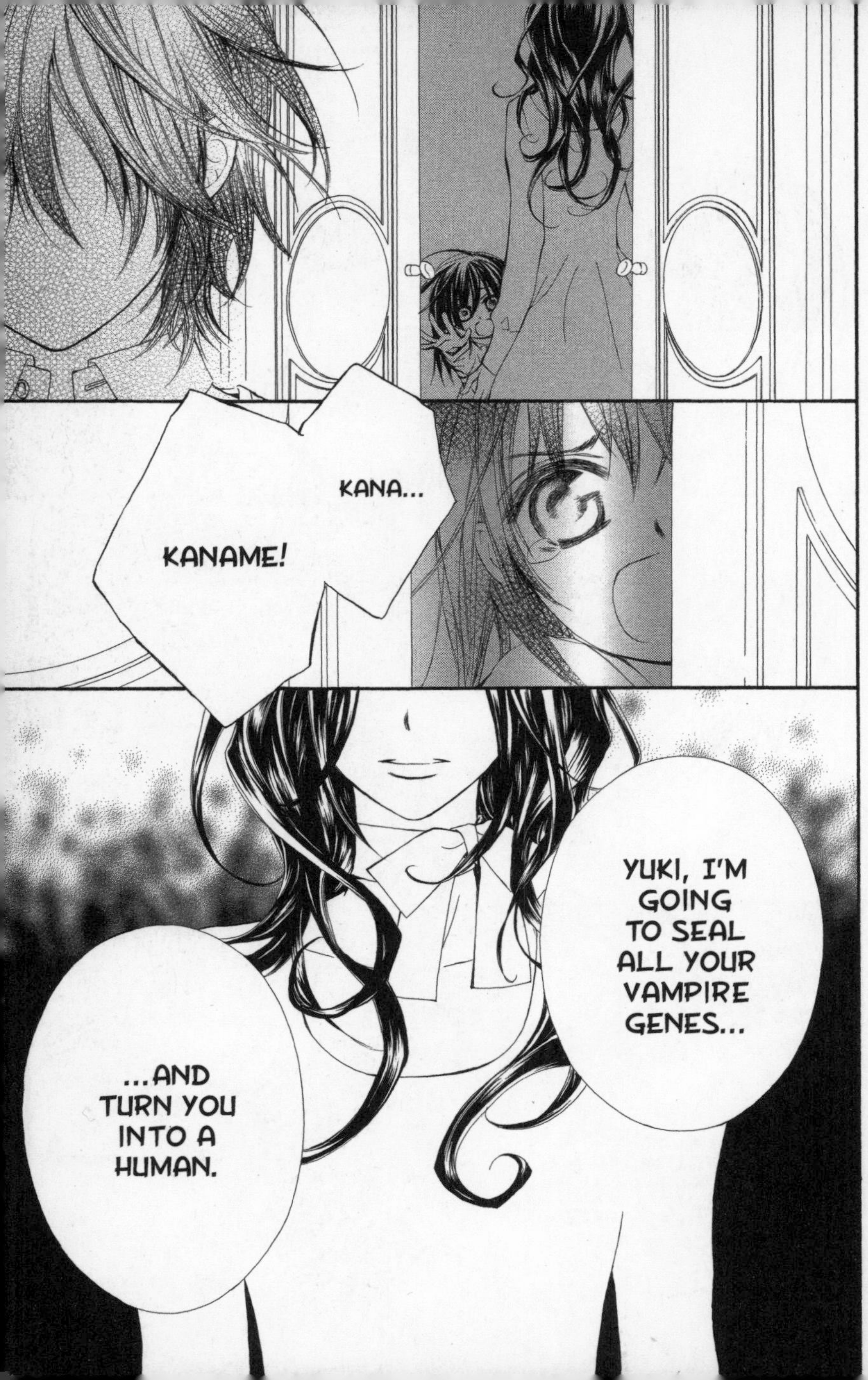
KANA...
KANAME!
YUKI, I'M GOING TO SEAL ALL YOUR VAMPIRE GENES...
...AND TURN YOU INTO A HUMAN.

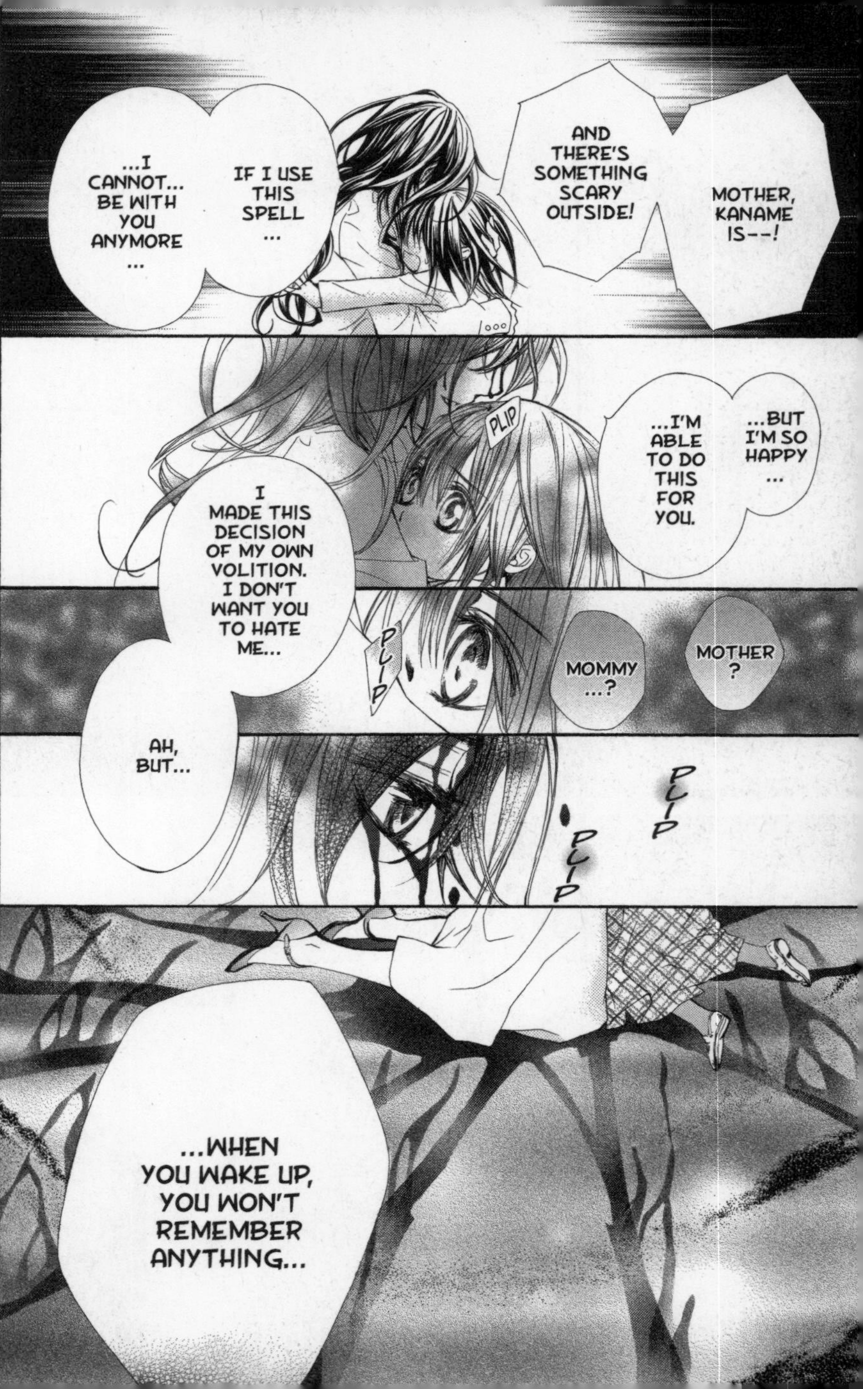
MOTHER, KANAME IS--!
AND THERE'S SOMETHING SCARY OUTSIDE!
IF I USE THIS SPELL ...
...I CANNOT... BE WITH YOU ANYMORE ...
...BUT I'M SO HAPPY ...
...I'M ABLE TO DO THIS FOR YOU.
PLIP
I MADE THIS DECISION OF MY OWN VOLITION. I DON'T WANT YOU TO HATE ME...
MOTHER ?
MOMMY ...?
PLIP
PLIP
PLIP
AH, BUT...
...WHEN YOU WAKE UP, YOU WON'T REMEMBER ANYTHING...

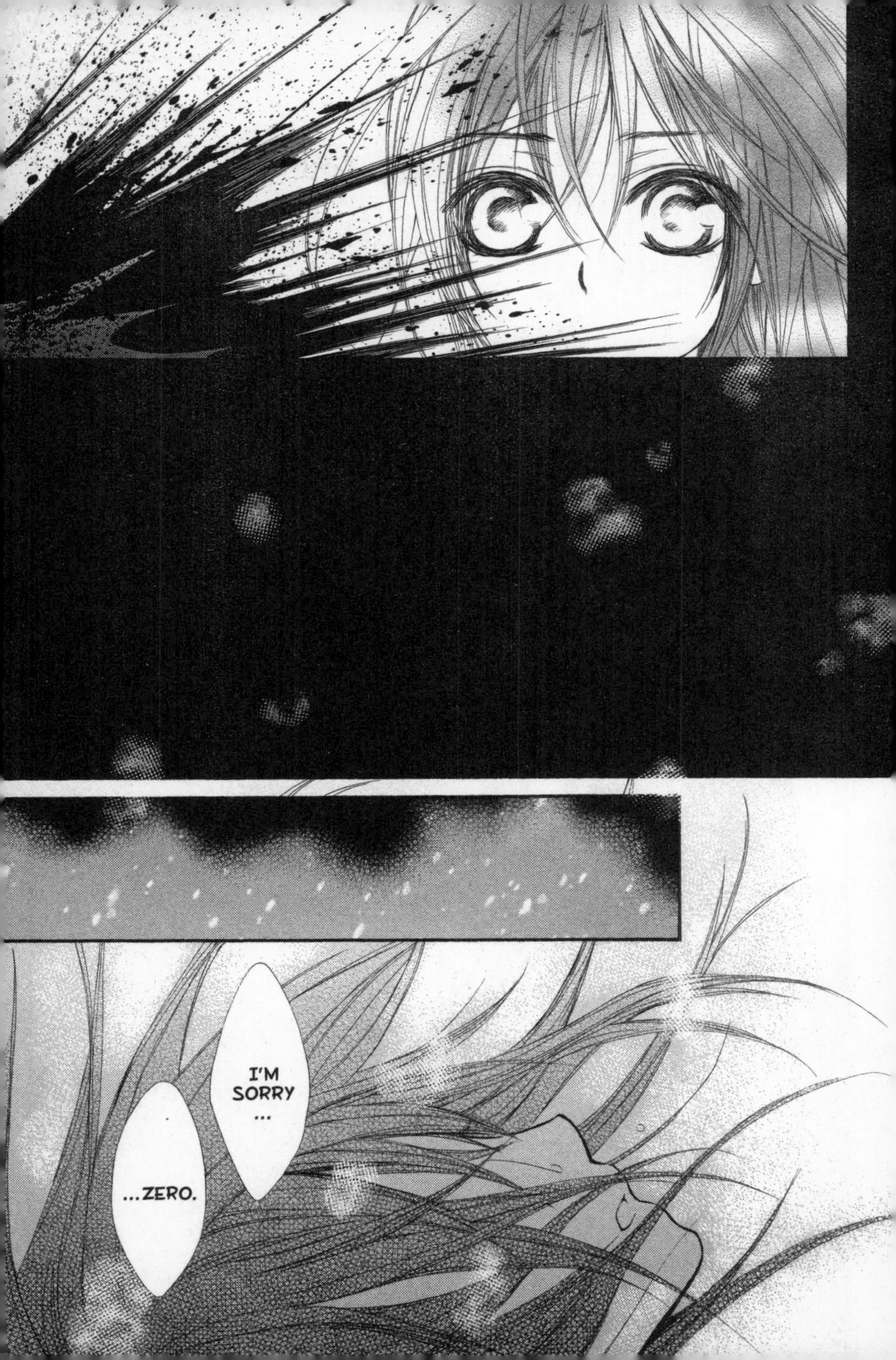
I'M SORRY ...
...ZERO.

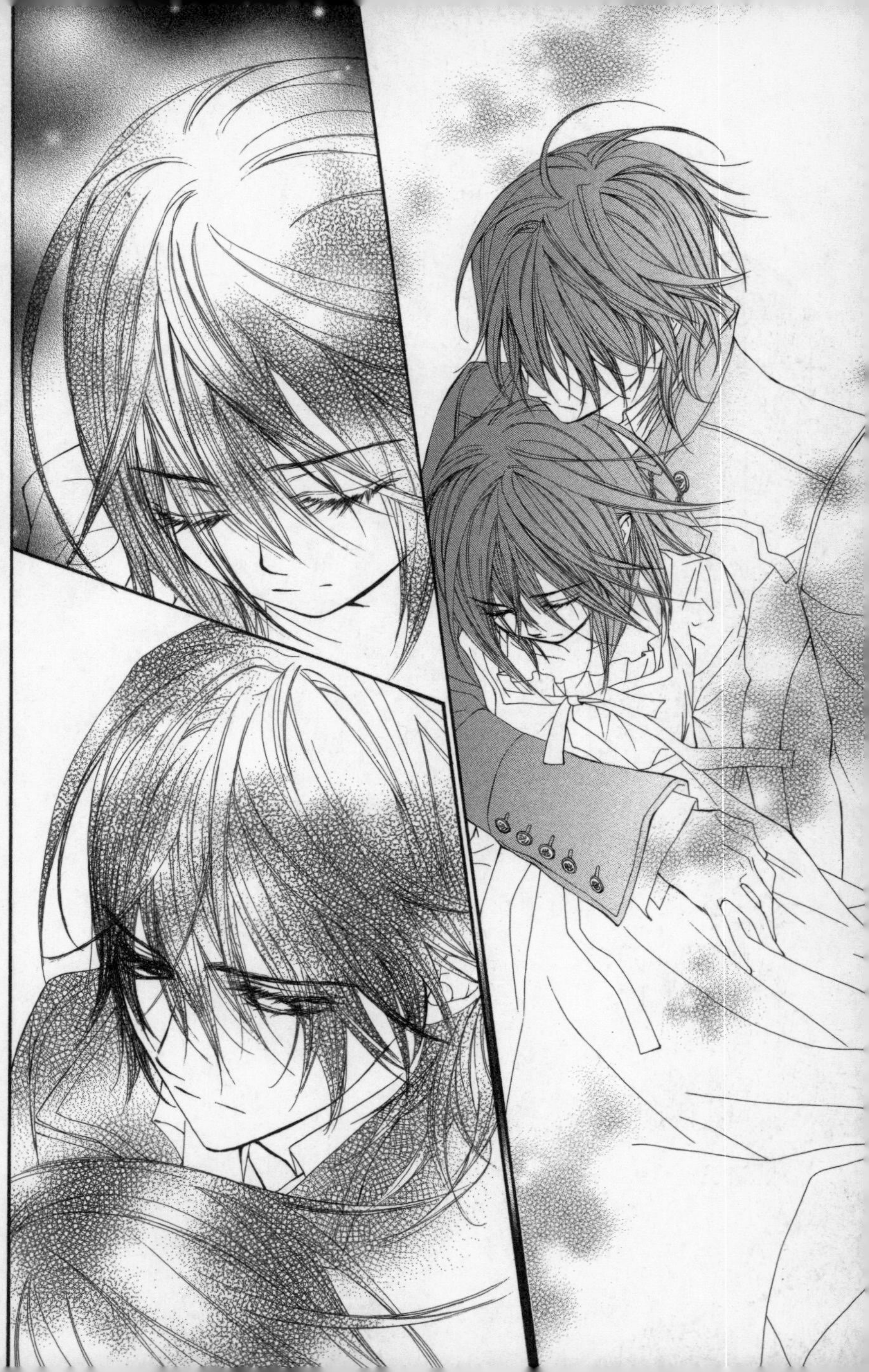

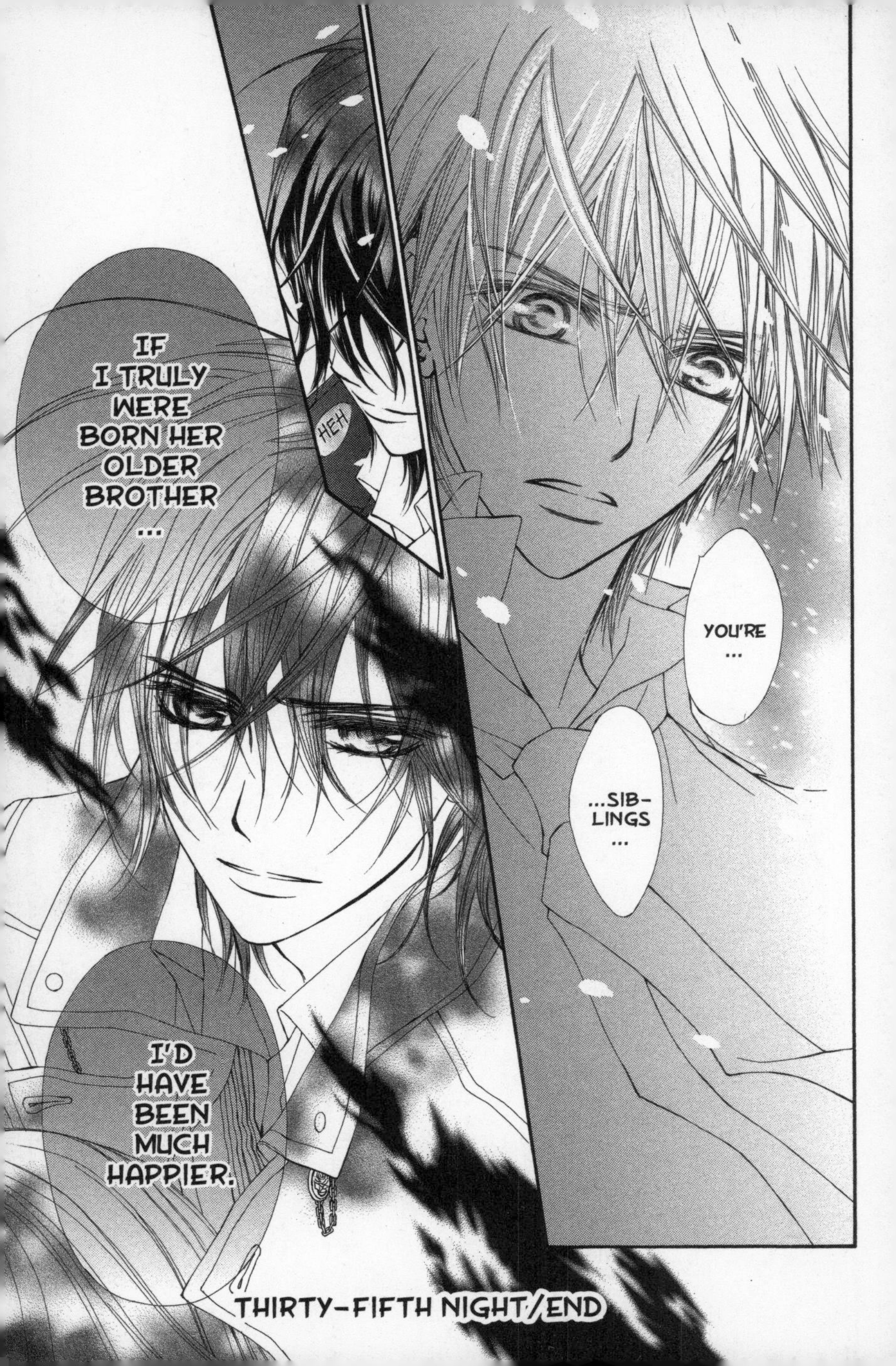
YOU'RE ...
...SIB-LINGS ...
HEH
IF I TRULY WERE BORN HER OLDER BROTHER ...
I'D HAVE BEEN MUCH HAPPIER.
THIRTY-FIFTH NIGHT/END

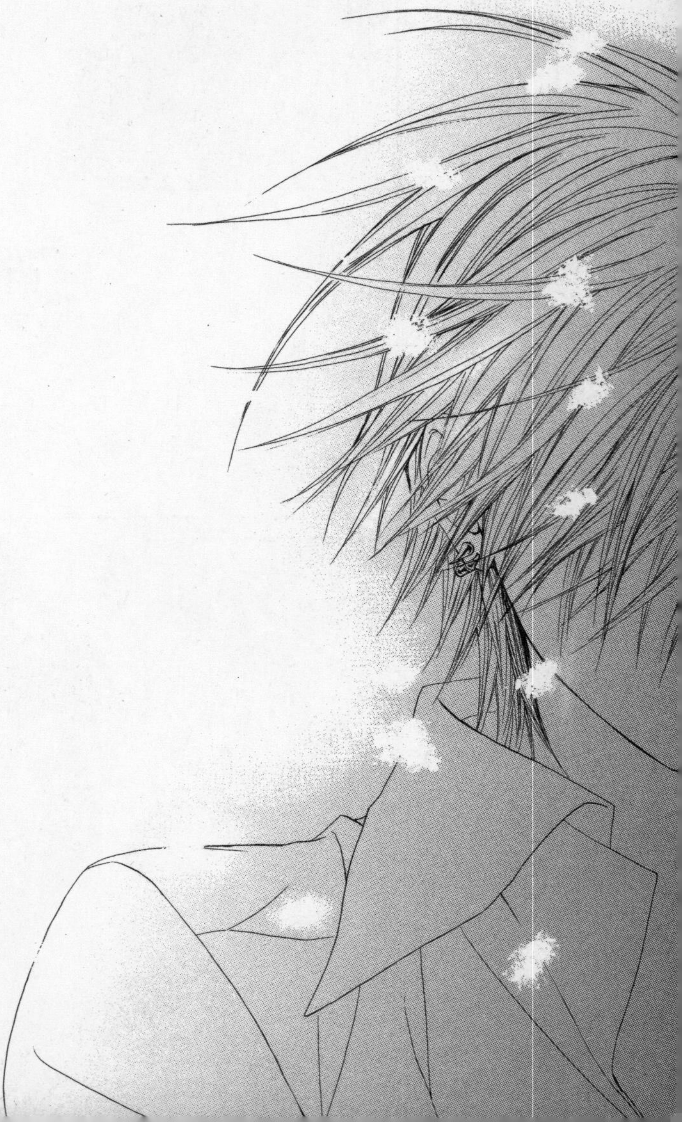

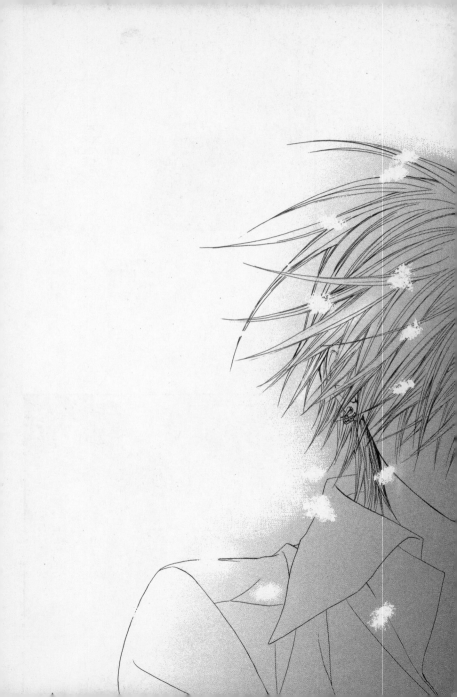

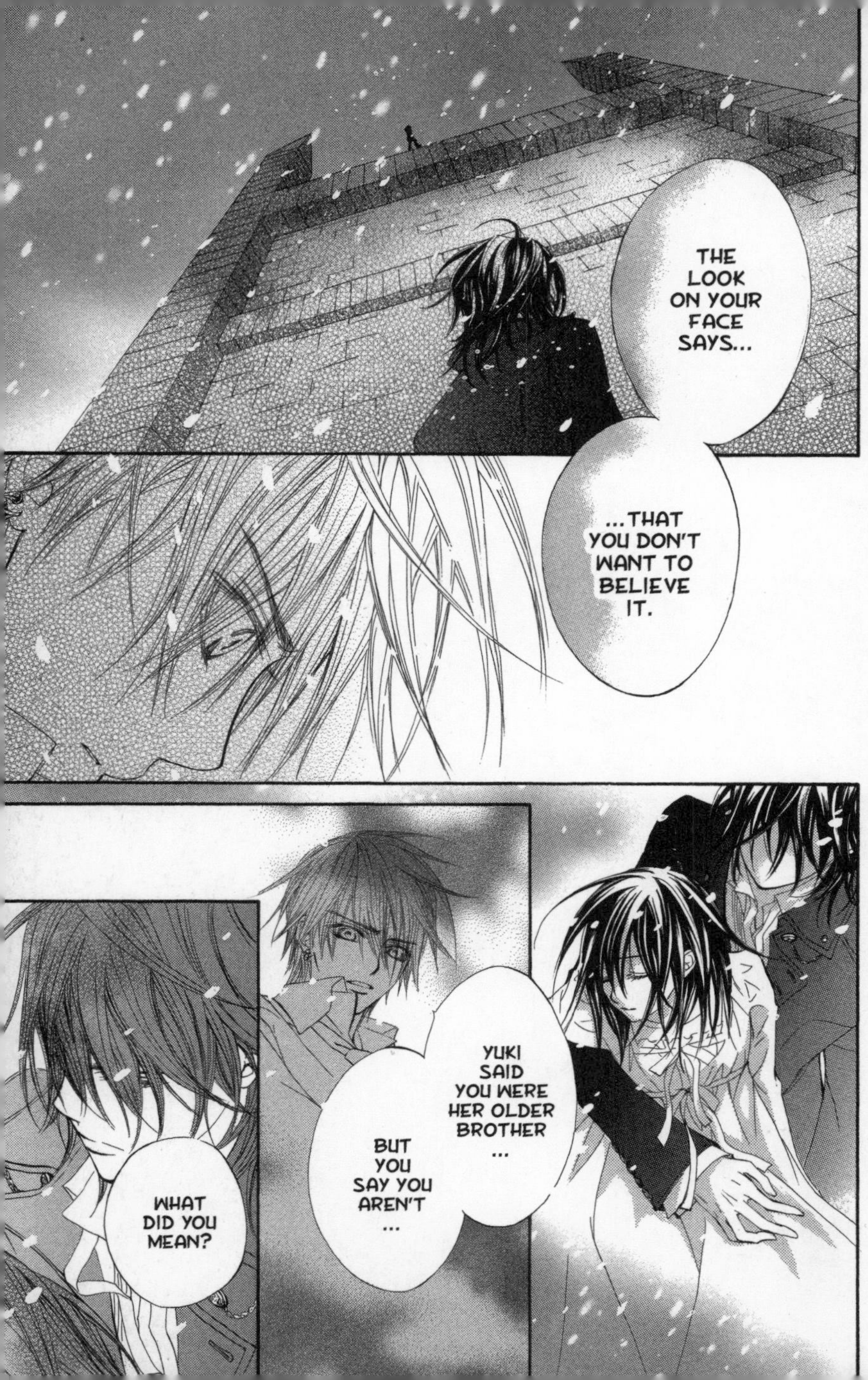
THE LOOK ON YOUR FACE SAYS...
...THAT YOU DON'T WANT TO BELIEVE IT.
YUKI SAID YOU WERE HER OLDER BROTHER ...
BUT YOU SAY YOU AREN'T ...
WHAT DID YOU MEAN?

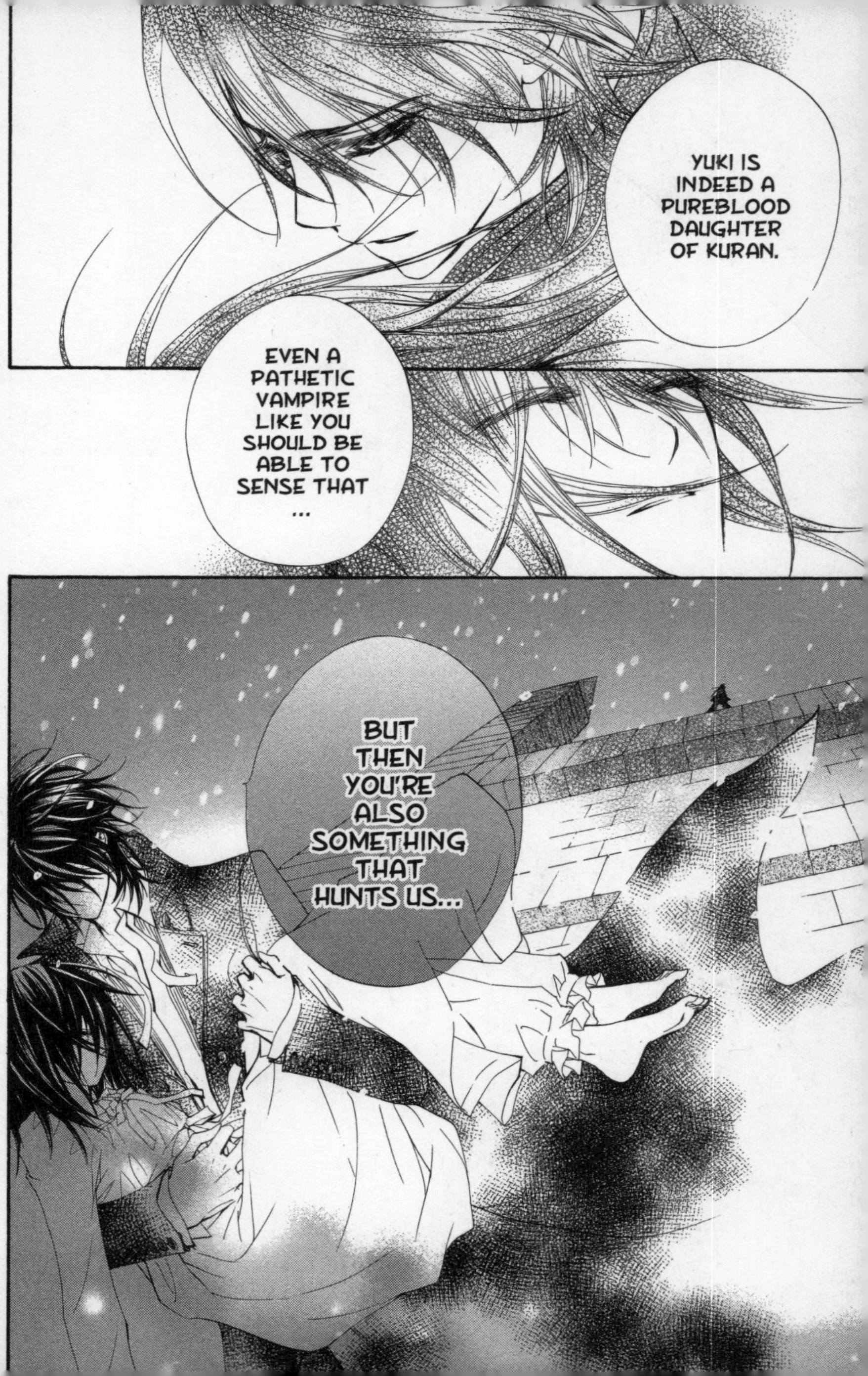
YUKI IS INDEED A PUREBLOOD DAUGHTER OF KURAN.
EVEN A PATHETIC VAMPIRE LIKE YOU SHOULD BE ABLE TO SENSE THAT ...
BUT THEN YOU'RE ALSO SOMETHING THAT HUNTS US...

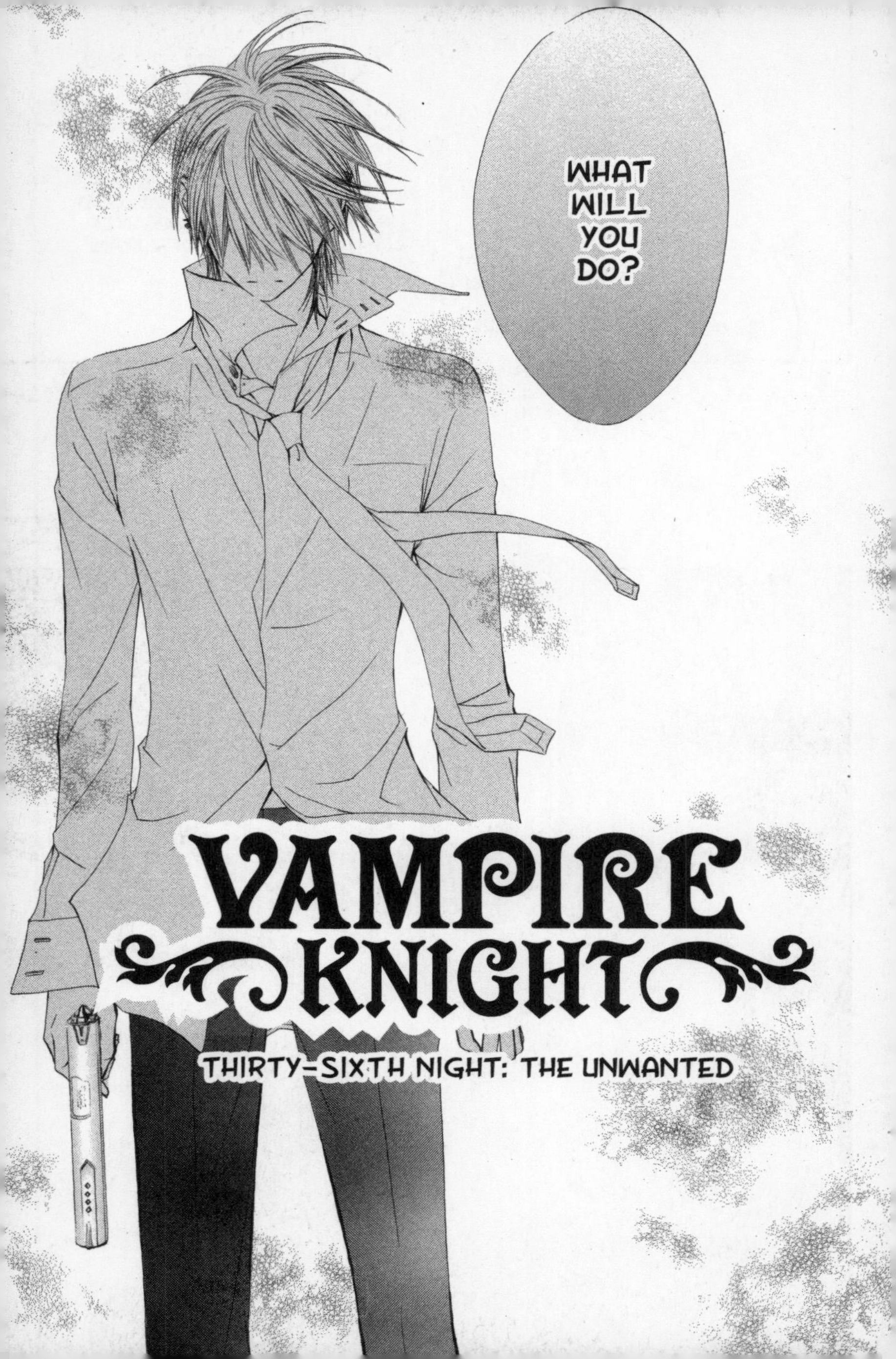
WHAT WILL YOU DO?
VAMPIRE KNIGHT
THIRTY-SIXTH NIGHT: THE UNWANTED

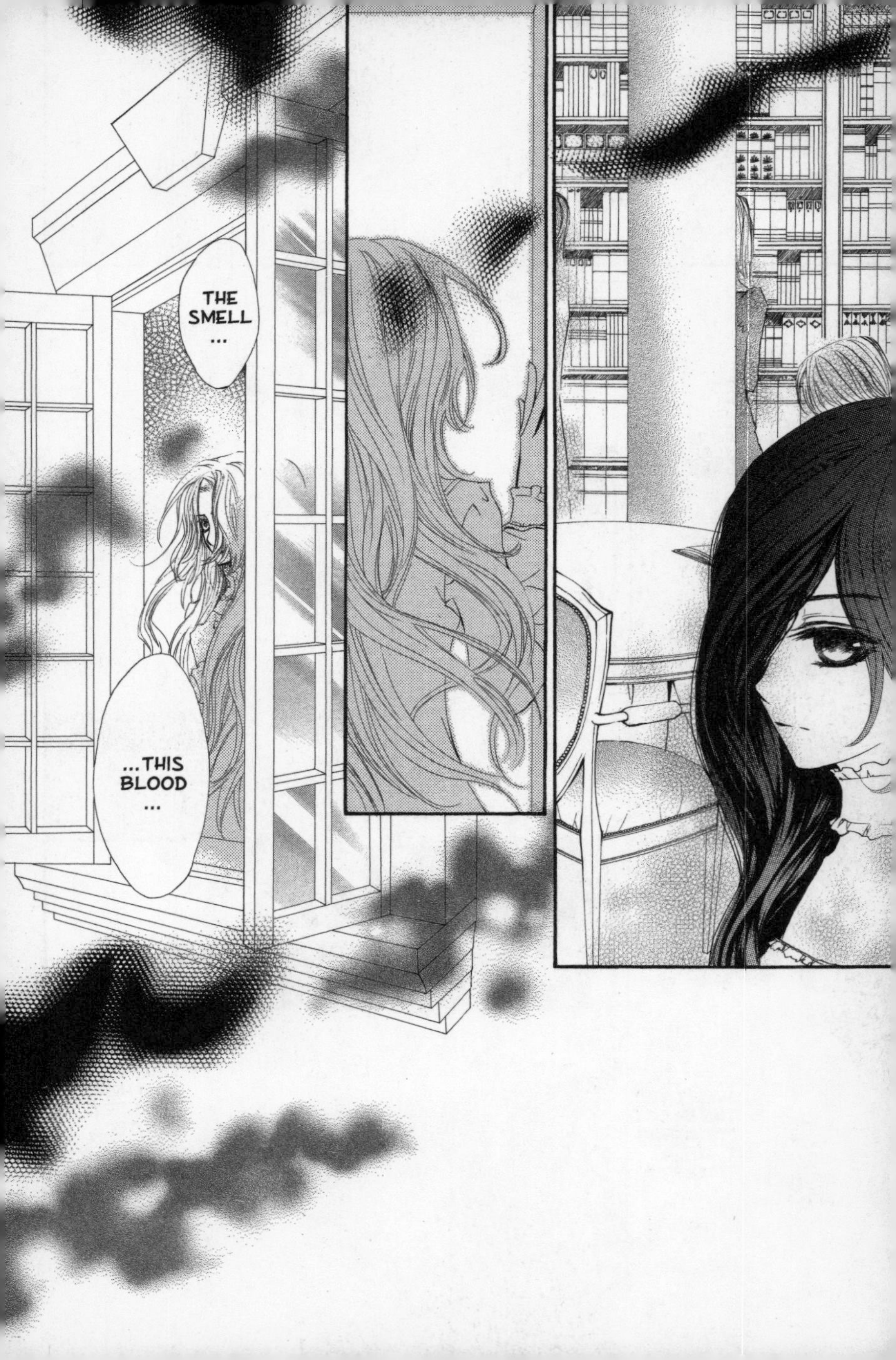
THE SMELL ...
...THIS BLOOD ...

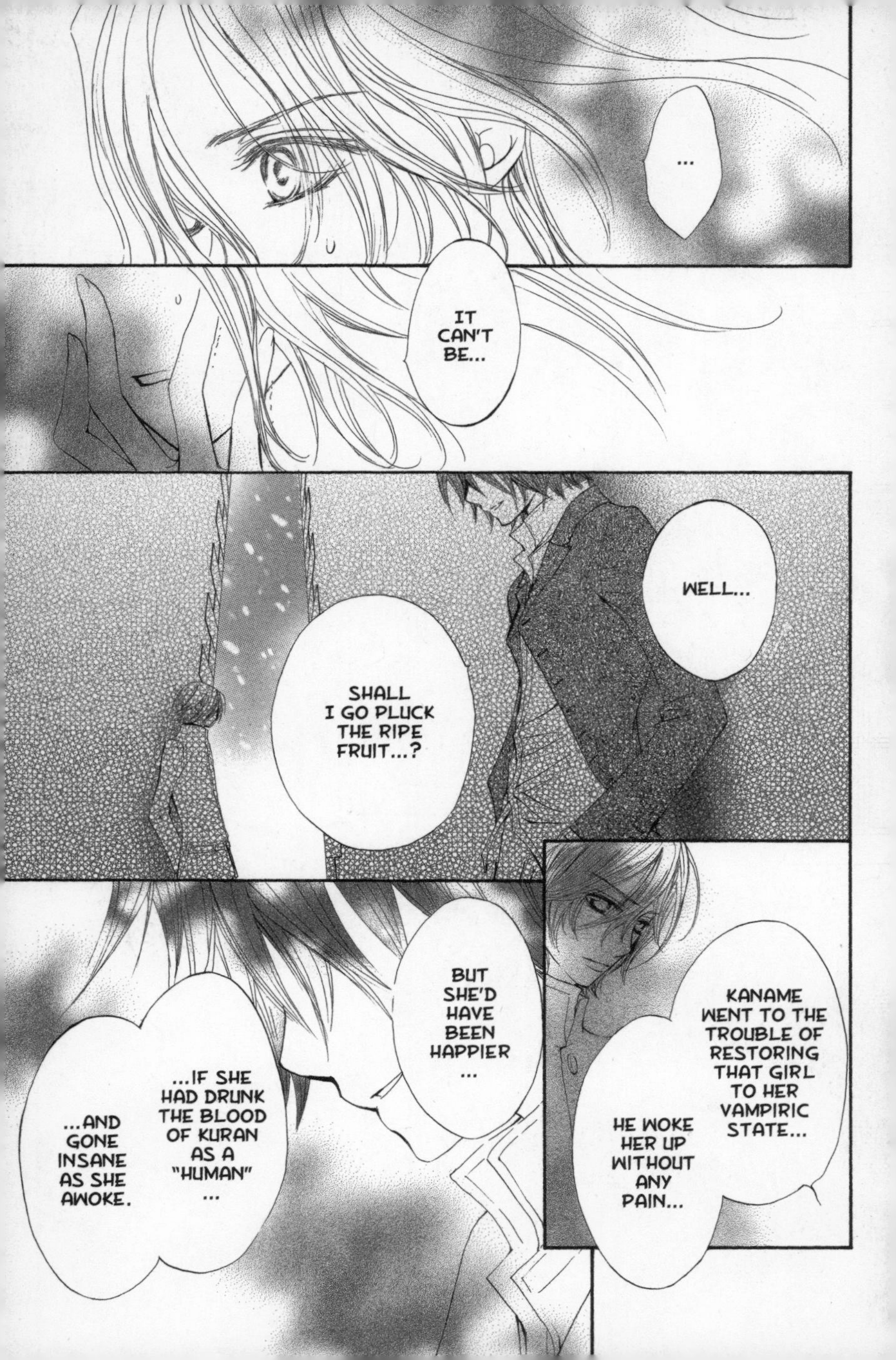
...
IT CAN'T BE...
WELL...
SHALL I GO PLUCK THE RIPE FRUIT...?
KANAME WENT TO THE TROUBLE OF RESTORING THAT GIRL TO HER VAMPIRIC STATE...
HE WOKE HER UP WITHOUT ANY PAIN...
BUT SHE'D HAVE BEEN HAPPIER ...
...IF SHE HAD DRUNK THE BLOOD OF KURAN AS A "HUMAN" ...
...AND GONE INSANE AS SHE AWOKE.

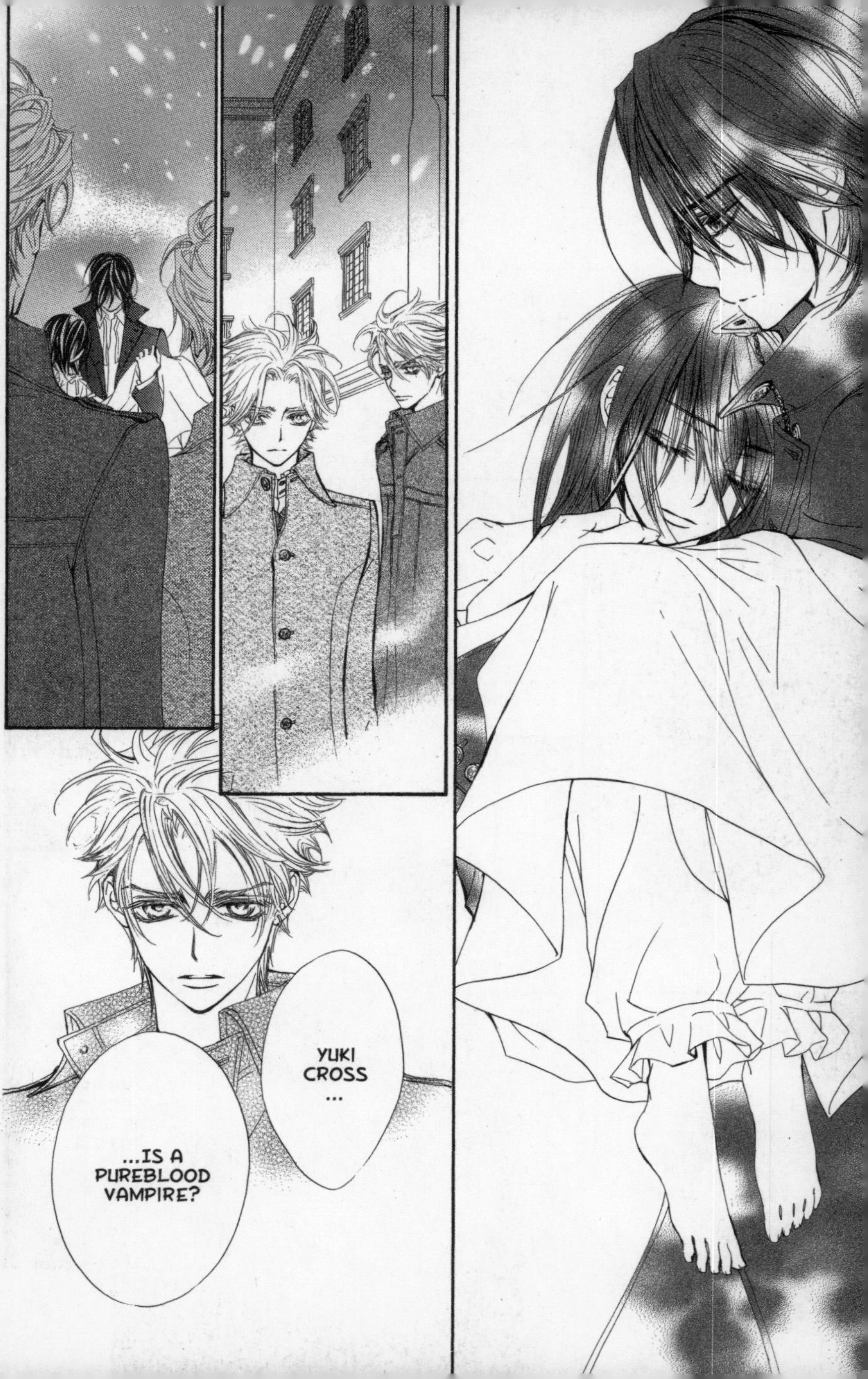
YUKI CROSS ...
...IS A PUREBLOOD VAMPIRE?

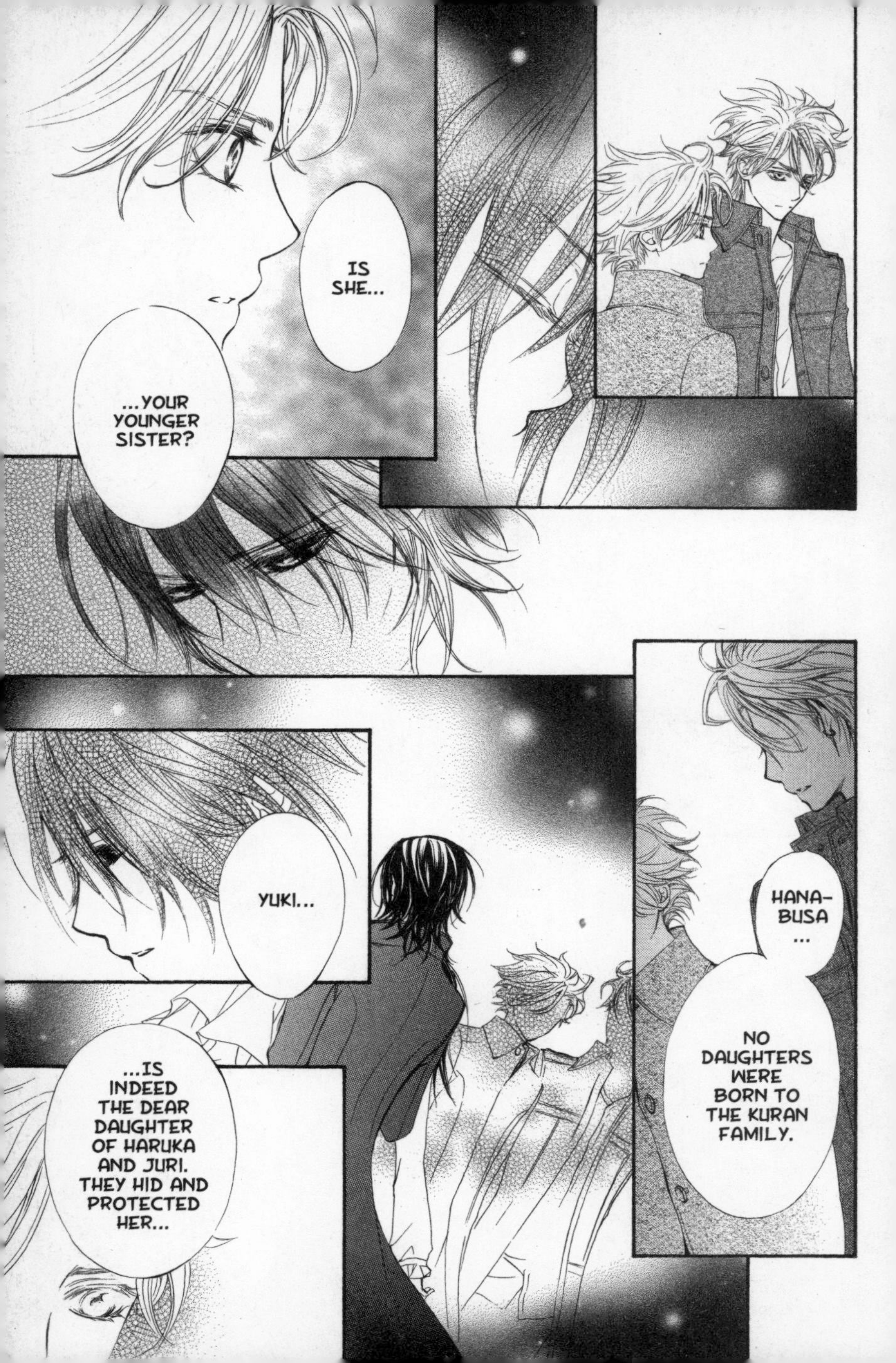
IS SHE...
...YOUR YOUNGER SISTER?
HANA-BUSA...
NO DAUGHTERS WERE BORN TO THE KURAN FAMILY.
YUKI...
...IS INDEED THE DEAR DAUGHTER OF HARUKA AND JURI. THEY HID AND PROTECTED HER...

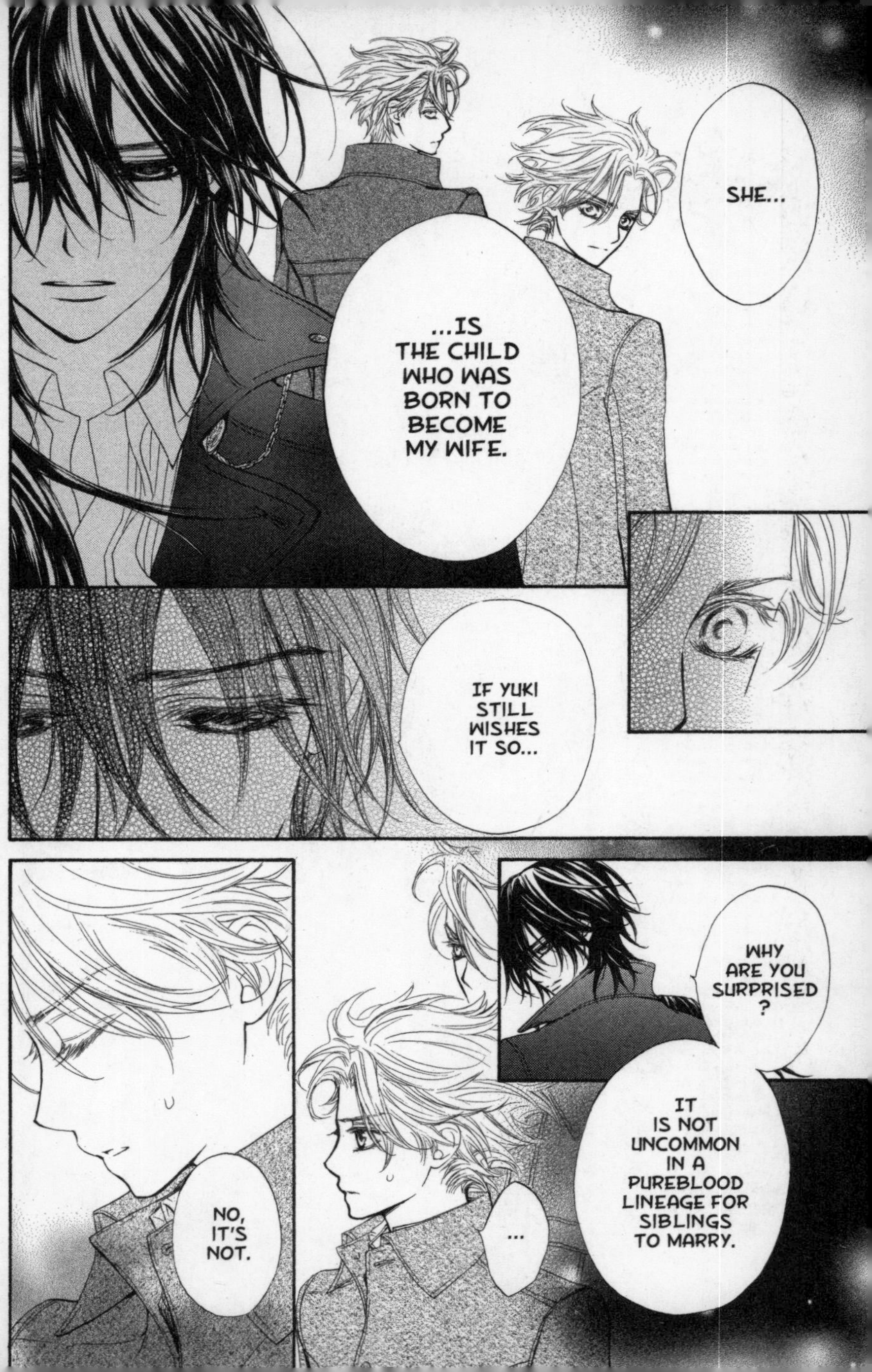
SHE...
...IS THE CHILD WHO WAS BORN TO BECOME MY WIFE.
IF YUKI STILL WISHES IT SO...
WHY ARE YOU SURPRISED?
IT IS NOT UNCOMMON IN A PUREBLOOD LINEAGE FOR SIBLINGS TO MARRY.
...
NO, IT'S NOT.

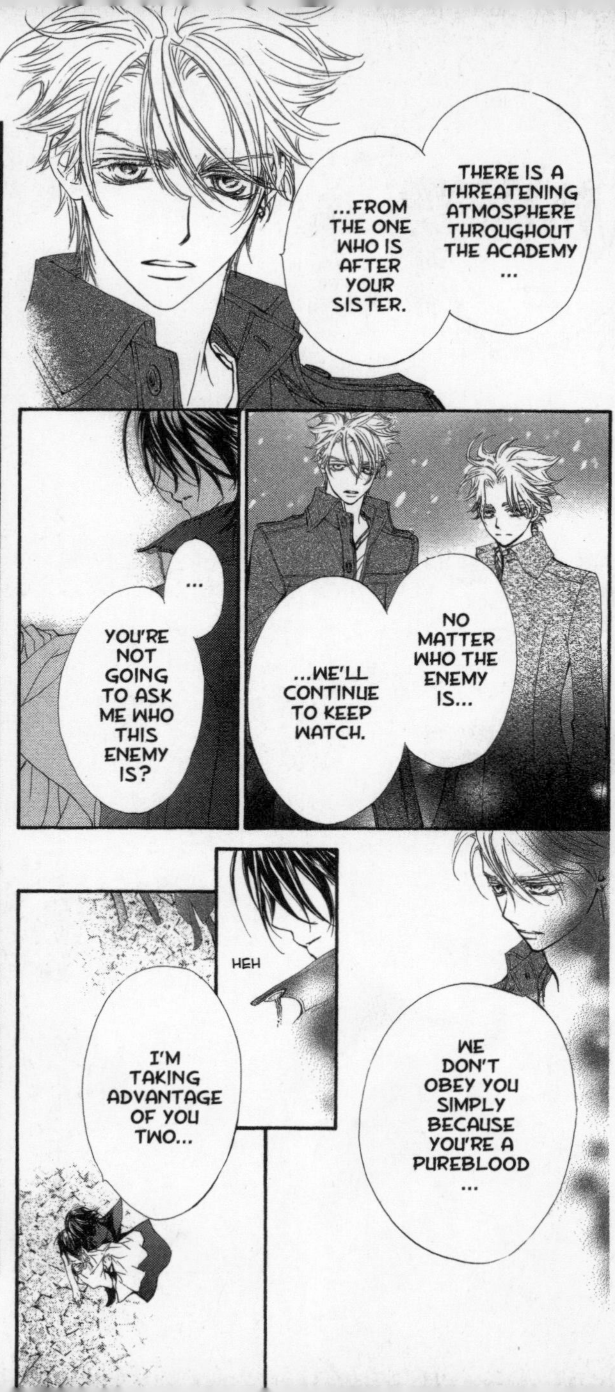
THERE IS A THREATENING ATMOSPHERE THROUGHOUT THE ACADEMY...
...FROM THE ONE WHO IS AFTER YOUR SISTER.
NO MATTER WHO THE ENEMY IS...
...WE'LL CONTINUE TO KEEP WATCH.
...
YOU'RE NOT GOING TO ASK ME WHO THIS ENEMY IS?
WE DON'T OBEY YOU SIMPLY BECAUSE YOU'RE A PUREBLOOD...
HEH
I'M TAKING ADVANTAGE OF YOU TWO...

II

I went to see the recording of the anime! My wishes came true! Here's a list of what was different from the drama CD and things I noticed for the first time.

- It takes over three hours to record a single episode. They record each scene with care, and everyone discusses things when necessary. (I participated in the discussion a little too.)
- I almost made my debut as a voice actress. Temporarily. (It was too difficult, and I said no right away.)
- I now realize that the scenes in which the character is always calm, where the Kaname-sama voice (played by Kishio-san) repeated himself were super-rare!! Thank you...! (I'm sorry. But they were usually interesting or smile-provoking, so the atmosphere became very relaxed...)
- I could only see the back of the voice actors while they were acting... when Miyano-san (who plays Zero and Ichiru) was acting out a wailing scene, his emotions were exploding from his back. I was able to observe an amazing amount of soul.

(continued)

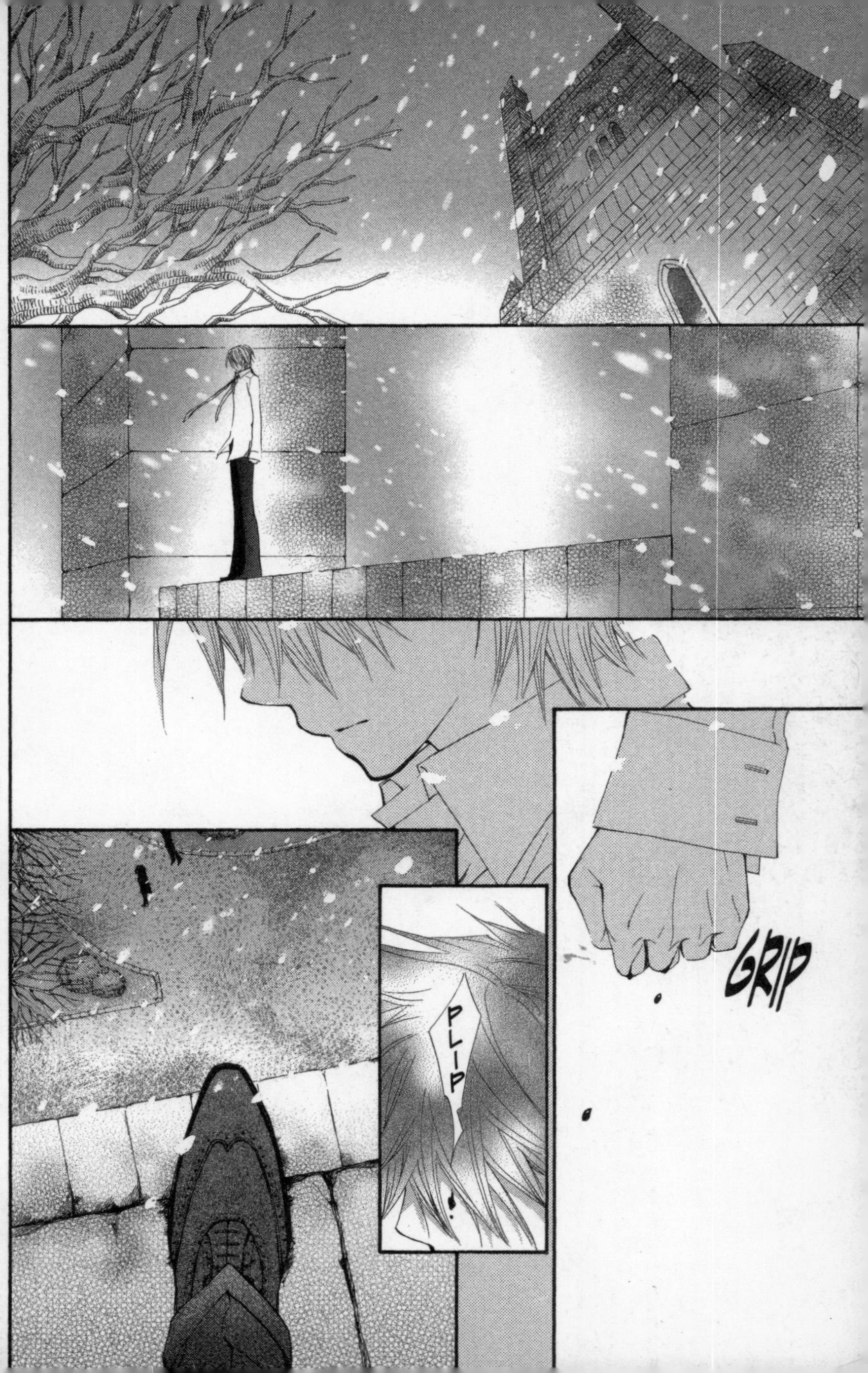
GRIP
PLIP

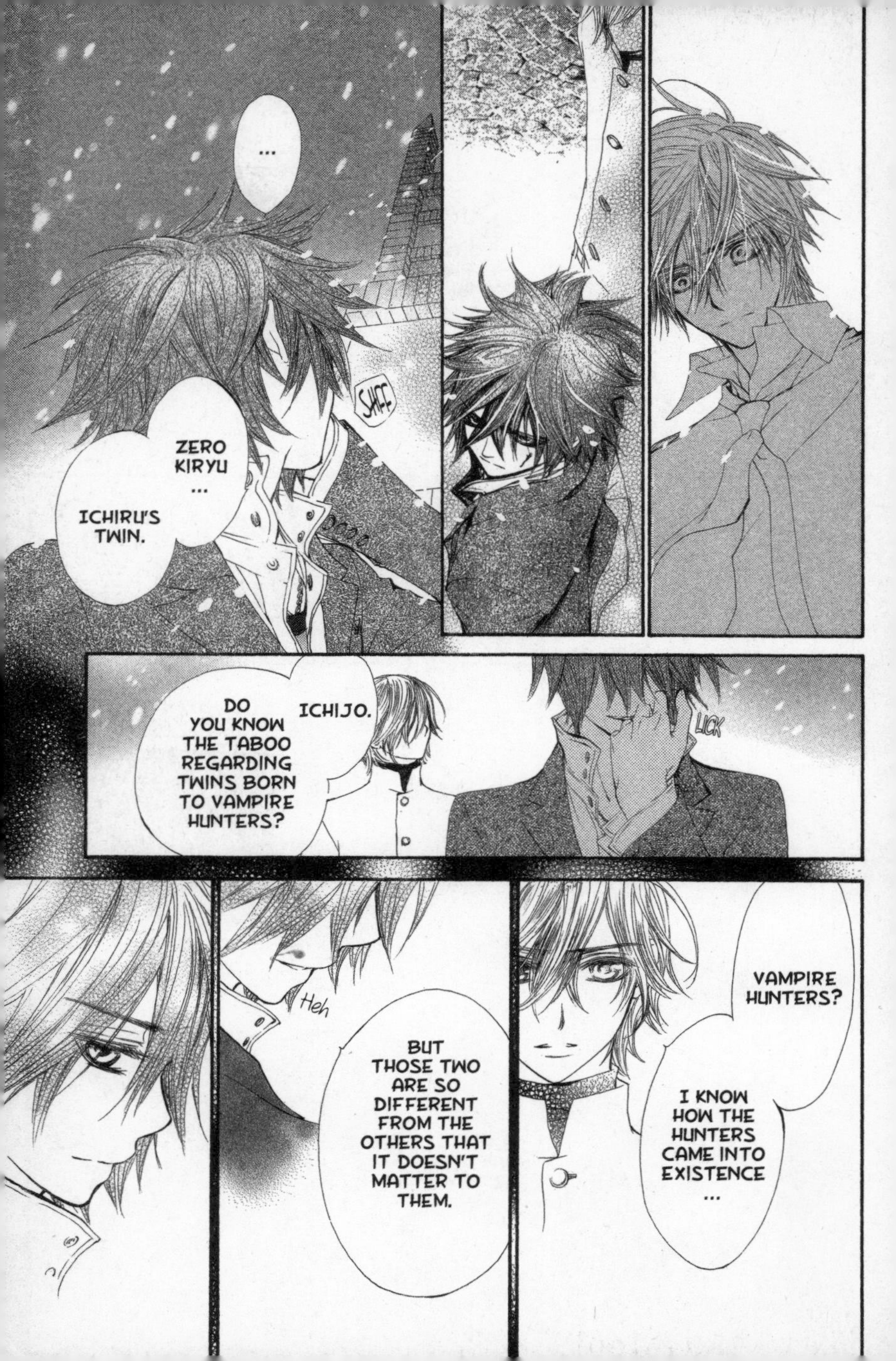
...
SHFF
ZERO KIRYU ... ICHIRU'S TWIN.
LICK
ICHIJO.
DO YOU KNOW THE TABOO REGARDING TWINS BORN TO VAMPIRE HUNTERS?
VAMPIRE HUNTERS?
I KNOW HOW THE HUNTERS CAME INTO EXISTENCE ...
Heh
BUT THOSE TWO ARE SO DIFFERENT FROM THE OTHERS THAT IT DOESN'T MATTER TO THEM.

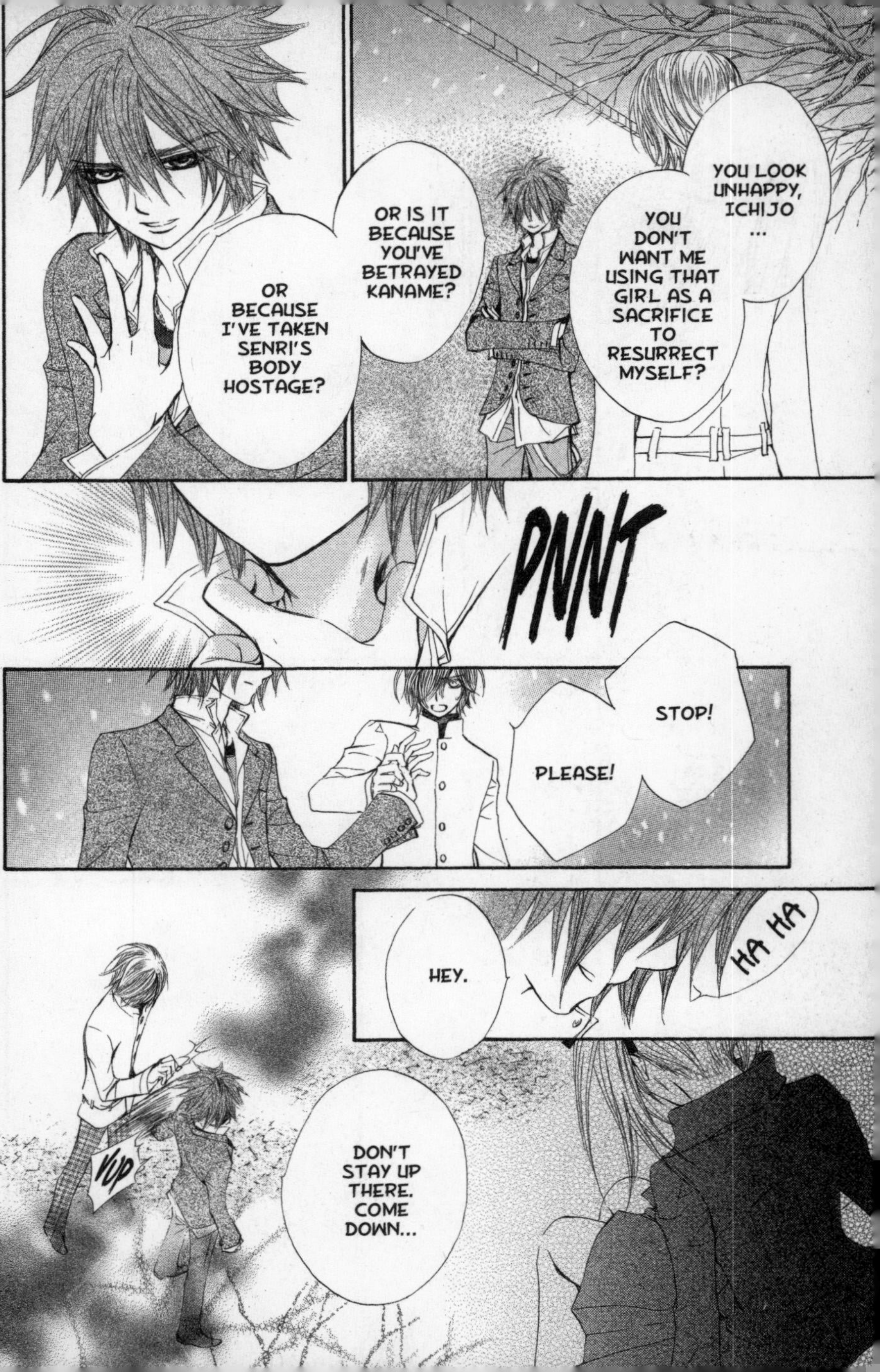
YOU LOOK UNHAPPY, ICHIJO ...
YOU DON'T WANT ME USING THAT GIRL AS A SACRIFICE TO RESURRECT MYSELF?
OR IS IT BECAUSE YOU'VE BETRAYED KANAME?
OR BECAUSE I'VE TAKEN SENRI'S BODY HOSTAGE?
PNNT
STOP!
PLEASE!
HA HA
HEY.
DON'T STAY UP THERE. COME DOWN...
VUP

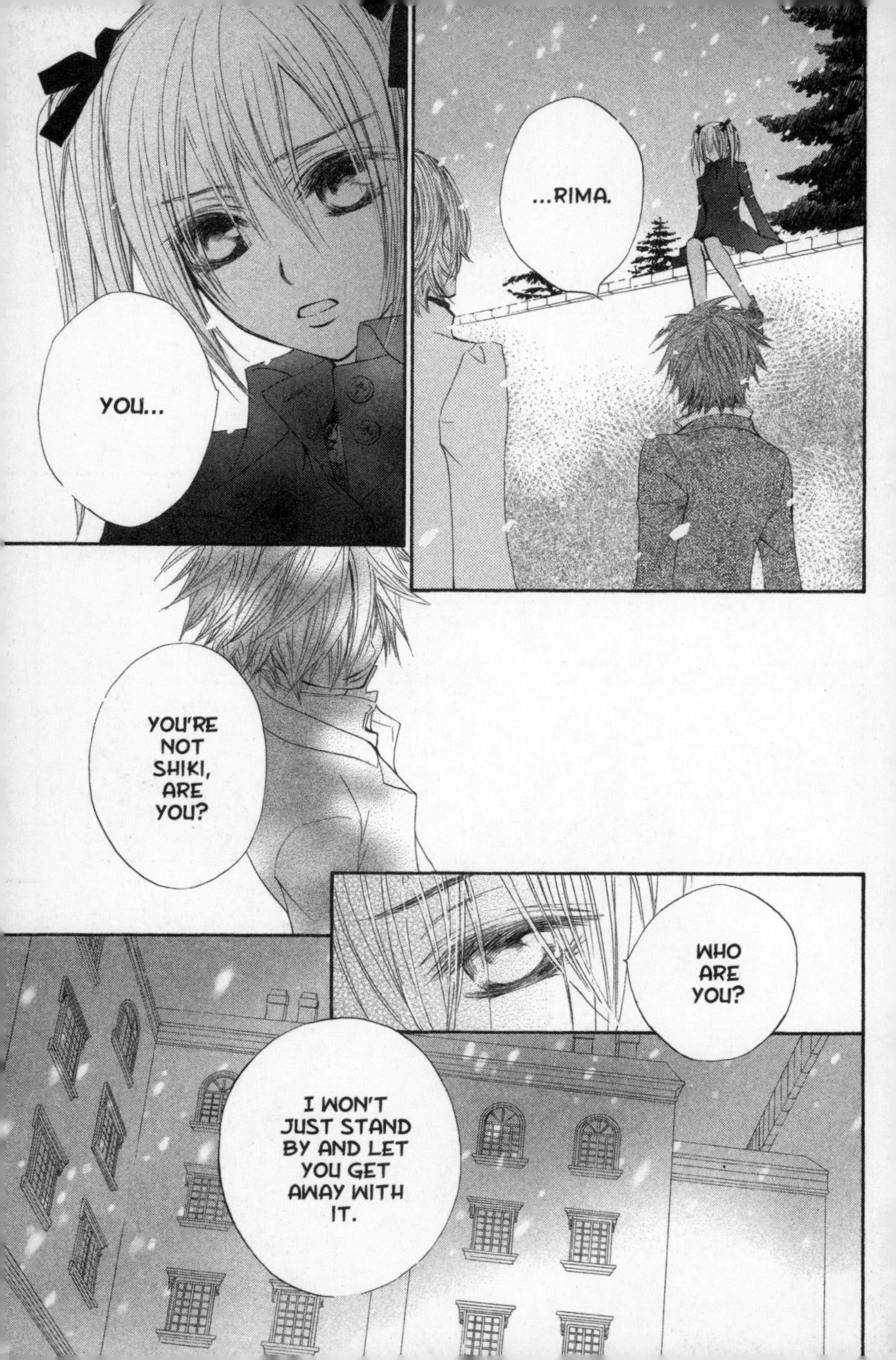
...RIMA.
YOU...
YOU'RE NOT SHIKI, ARE YOU?
WHO ARE YOU?
I WON'T JUST STAND BY AND LET YOU GET AWAY WITH IT.

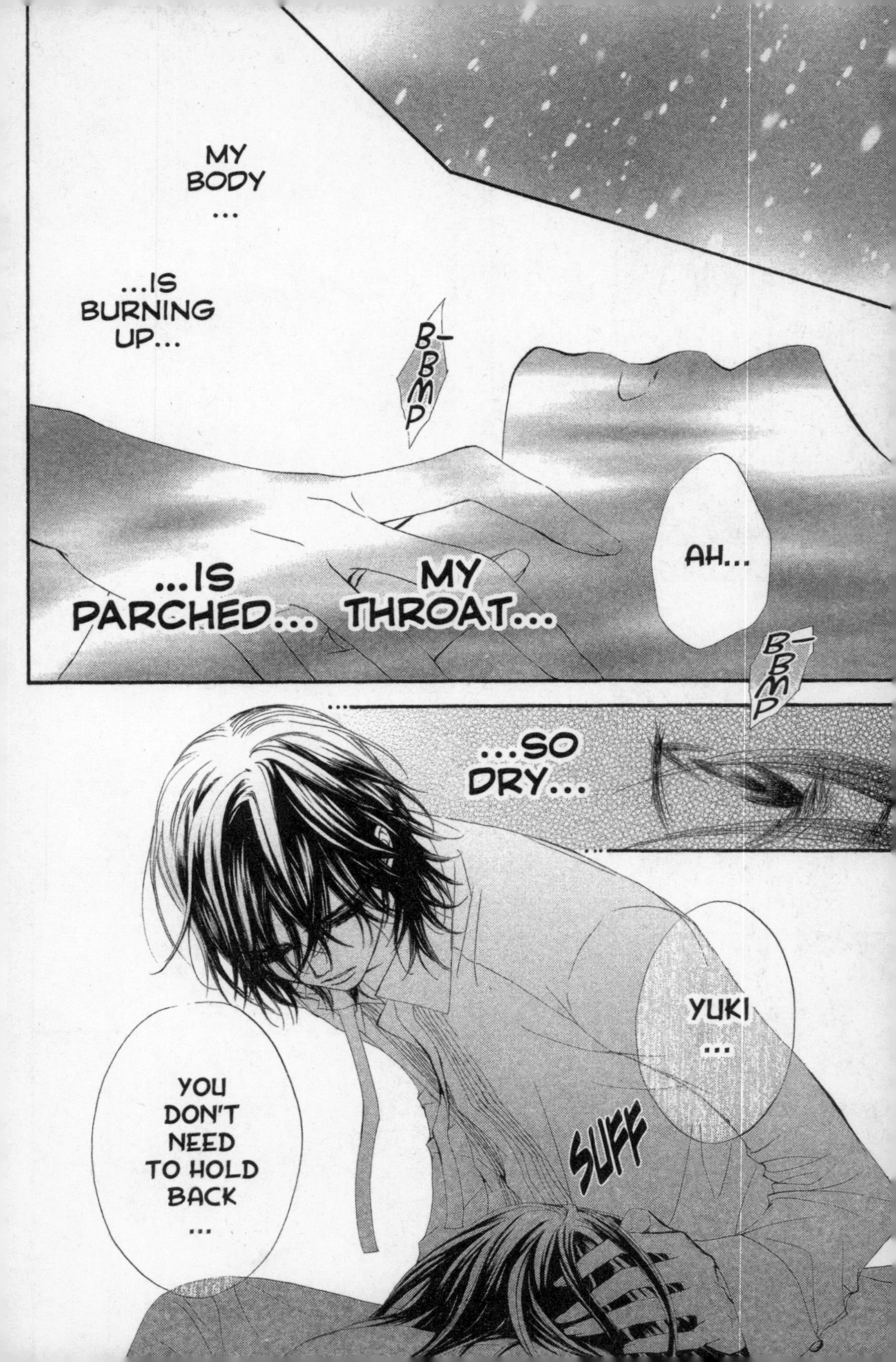

MY BODY ...
...IS BURNING UP...
B-BMP
AH...
MY THROAT...
...IS PARCHED...
B-BMP
...SO DRY...
YUKI ...
SUFF
YOU DON'T NEED TO HOLD BACK ...

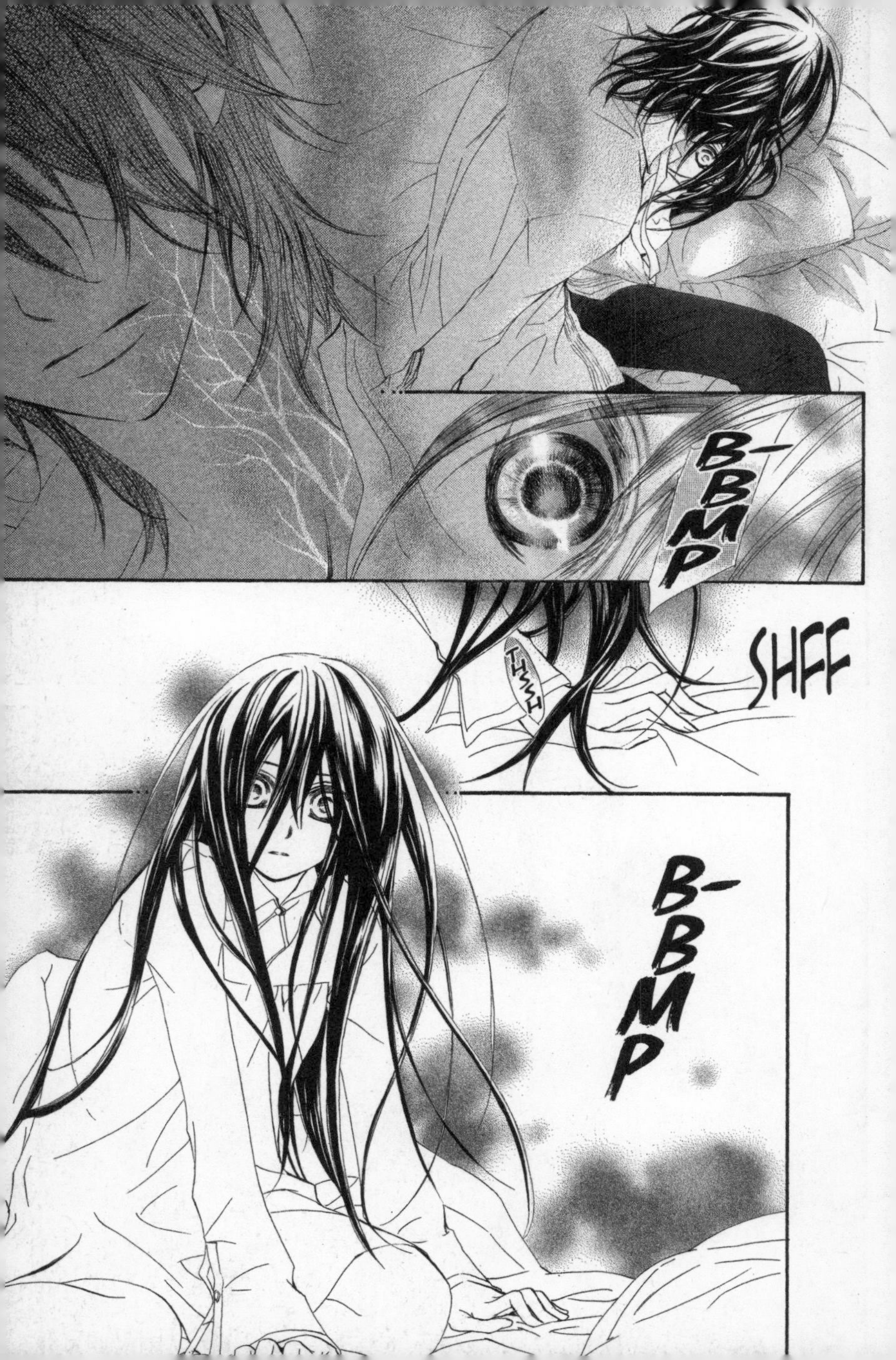
B-BBMP
SHFF
THSSH
B-BBMP

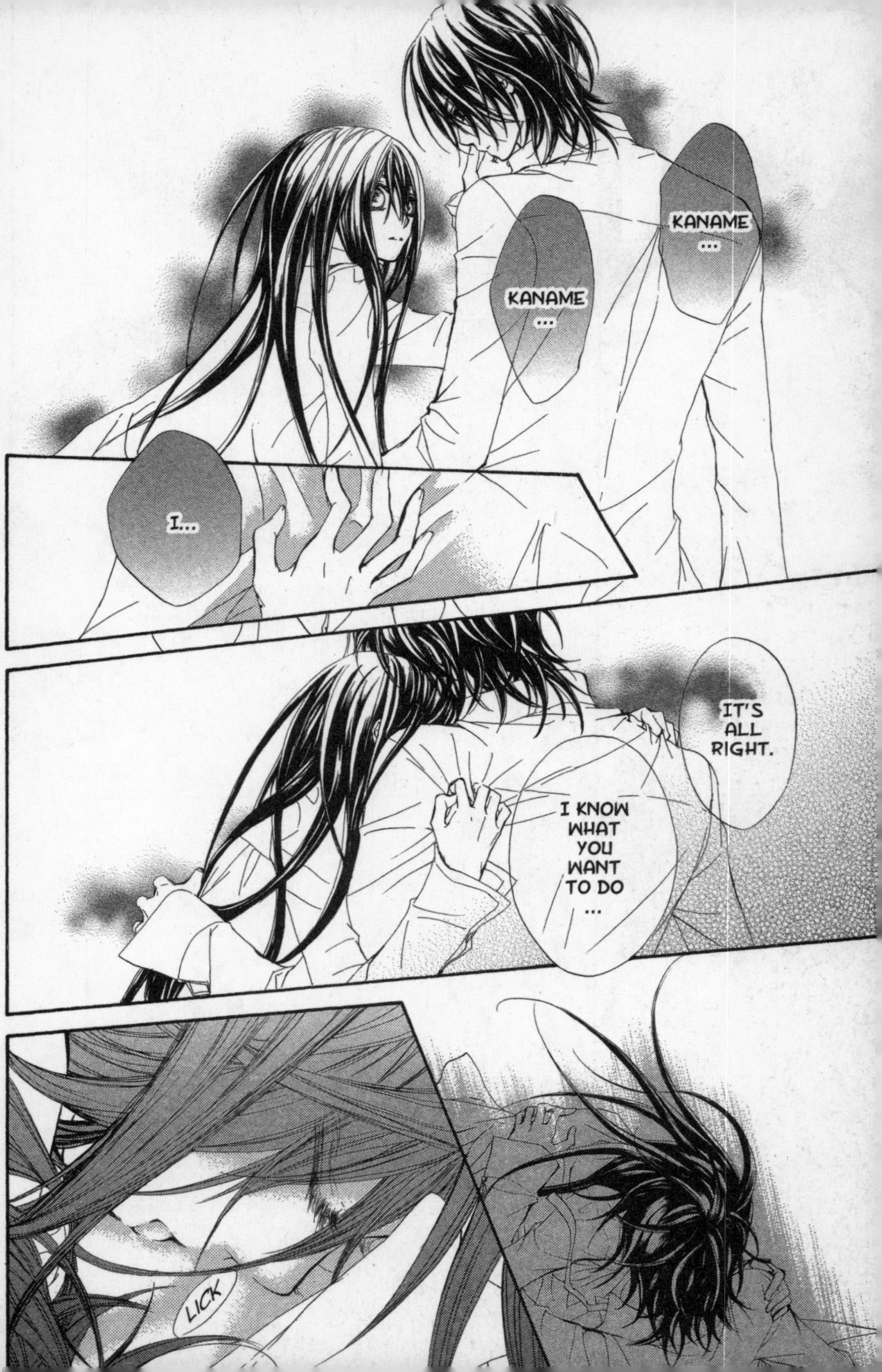
KANAME ...
KANAME ...
I...
IT'S ALL RIGHT.
I KNOW WHAT YOU WANT TO DO ...
LICK

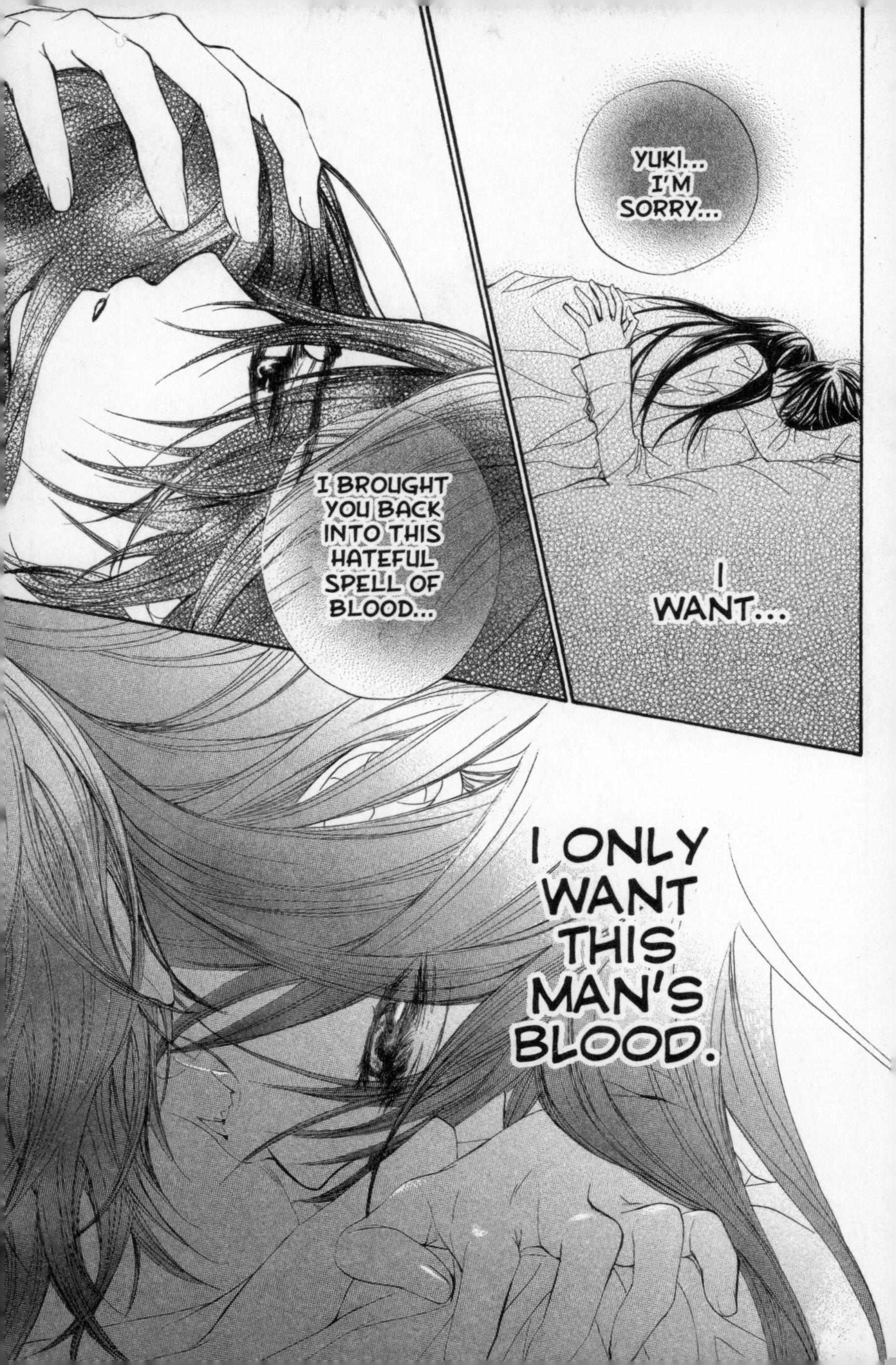
YUKI... I'M SORRY...
I WANT...
I BROUGHT YOU BACK INTO THIS HATEFUL SPELL OF BLOOD...
I ONLY WANT THIS MAN'S BLOOD.

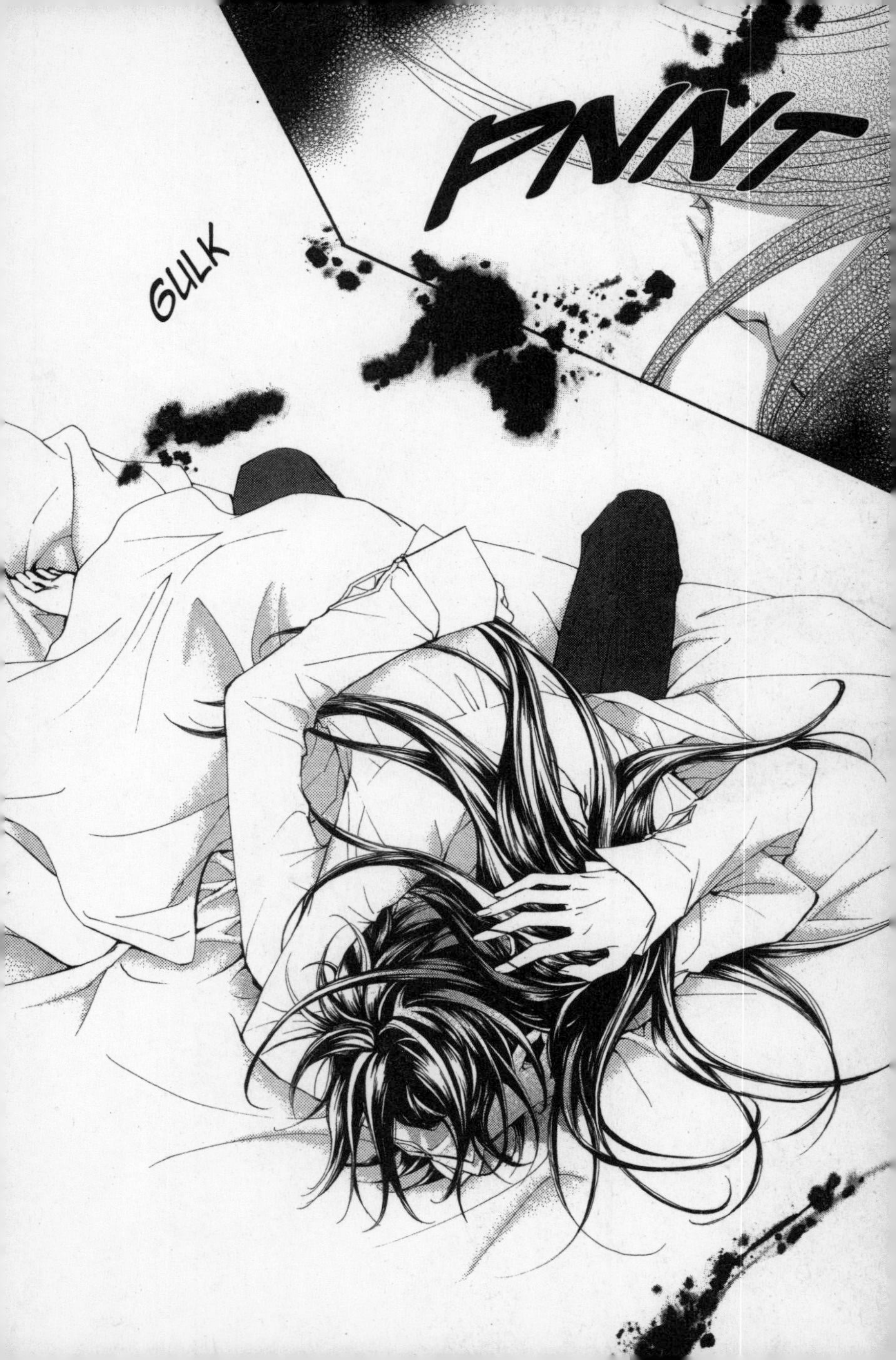
PNNT
GULK

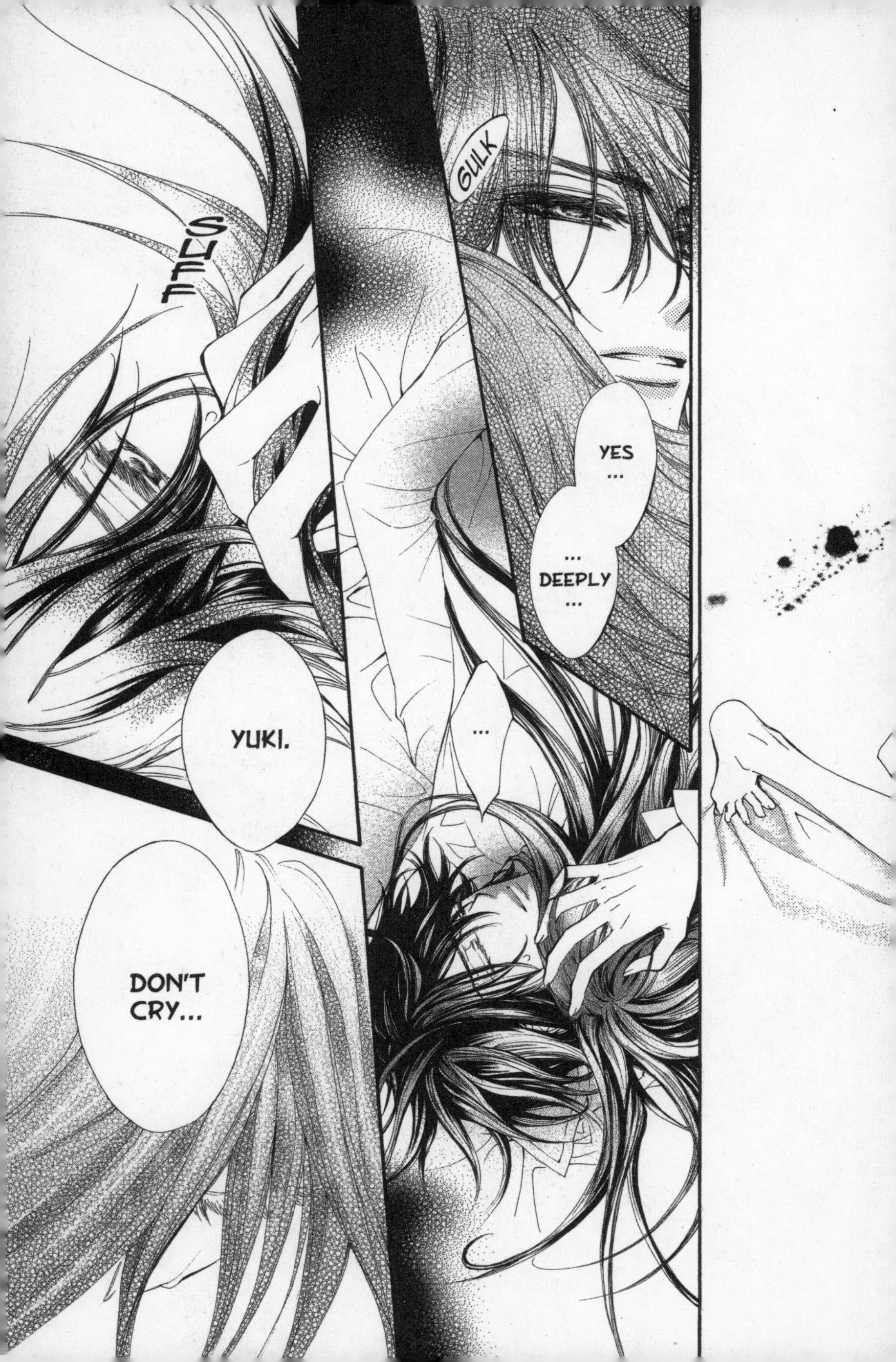
GULK
YES ...
... DEEPLY ...
...
SUFF
YUKI.
DON'T CRY...

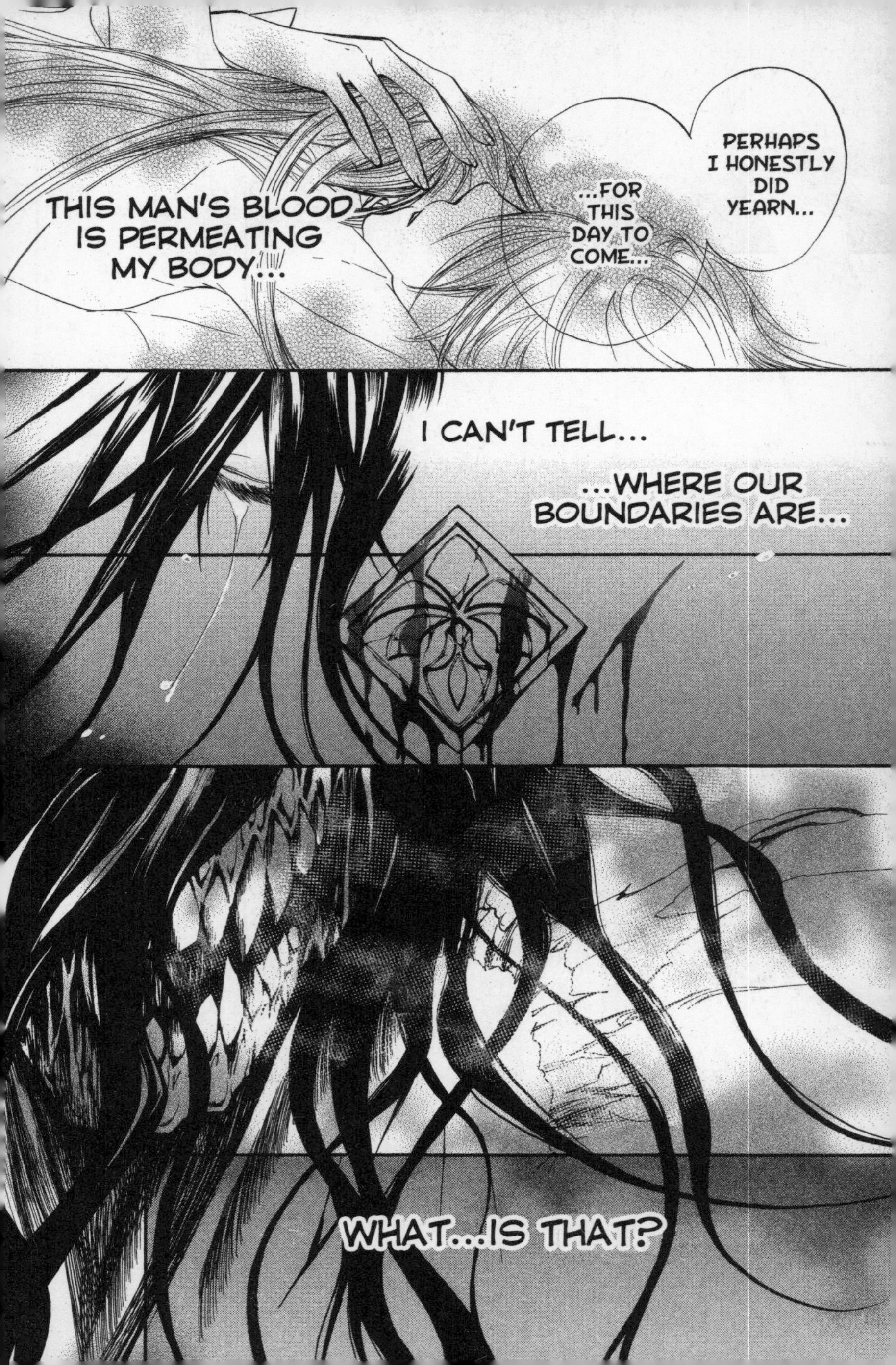
PERHAPS I HONESTLY DID YEARN...
...FOR THIS DAY TO COME...
THIS MAN'S BLOOD IS PERMEATING MY BODY...
I CAN'T TELL...
...WHERE OUR BOUNDARIES ARE...
WHAT...IS THAT?

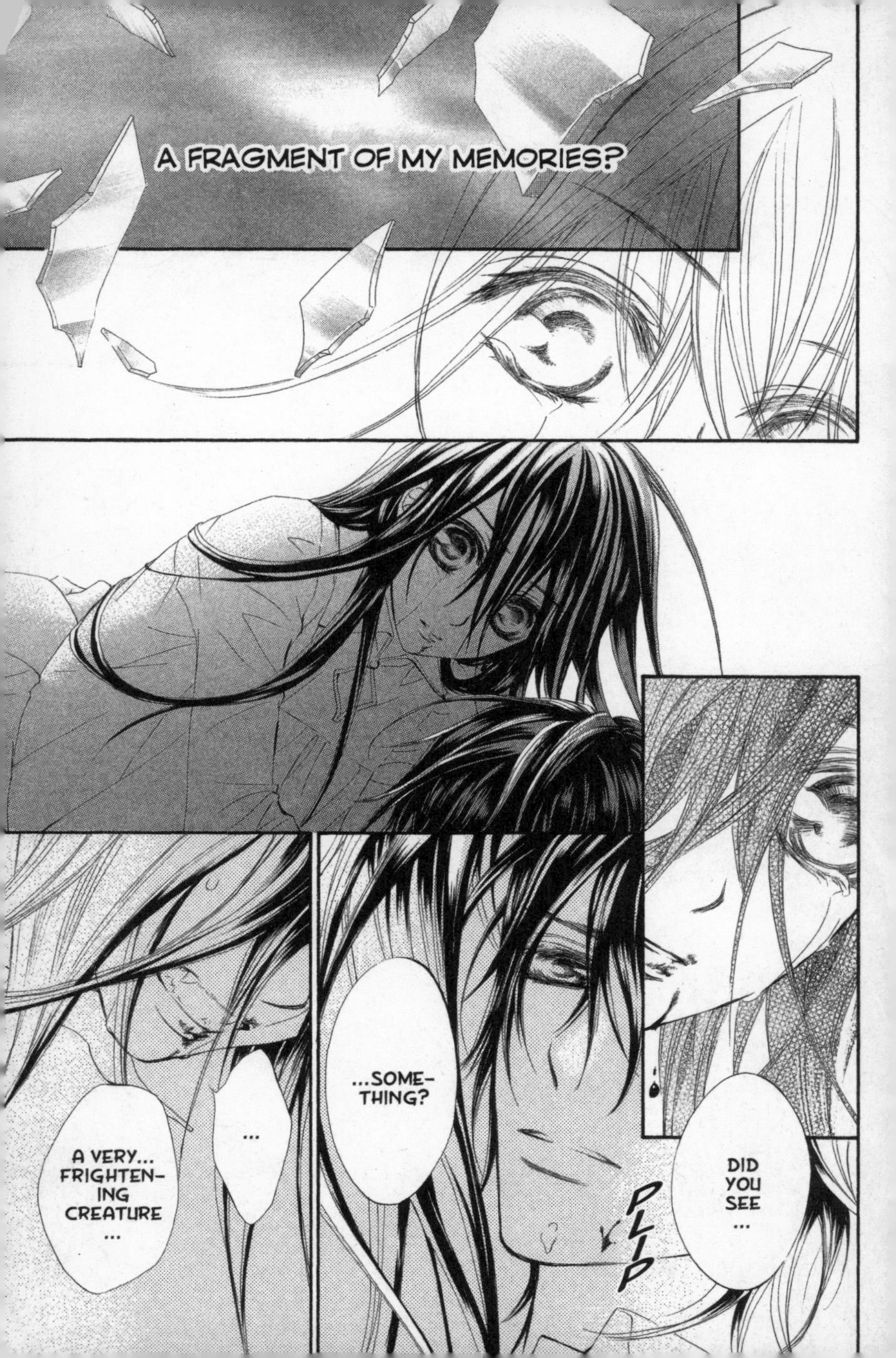
A FRAGMENT OF MY MEMORIES?
DID YOU SEE ...
PLIP
...SOME-THING?
...
A VERY... FRIGHTEN-ING CREATURE ...

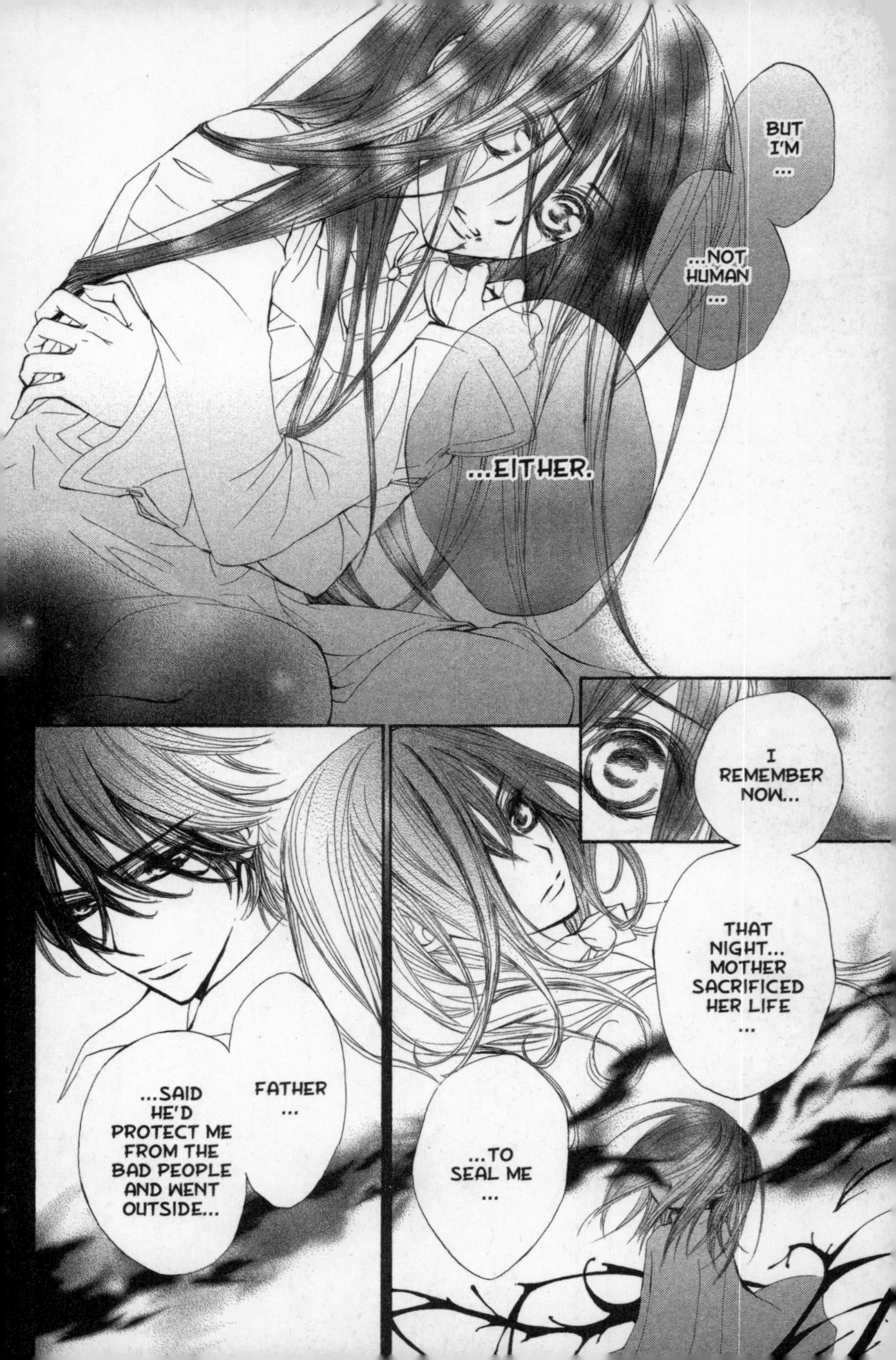
BUT I'M ...
...NOT HUMAN ...
...EITHER.
I REMEMBER NOW...
THAT NIGHT... MOTHER SACRIFICED HER LIFE ...
...TO SEAL ME ...
FATHER ...
...SAID HE'D PROTECT ME FROM THE BAD PEOPLE AND WENT OUTSIDE...

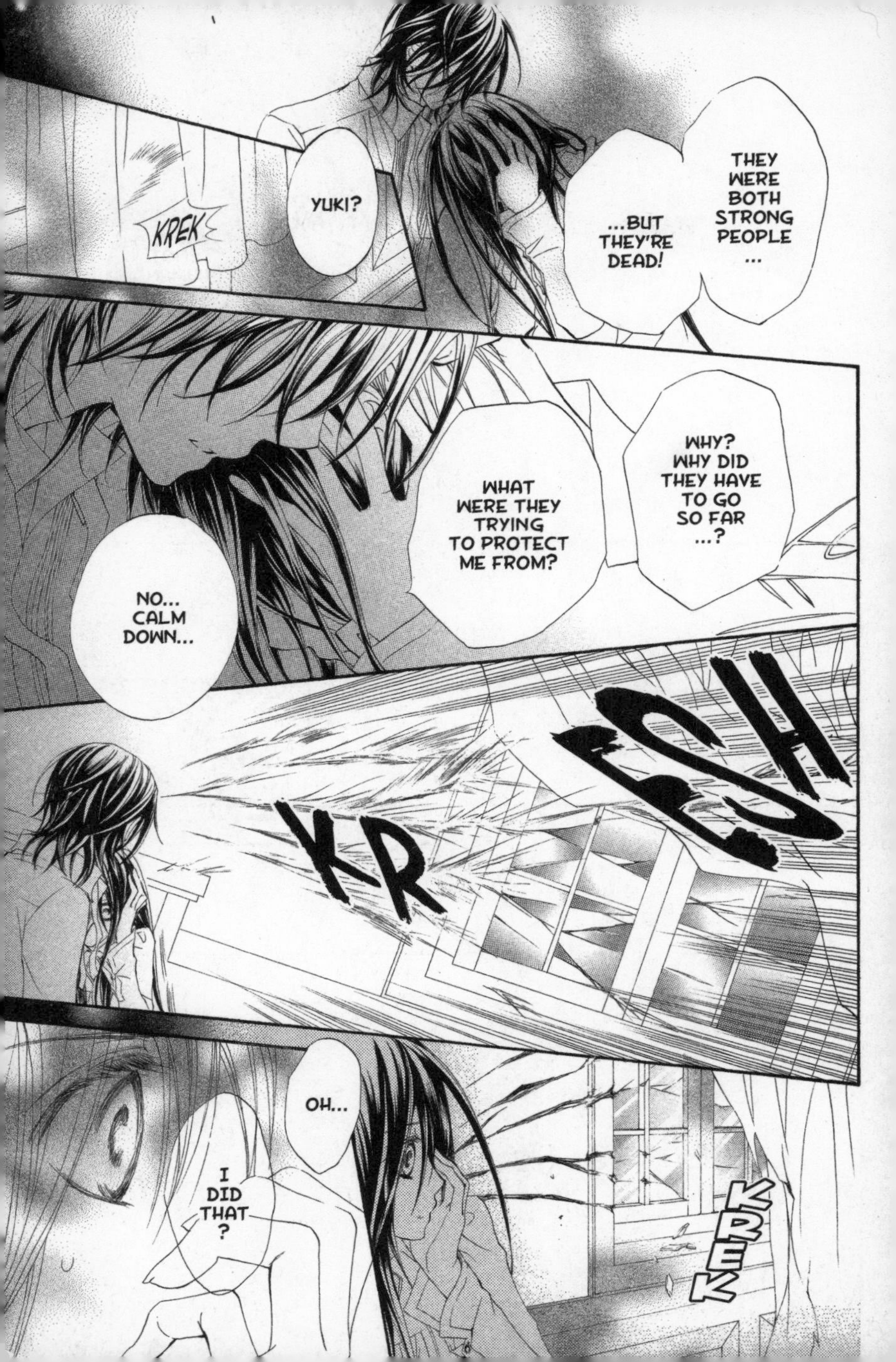
THEY WERE BOTH STRONG PEOPLE ...
...BUT THEY'RE DEAD!
YUKI?
KREK
WHY? WHY DID THEY HAVE TO GO SO FAR ...?
WHAT WERE THEY TRYING TO PROTECT ME FROM?
NO... CALM DOWN...
KRESH
KREK
OH...
I DID THAT?

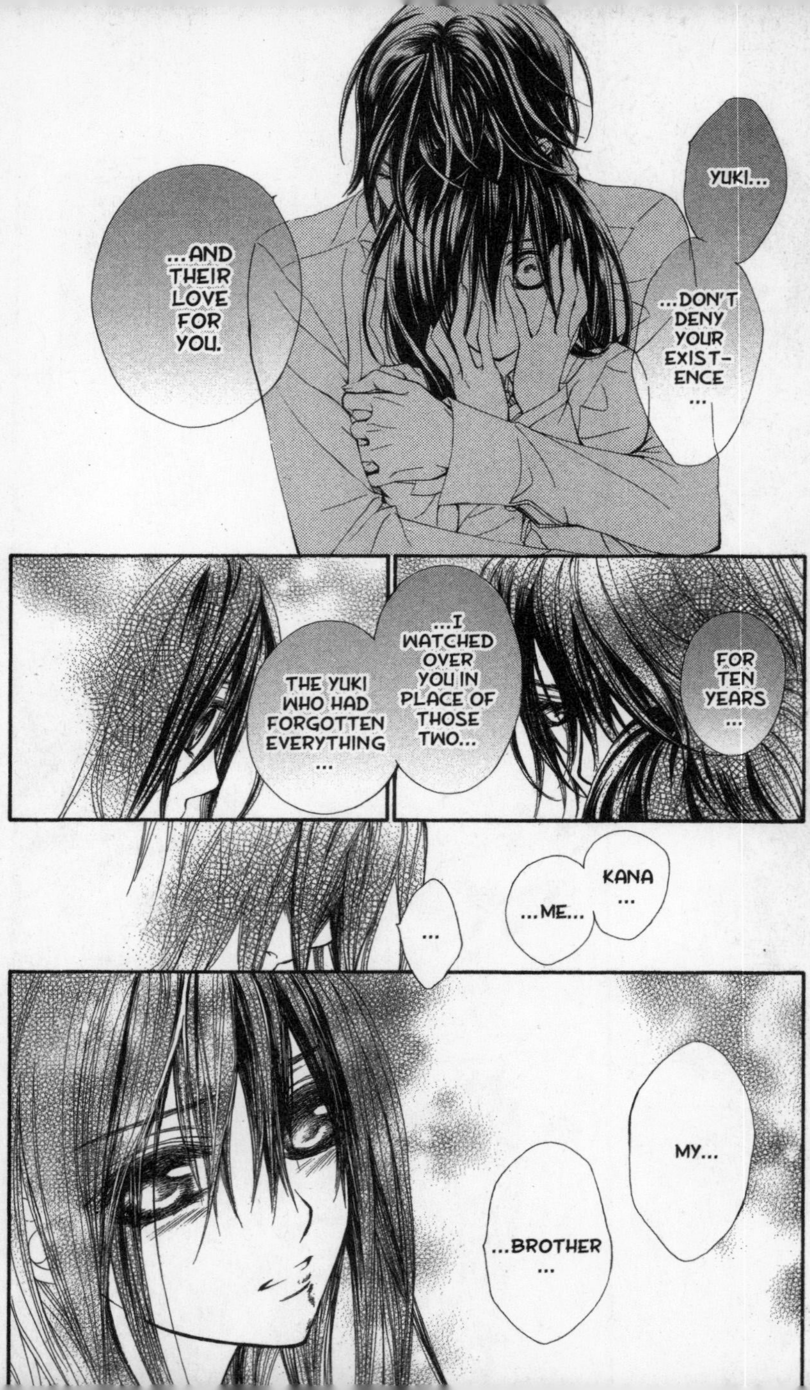
YUKI...
...DON'T DENY YOUR EXIST-ENCE...
...AND THEIR LOVE FOR YOU.
FOR TEN YEARS...
...I WATCHED OVER YOU IN PLACE OF THOSE TWO...
THE YUKI WHO HAD FORGOTTEN EVERYTHING...
KANA...
...ME...
...
MY...
...BROTHER...

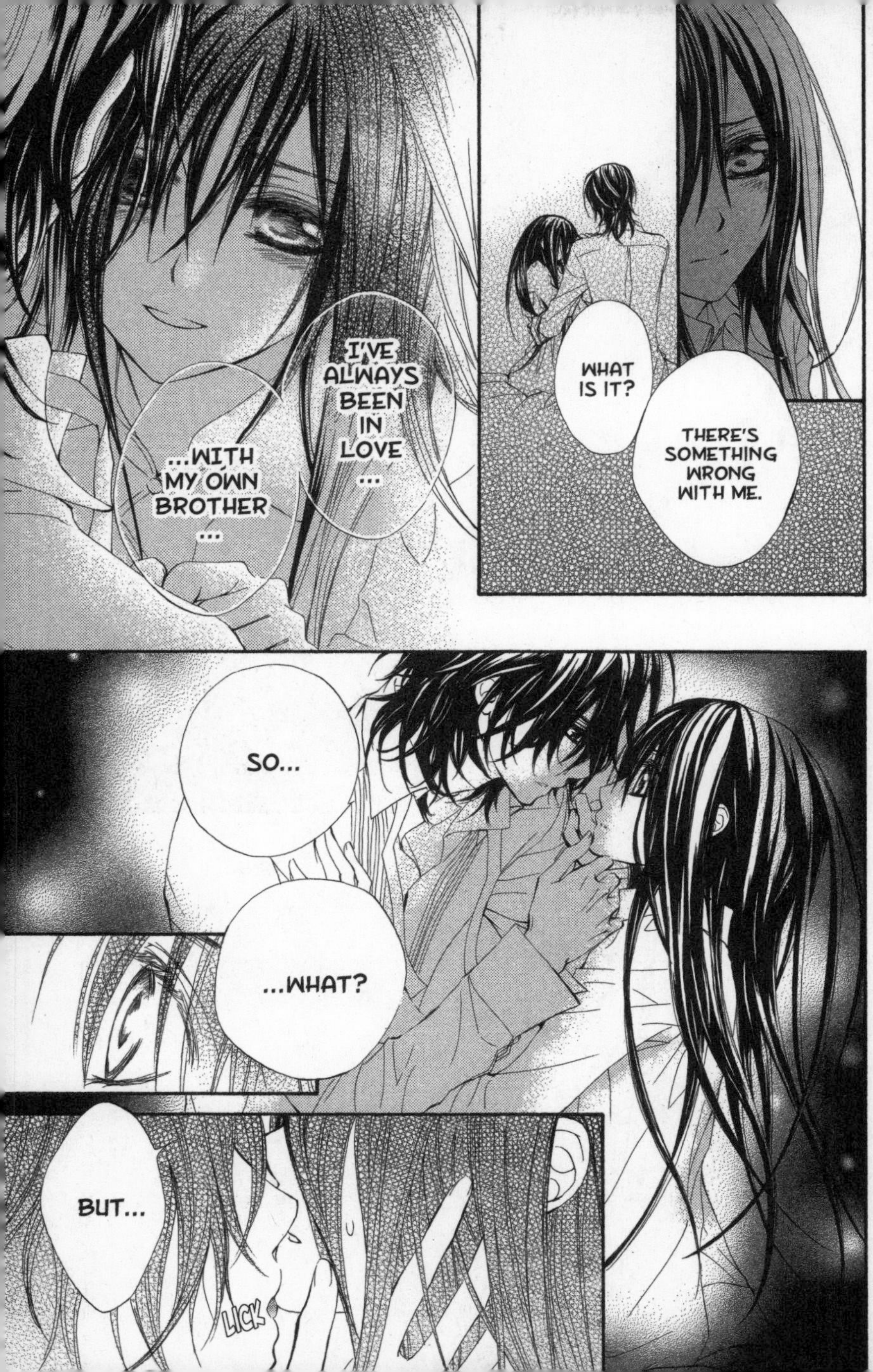
WHAT IS IT?
THERE'S SOMETHING WRONG WITH ME.
I'VE ALWAYS BEEN IN LOVE...
...WITH MY OWN BROTHER...
SO...
...WHAT?
BUT...
LICK

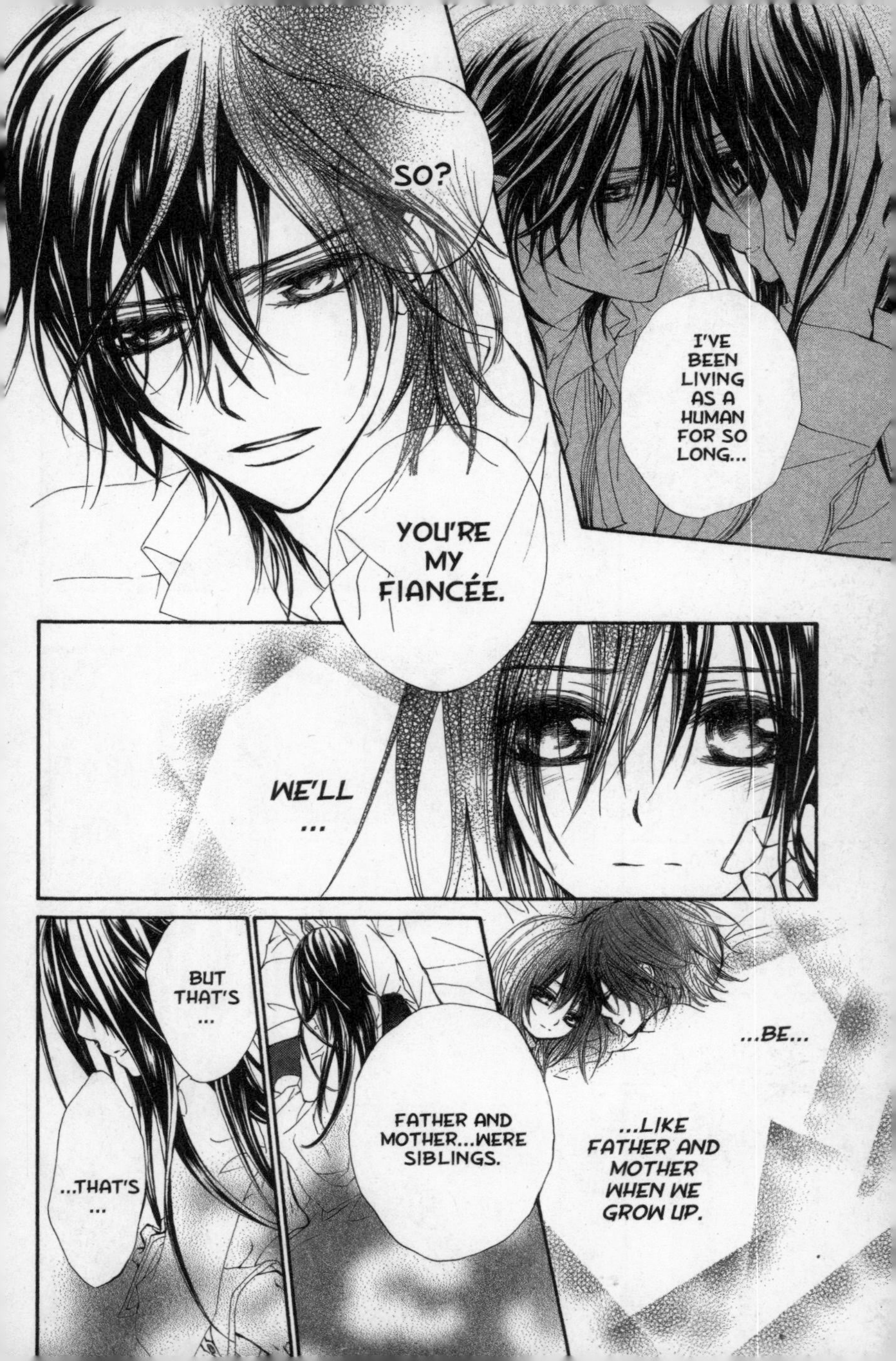
I'VE BEEN LIVING AS A HUMAN FOR SO LONG...
SO?
YOU'RE MY FIANCÉE.
WE'LL ...
...BE...
...LIKE FATHER AND MOTHER WHEN WE GROW UP.
FATHER AND MOTHER...WERE SIBLINGS.
BUT THAT'S ...
...THAT'S ...

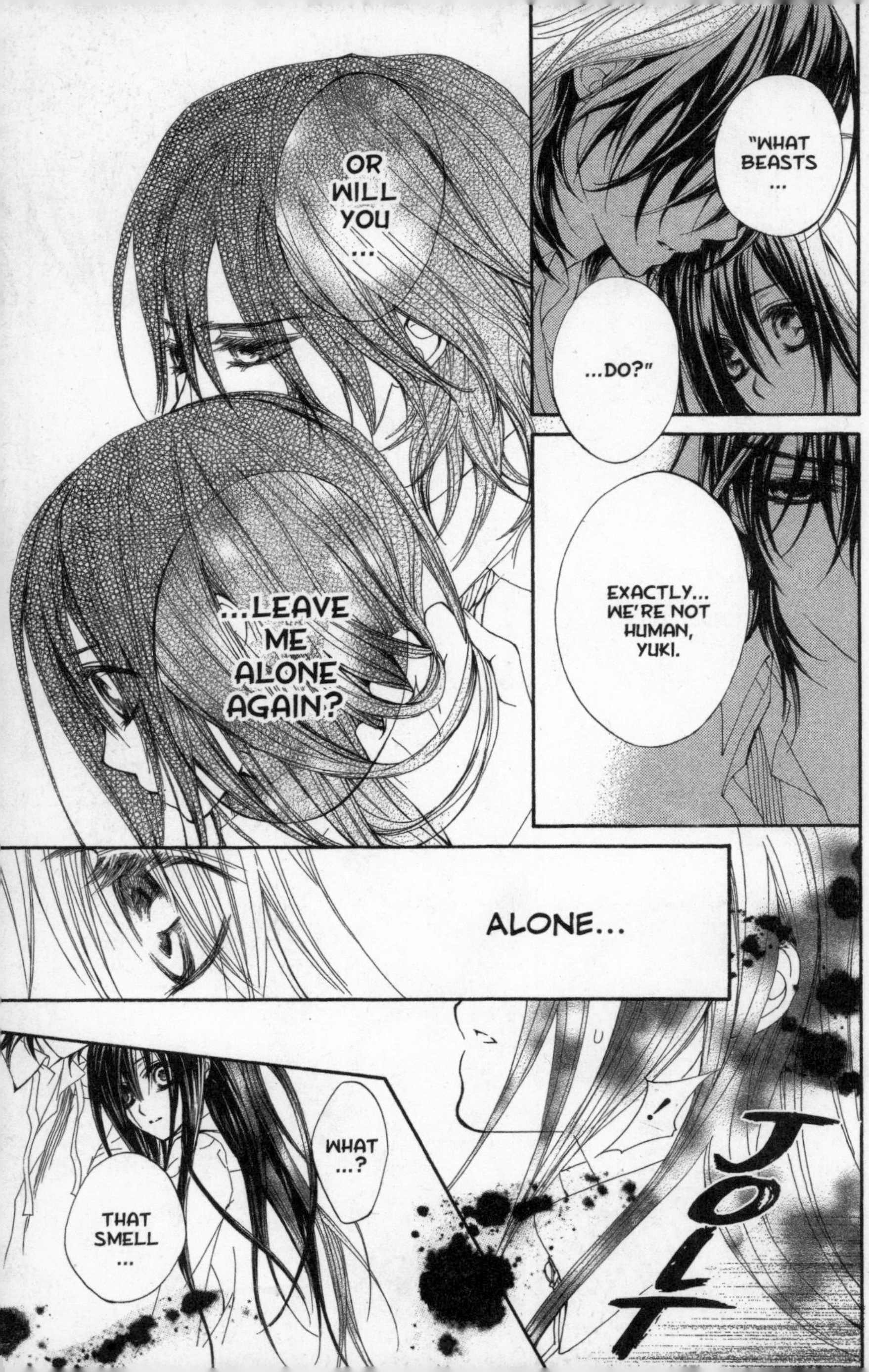
"WHAT BEASTS ...
...DO?"
EXACTLY... WE'RE NOT HUMAN, YUKI.
OR WILL YOU ...
...LEAVE ME ALONE AGAIN?
ALONE...
!
JOLT
WHAT ...?
THAT SMELL ...

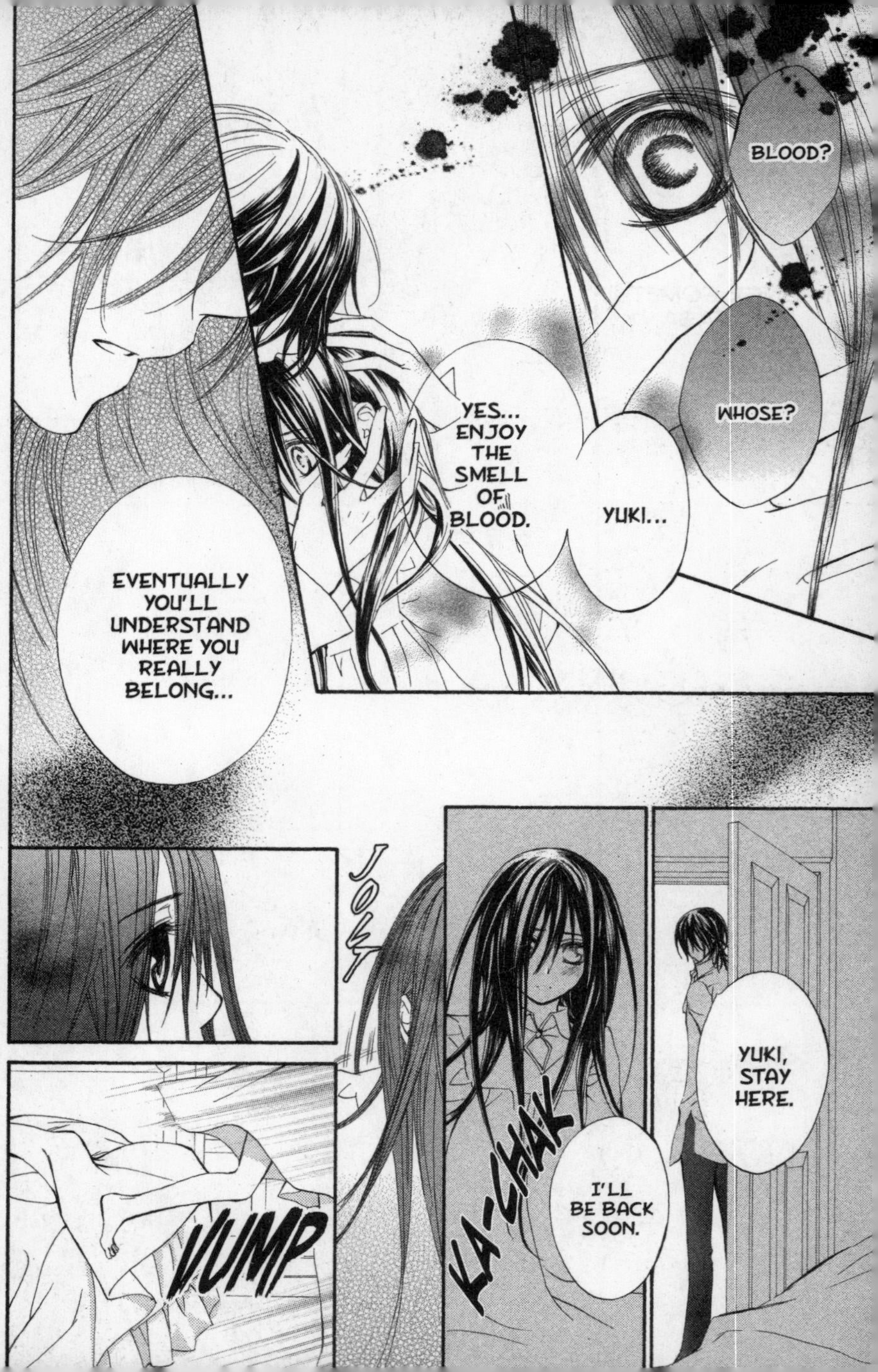
BLOOD?
WHOSE?
YUKI...
YES... ENJOY THE SMELL OF BLOOD.
EVENTUALLY YOU'LL UNDERSTAND WHERE YOU REALLY BELONG...
YUKI, STAY HERE.
KA-CHAK
I'LL BE BACK SOON.
JOLT
VUMP

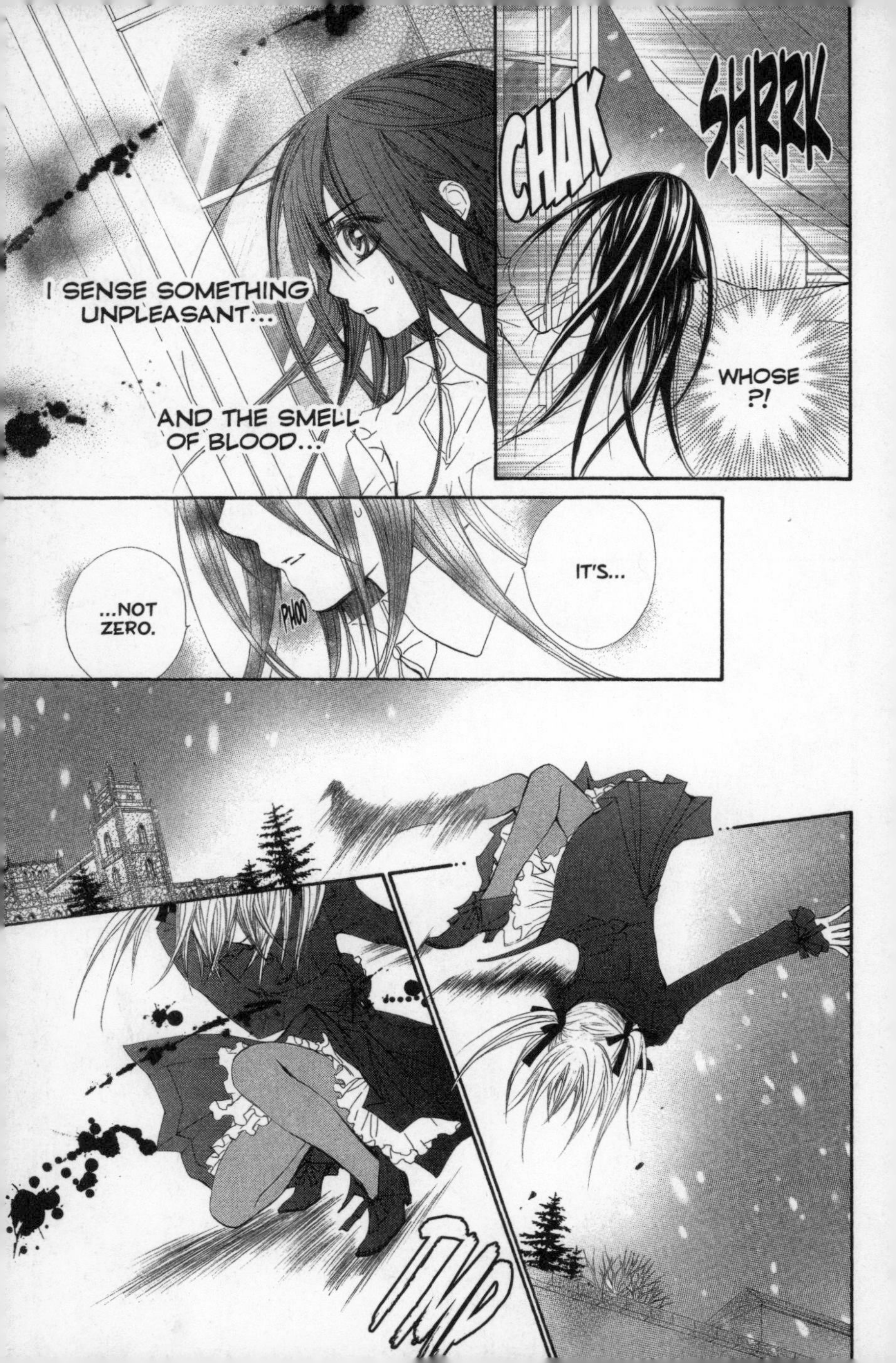
CHAK
SHRRK
WHOSE ?!
I SENSE SOMETHING UNPLEASANT...
AND THE SMELL OF BLOOD...
IT'S...
PHOO
...NOT ZERO.
...
...
TMP

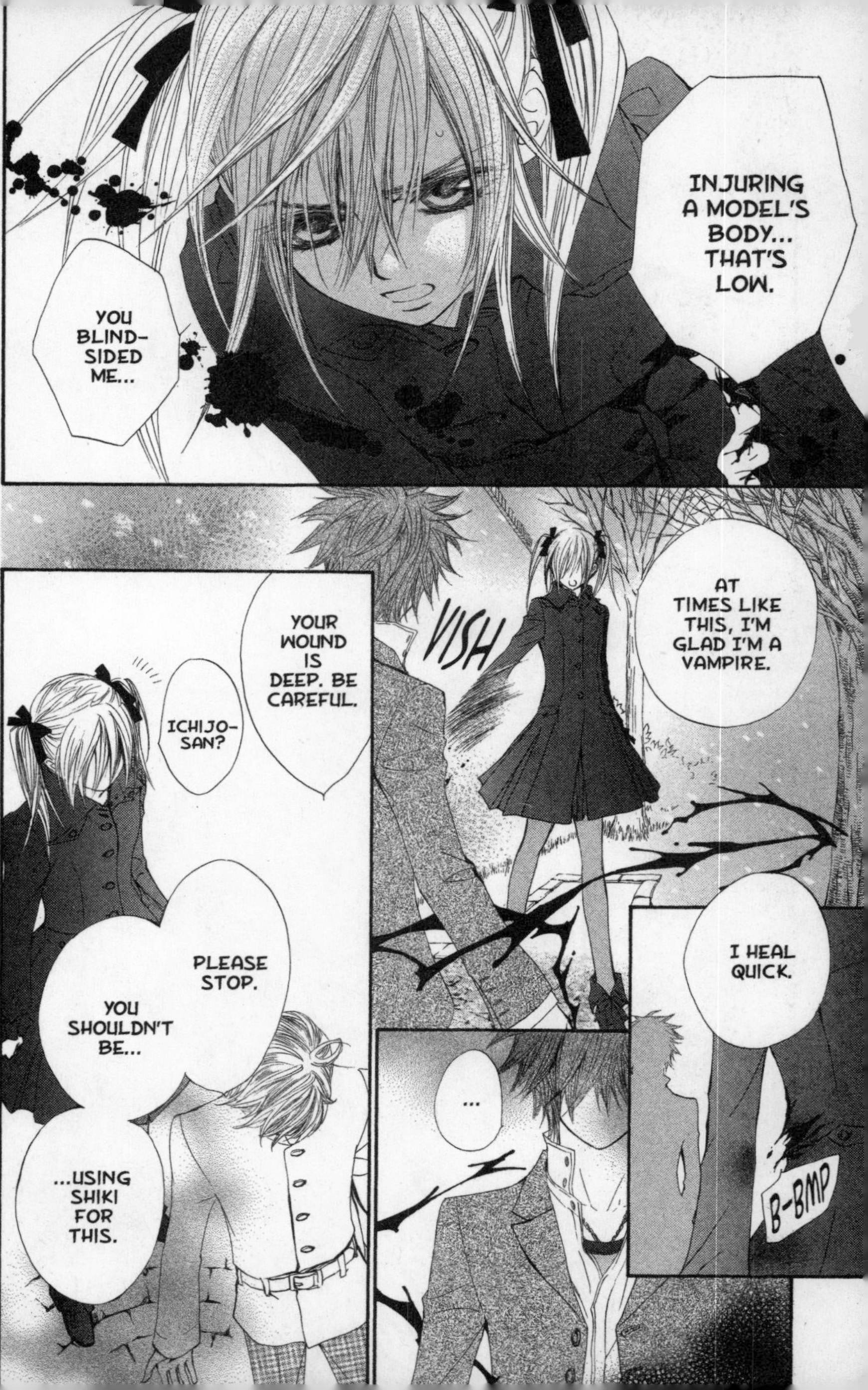
INJURING A MODEL'S BODY... THAT'S LOW.
YOU BLIND-SIDED ME...
AT TIMES LIKE THIS, I'M GLAD I'M A VAMPIRE.
VISH
YOUR WOUND IS DEEP. BE CAREFUL.
ICHIJO-SAN?
I HEAL QUICK.
B-BMP
...
PLEASE STOP.
YOU SHOULDN'T BE...
...USING SHIKI FOR THIS.

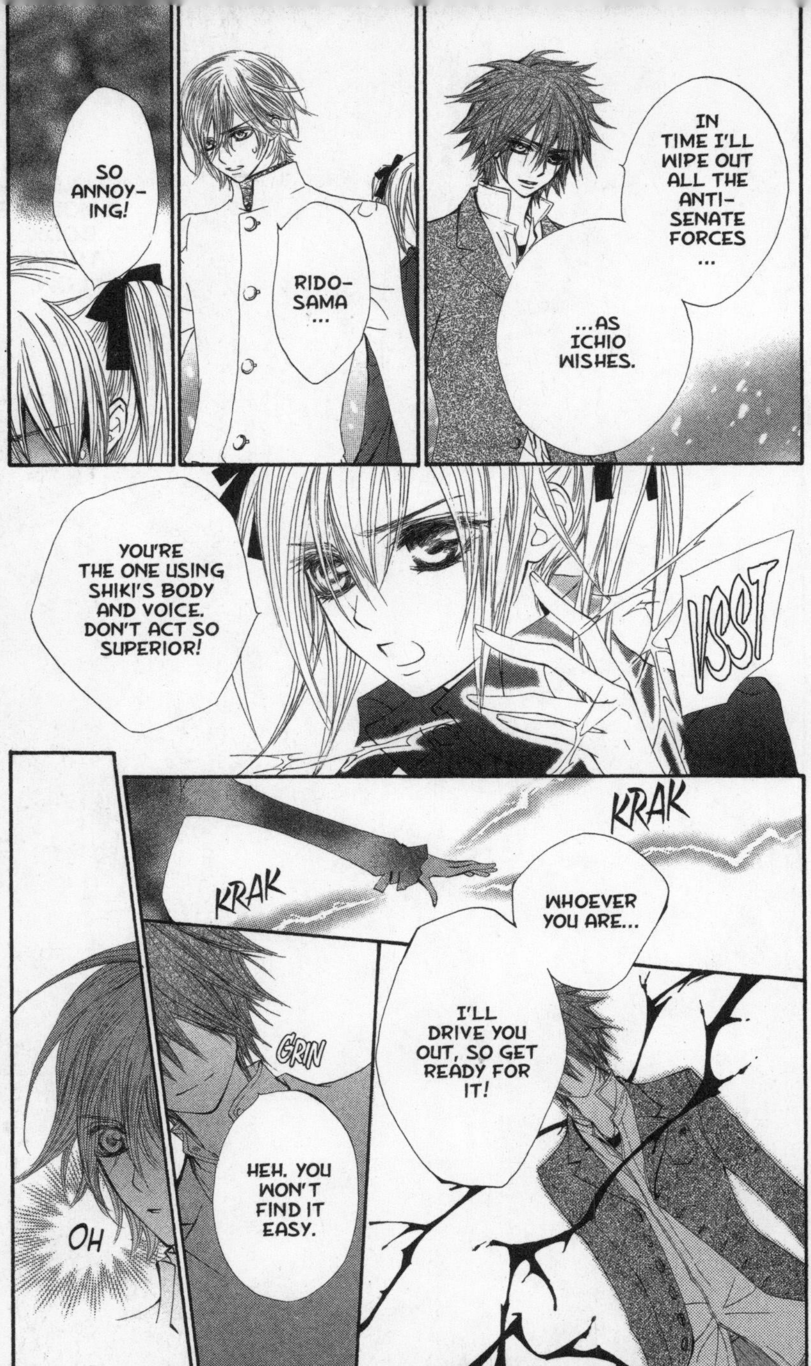
IN TIME I'LL WIPE OUT ALL THE ANTI-SENATE FORCES...
...AS ICHIO WISHES.
RIDO-SAMA...
SO ANNOYING!
YOU'RE THE ONE USING SHIKI'S BODY AND VOICE. DON'T ACT SO SUPERIOR!
VSST
KRAK
KRAK
WHOEVER YOU ARE...
I'LL DRIVE YOU OUT, SO GET READY FOR IT!
GRIN
HEH. YOU WON'T FIND IT EASY.
OH

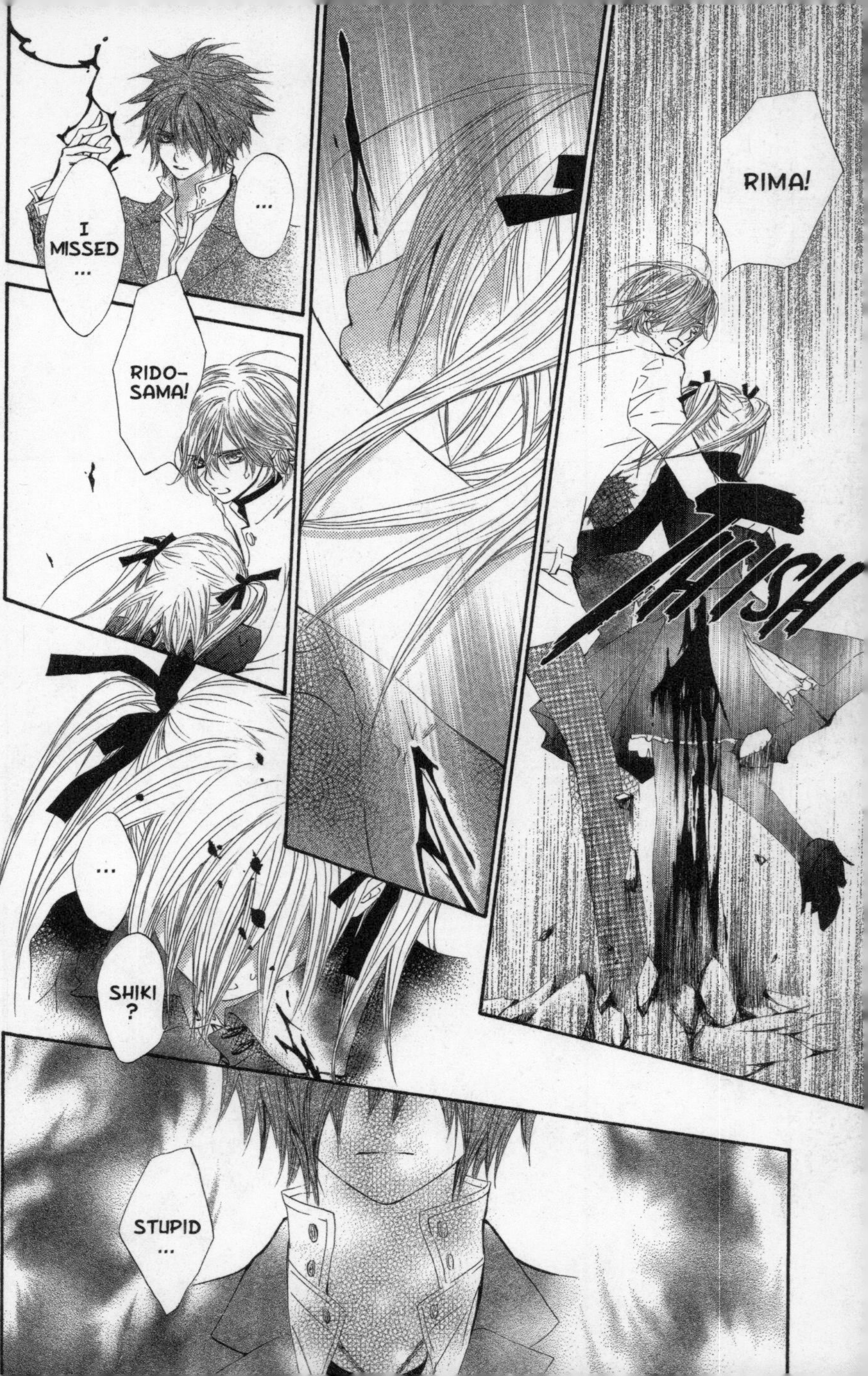
RIMA!
THISH
...
I MISSED ...
RIDO-SAMA!
...
SHIKI ?
STUPID ...

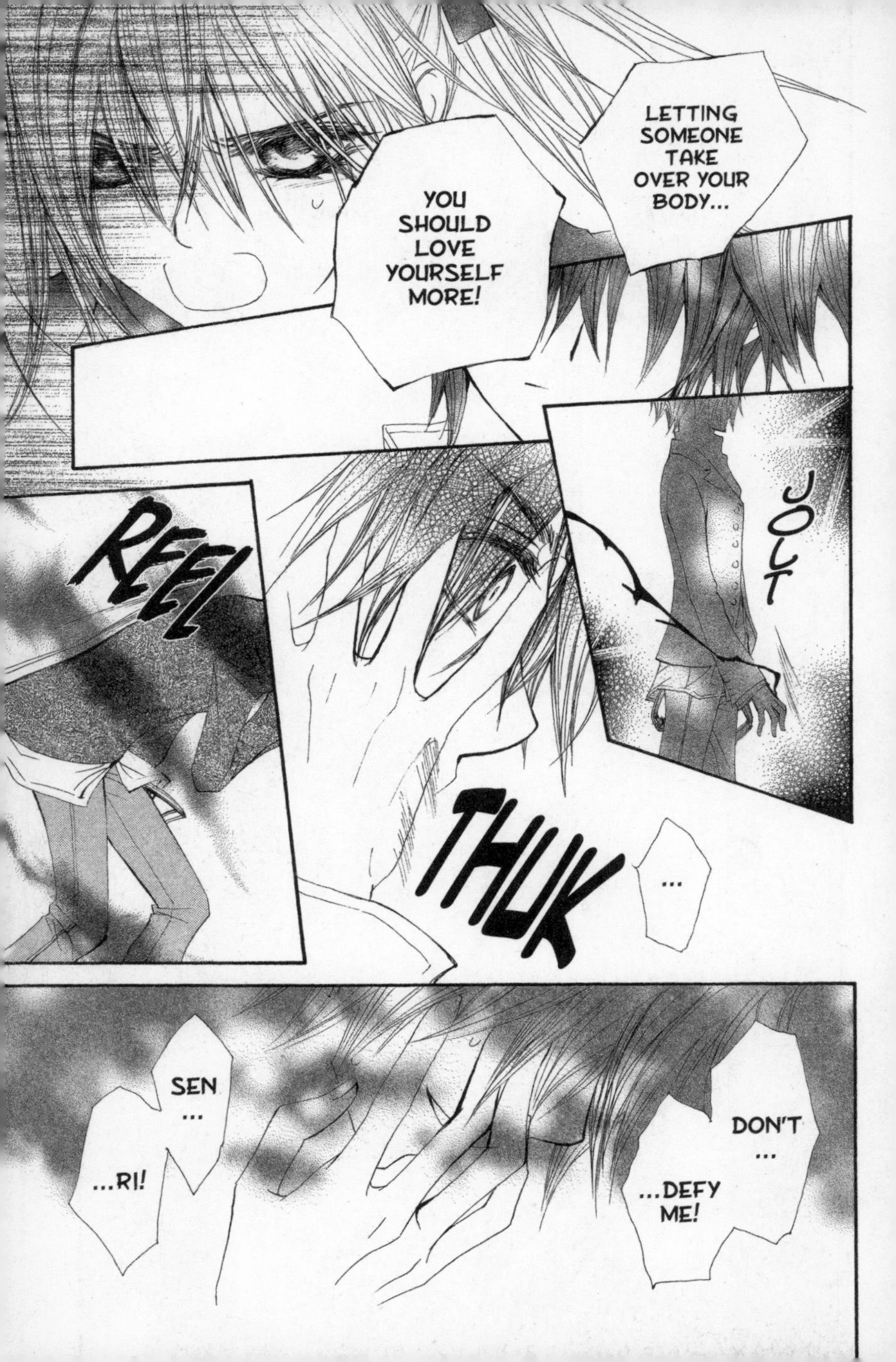
LETTING SOMEONE TAKE OVER YOUR BODY...
YOU SHOULD LOVE YOURSELF MORE!
JOLT
...
THUK
REEL
DON'T ...
...DEFY ME!
SEN ...
...RI!

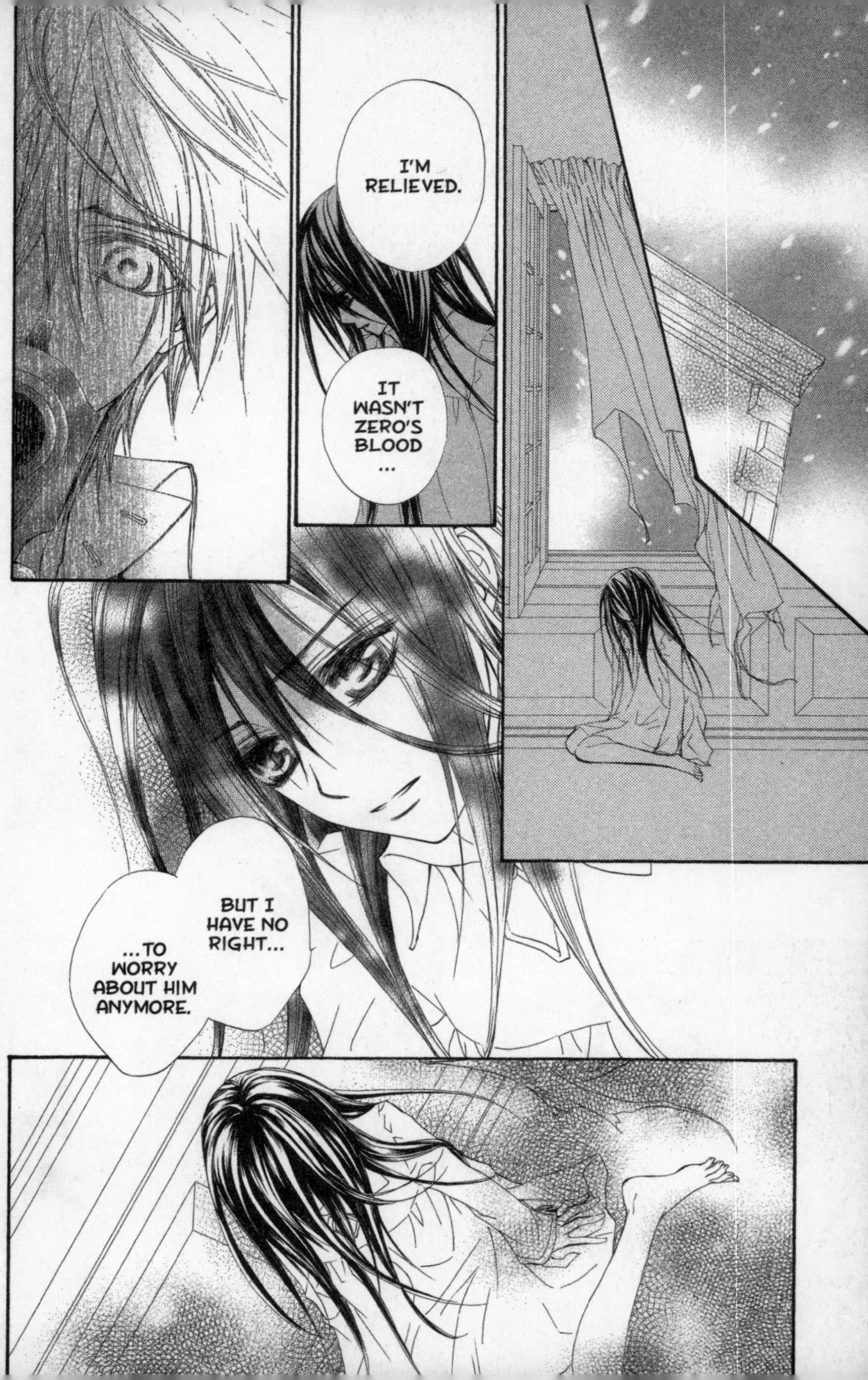
I'M RELIEVED.
IT WASN'T ZERO'S BLOOD ...
BUT I HAVE NO RIGHT...
...TO WORRY ABOUT HIM ANYMORE.

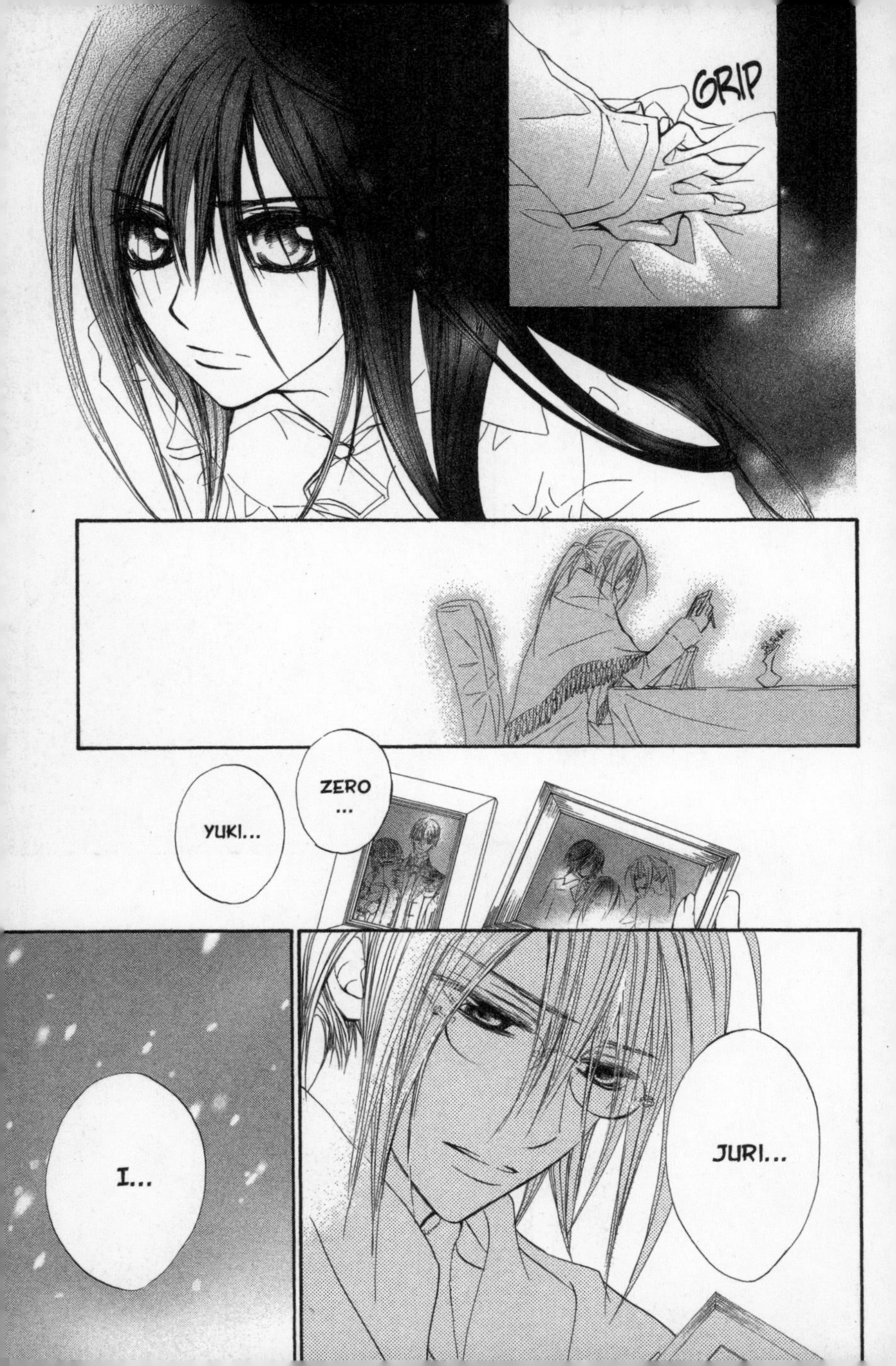
GRIP
ZERO...
YUKI...
JURI...
I...

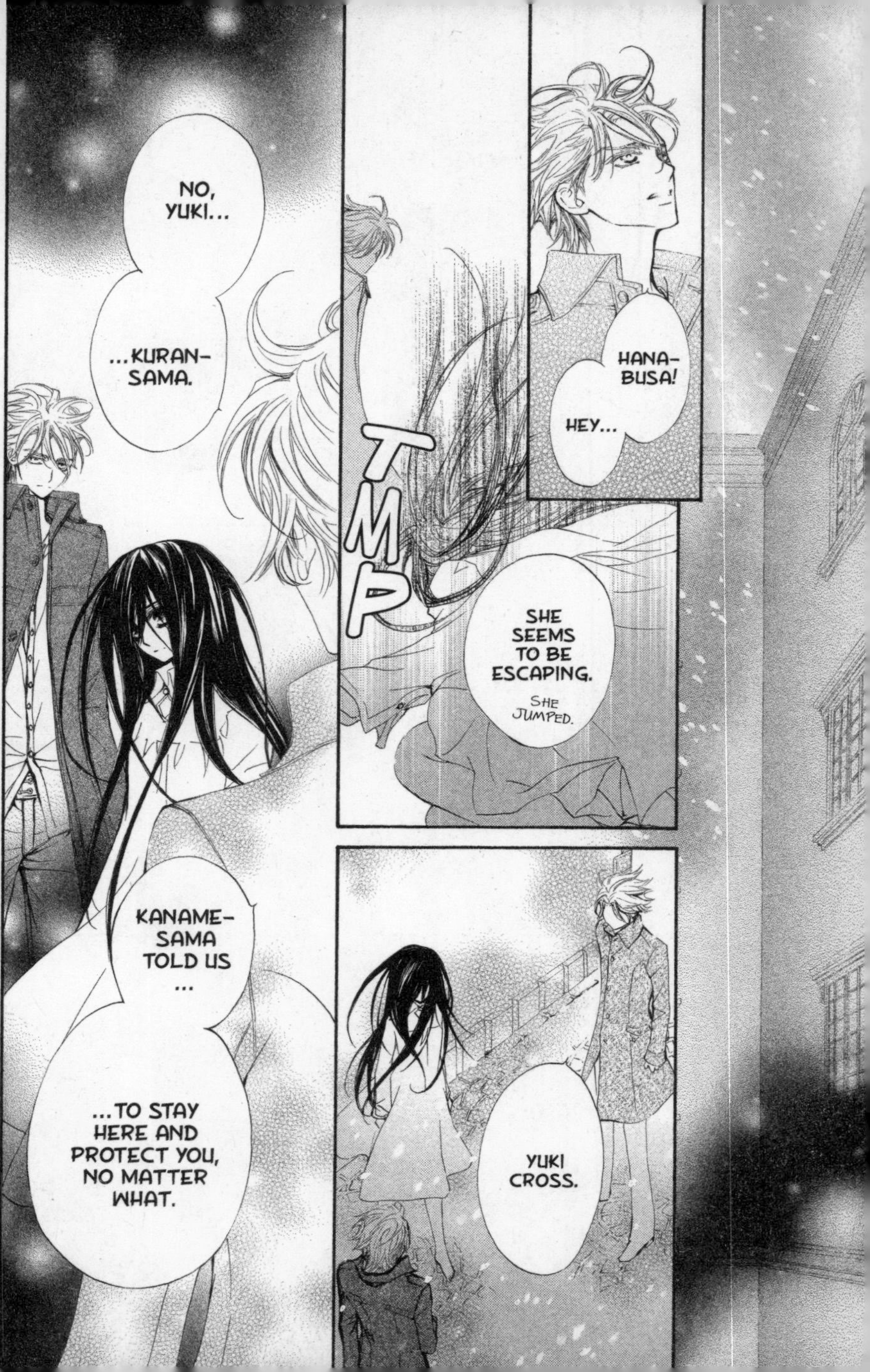
HANA-BUSA!
HEY...
TMP
SHE SEEMS TO BE ESCAPING.
SHE JUMPED.
YUKI CROSS.
NO, YUKI...
...KURAN-SAMA.
KANAME-SAMA TOLD US ...
...TO STAY HERE AND PROTECT YOU, NO MATTER WHAT.

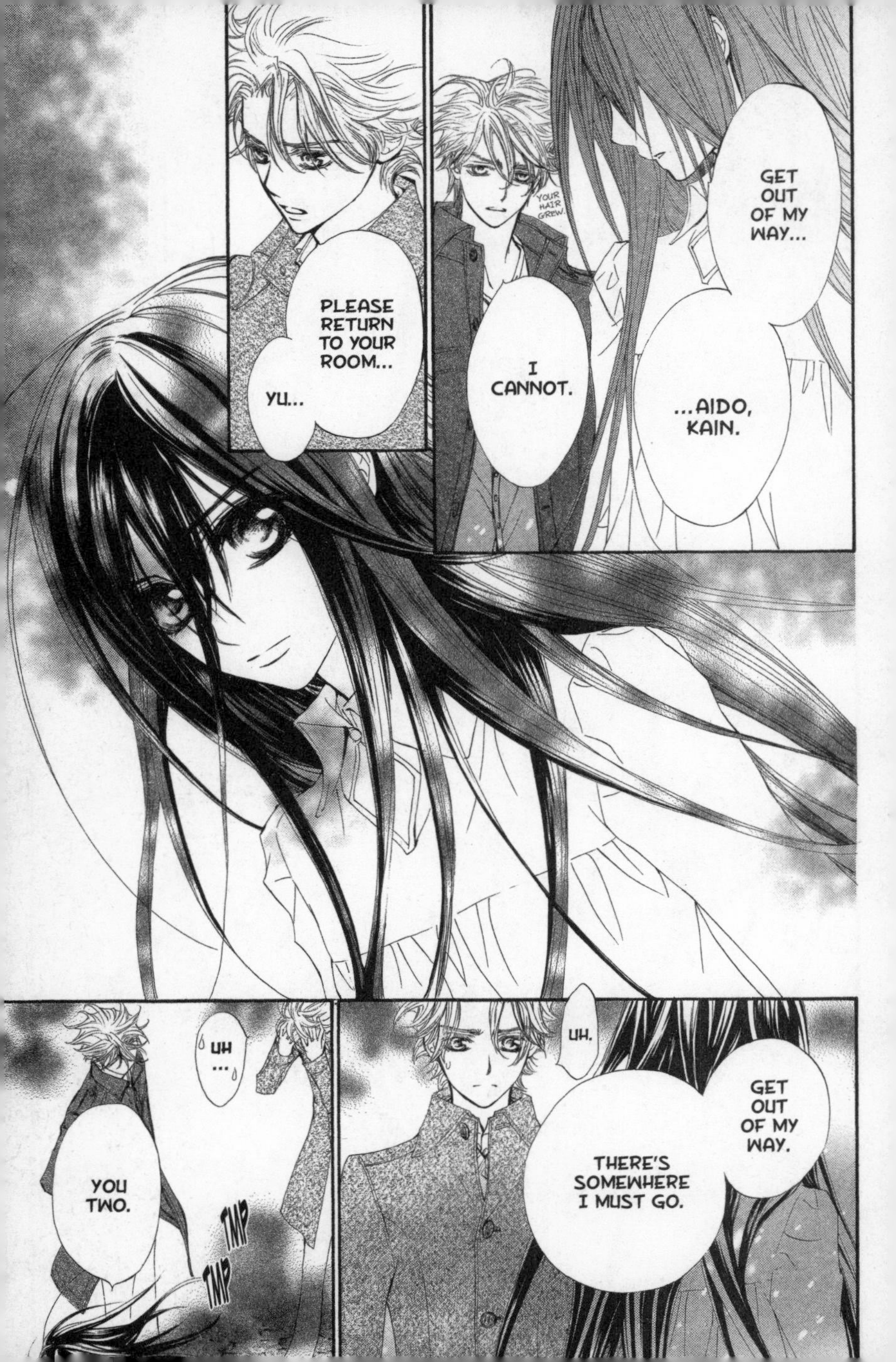
GET OUT OF MY WAY...
...AIDO, KAIN.
YOUR HAIR GREW.
I CANNOT.
PLEASE RETURN TO YOUR ROOM...
YU...
GET OUT OF MY WAY.
THERE'S SOMEWHERE I MUST GO.
UH.
UH ...
YOU TWO.
TMP
TMP

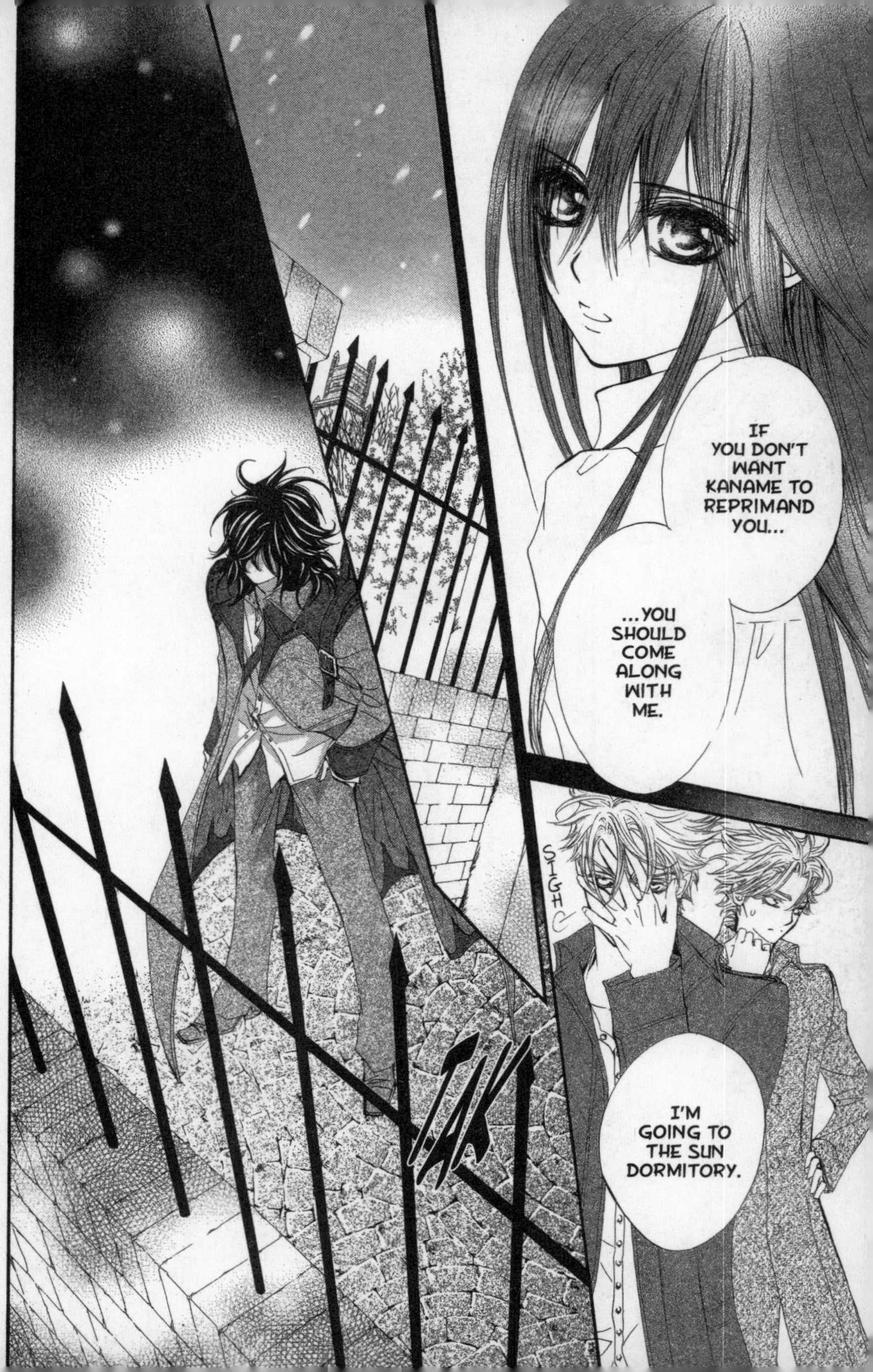
IF YOU DON'T WANT KANAME TO REPRIMAND YOU...
...YOU SHOULD COME ALONG WITH ME.
SIGH
I'M GOING TO THE SUN DORMITORY.
TAK

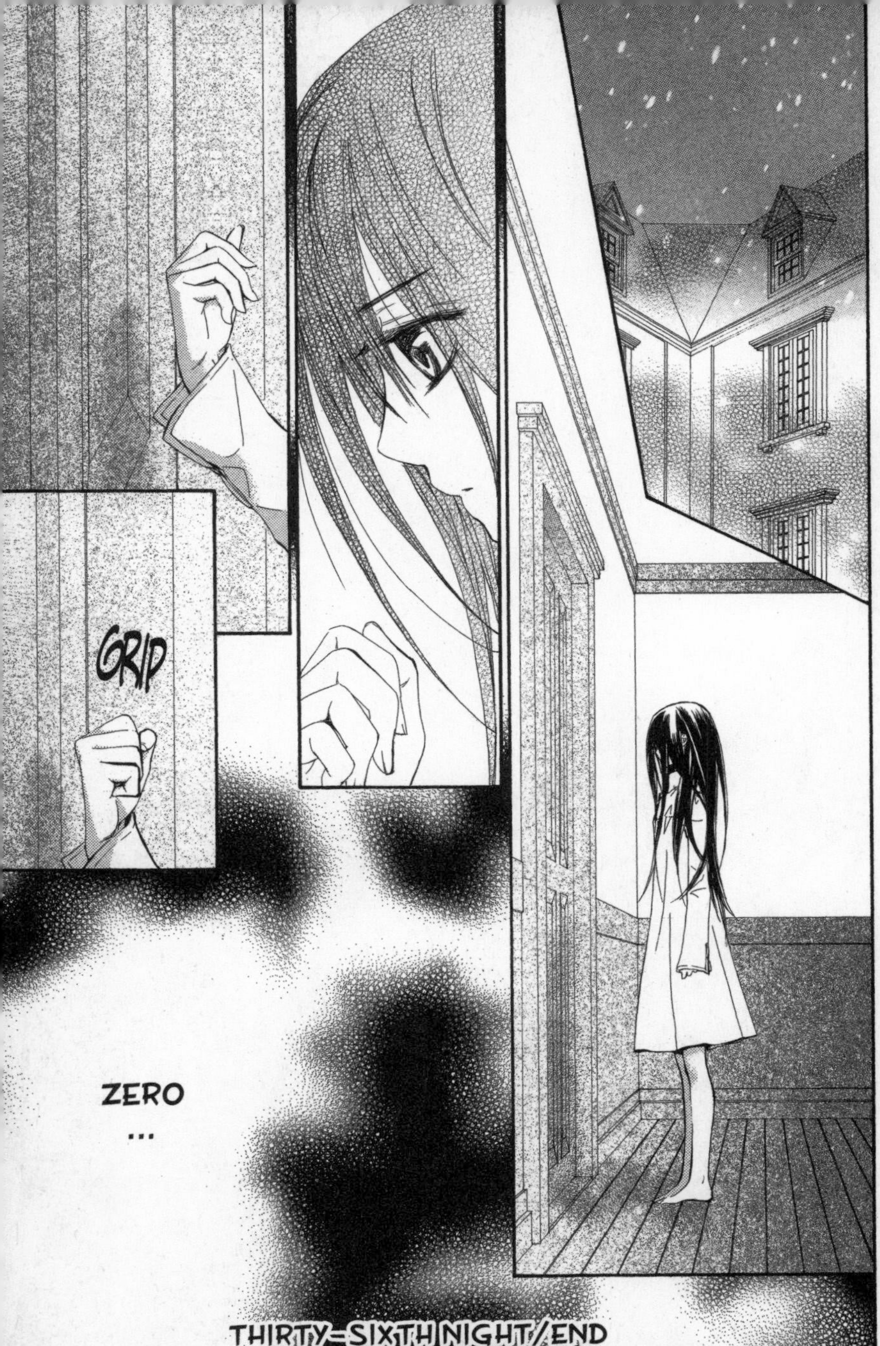
GRIP
ZERO
...

THIRTY-SIXTH NIGHT/END

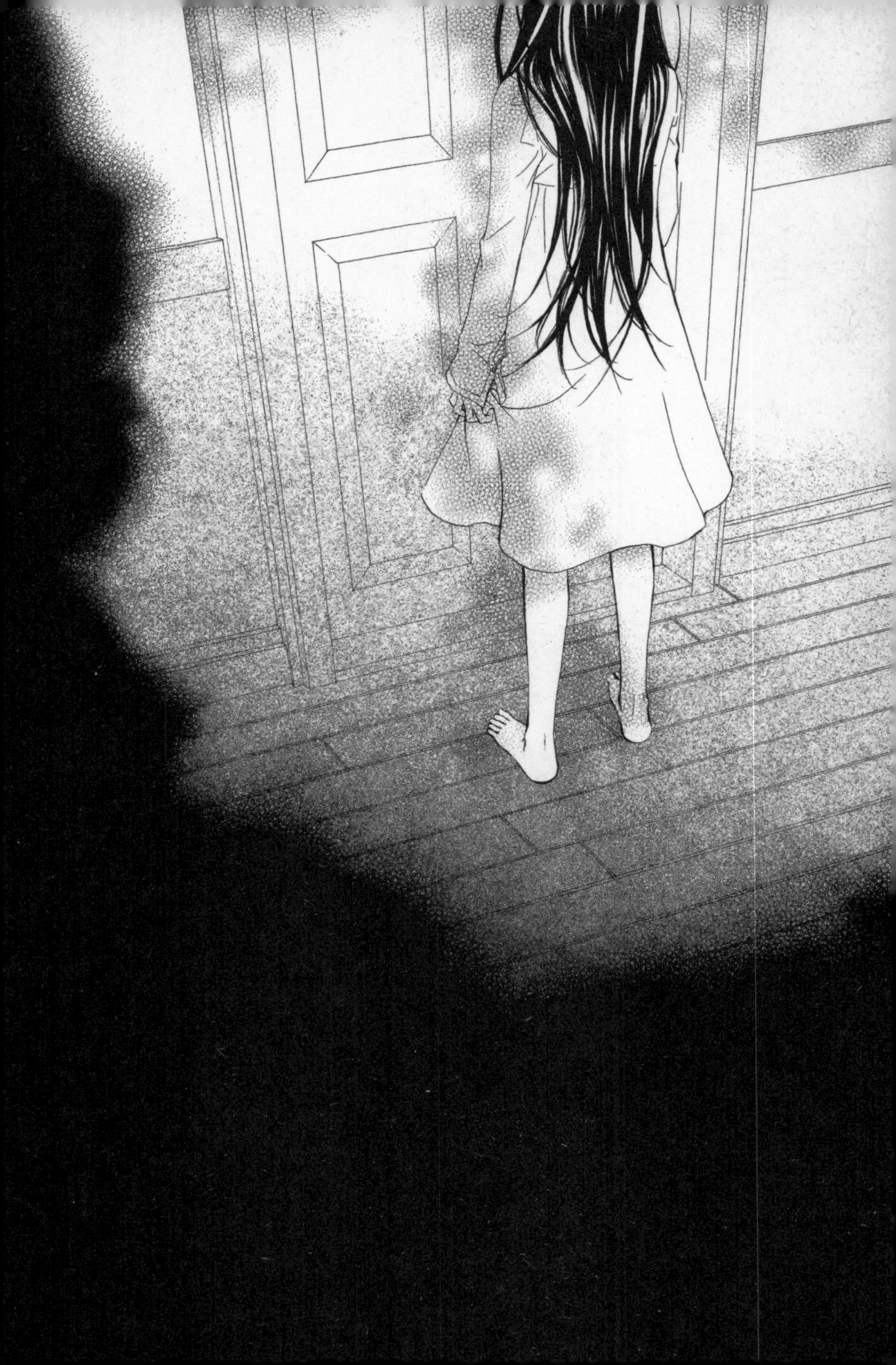

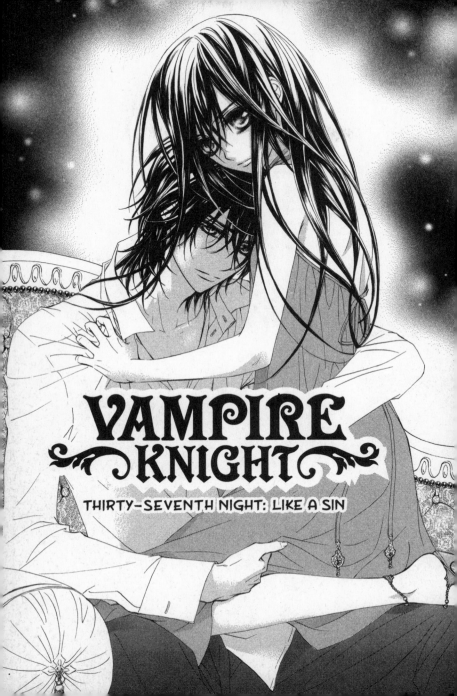

VAMPIRE KNIGHT

THIRTY-SEVENTH NIGHT: LIKE A SIN

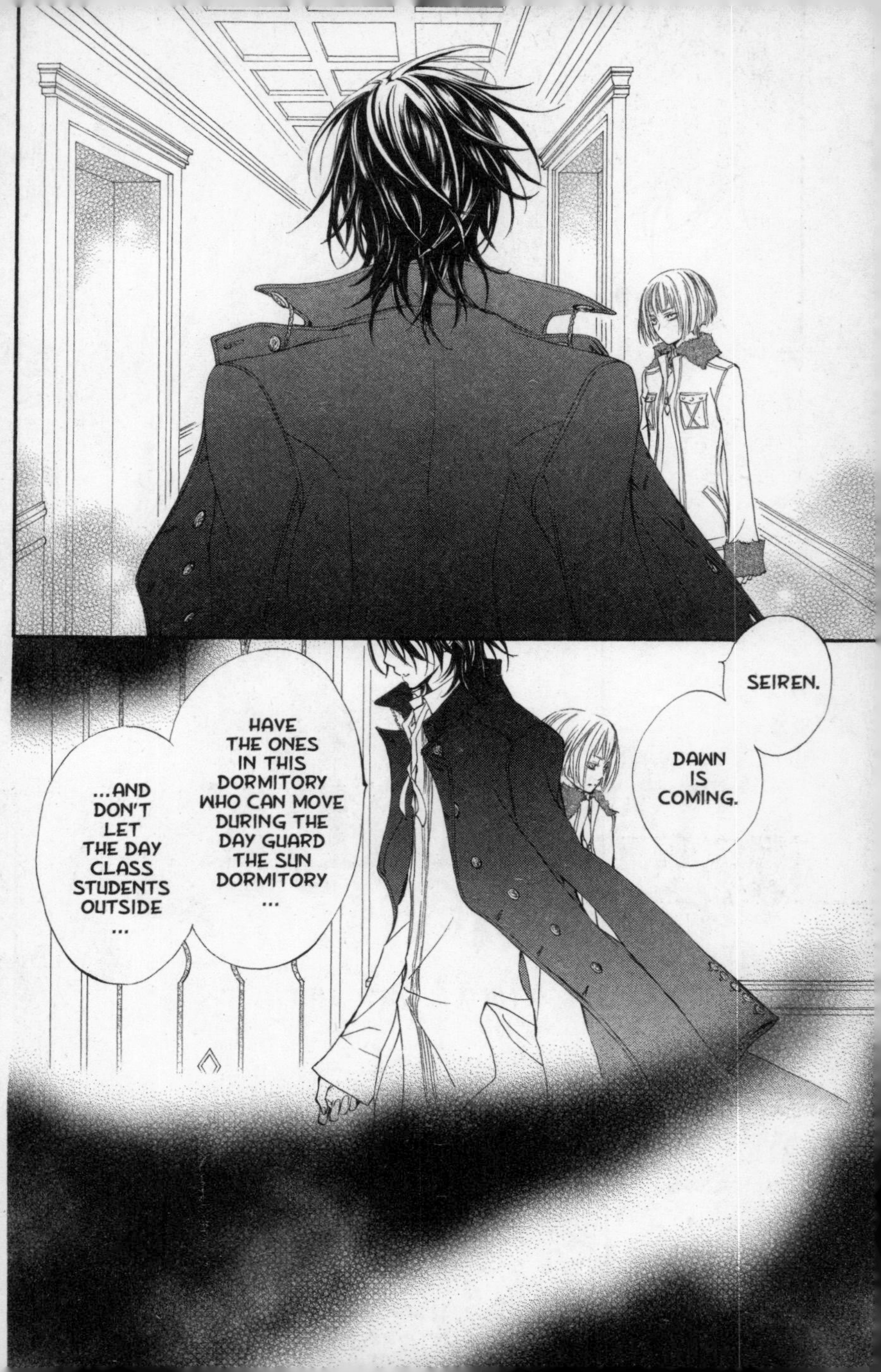
SEIREN.
DAWN IS COMING.
HAVE THE ONES IN THIS DORMITORY WHO CAN MOVE DURING THE DAY GUARD THE SUN DORMITORY ...
...AND DON'T LET THE DAY CLASS STUDENTS OUTSIDE ...

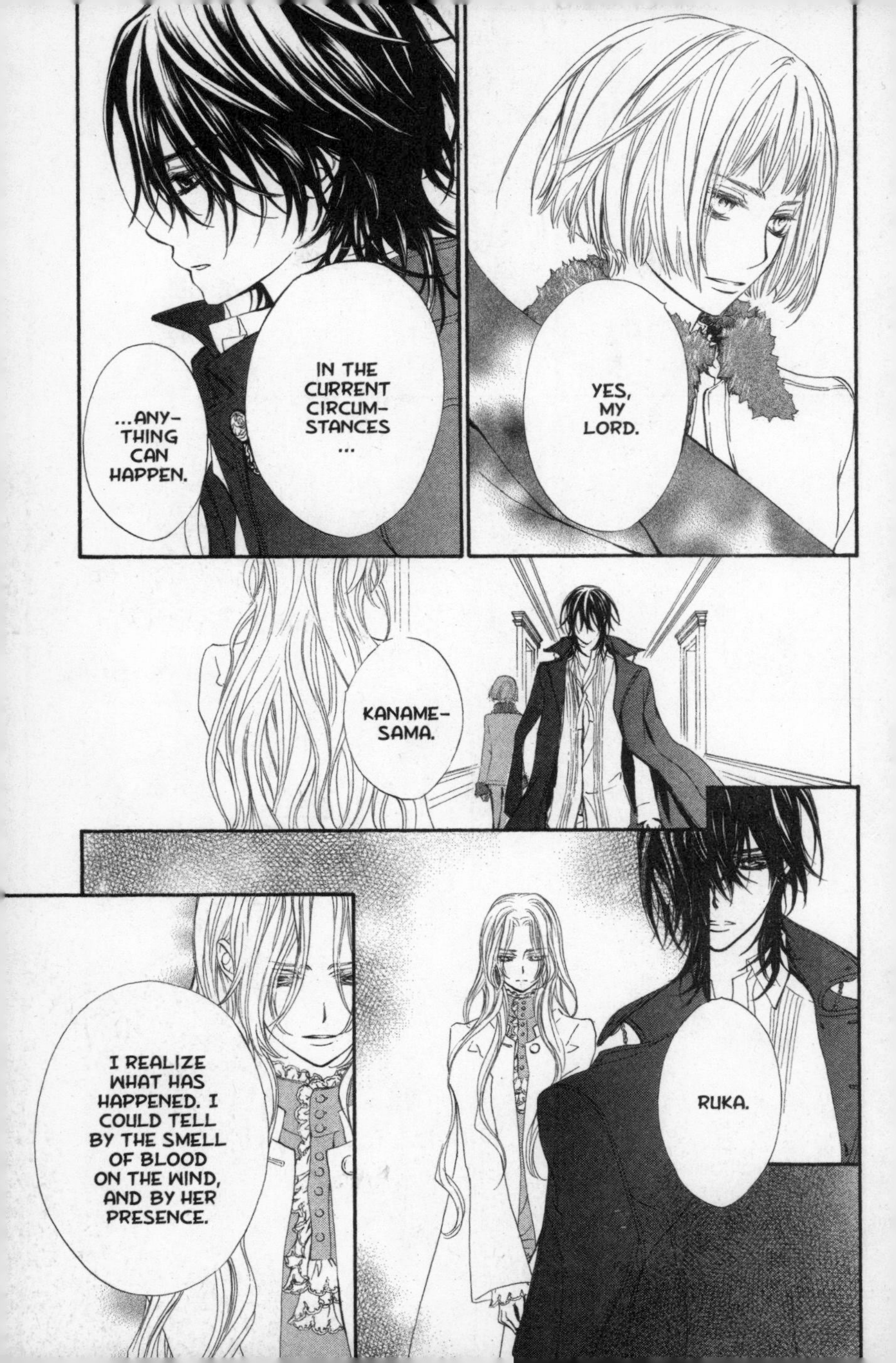
YES, MY LORD.
IN THE CURRENT CIRCUM-STANCES ...
...ANY-THING CAN HAPPEN.
KANAME-SAMA.
RUKA.
I REALIZE WHAT HAS HAPPENED. I COULD TELL BY THE SMELL OF BLOOD ON THE WIND, AND BY HER PRESENCE.

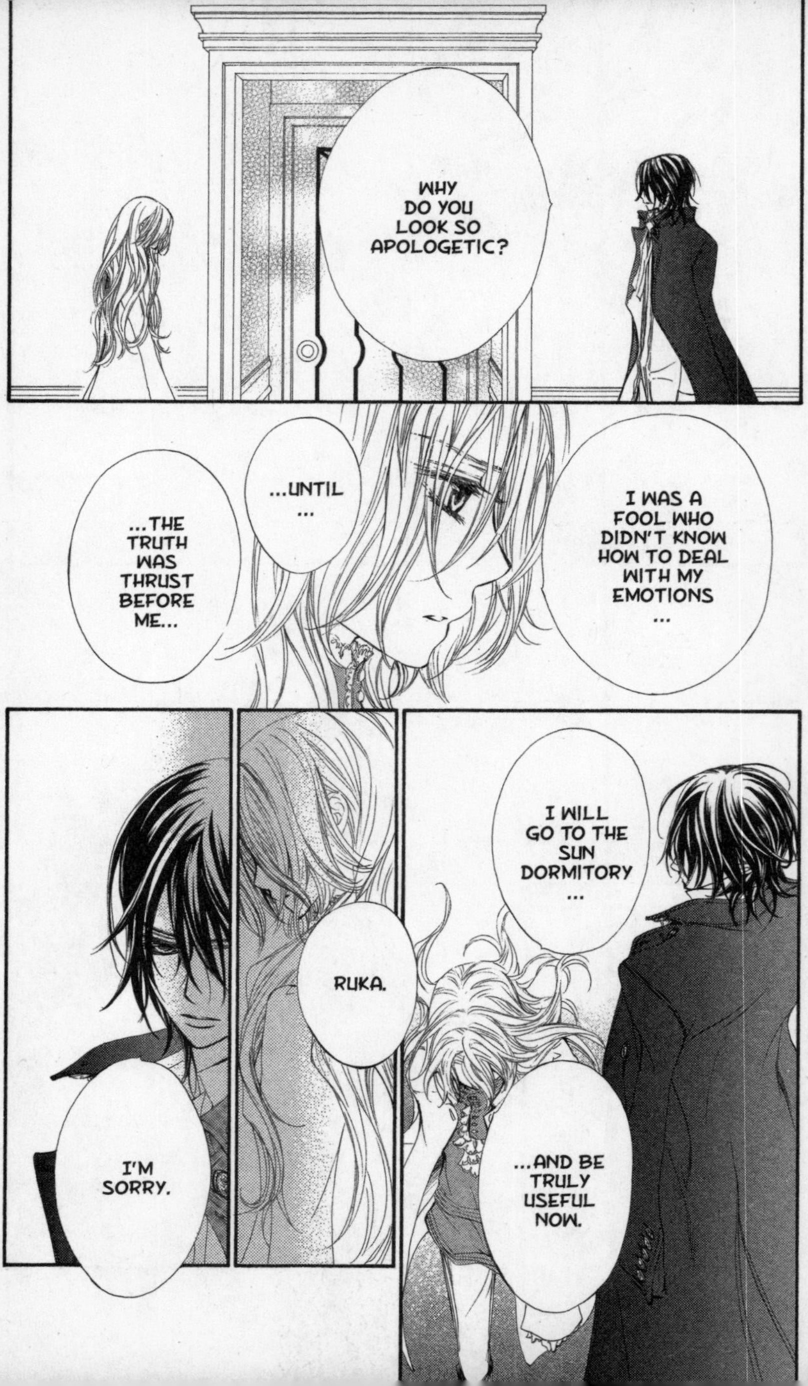
WHY DO YOU LOOK SO APOLOGETIC?
I WAS A FOOL WHO DIDN'T KNOW HOW TO DEAL WITH MY EMOTIONS ...
...UNTIL ...
...THE TRUTH WAS THRUST BEFORE ME...
I WILL GO TO THE SUN DORMITORY ...
...AND BE TRULY USEFUL NOW.
RUKA.
I'M SORRY.

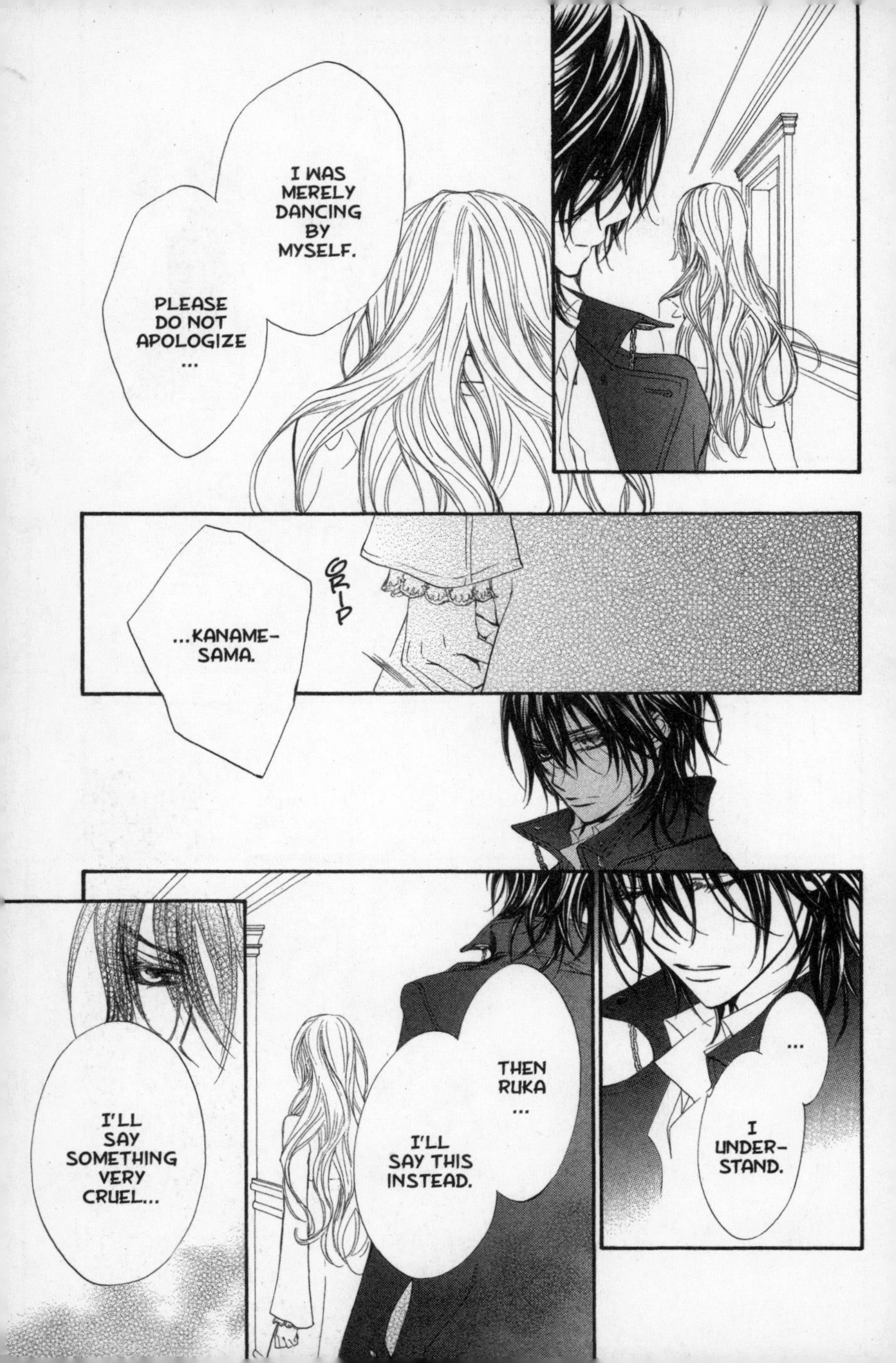
I WAS MERELY DANCING BY MYSELF.
PLEASE DO NOT APOLOGIZE ...
GRIP
...KANAME-SAMA.
...
I UNDERSTAND.
THEN RUKA ...
I'LL SAY THIS INSTEAD.
I'LL SAY SOMETHING VERY CRUEL...

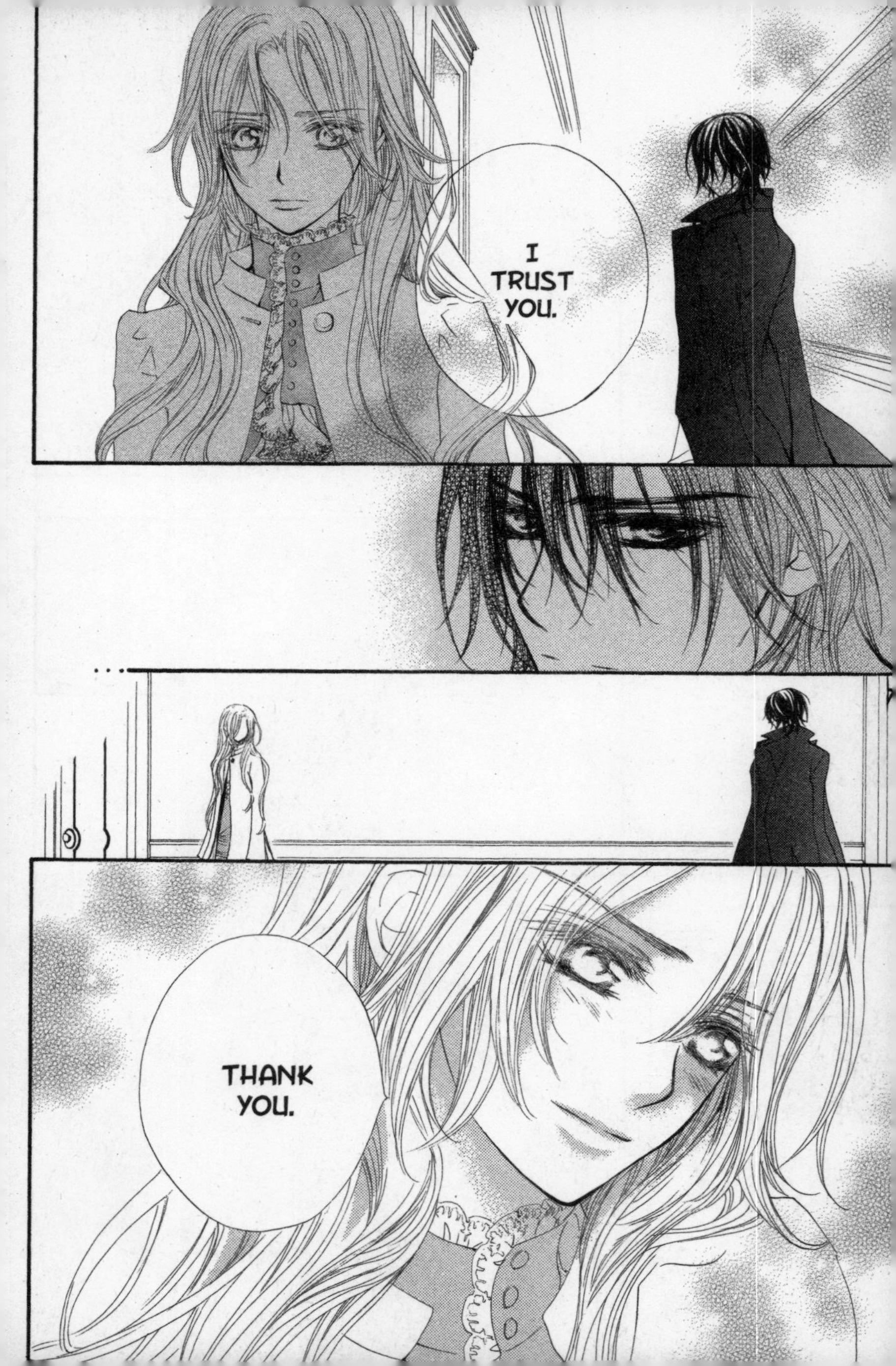
I TRUST YOU.
...
THANK YOU.

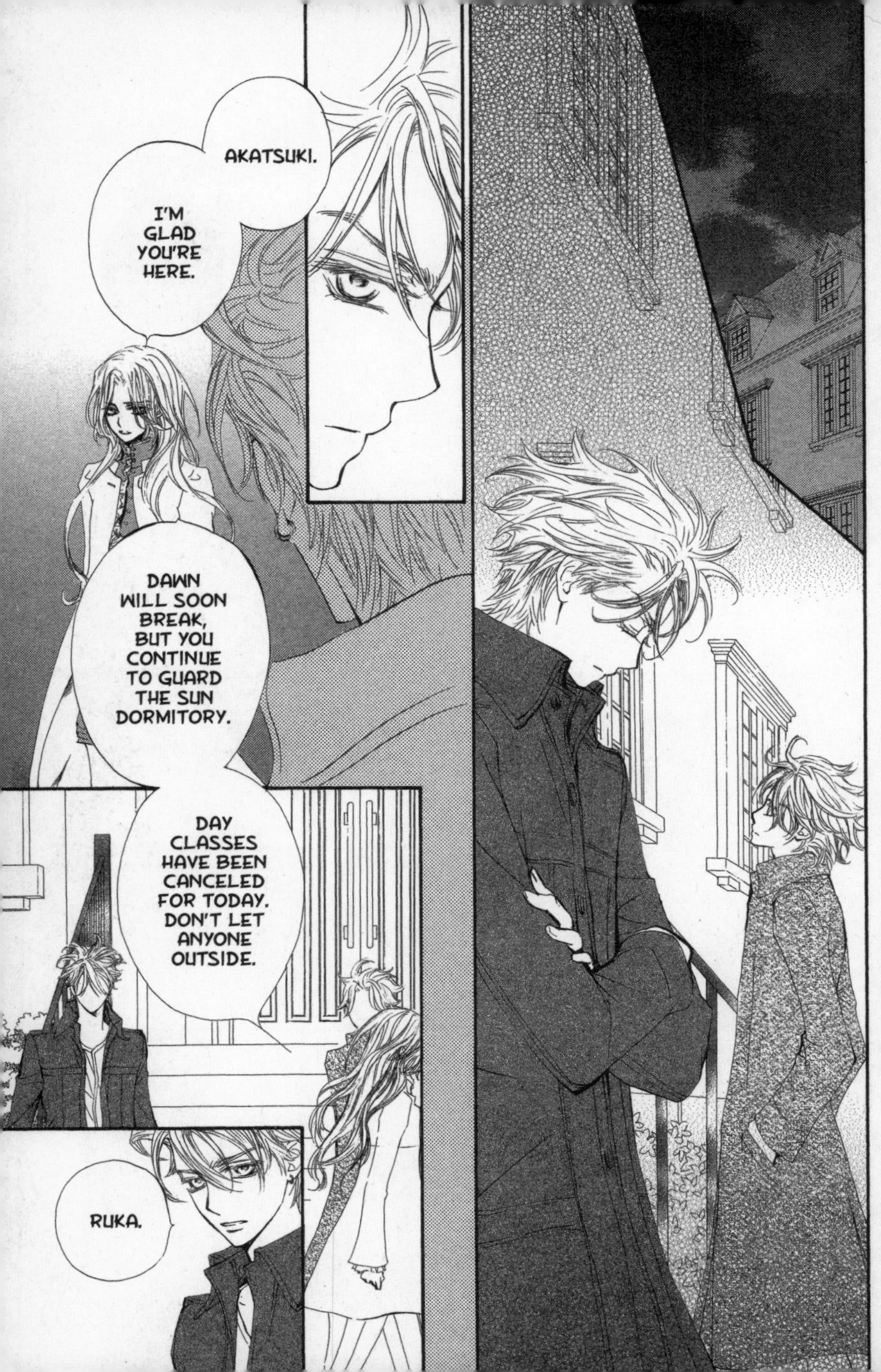
AKATSUKI.
I'M GLAD YOU'RE HERE.
DAWN WILL SOON BREAK, BUT YOU CONTINUE TO GUARD THE SUN DORMITORY.
DAY CLASSES HAVE BEEN CANCELED FOR TODAY. DON'T LET ANYONE OUTSIDE.
RUKA.

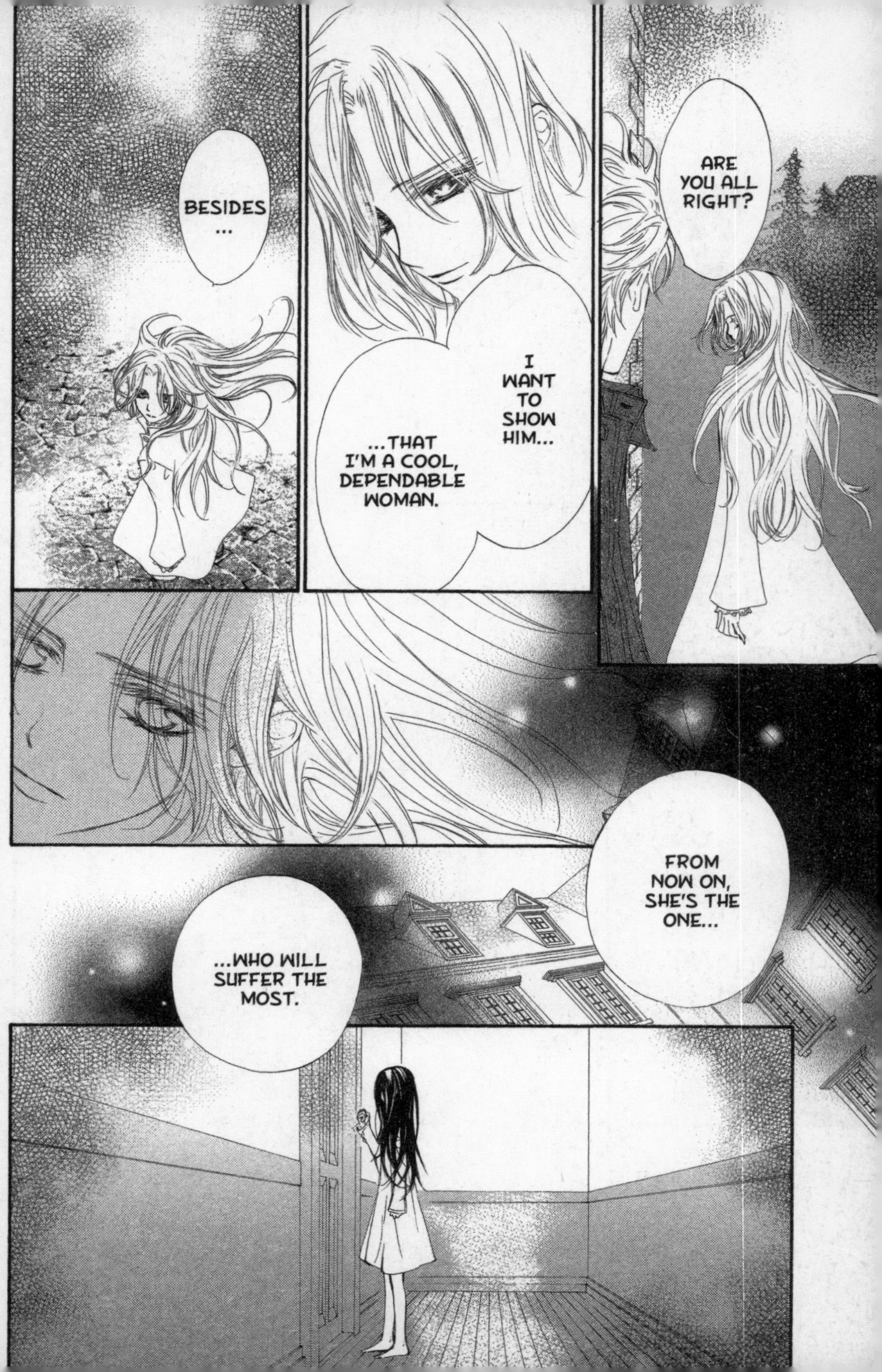
ARE YOU ALL RIGHT?
I WANT TO SHOW HIM...
...THAT I'M A COOL, DEPENDABLE WOMAN.
BESIDES...
FROM NOW ON, SHE'S THE ONE...
...WHO WILL SUFFER THE MOST.

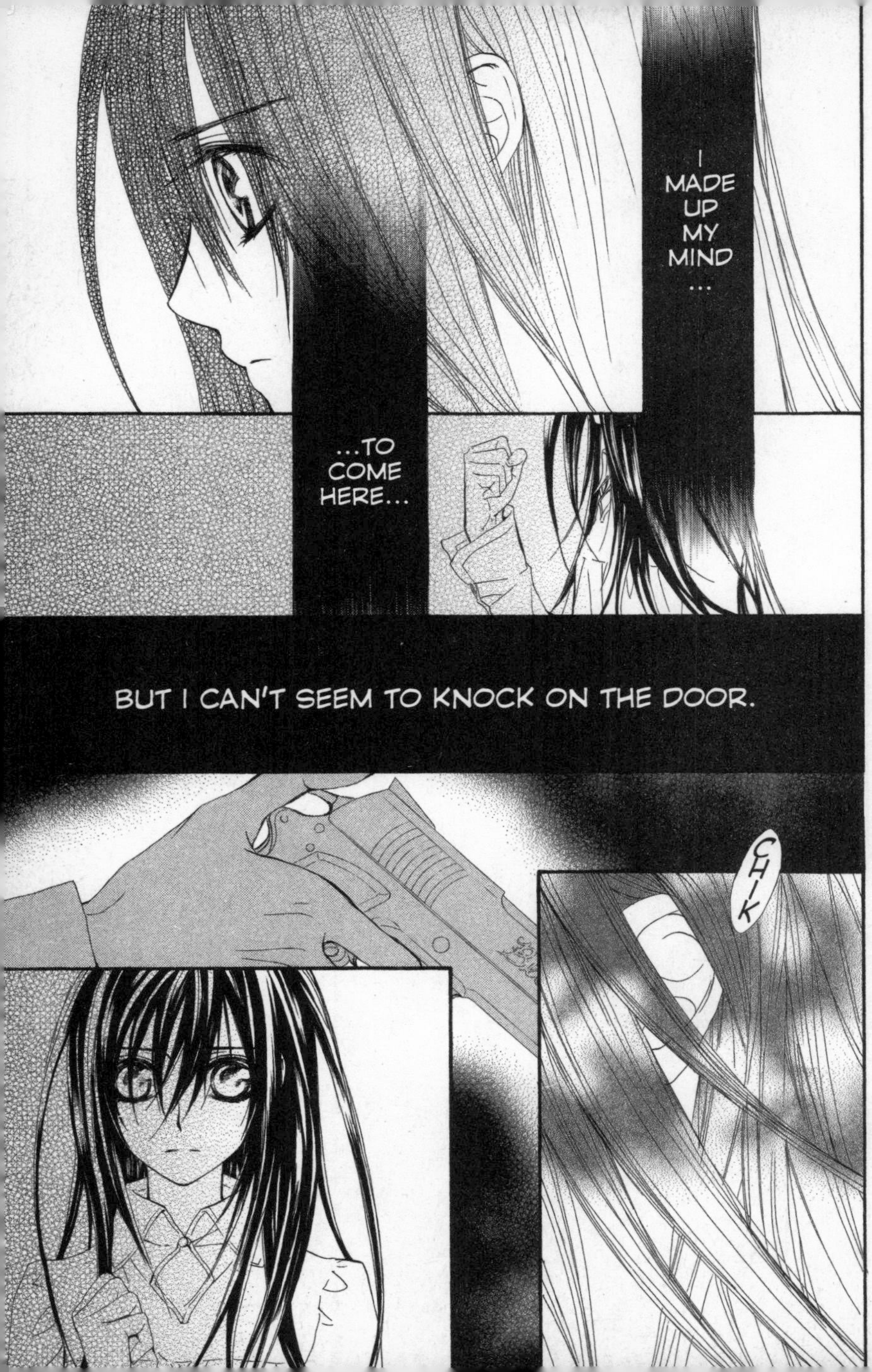
I MADE UP MY MIND...
...TO COME HERE...
BUT I CAN'T SEEM TO KNOCK ON THE DOOR.
CHIK

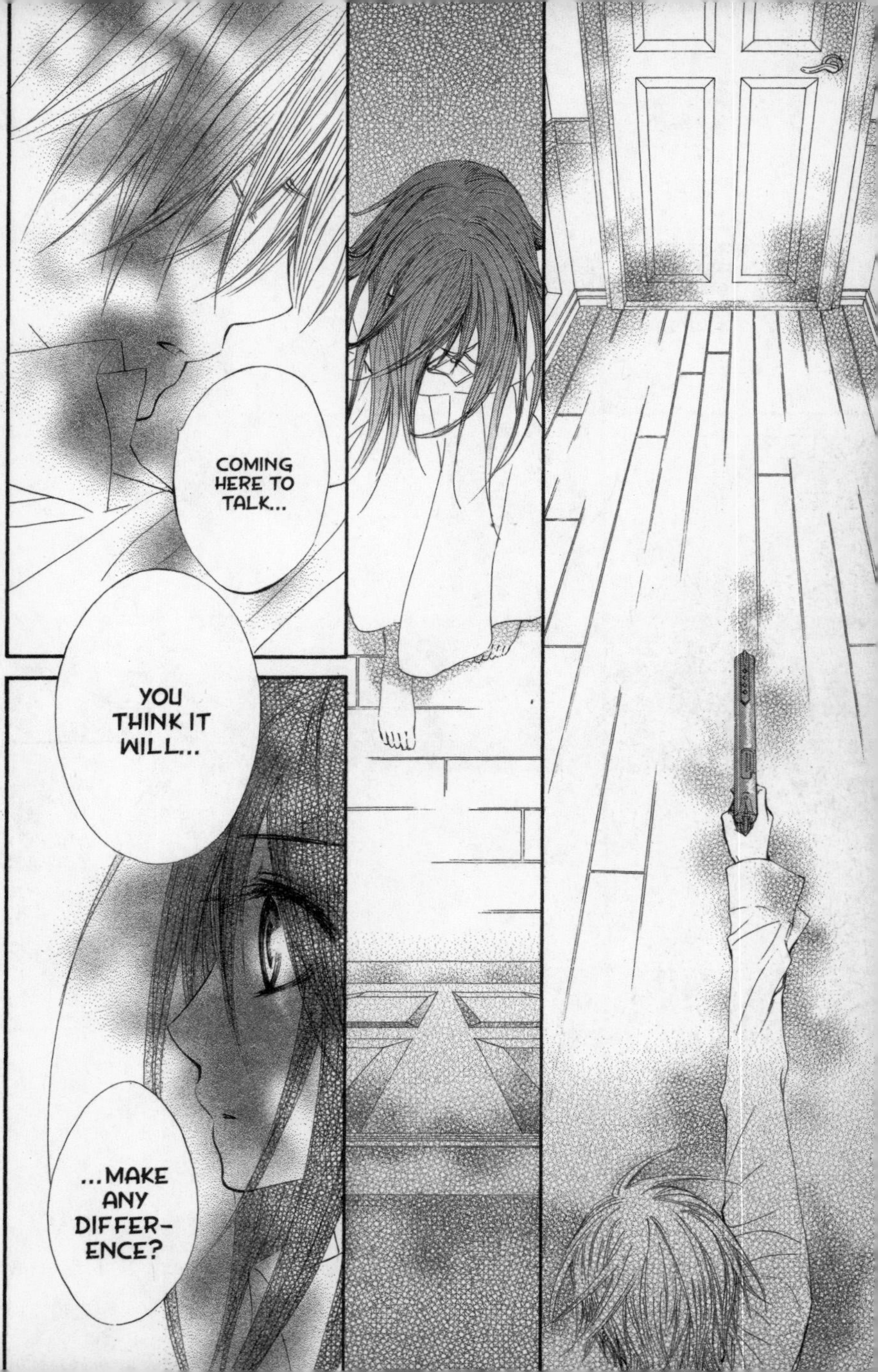
COMING HERE TO TALK...
YOU THINK IT WILL...
...MAKE ANY DIFFERENCE?

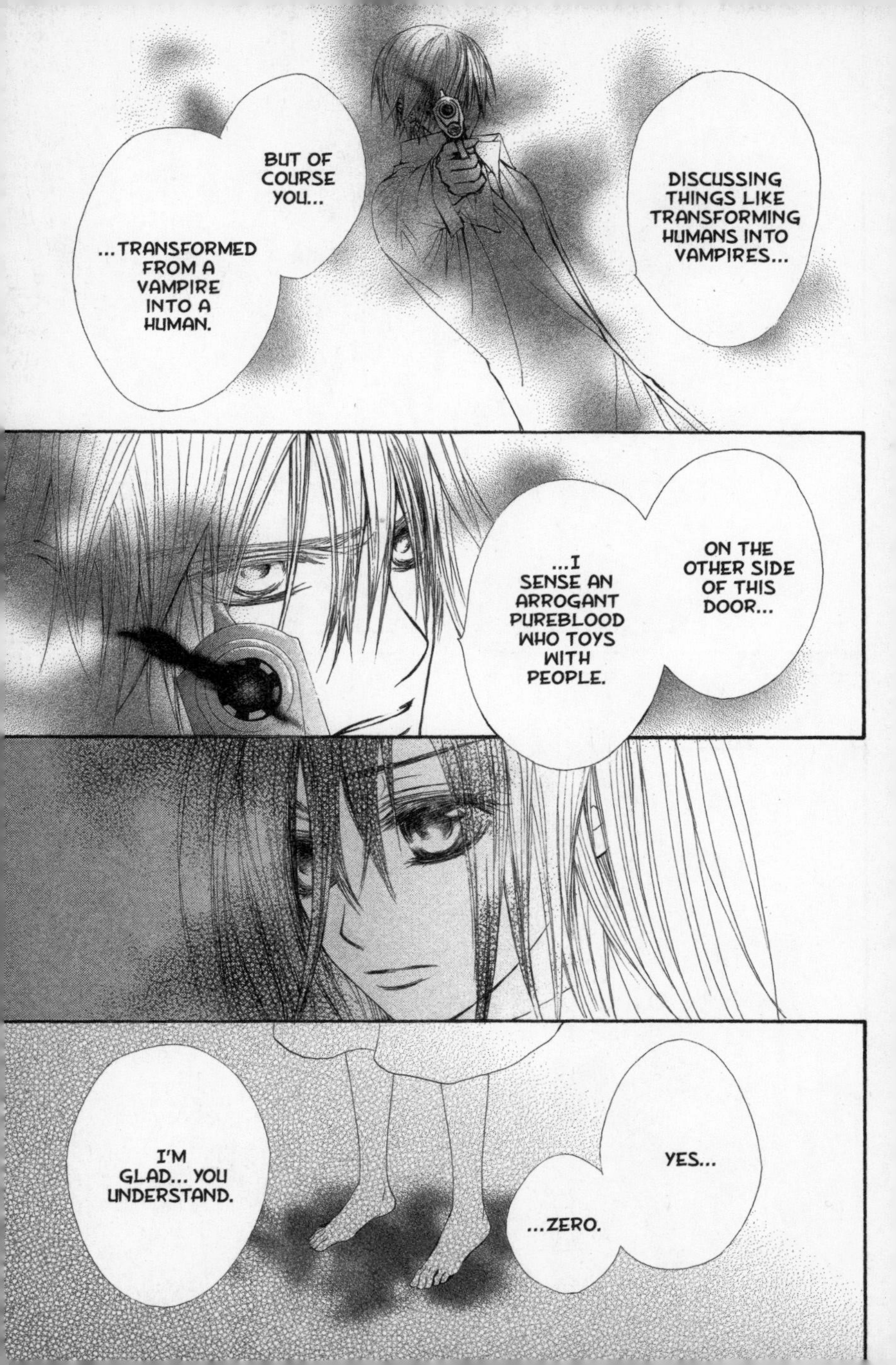
DISCUSSING THINGS LIKE TRANSFORMING HUMANS INTO VAMPIRES...
BUT OF COURSE YOU...
...TRANSFORMED FROM A VAMPIRE INTO A HUMAN.
ON THE OTHER SIDE OF THIS DOOR...
...I SENSE AN ARROGANT PUREBLOOD WHO TOYS WITH PEOPLE.
YES...
...ZERO.
I'M GLAD... YOU UNDERSTAND.

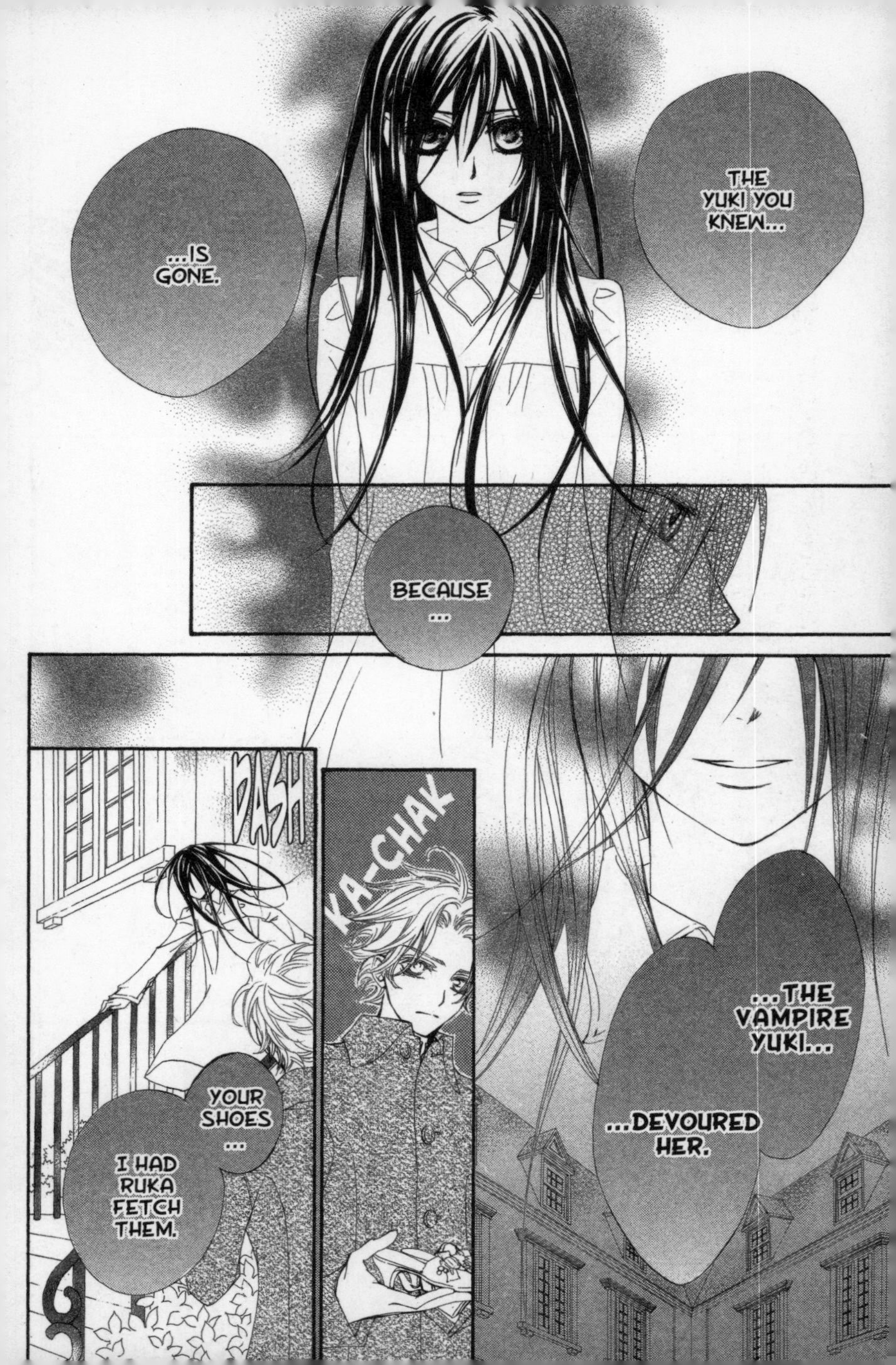

THE YUKI YOU KNEW...
...IS GONE.
BECAUSE ...
...THE VAMPIRE YUKI...
...DEVOURED HER.
KA-CHAK
DASH
YOUR SHOES ...
I HAD RUKA FETCH THEM.

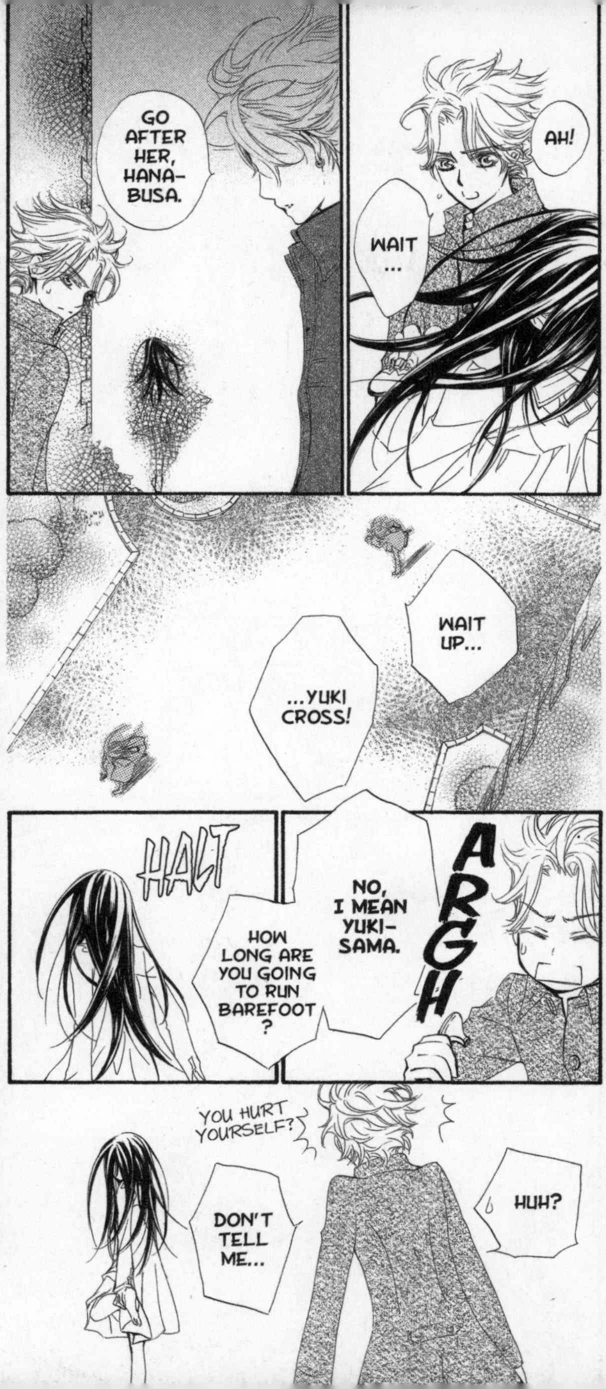
AH!
WAIT...
GO AFTER HER, HANA-BUSA.
WAIT UP...
...YUKI CROSS!
ARGH
NO, I MEAN YUKI-SAMA.
HALT
HOW LONG ARE YOU GOING TO RUN BAREFOOT?
YOU HURT YOURSELF?
HUH?
DON'T TELL ME...

III

My heart was touched, and I felt respect for people who are voice actors once again. Suddenly, something like a musical, which I could not decipher, began. It was too funny, and watching it from the side, I couldn't help running up and asking the staff to help(?). I was then told, "It's always like this when we're recording Vampire Knight. They're funny."

● I happened to observe Miyano-san, who mischievously asked something in a mysterious language to dear Horie-san (who plays Yuki), and she was like "Uh?? ʒ Um... ʒ," not knowing how to respond. I believe I was able to grasp the atmosphere of the studio quite well. There are lots of playful people about!

● The anime is almost always serious. Thank you everyone for sticking with it and holding back your playfulness!! I'm really glad everyone seemed to be enjoying it.♡ I'm looking forward to the second season of the anime too!!

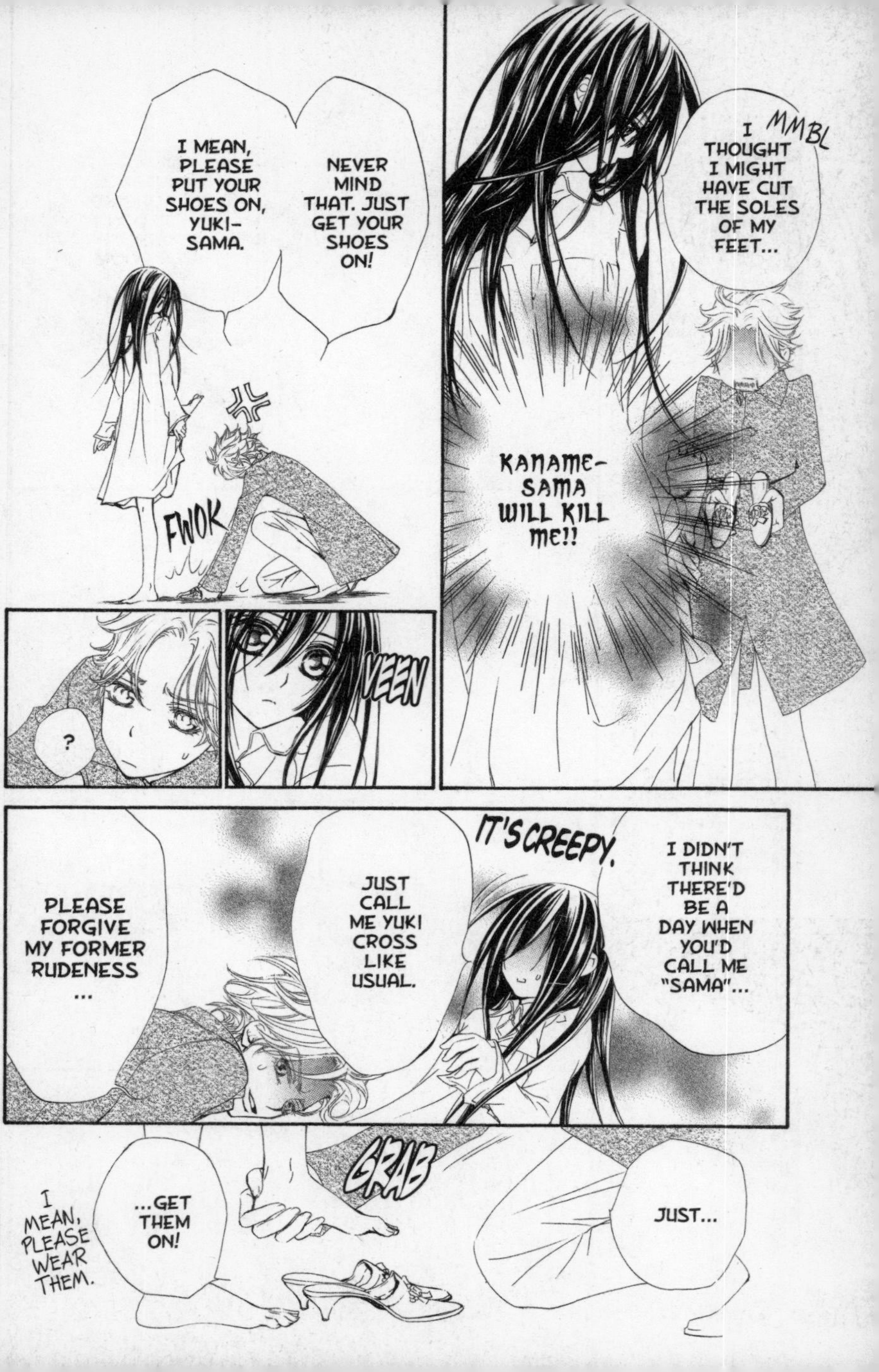
I THOUGHT I MIGHT HAVE CUT THE SOLES OF MY FEET...
MMBL
KANAME-SAMA WILL KILL ME!!
NEVER MIND THAT. JUST GET YOUR SHOES ON!
I MEAN, PLEASE PUT YOUR SHOES ON, YUKI-SAMA.
FWOK
VEEN
?
I DIDN'T THINK THERE'D BE A DAY WHEN YOU'D CALL ME "SAMA"...
IT'S CREEPY.
JUST CALL ME YUKI CROSS LIKE USUAL.
PLEASE FORGIVE MY FORMER RUDENESS ...
JUST...
GRAB
...GET THEM ON!
I MEAN, PLEASE WEAR THEM.

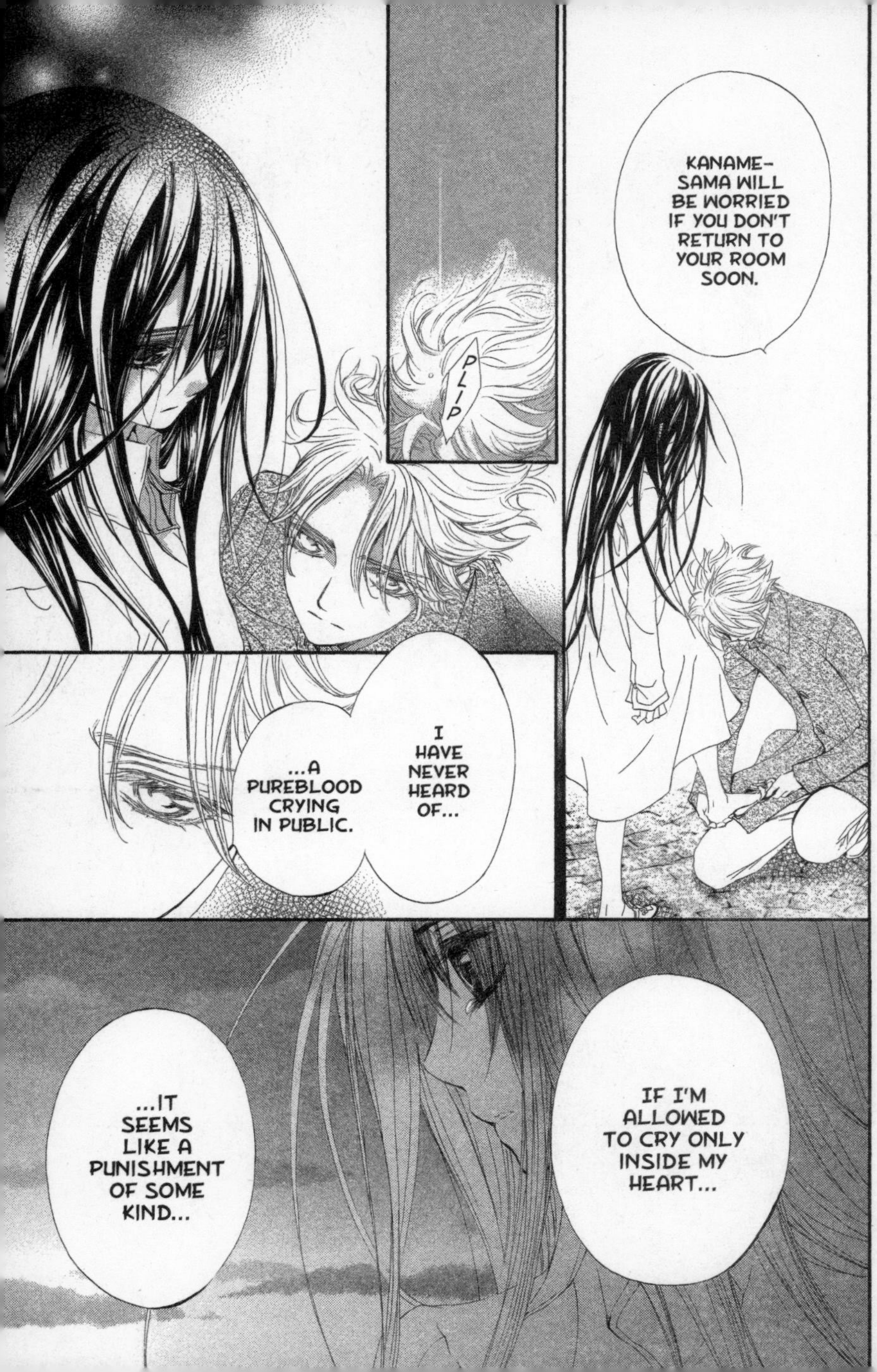
KANAME-SAMA WILL BE WORRIED IF YOU DON'T RETURN TO YOUR ROOM SOON.
PLIP
I HAVE NEVER HEARD OF...
...A PUREBLOOD CRYING IN PUBLIC.
IF I'M ALLOWED TO CRY ONLY INSIDE MY HEART...
...IT SEEMS LIKE A PUNISHMENT OF SOME KIND...

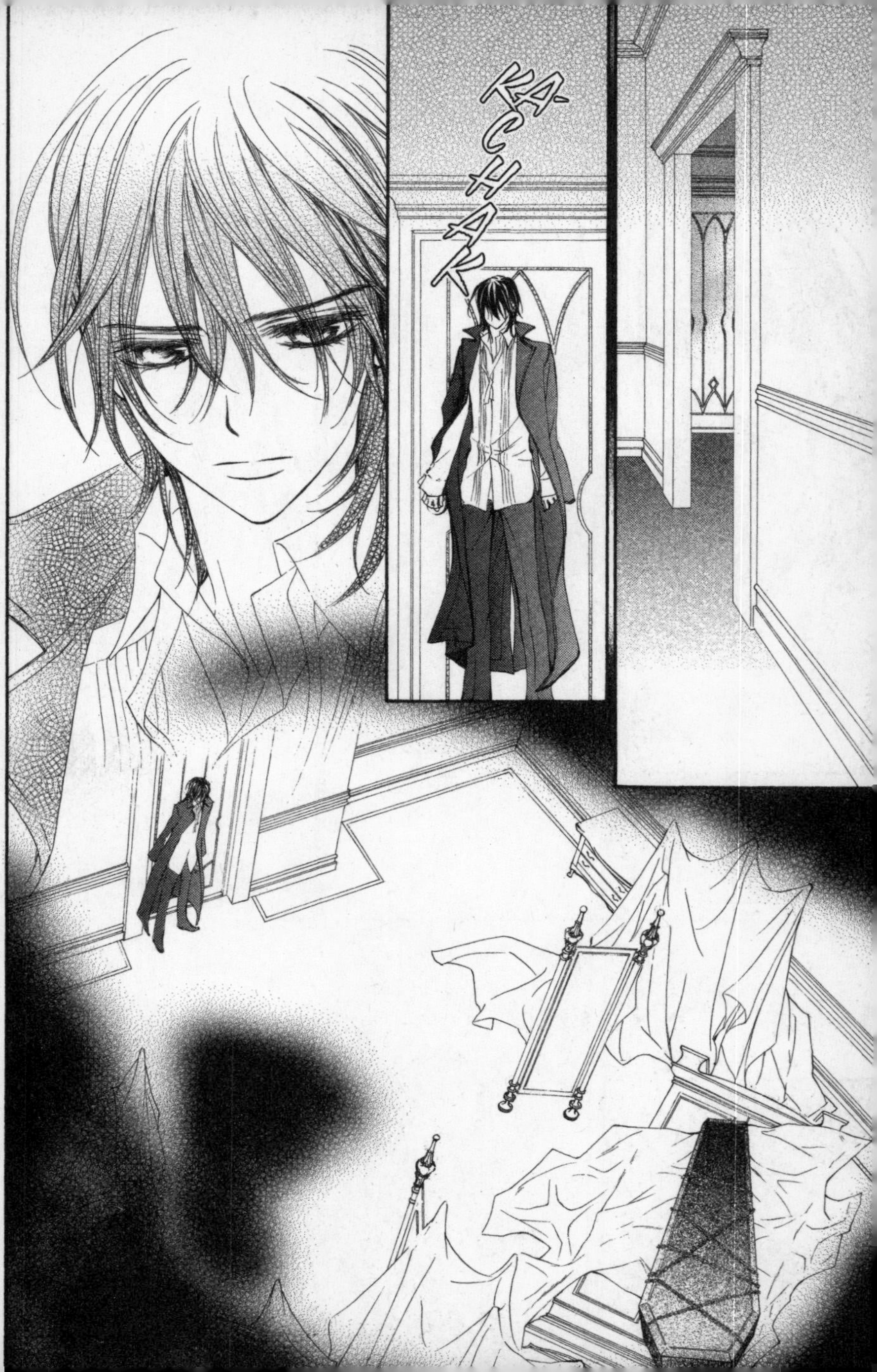
KA-CHAK

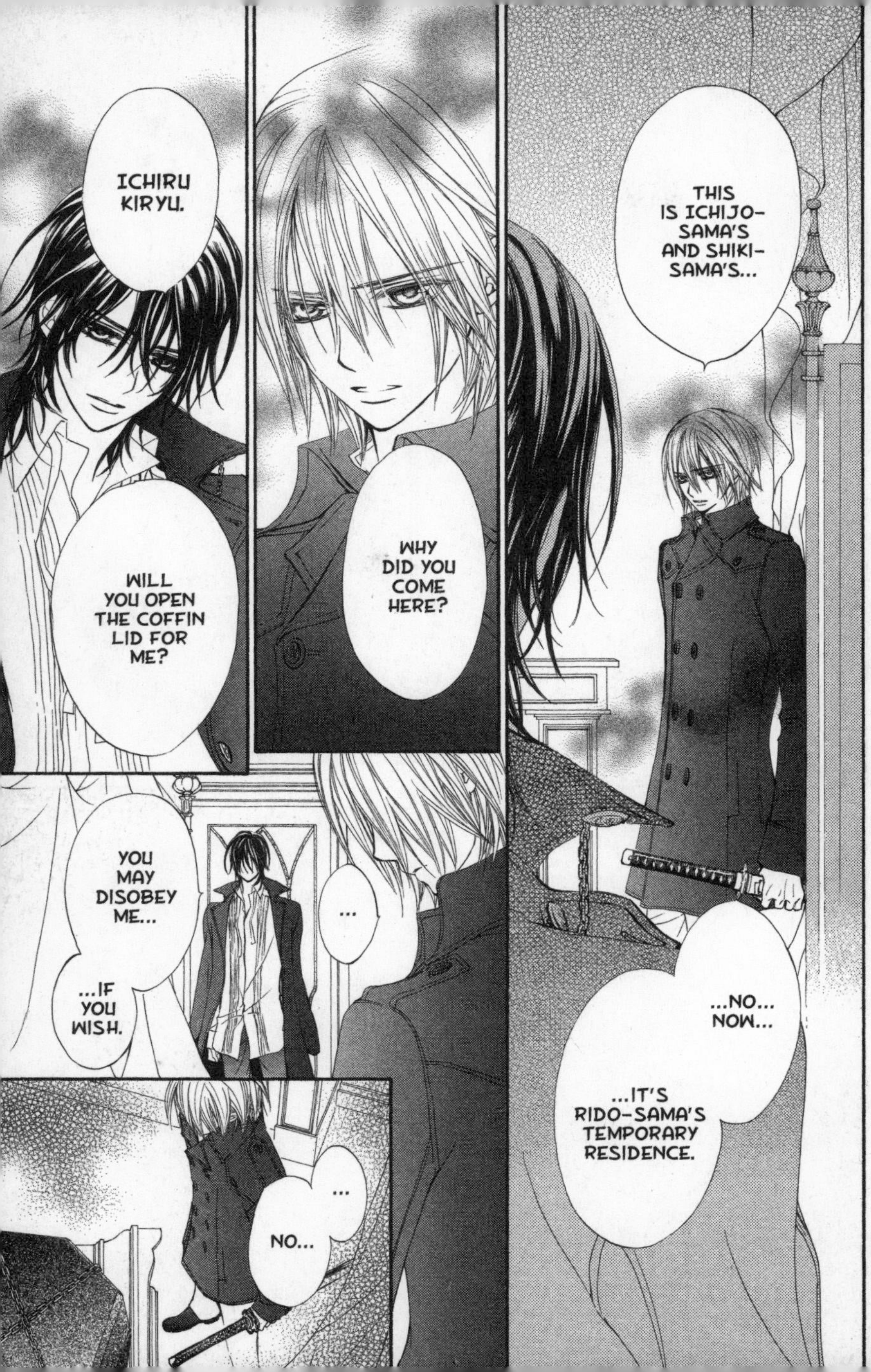
THIS IS ICHIJO-SAMA'S AND SHIKI-SAMA'S...
...NO... NOW...
...IT'S RIDO-SAMA'S TEMPORARY RESIDENCE.
WHY DID YOU COME HERE?
ICHIRU KIRYU.
WILL YOU OPEN THE COFFIN LID FOR ME?
...
YOU MAY DISOBEY ME...
...IF YOU WISH.
...
NO...

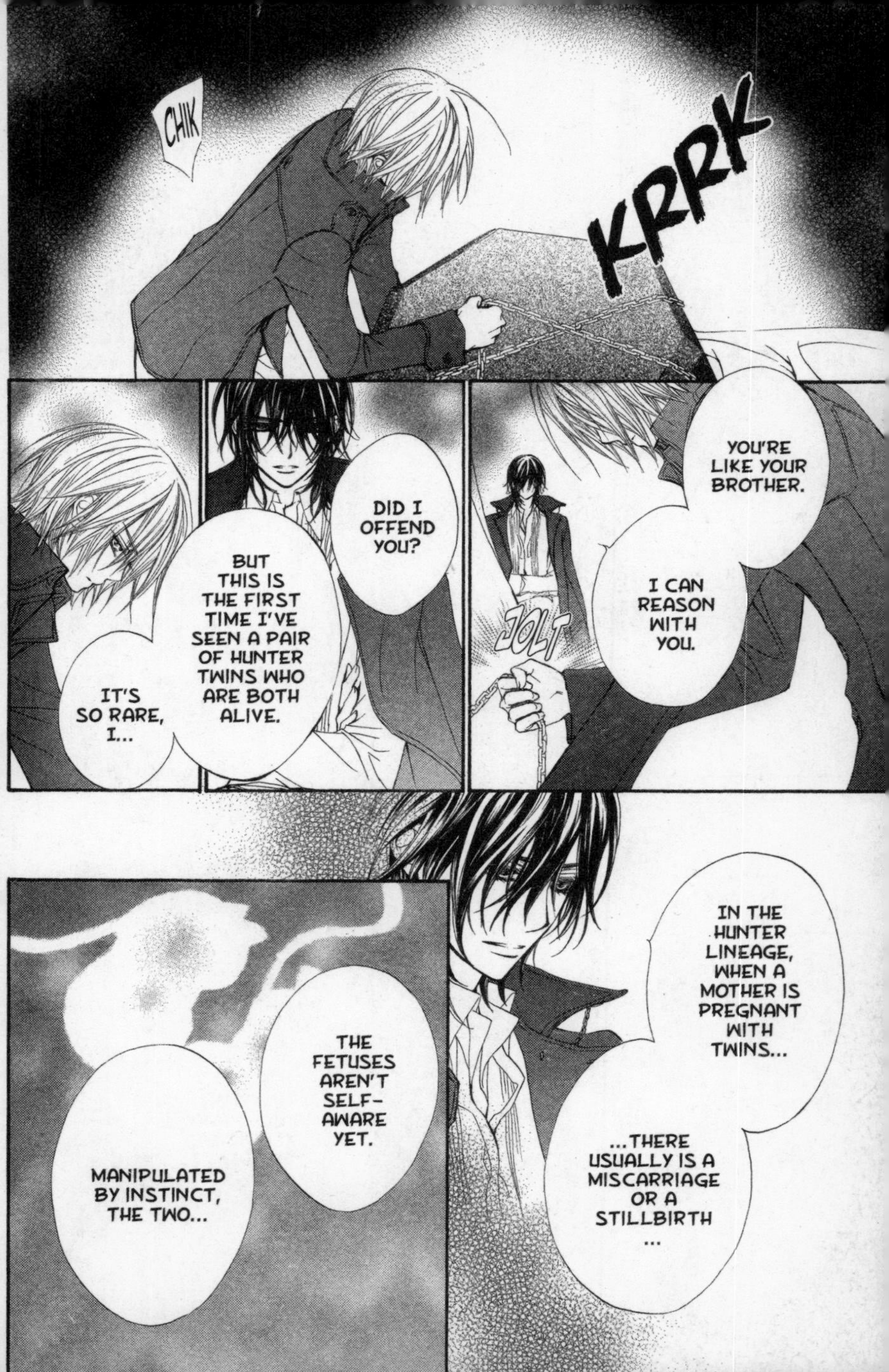

KRRK
CHIK
YOU'RE LIKE YOUR BROTHER.
I CAN REASON WITH YOU.
JOLT
DID I OFFEND YOU?
BUT THIS IS THE FIRST TIME I'VE SEEN A PAIR OF HUNTER TWINS WHO ARE BOTH ALIVE.
IT'S SO RARE, I...
IN THE HUNTER LINEAGE, WHEN A MOTHER IS PREGNANT WITH TWINS...
...THERE USUALLY IS A MISCARRIAGE OR A STILLBIRTH ...
THE FETUSES AREN'T SELF-AWARE YET.
MANIPULATED BY INSTINCT, THE TWO...

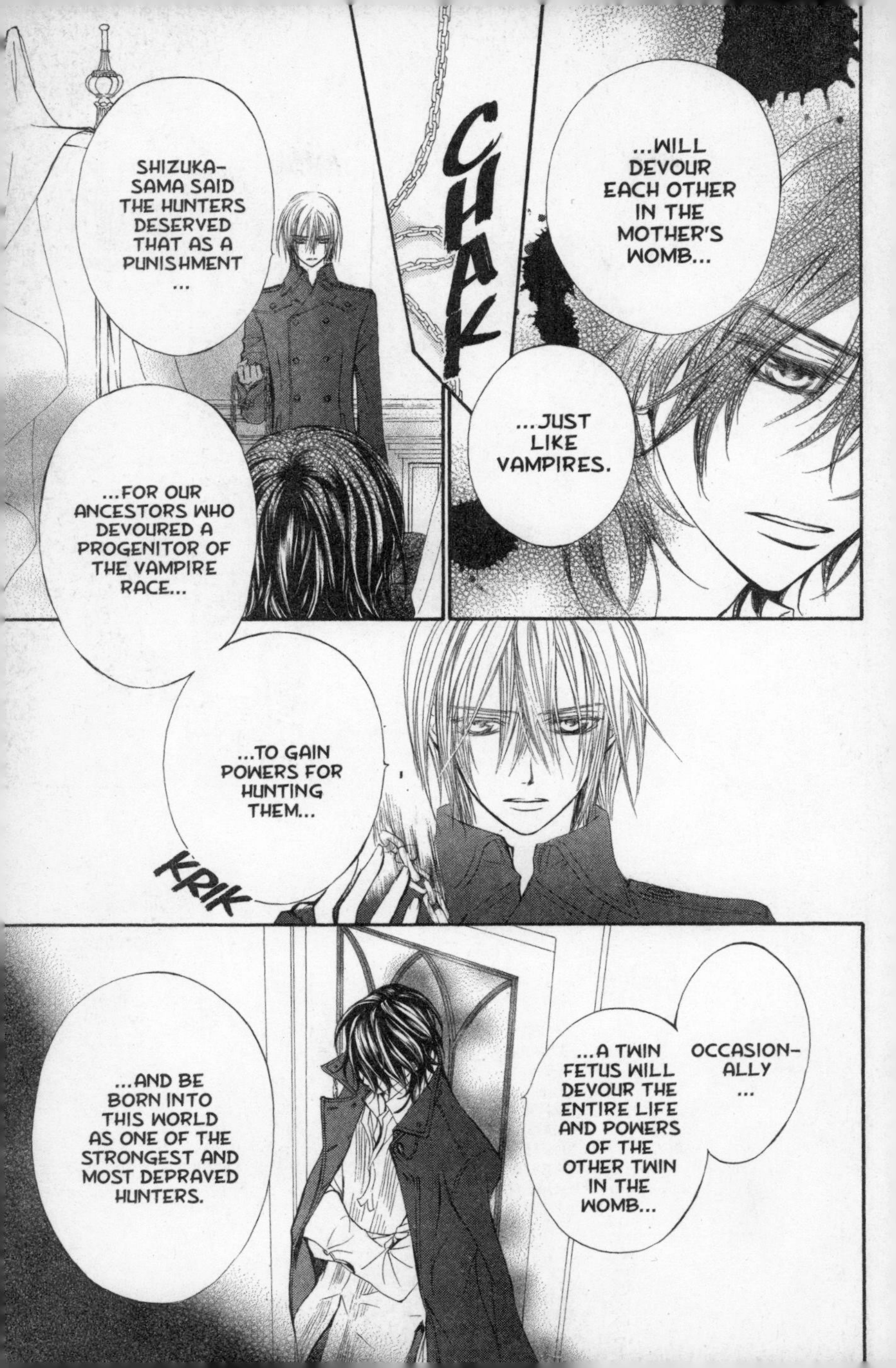
...WILL DEVOUR EACH OTHER IN THE MOTHER'S WOMB...
...JUST LIKE VAMPIRES.
CHAK
SHIZUKA-SAMA SAID THE HUNTERS DESERVED THAT AS A PUNISHMENT...
...FOR OUR ANCESTORS WHO DEVOURED A PROGENITOR OF THE VAMPIRE RACE...
...TO GAIN POWERS FOR HUNTING THEM...
KRIK
OCCASION-ALLY...
...A TWIN FETUS WILL DEVOUR THE ENTIRE LIFE AND POWERS OF THE OTHER TWIN IN THE WOMB...
...AND BE BORN INTO THIS WORLD AS ONE OF THE STRONGEST AND MOST DEPRAVED HUNTERS.

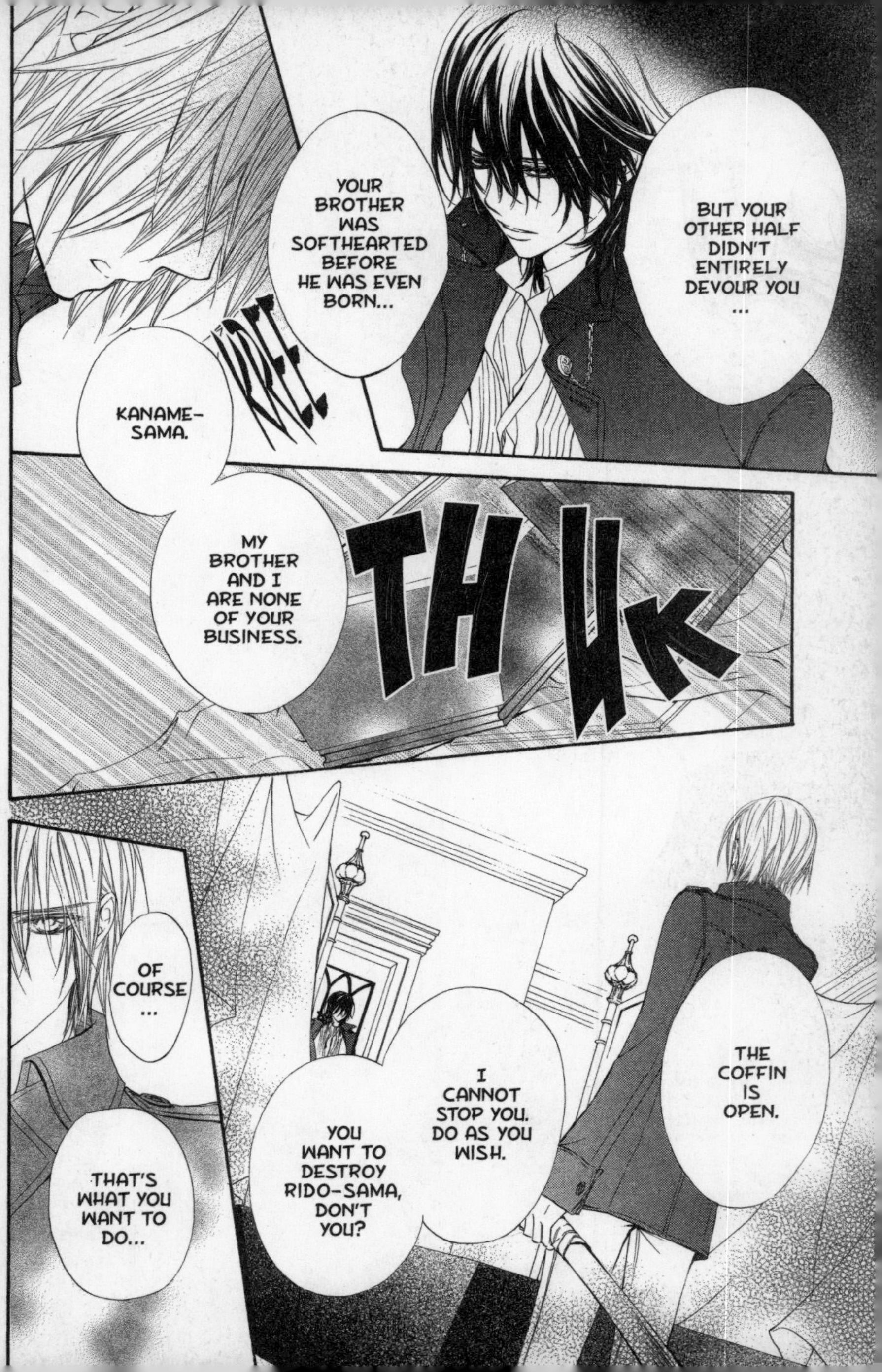
BUT YOUR OTHER HALF DIDN'T ENTIRELY DEVOUR YOU ...
YOUR BROTHER WAS SOFTHEARTED BEFORE HE WAS EVEN BORN...
KANAME-SAMA.
MY BROTHER AND I ARE NONE OF YOUR BUSINESS.
THUK
THE COFFIN IS OPEN.
I CANNOT STOP YOU. DO AS YOU WISH.
YOU WANT TO DESTROY RIDO-SAMA, DON'T YOU?
OF COURSE ...
THAT'S WHAT YOU WANT TO DO...

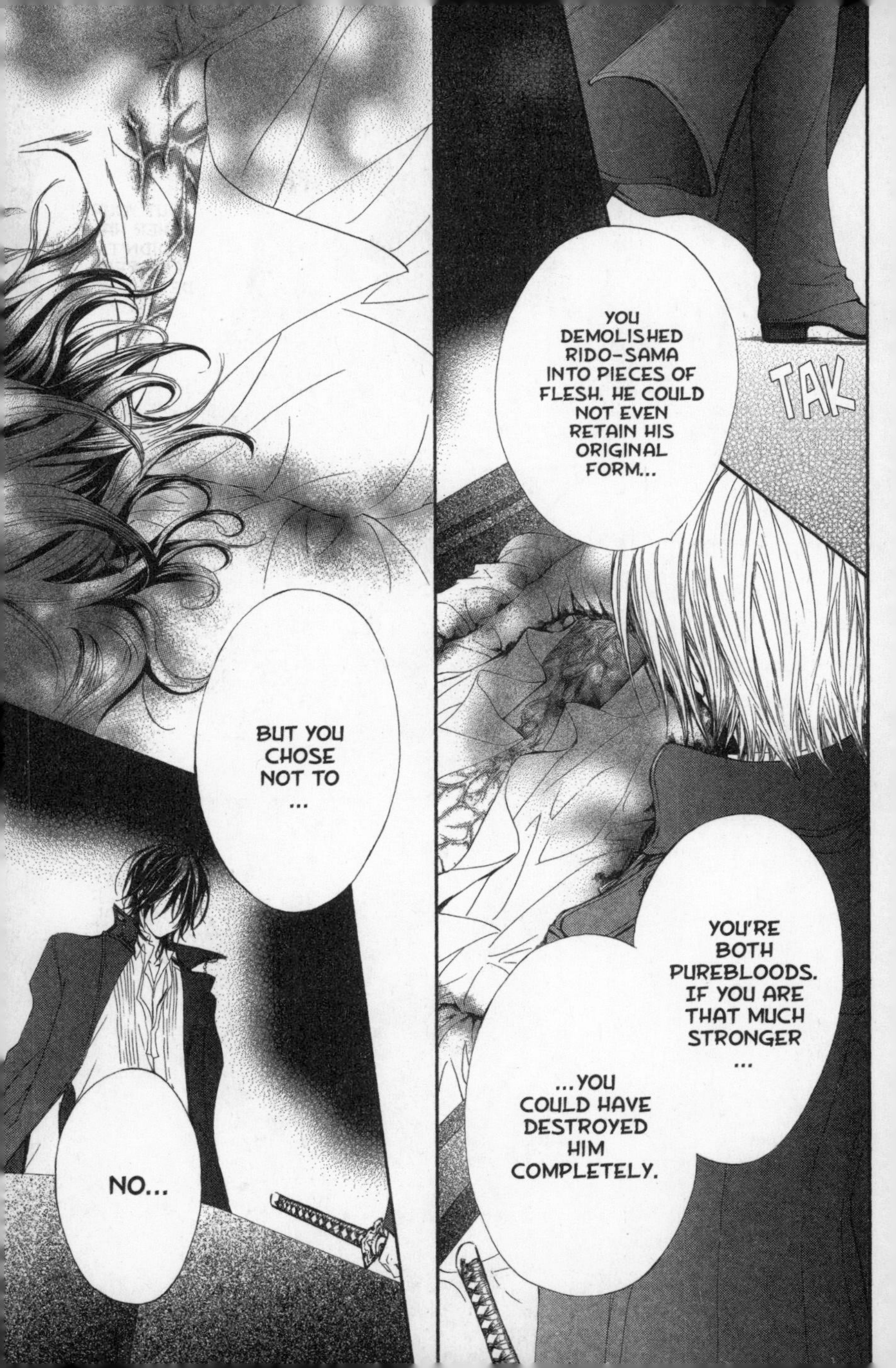
YOU DEMOLISHED RIDO-SAMA INTO PIECES OF FLESH. HE COULD NOT EVEN RETAIN HIS ORIGINAL FORM...
TAK
YOU'RE BOTH PUREBLOODS. IF YOU ARE THAT MUCH STRONGER ...
...YOU COULD HAVE DESTROYED HIM COMPLETELY.
BUT YOU CHOSE NOT TO ...
NO...

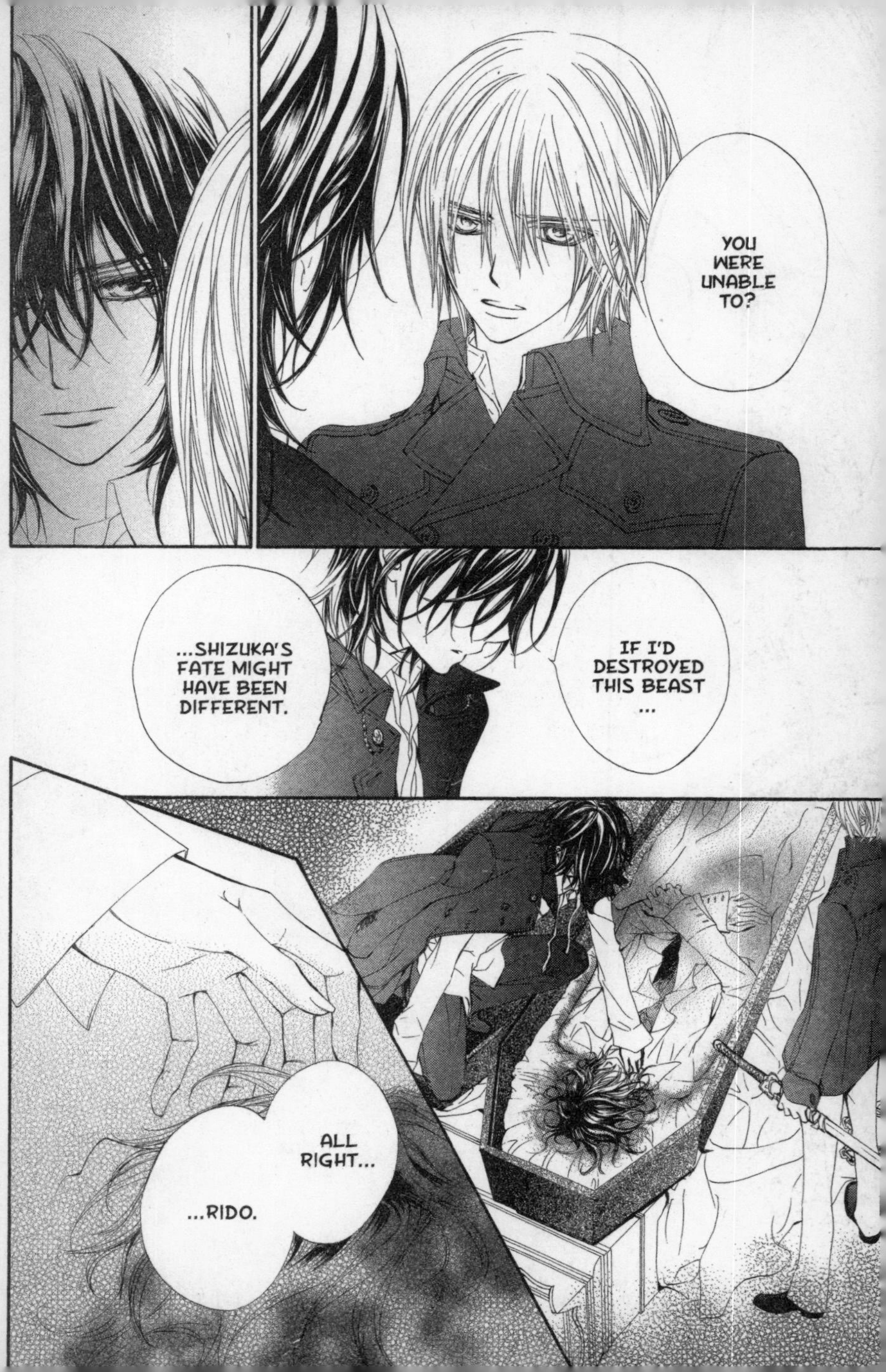
YOU WERE UNABLE TO?
IF I'D DESTROYED THIS BEAST ...
...SHIZUKA'S FATE MIGHT HAVE BEEN DIFFERENT.
ALL RIGHT...
...RIDO.

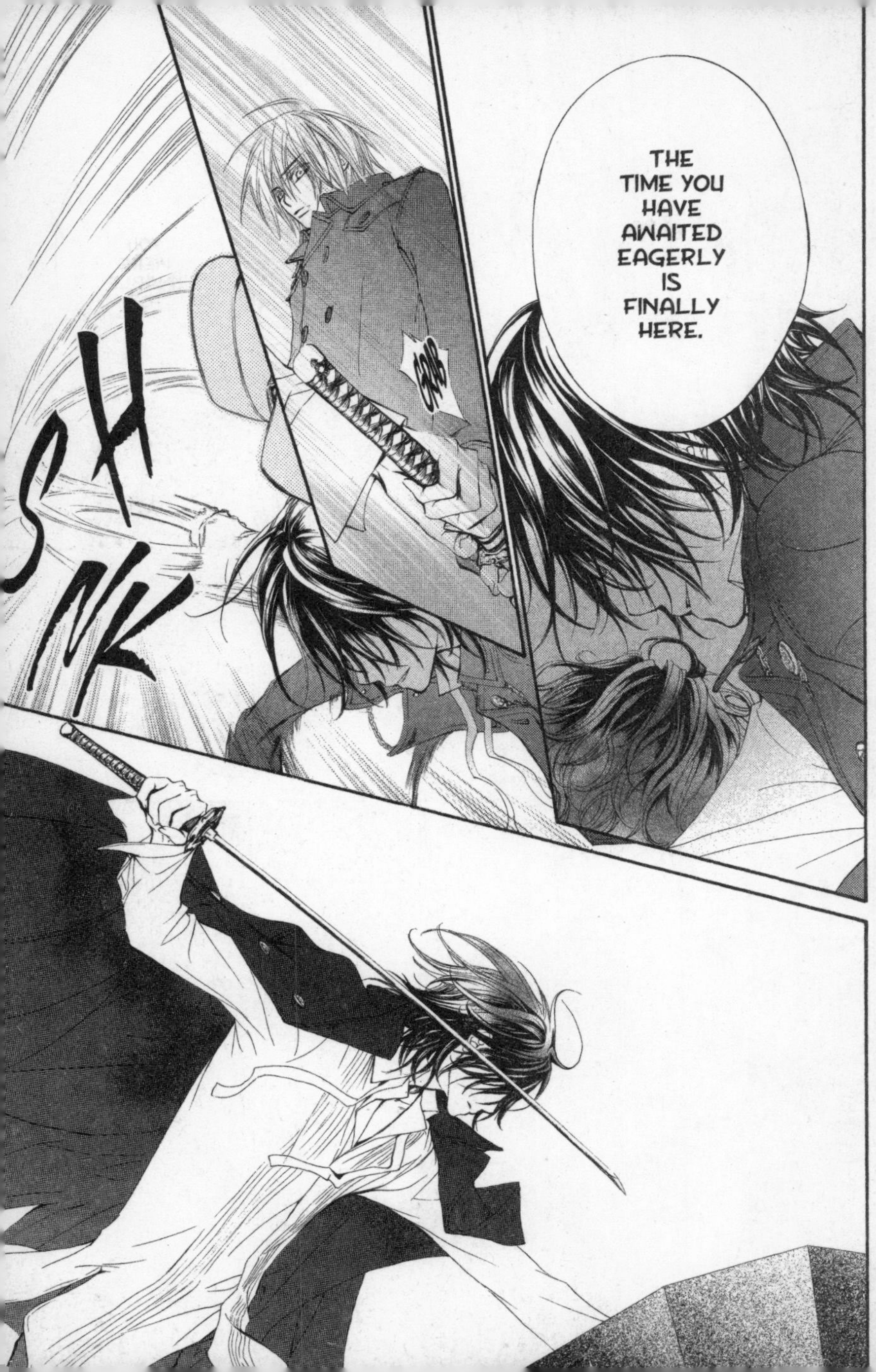
THE TIME YOU HAVE AWAITED EAGERLY IS FINALLY HERE.
GRAB
SHNK

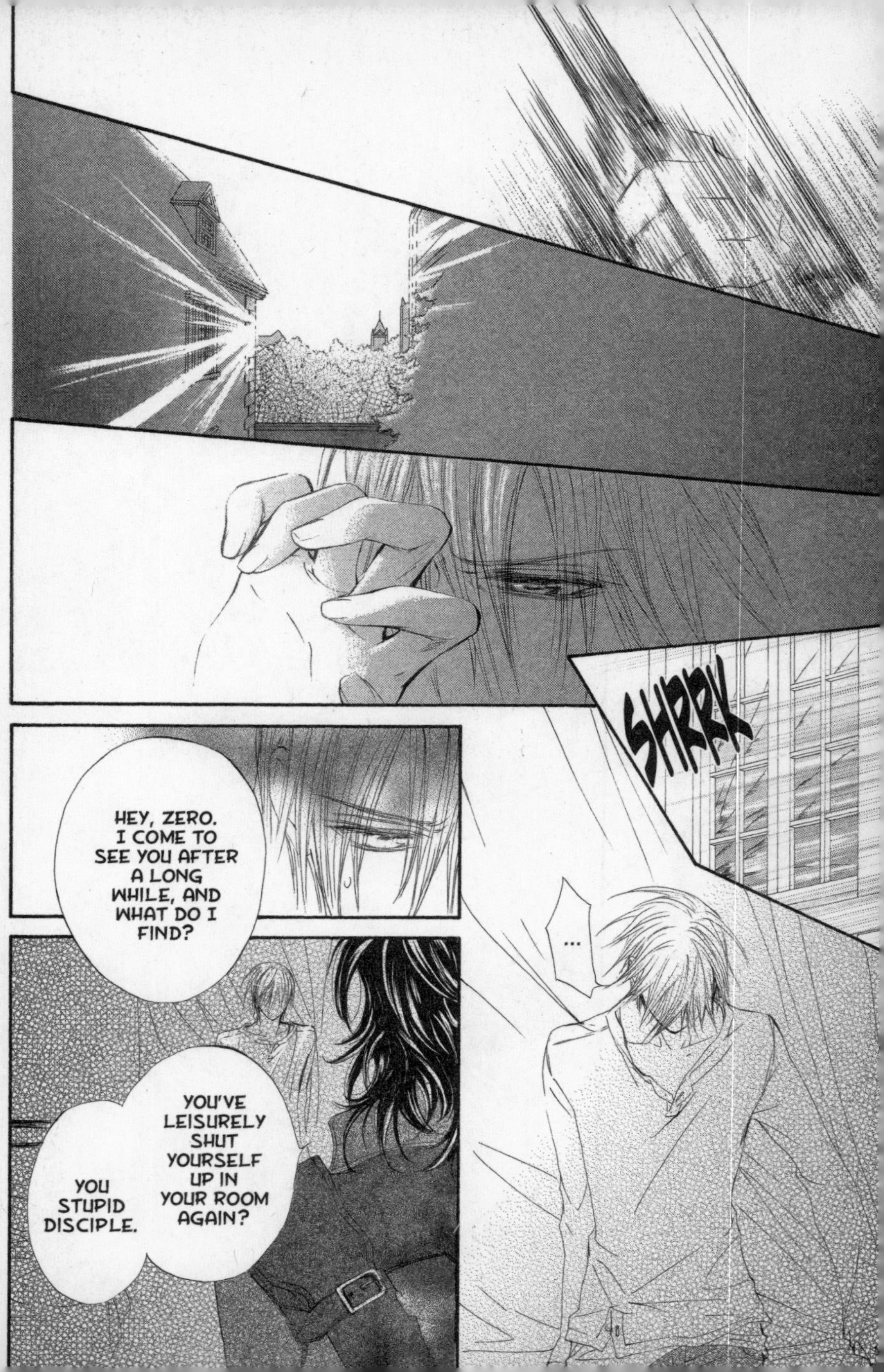
SHRRK
...
HEY, ZERO. I COME TO SEE YOU AFTER A LONG WHILE, AND WHAT DO I FIND?
YOU'VE LEISURELY SHUT YOURSELF UP IN YOUR ROOM AGAIN?
YOU STUPID DISCIPLE.

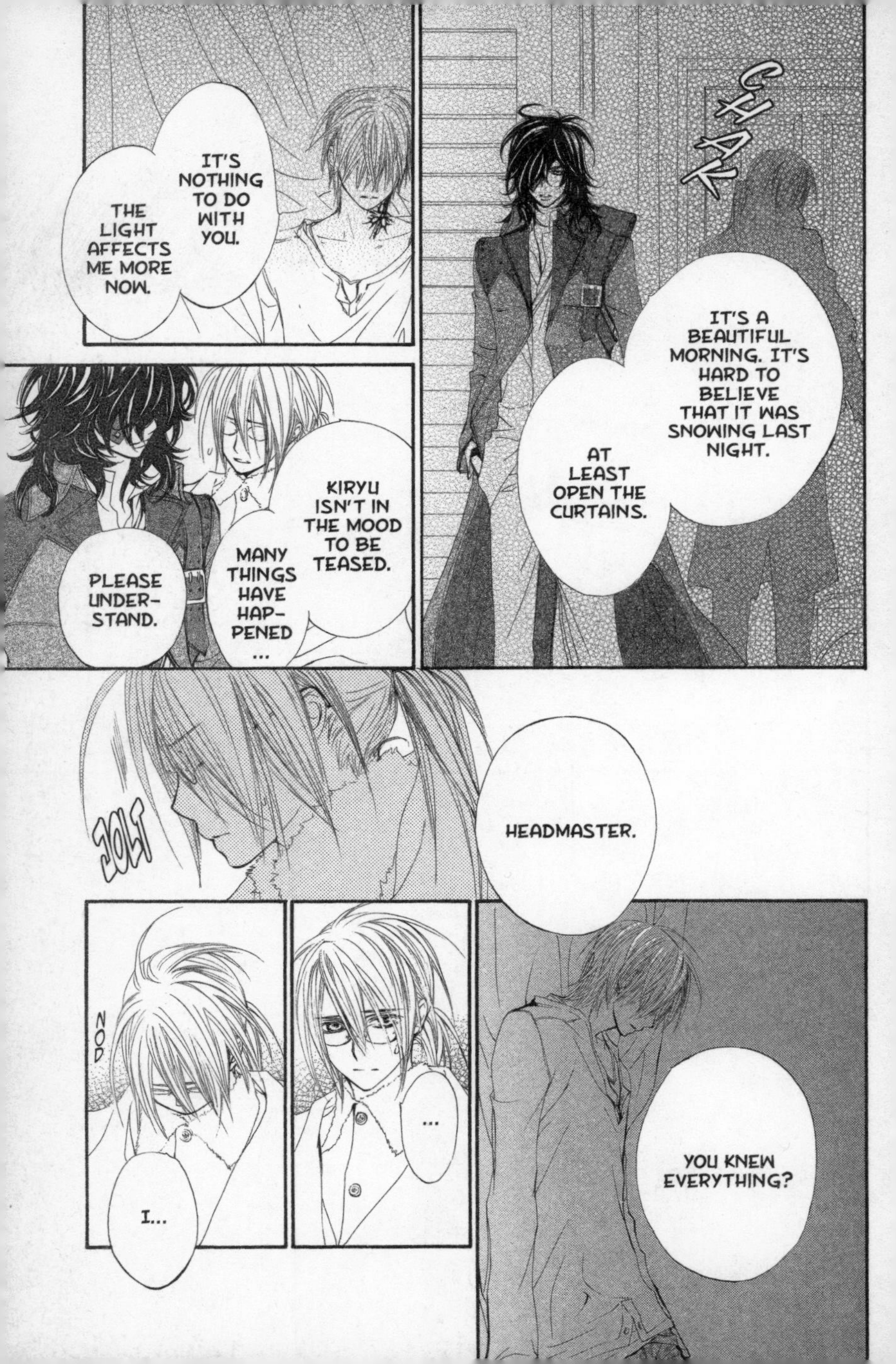
CHAK
IT'S A BEAUTIFUL MORNING. IT'S HARD TO BELIEVE THAT IT WAS SNOWING LAST NIGHT.
AT LEAST OPEN THE CURTAINS.
IT'S NOTHING TO DO WITH YOU.
THE LIGHT AFFECTS ME MORE NOW.
KIRYU ISN'T IN THE MOOD TO BE TEASED.
MANY THINGS HAVE HAP-PENED ...
PLEASE UNDER-STAND.
JOLT
HEADMASTER.
YOU KNEW EVERYTHING?
...
NOD
I...

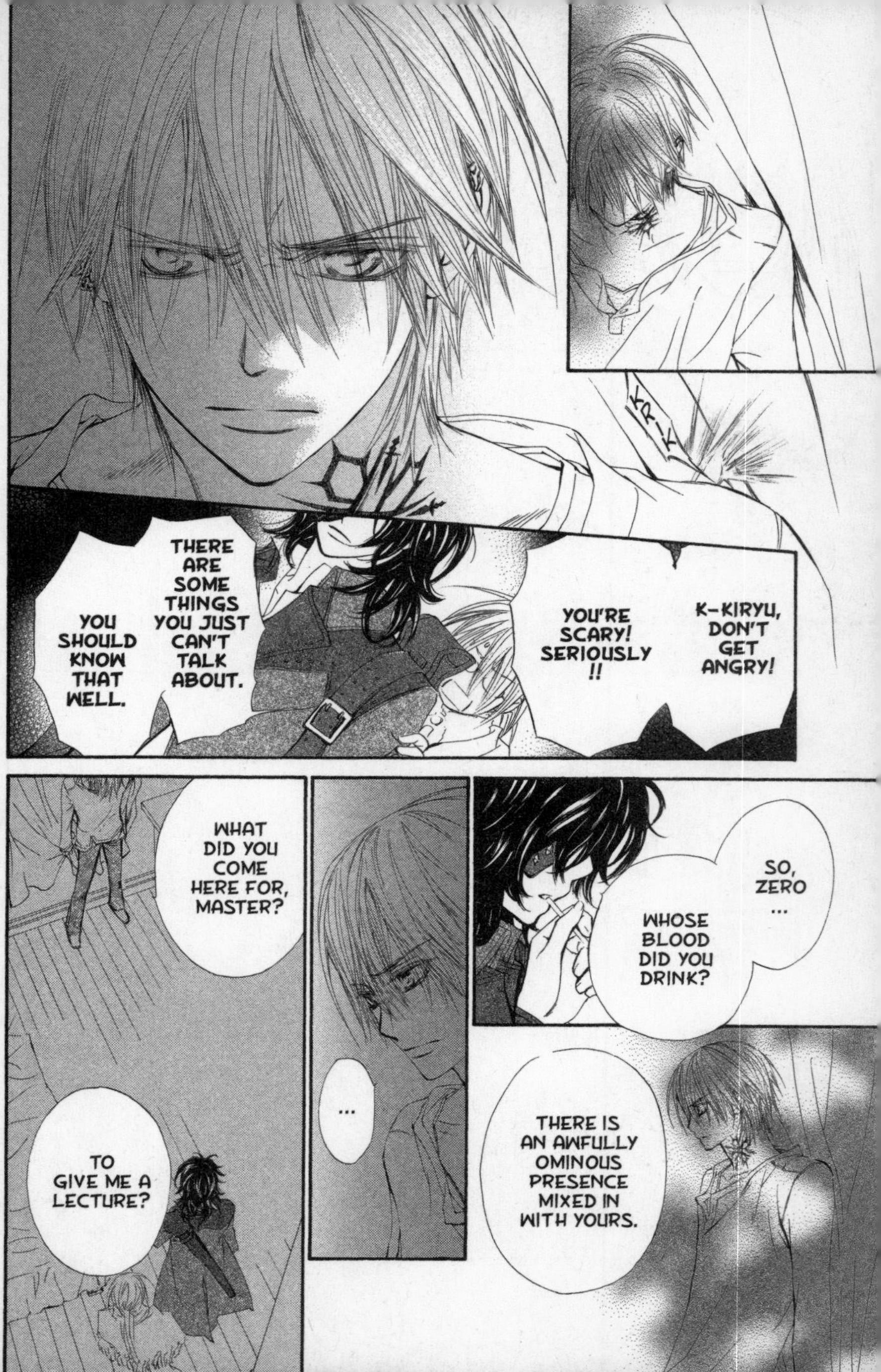
KR-K
K-KIRYU, DON'T GET ANGRY!
YOU'RE SCARY! SERIOUSLY !!
THERE ARE SOME THINGS YOU JUST CAN'T TALK ABOUT.
YOU SHOULD KNOW THAT WELL.
SO, ZERO ...
WHOSE BLOOD DID YOU DRINK?
THERE IS AN AWFULLY OMINOUS PRESENCE MIXED IN WITH YOURS.
...
WHAT DID YOU COME HERE FOR, MASTER?
TO GIVE ME A LECTURE?

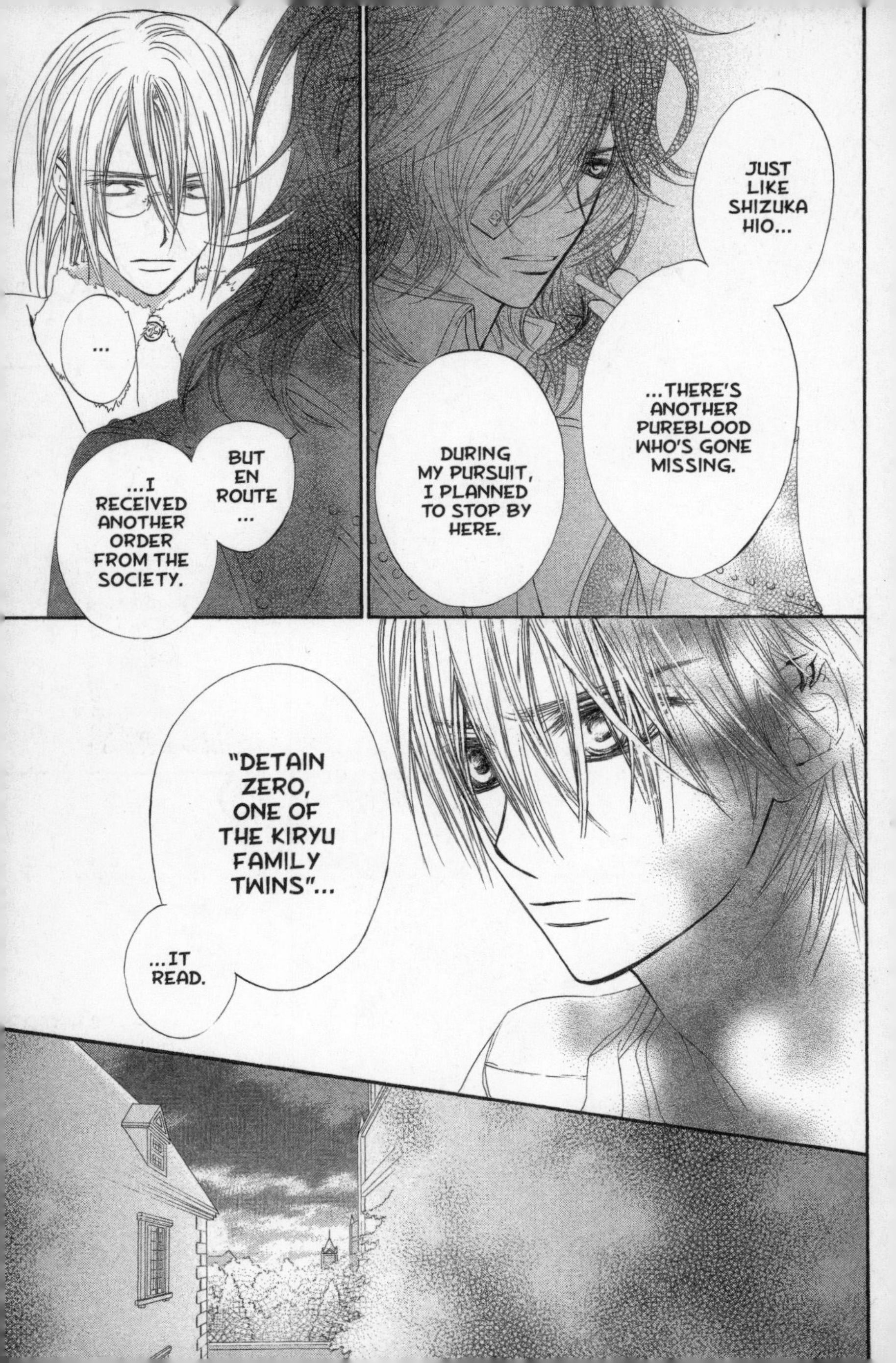
JUST LIKE SHIZUKA HIO...
...THERE'S ANOTHER PUREBLOOD WHO'S GONE MISSING.
DURING MY PURSUIT, I PLANNED TO STOP BY HERE.
...
BUT EN ROUTE...
...I RECEIVED ANOTHER ORDER FROM THE SOCIETY.
"DETAIN ZERO, ONE OF THE KIRYU FAMILY TWINS"...
...IT READ.

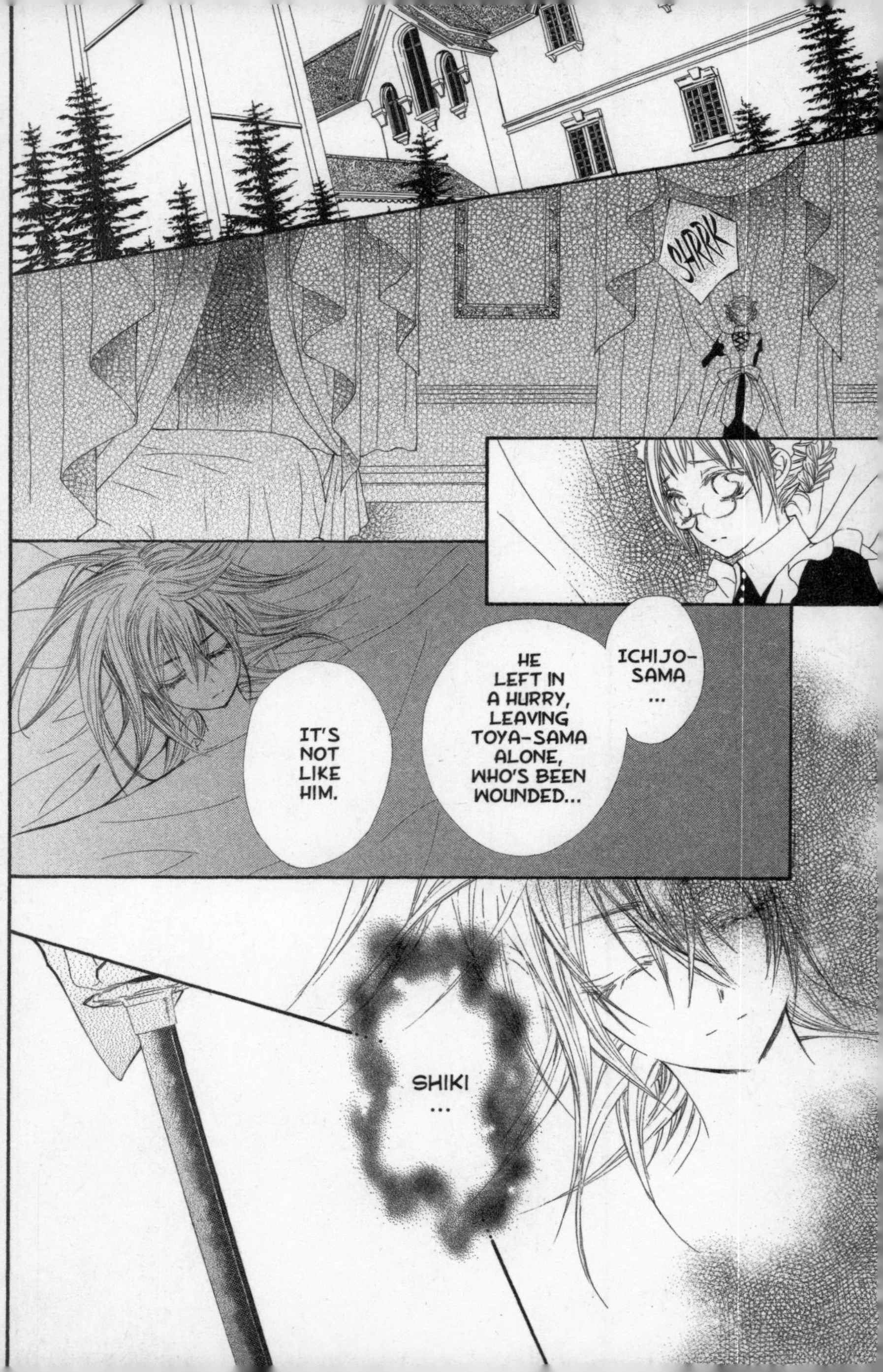
SHRRK
ICHIJO-SAMA...
HE LEFT IN A HURRY, LEAVING TOYA-SAMA ALONE, WHO'S BEEN WOUNDED...
IT'S NOT LIKE HIM.
SHIKI...

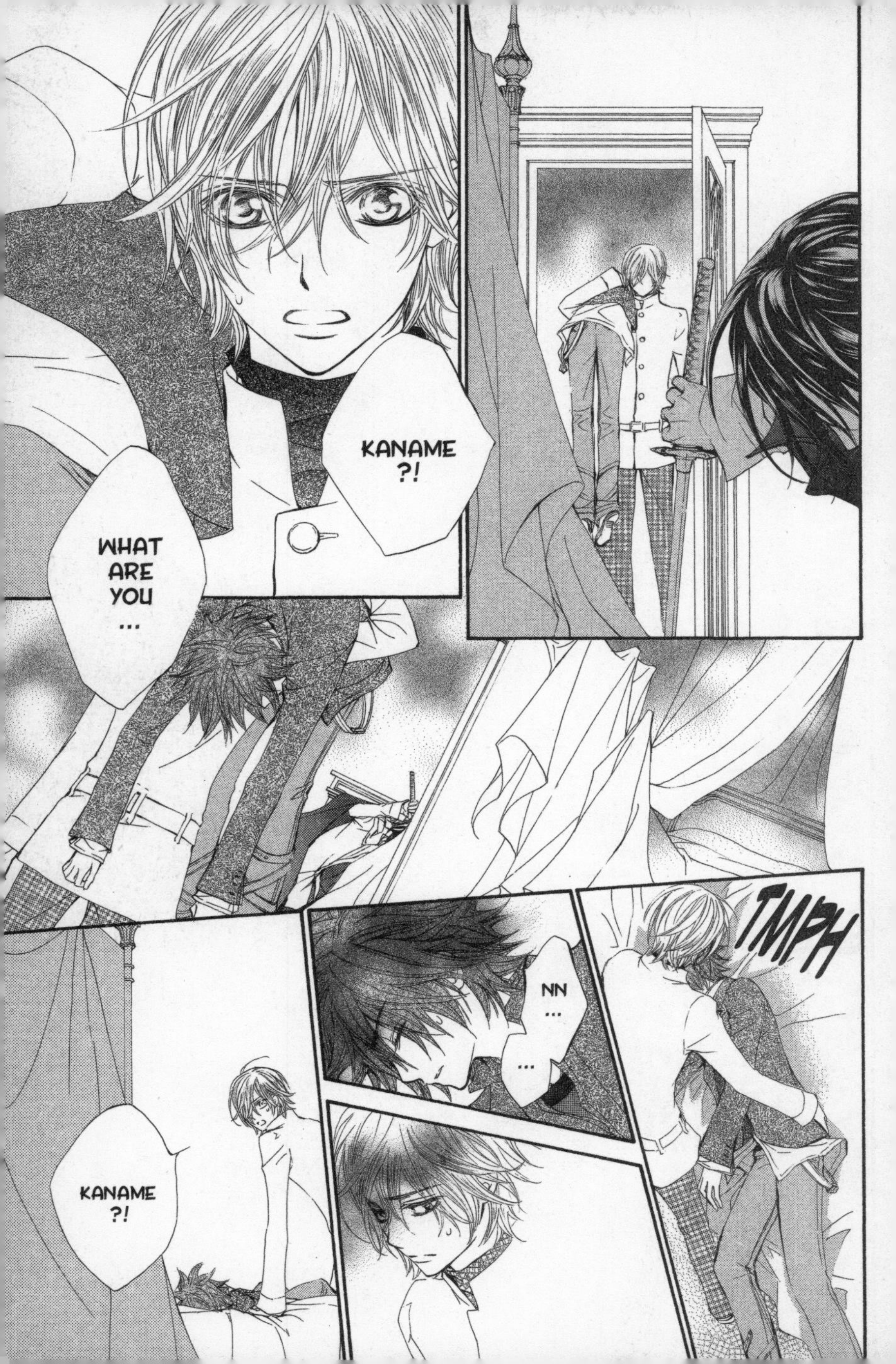
KANAME ?!
WHAT ARE YOU ...
TMPH
NN ...
...
KANAME ?!

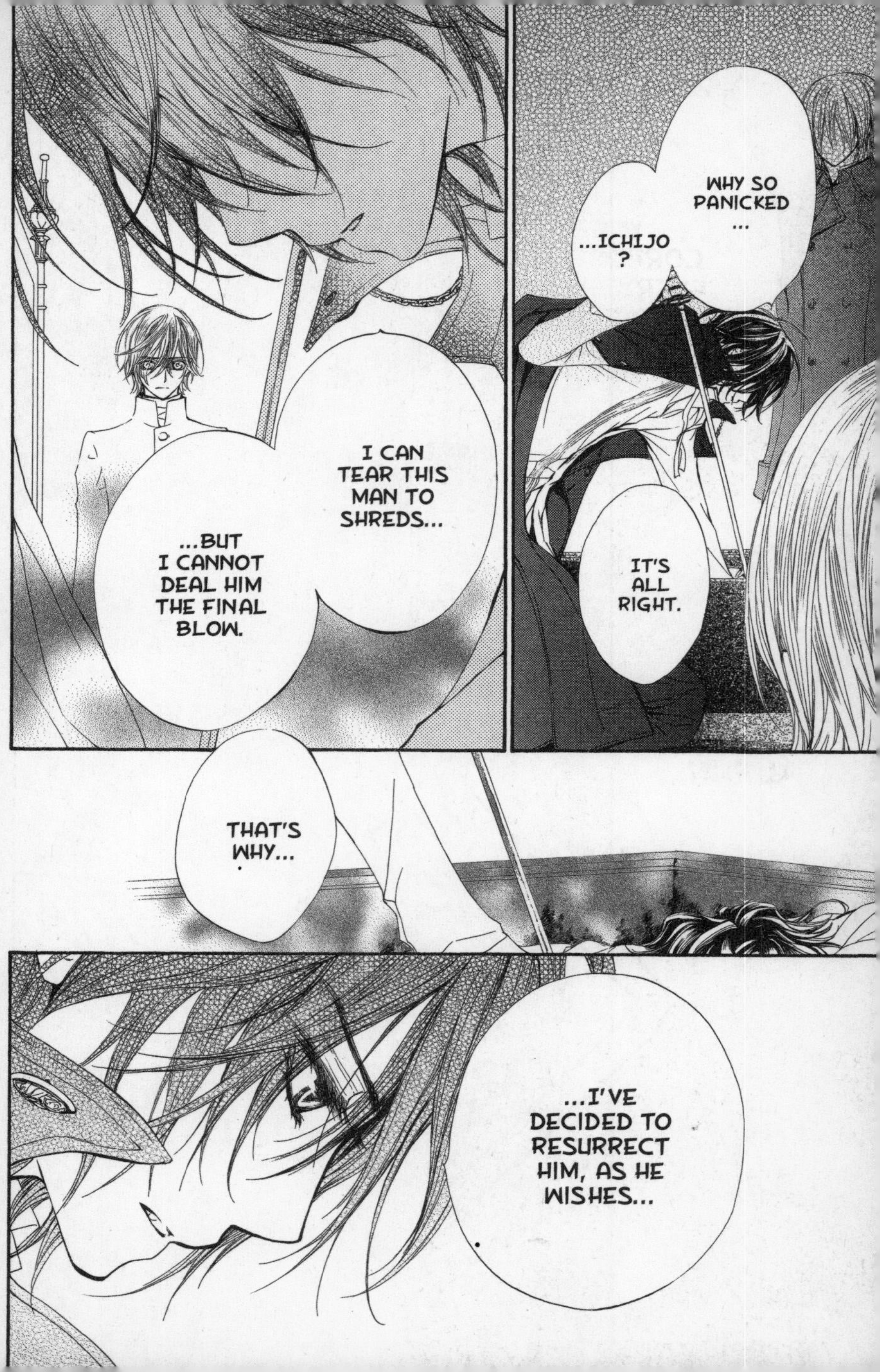
WHY SO PANICKED ...
...ICHIJO ?
IT'S ALL RIGHT.
I CAN TEAR THIS MAN TO SHREDS...
...BUT I CANNOT DEAL HIM THE FINAL BLOW.
THAT'S WHY...
...I'VE DECIDED TO RESURRECT HIM, AS HE WISHES...

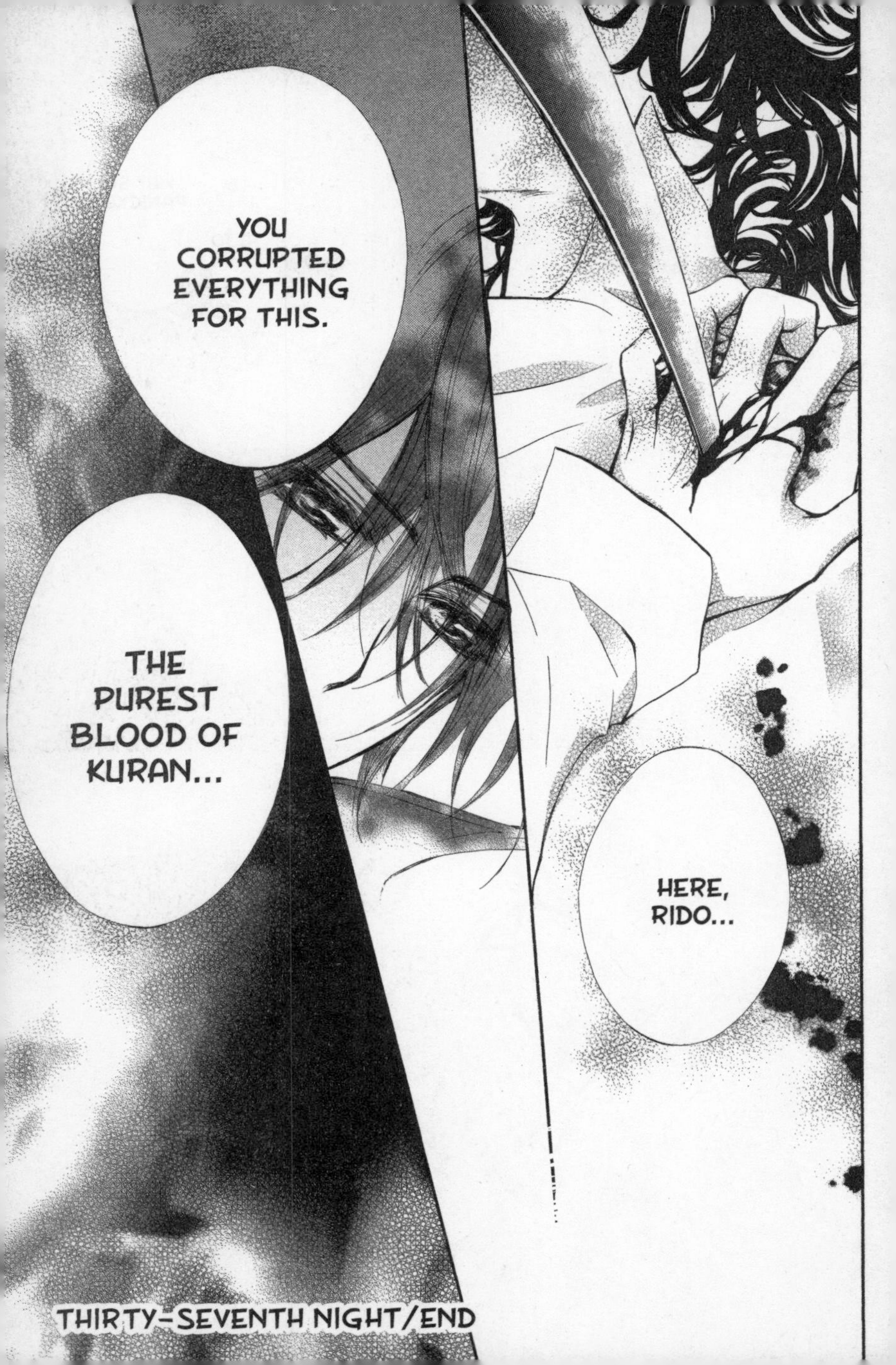
HERE, RIDO...
YOU CORRUPTED EVERYTHING FOR THIS.
THE PUREST BLOOD OF KURAN...
THIRTY-SEVENTH NIGHT/END

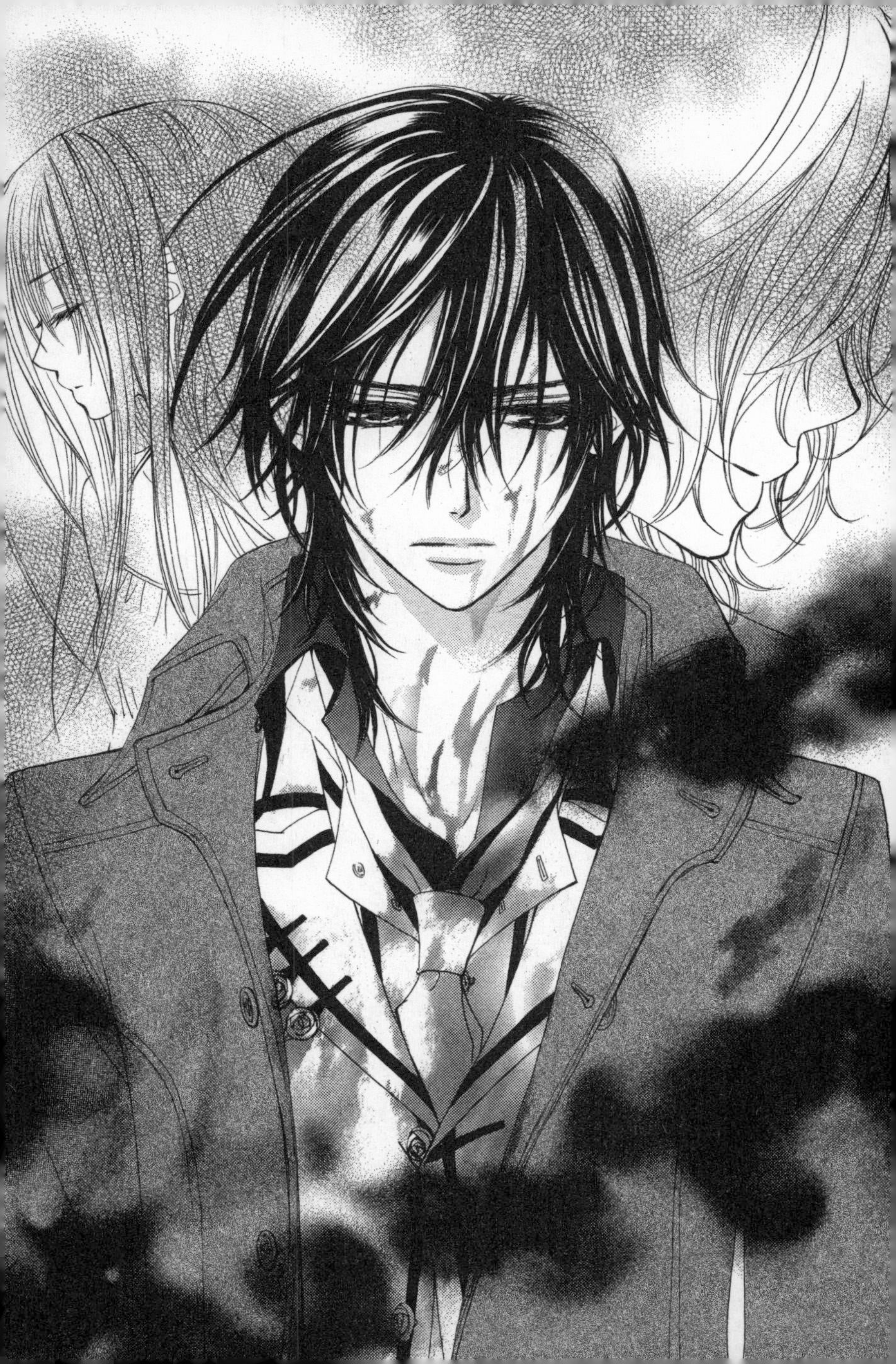

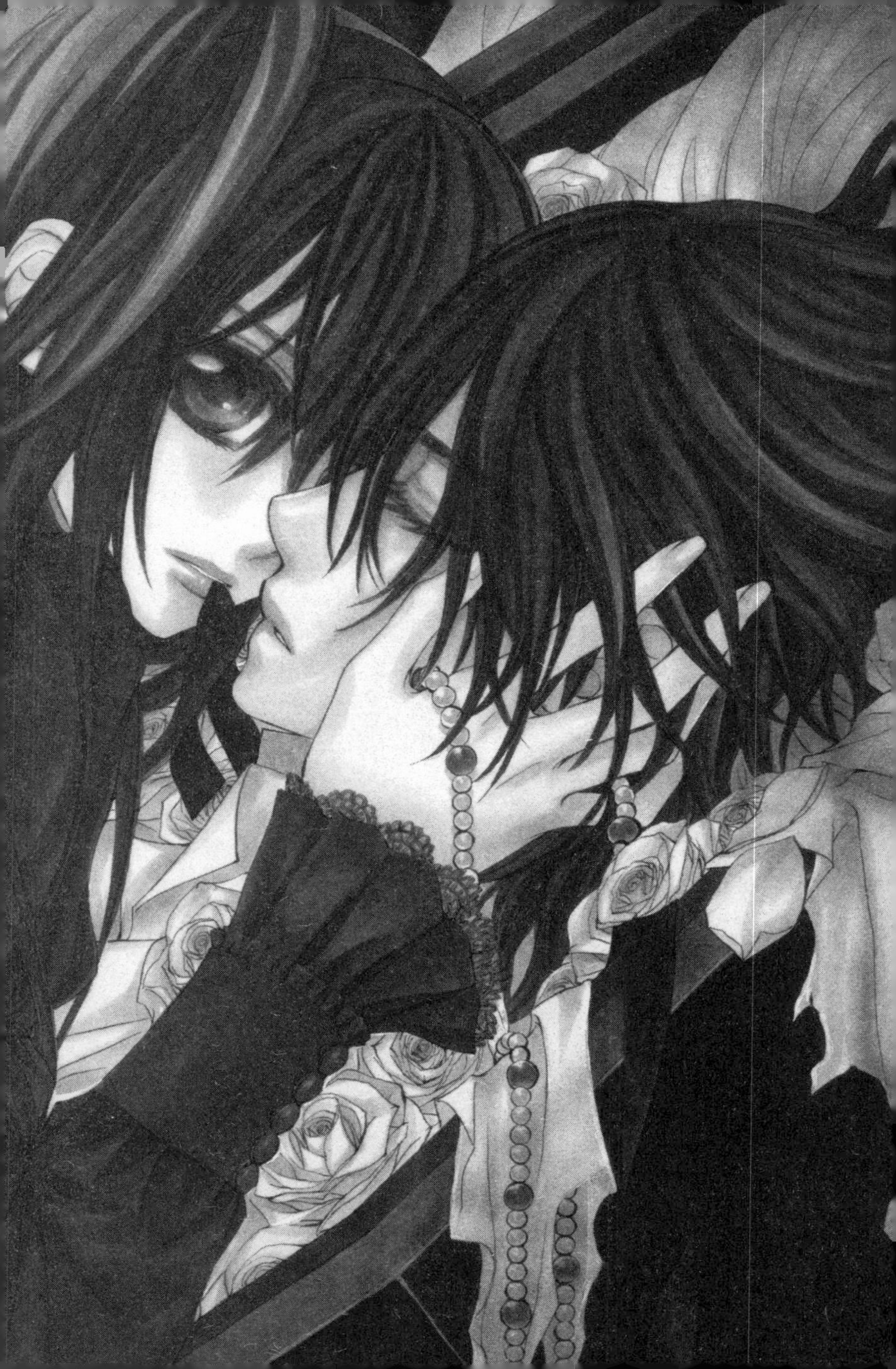

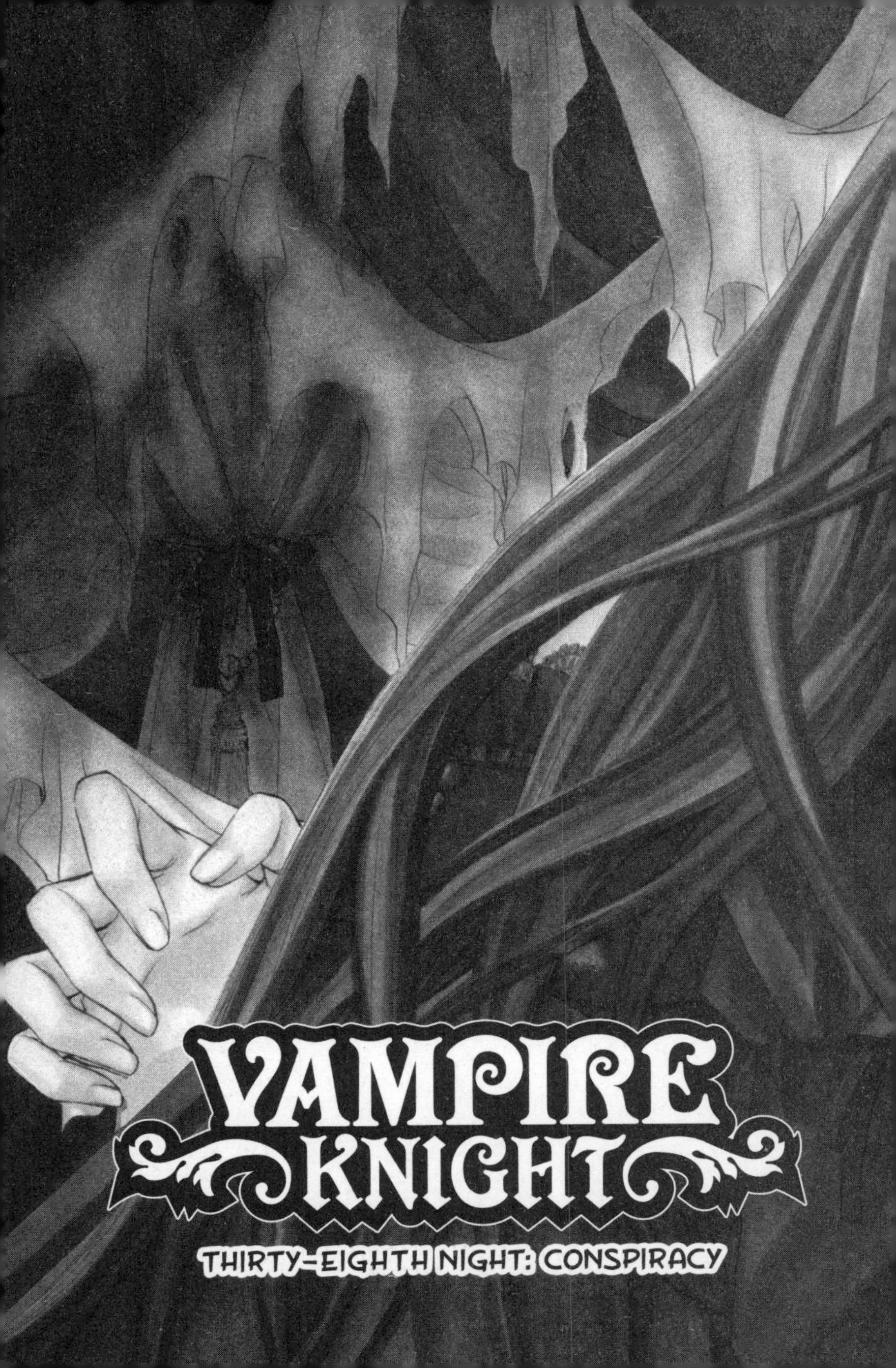
VAMPIRE KNIGHT
THIRTY-EIGHTH NIGHT: CONSPIRACY

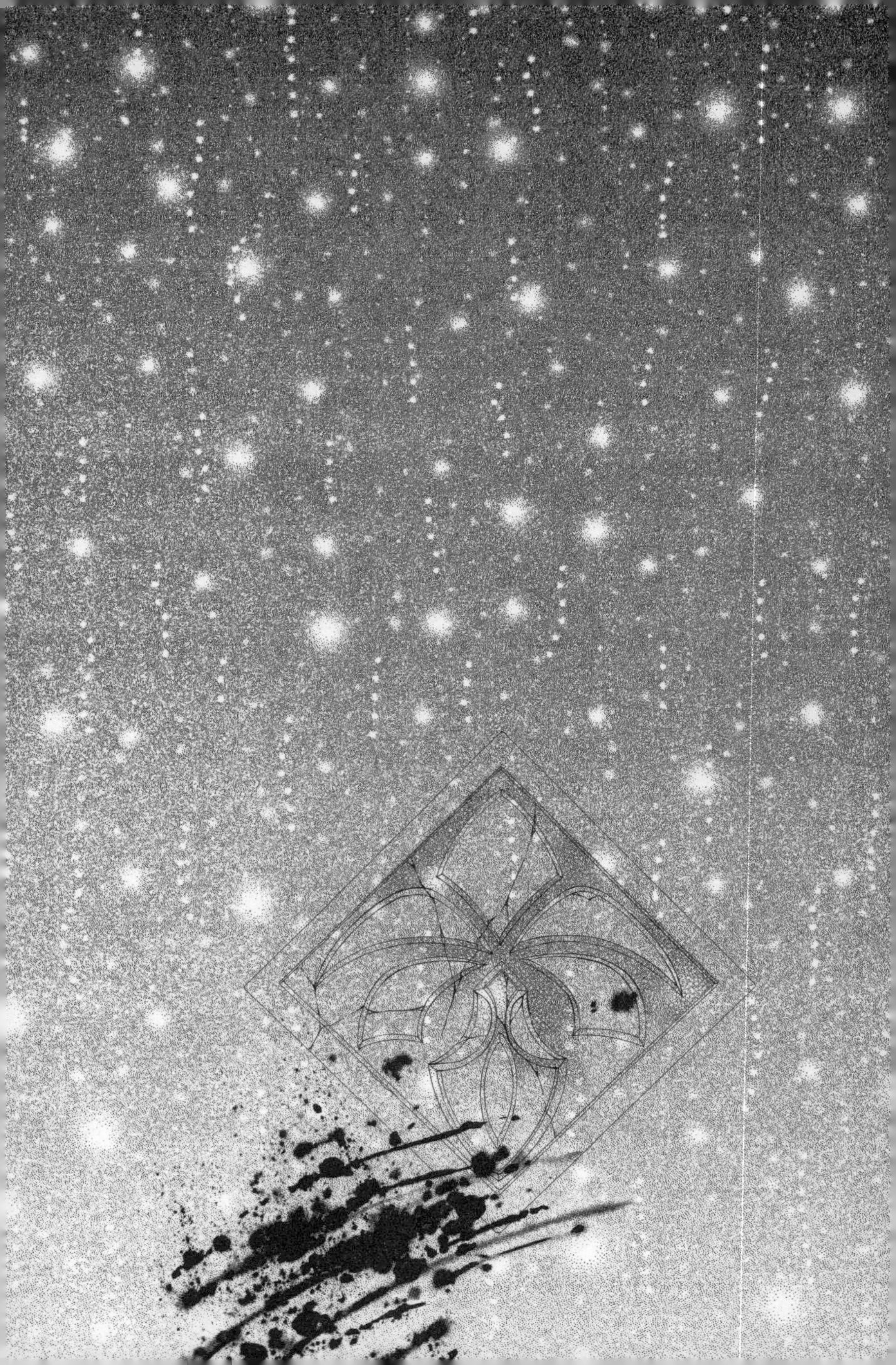

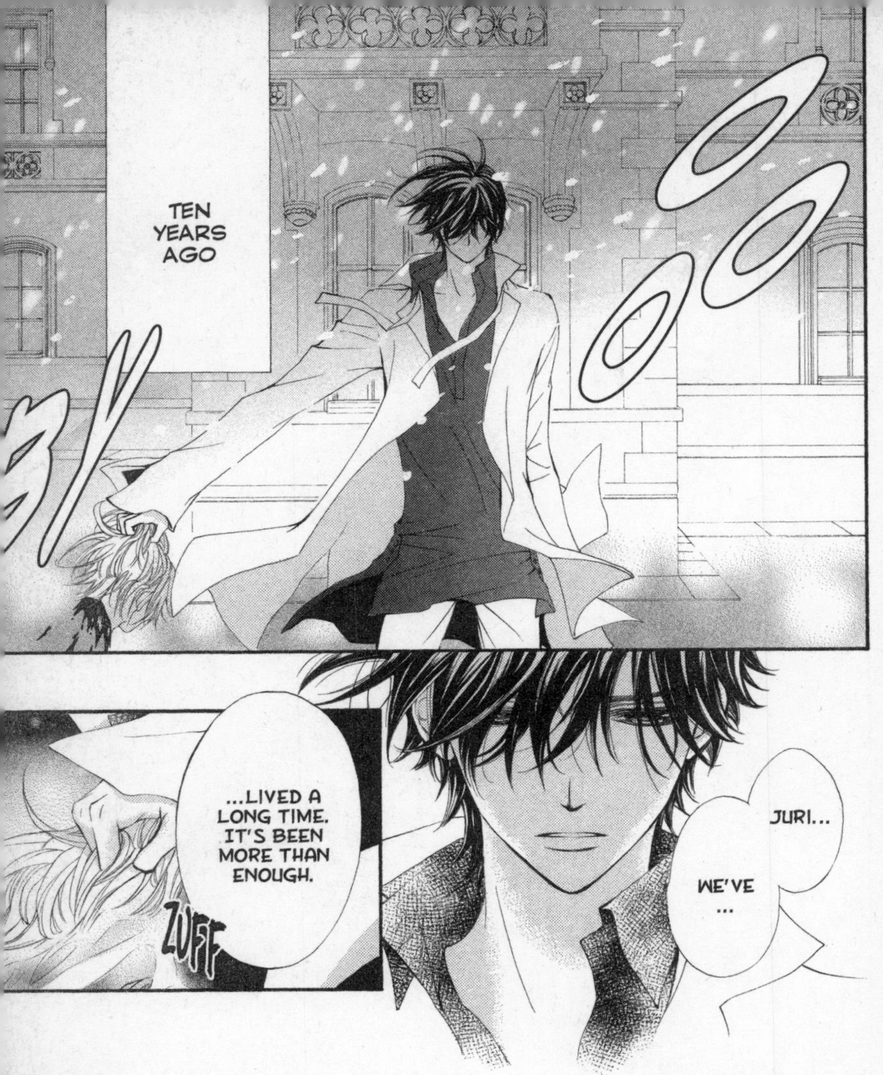
TEN YEARS AGO
JURI...
WE'VE ...
...LIVED A LONG TIME. IT'S BEEN MORE THAN ENOUGH.
ZUFF

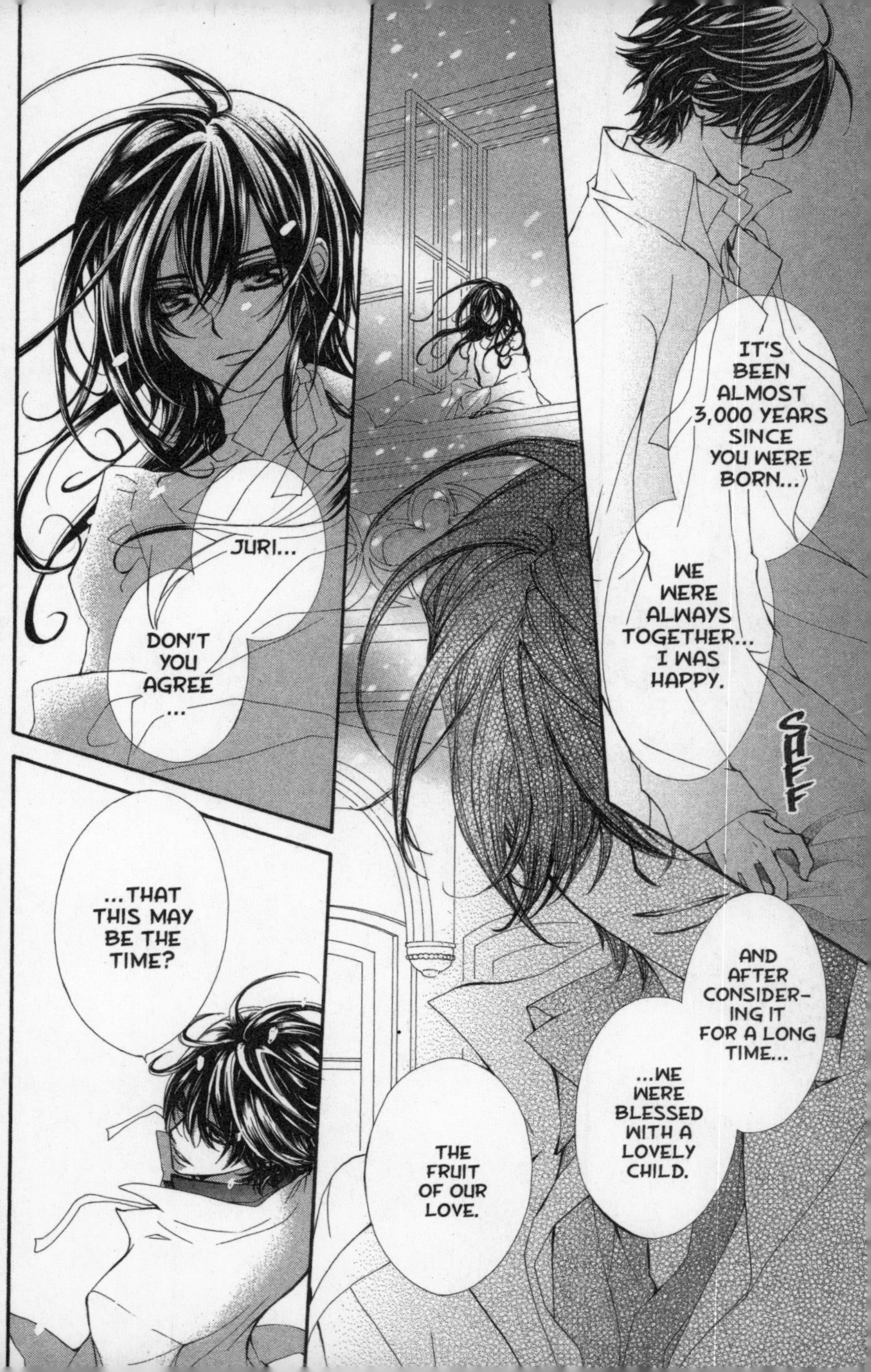
IT'S BEEN ALMOST 3,000 YEARS SINCE YOU WERE BORN...
WE WERE ALWAYS TOGETHER... I WAS HAPPY.
SHFF
AND AFTER CONSIDERING-ING IT FOR A LONG TIME...
...WE WERE BLESSED WITH A LOVELY CHILD.
THE FRUIT OF OUR LOVE.
JURI...
DON'T YOU AGREE ...
...THAT THIS MAY BE THE TIME?

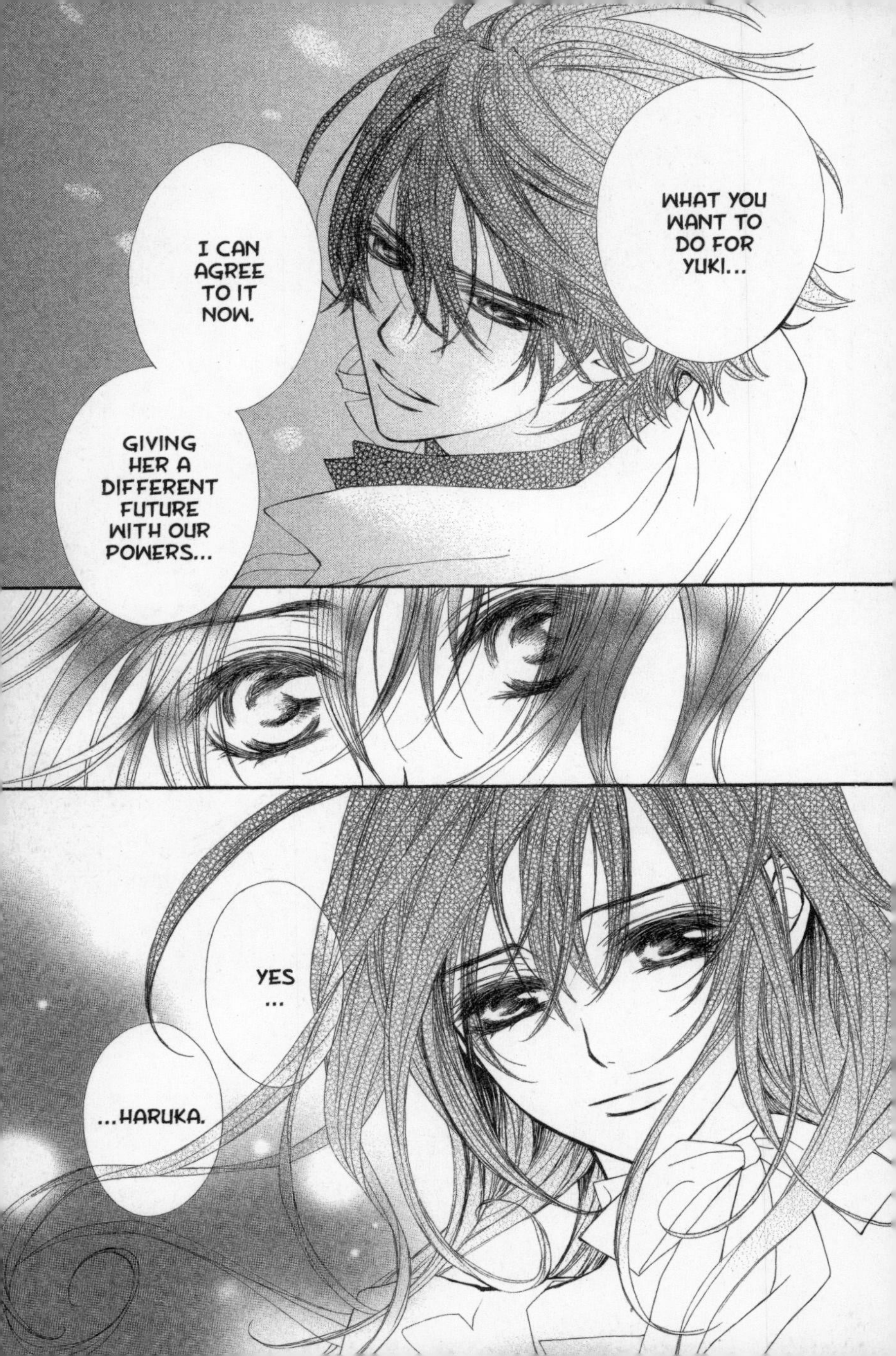
WHAT YOU WANT TO DO FOR YUKI...
I CAN AGREE TO IT NOW.
GIVING HER A DIFFERENT FUTURE WITH OUR POWERS...
YES ...
...HARUKA.

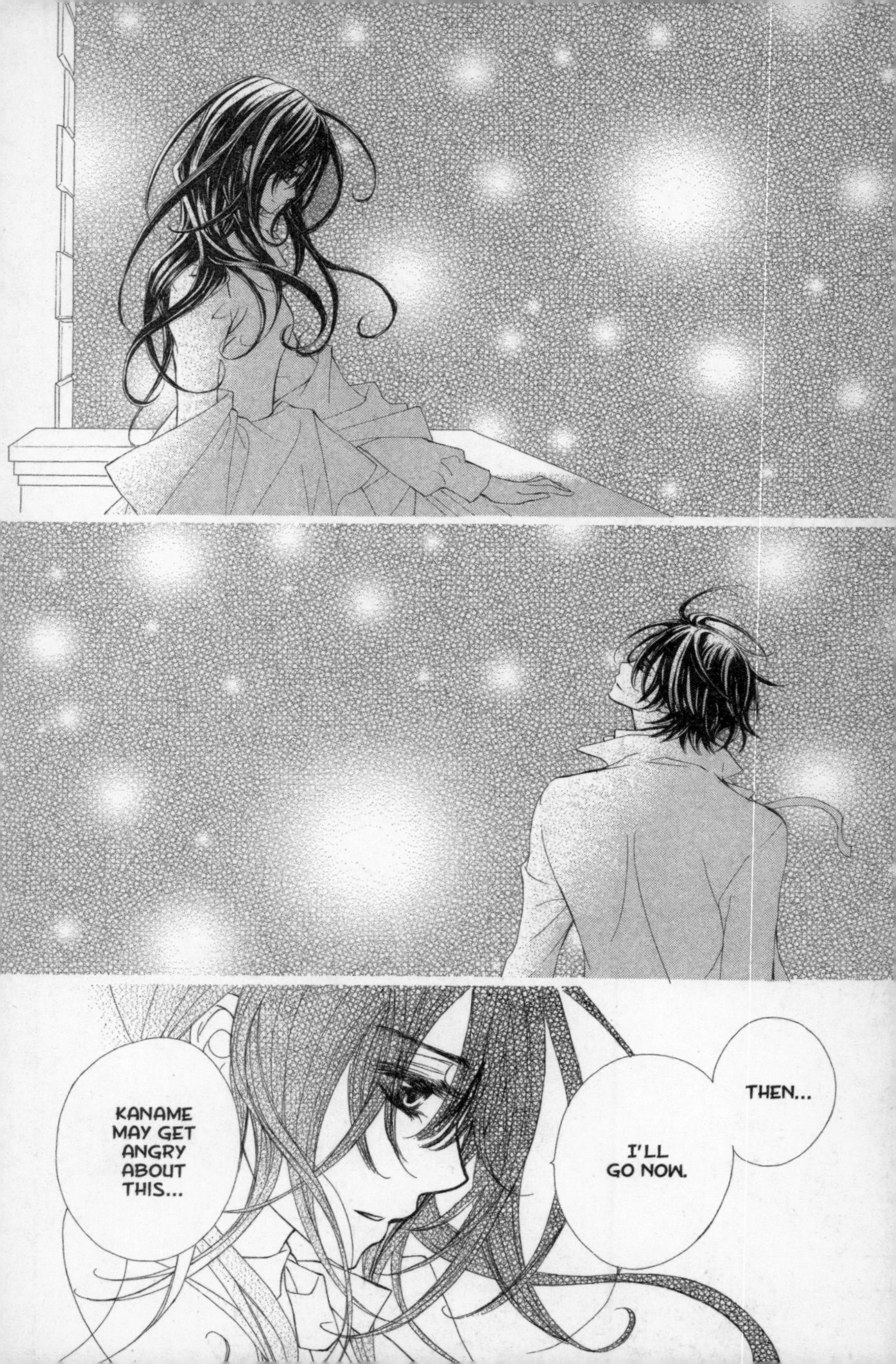
THEN...
I'LL GO NOW.
KANAME MAY GET ANGRY ABOUT THIS...

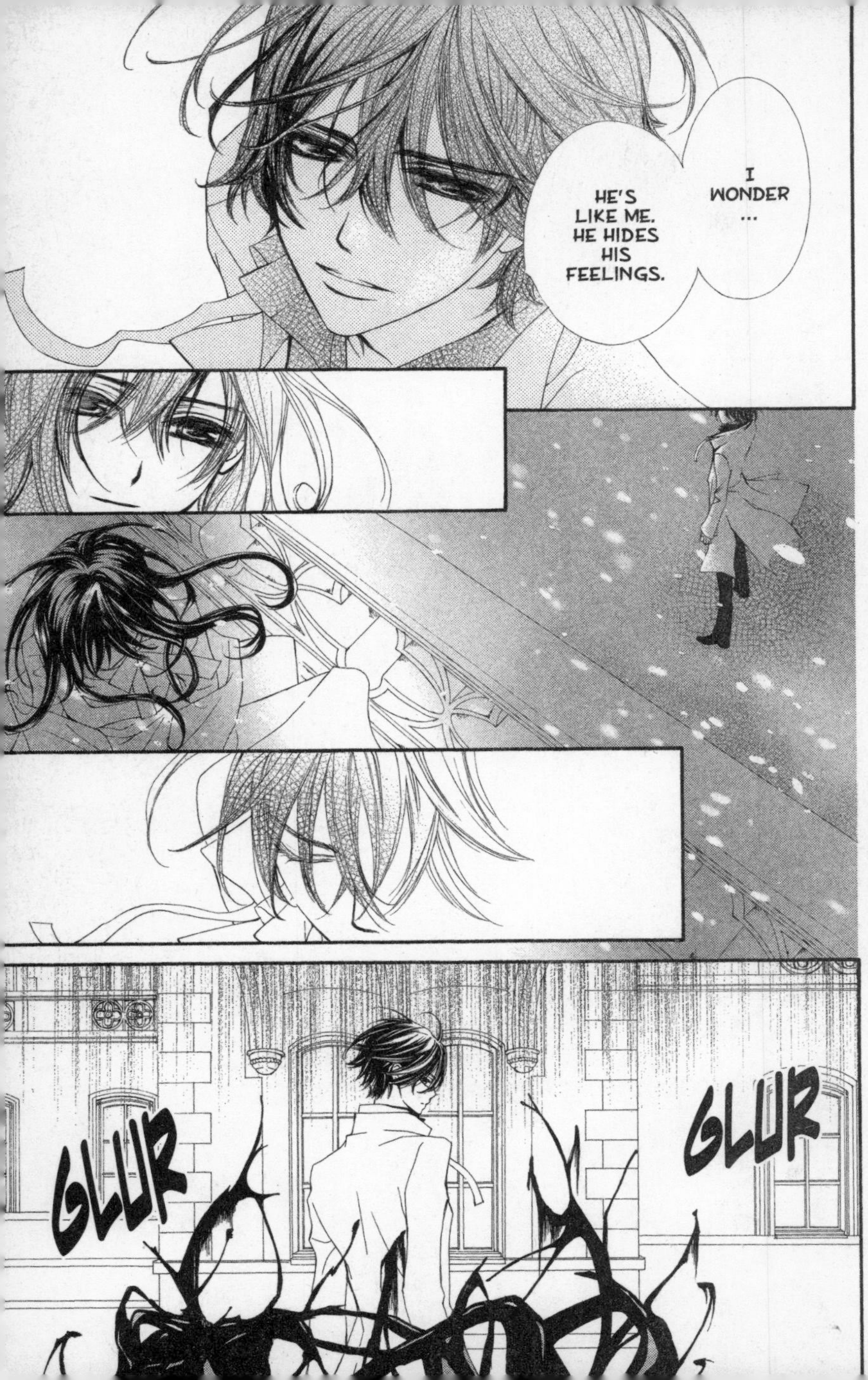
I WONDER ...
HE'S LIKE ME. HE HIDES HIS FEELINGS.
GLUR
GLUR

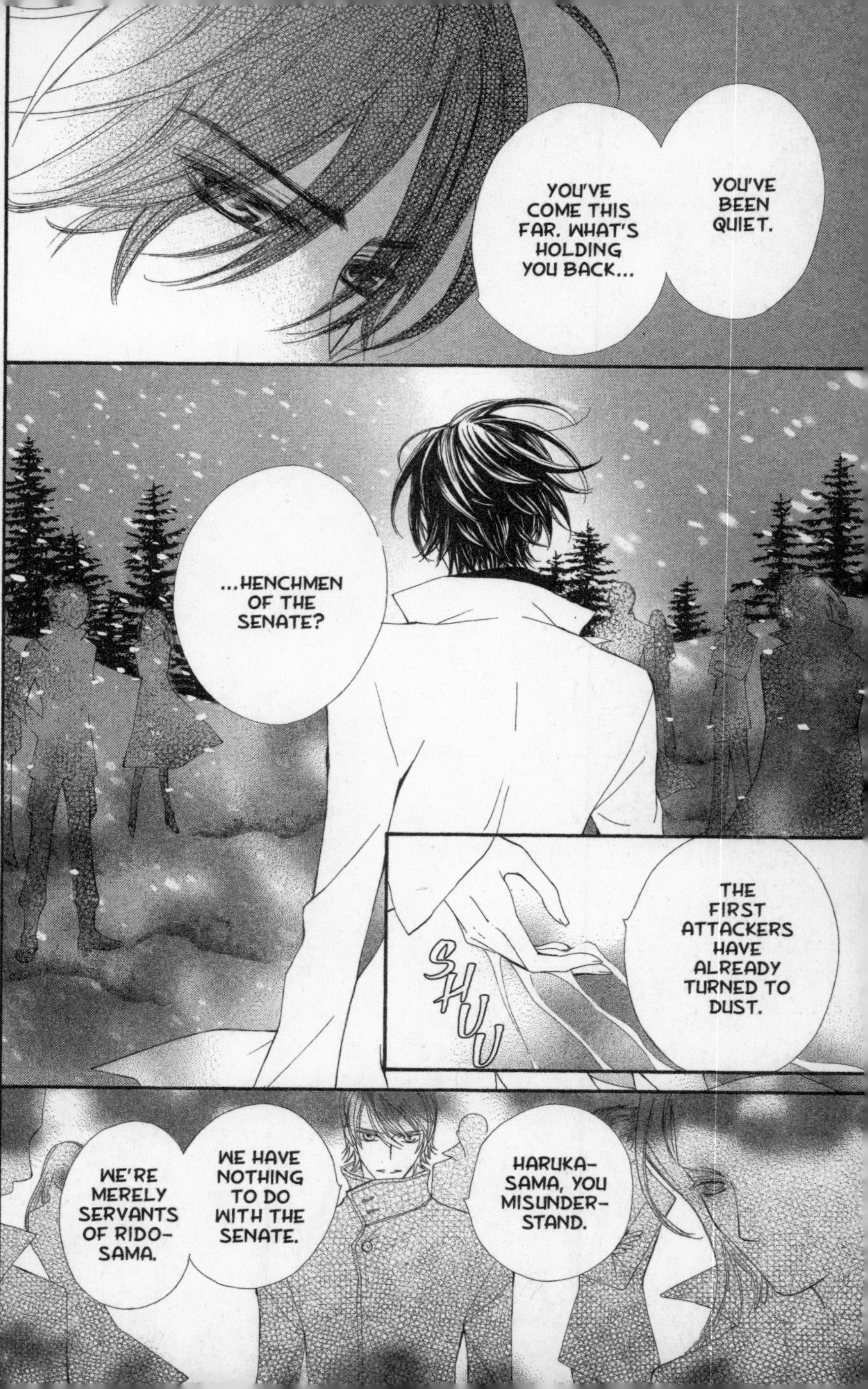
YOU'VE BEEN QUIET.
YOU'VE COME THIS FAR. WHAT'S HOLDING YOU BACK...
...HENCHMEN OF THE SENATE?
THE FIRST ATTACKERS HAVE ALREADY TURNED TO DUST.
SHUU
HARUKA-SAMA, YOU MISUNDER-STAND.
WE HAVE NOTHING TO DO WITH THE SENATE.
WE'RE MERELY SERVANTS OF RIDO-SAMA.

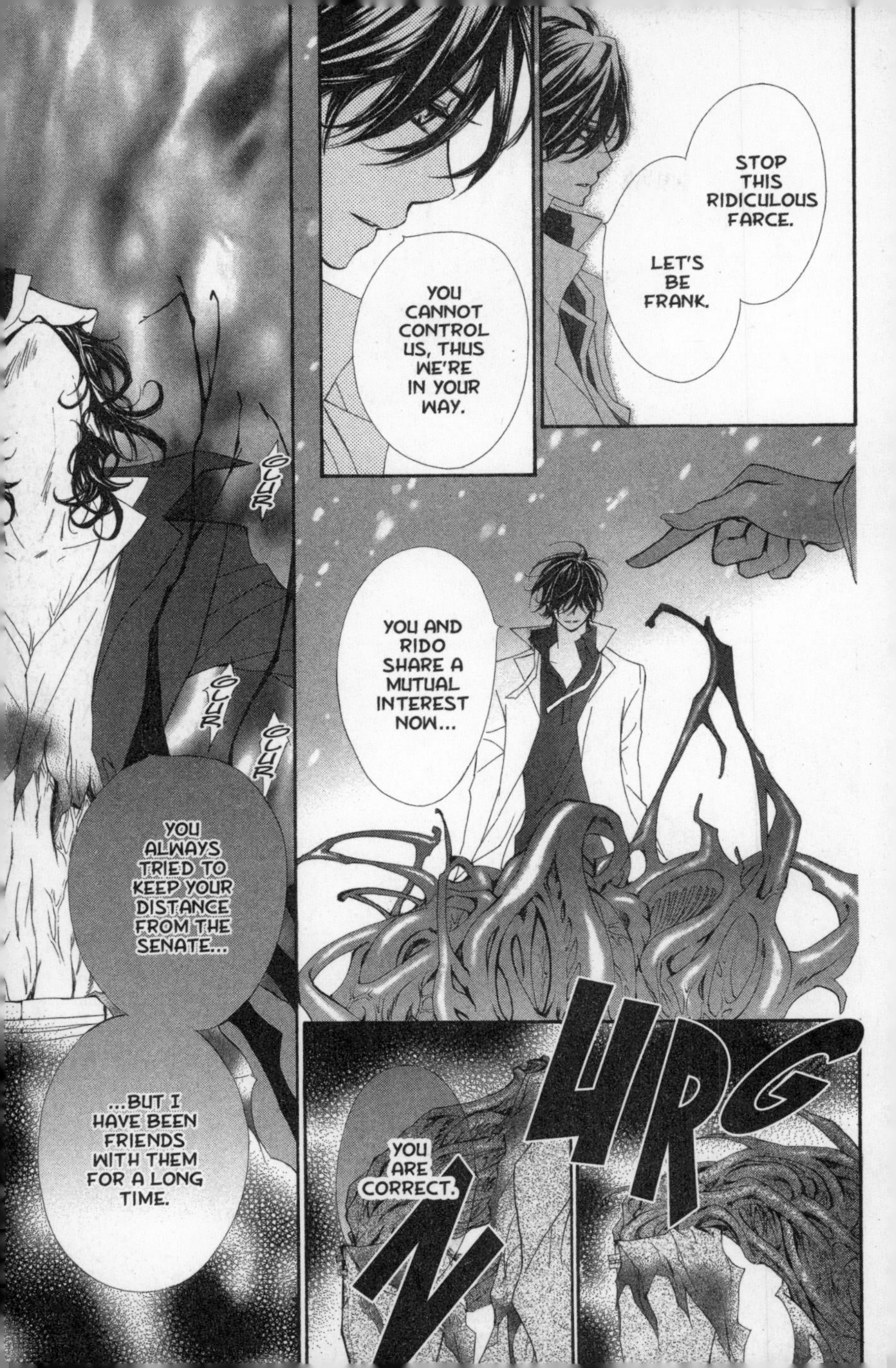
STOP THIS RIDICULOUS FARCE.
LET'S BE FRANK.
YOU CANNOT CONTROL US, THUS WE'RE IN YOUR WAY.
YOU AND RIDO SHARE A MUTUAL INTEREST NOW...
NURG
YOU ARE CORRECT.
GLUR
GLUR
GLUR
YOU ALWAYS TRIED TO KEEP YOUR DISTANCE FROM THE SENATE...
...BUT I HAVE BEEN FRIENDS WITH THEM FOR A LONG TIME.

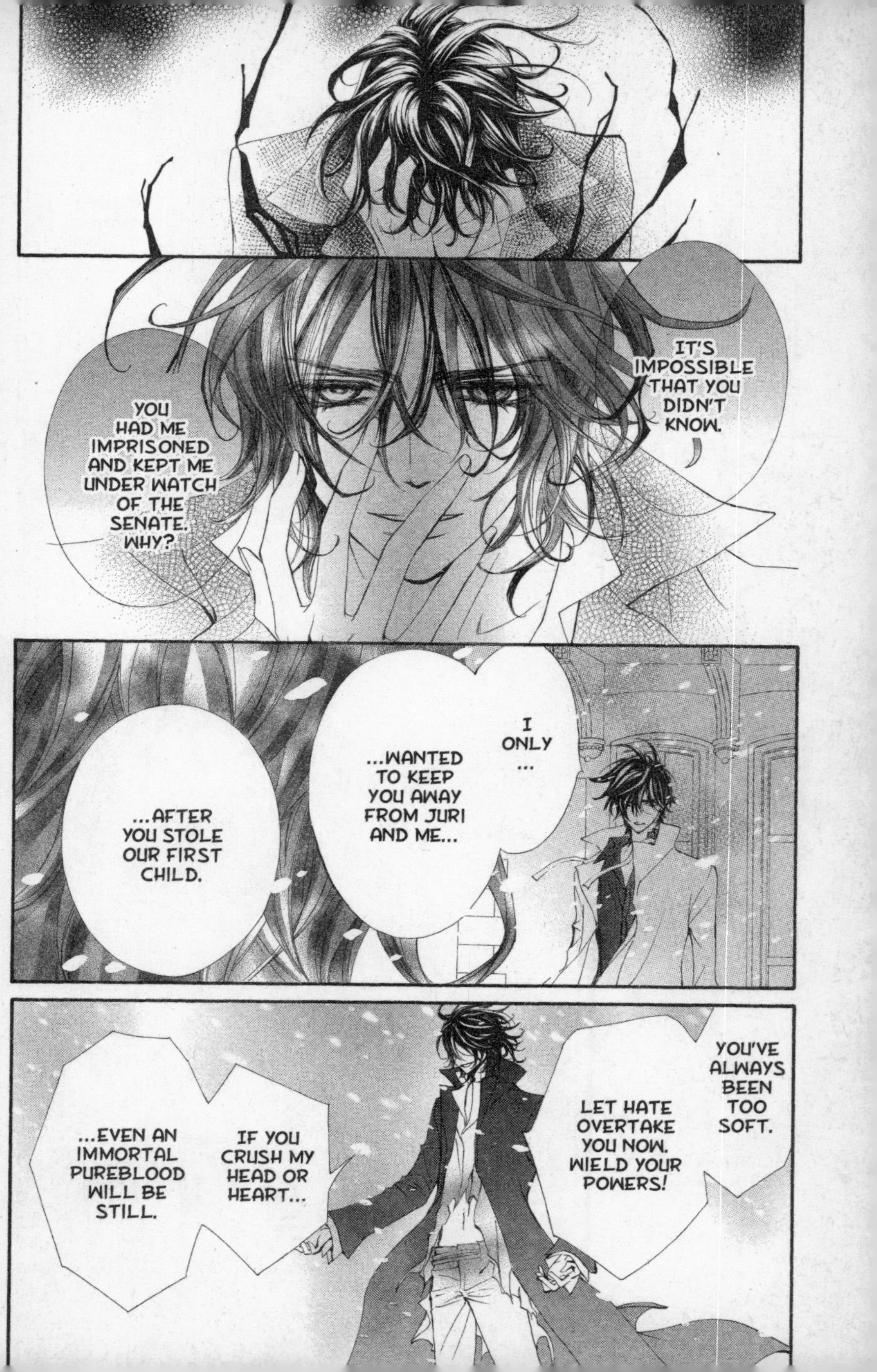

IT'S IMPOSSIBLE THAT YOU DIDN'T KNOW.
YOU HAD ME IMPRISONED AND KEPT ME UNDER WATCH OF THE SENATE. WHY?
I ONLY...
...WANTED TO KEEP YOU AWAY FROM JURI AND ME...
...AFTER YOU STOLE OUR FIRST CHILD.
YOU'VE ALWAYS BEEN TOO SOFT.
LET HATE OVERTAKE YOU NOW. WIELD YOUR POWERS!
IF YOU CRUSH MY HEAD OR HEART...
...EVEN AN IMMORTAL PUREBLOOD WILL BE STILL.

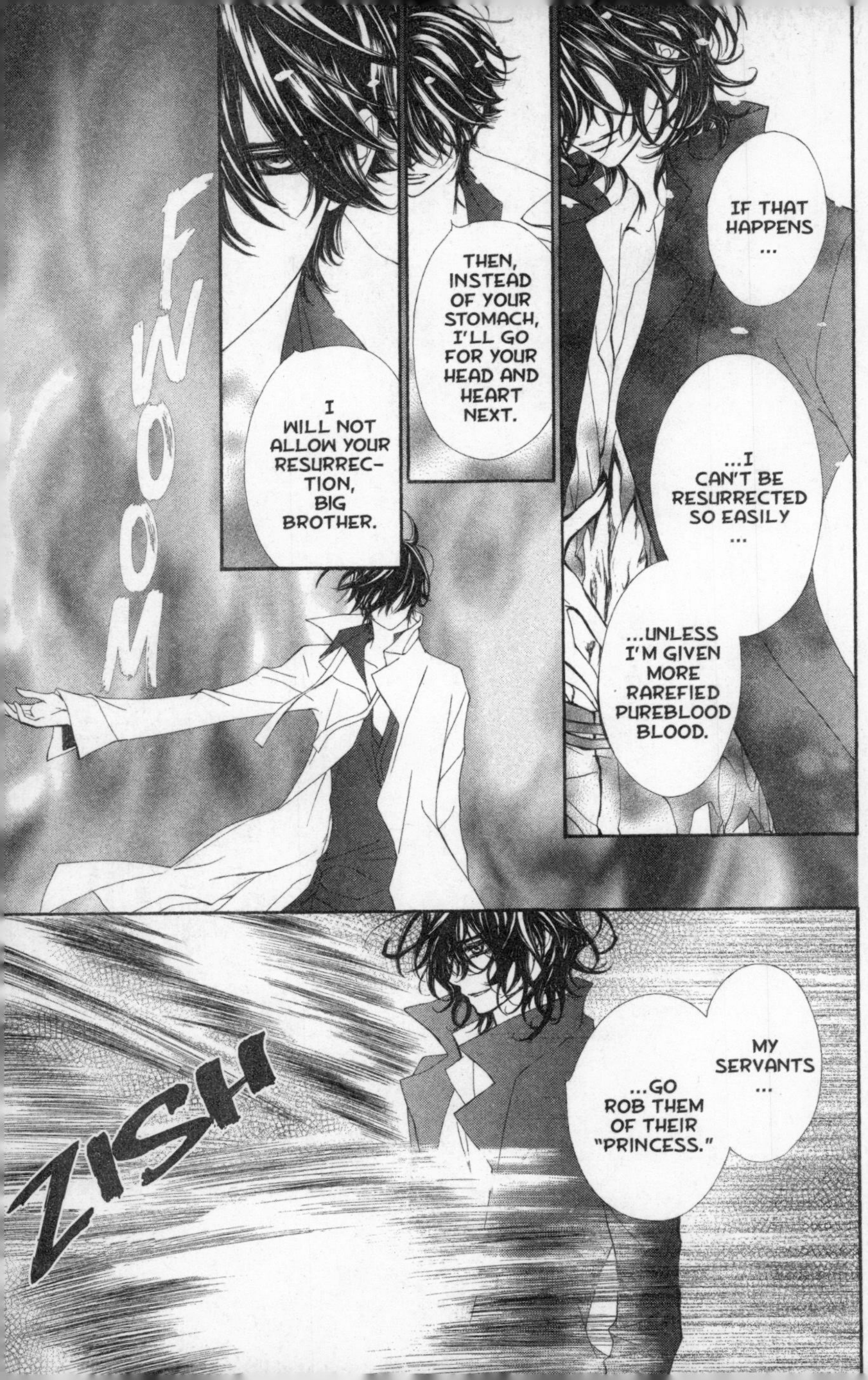
IF THAT HAPPENS ...
...I CAN'T BE RESURRECTED SO EASILY ...
...UNLESS I'M GIVEN MORE RAREFIED PUREBLOOD BLOOD.
THEN, INSTEAD OF YOUR STOMACH, I'LL GO FOR YOUR HEAD AND HEART NEXT.
I WILL NOT ALLOW YOUR RESURREC-TION, BIG BROTHER.
FWOOM
MY SERVANTS ...
...GO ROB THEM OF THEIR "PRINCESS."
ZISH

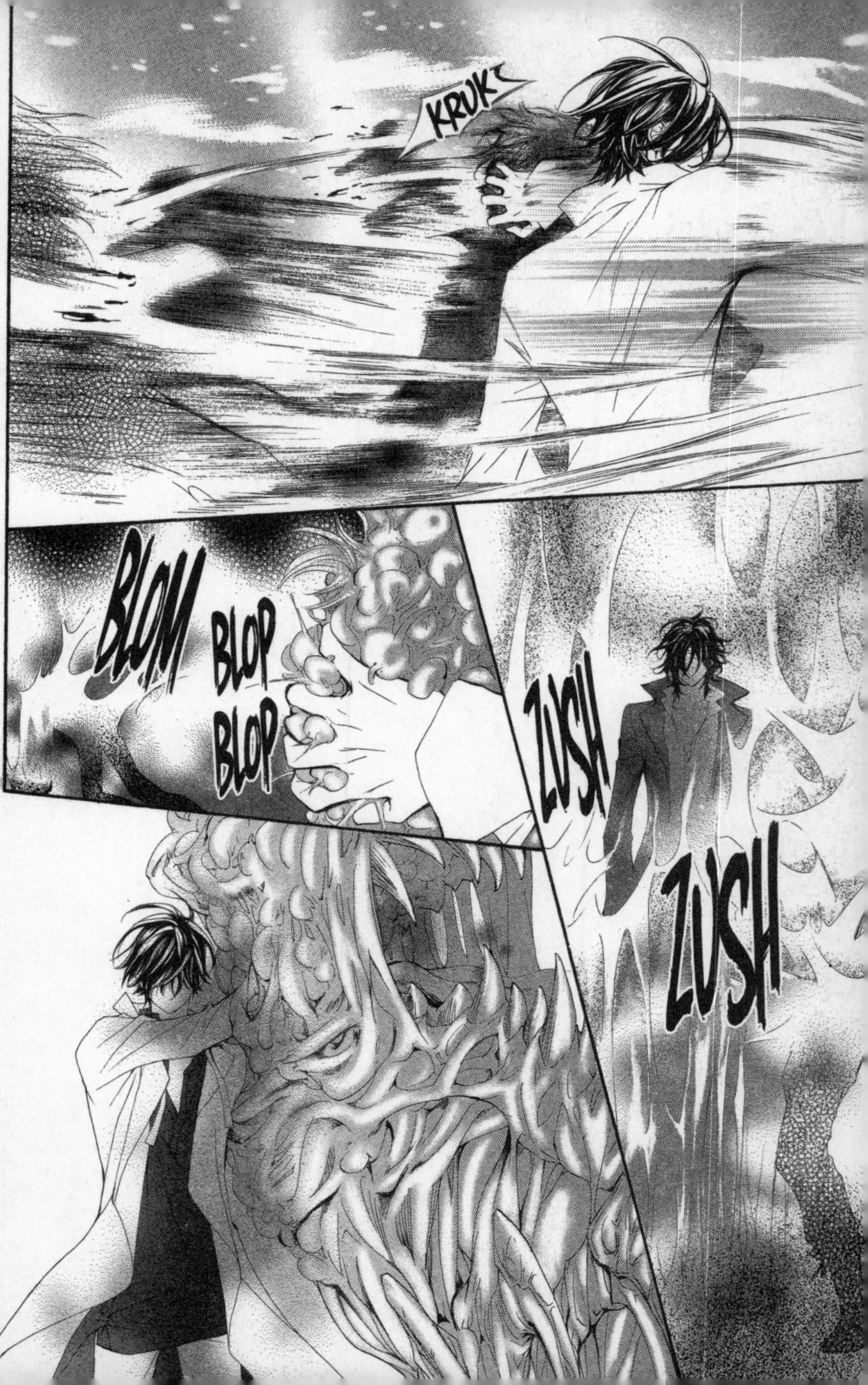
KRUK
ZUSH
ZUSH
BLOM
BLOP
BLOP

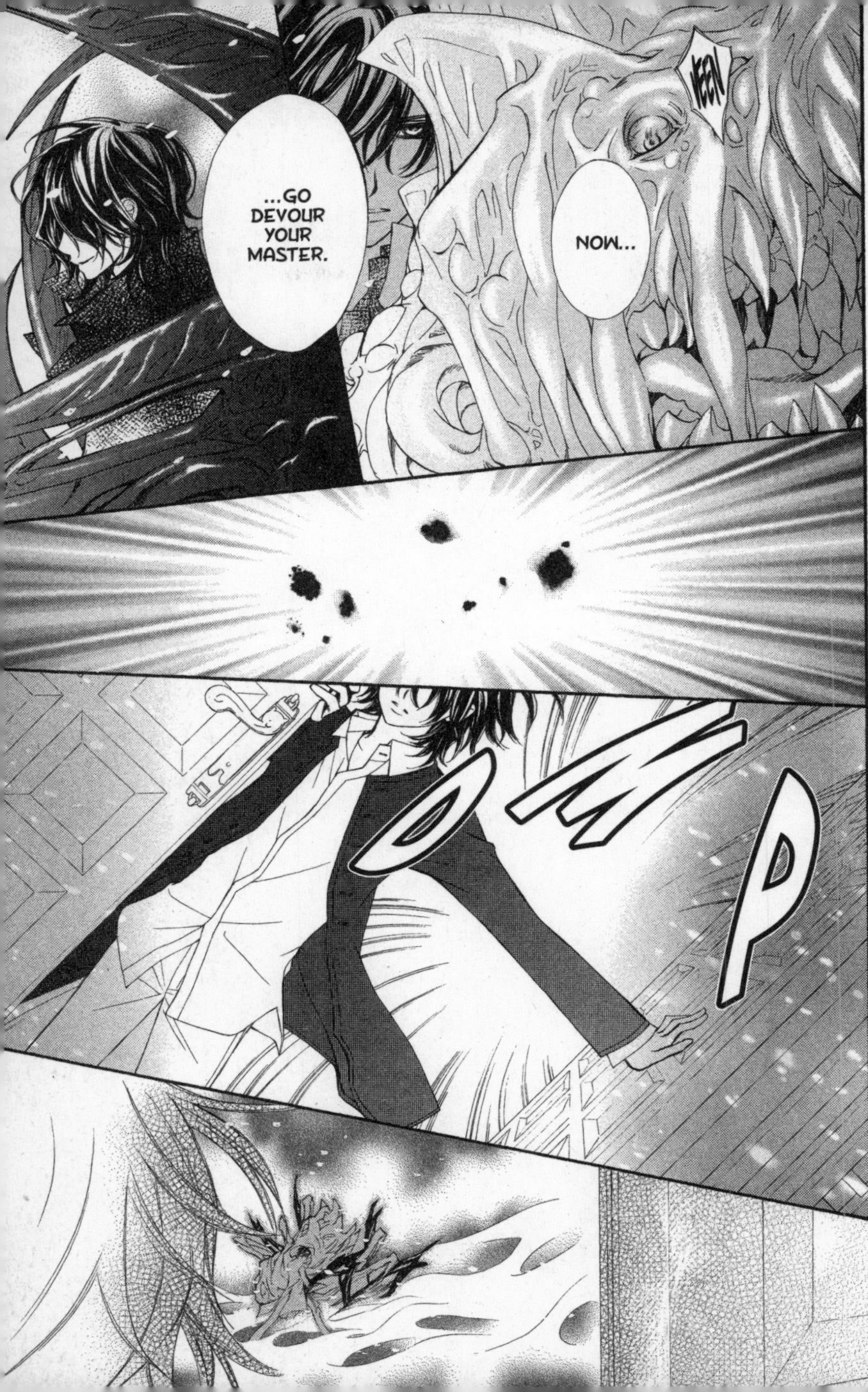
VEEN
NOW...
...GO DEVOUR YOUR MASTER.
DOMP

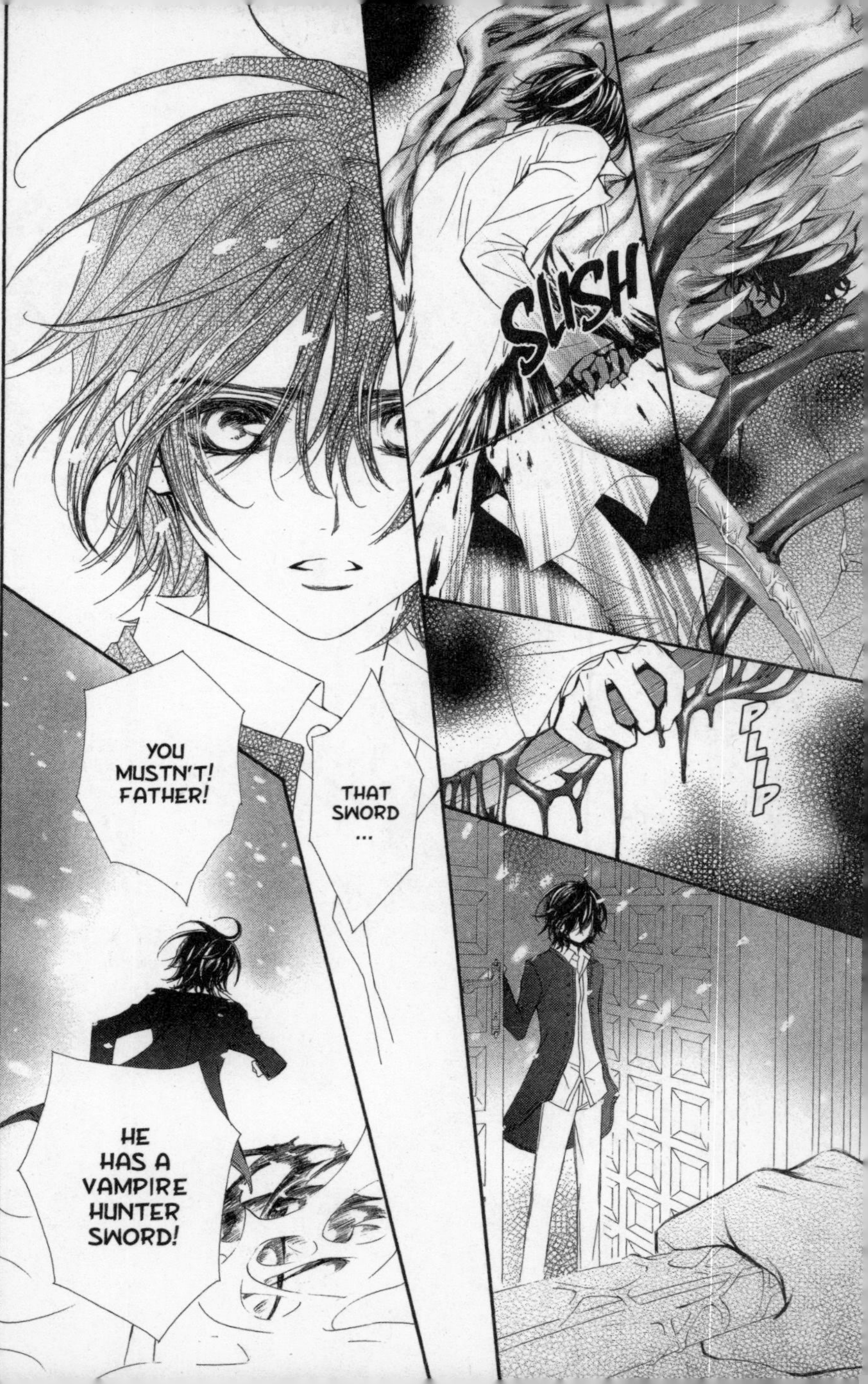
SLISH
PLIP
THAT SWORD ...
YOU MUSTN'T! FATHER!
HE HAS A VAMPIRE HUNTER SWORD!

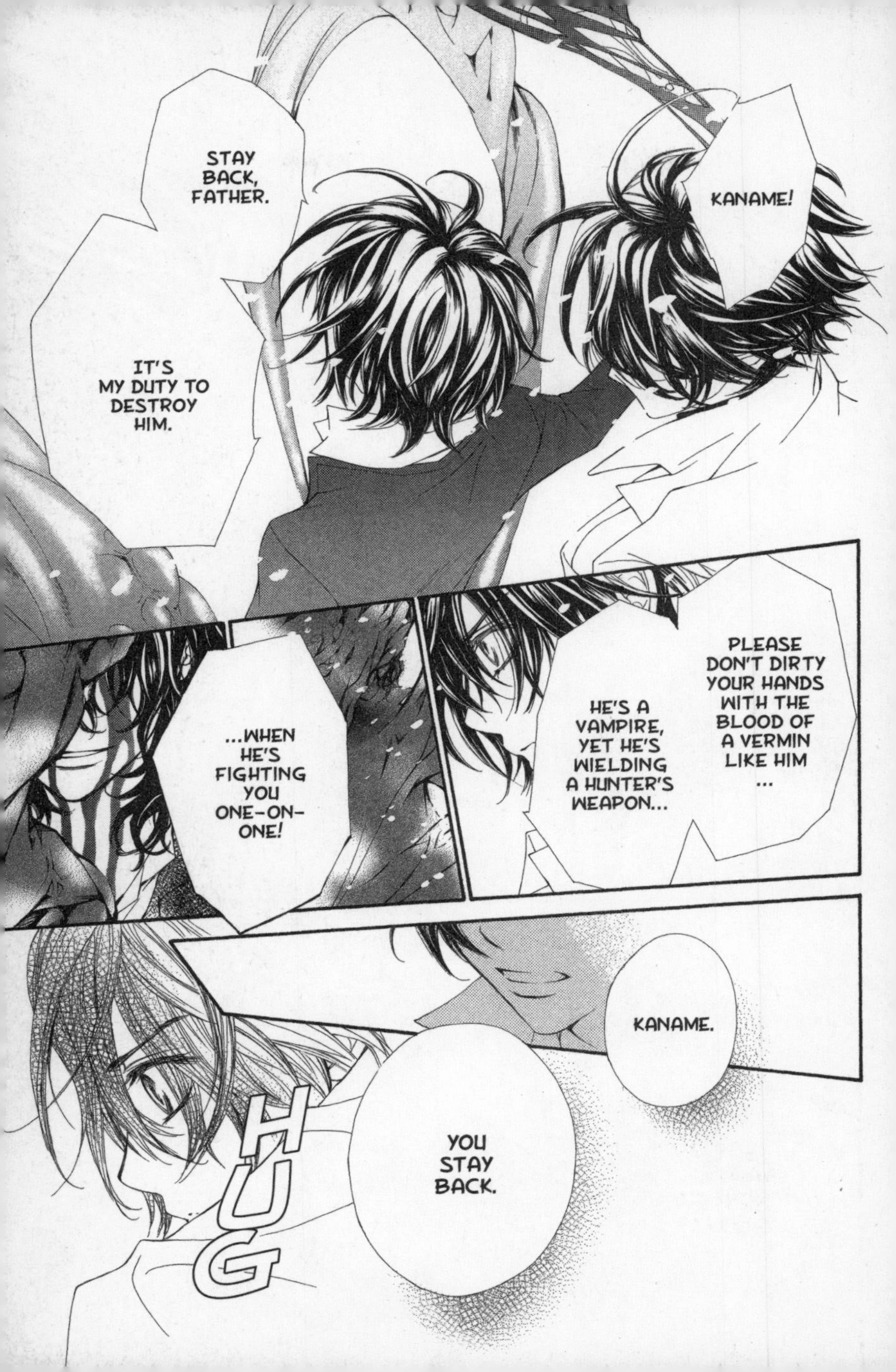
KANAME!
STAY BACK, FATHER.
IT'S MY DUTY TO DESTROY HIM.
PLEASE DON'T DIRTY YOUR HANDS WITH THE BLOOD OF A VERMIN LIKE HIM ...
HE'S A VAMPIRE, YET HE'S WIELDING A HUNTER'S WEAPON...
...WHEN HE'S FIGHTING YOU ONE-ON-ONE!
KANAME.
YOU STAY BACK.
HUG

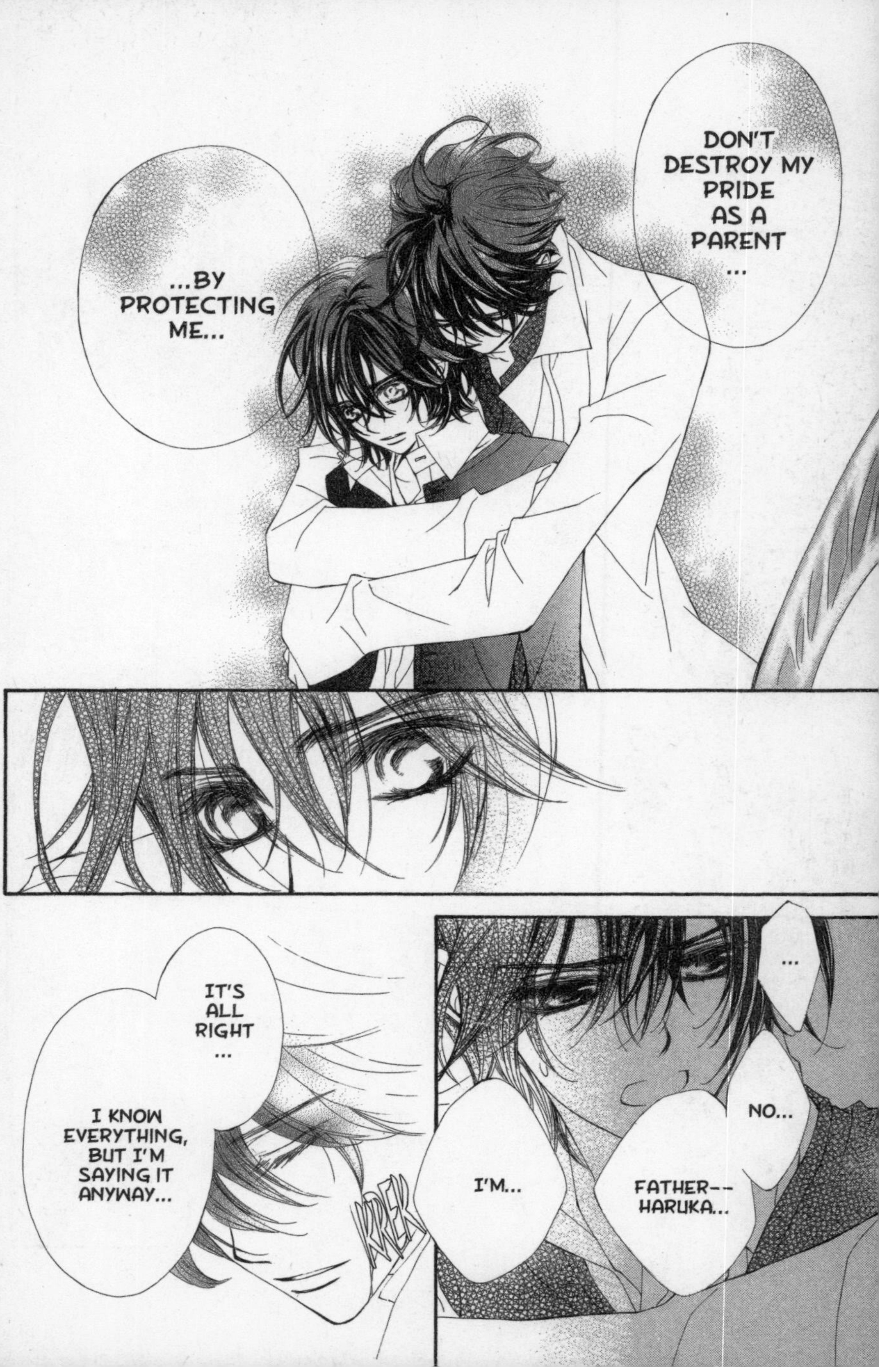
DON'T DESTROY MY PRIDE AS A PARENT ...
...BY PROTECTING ME...
...
NO...
FATHER-- HARUKA...
I'M...
IT'S ALL RIGHT ...
I KNOW EVERYTHING, BUT I'M SAYING IT ANYWAY...

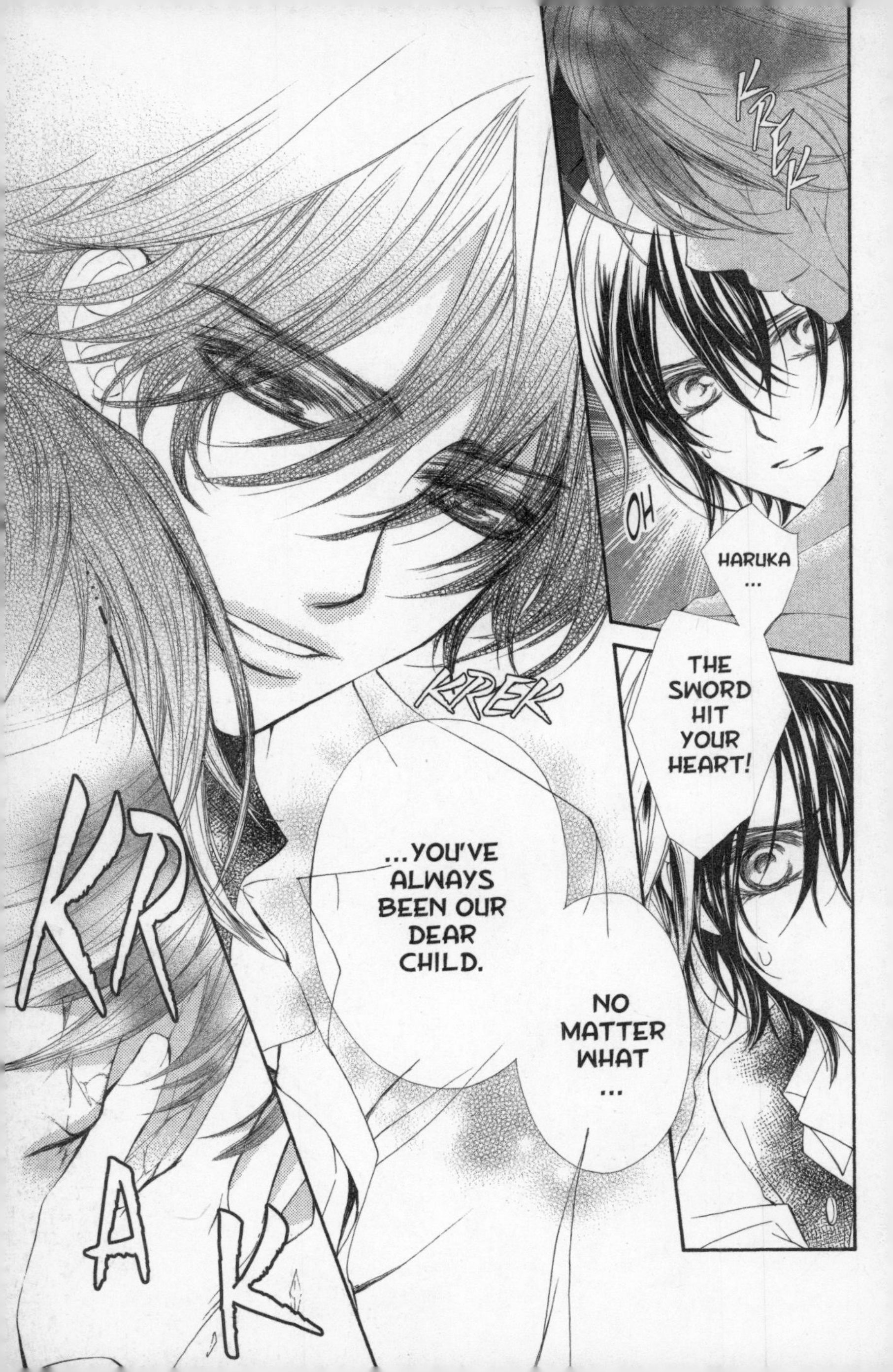
KREK
OH
HARUKA ...
THE SWORD HIT YOUR HEART!
KREK
NO MATTER WHAT ...
...YOU'VE ALWAYS BEEN OUR DEAR CHILD.
KRAK

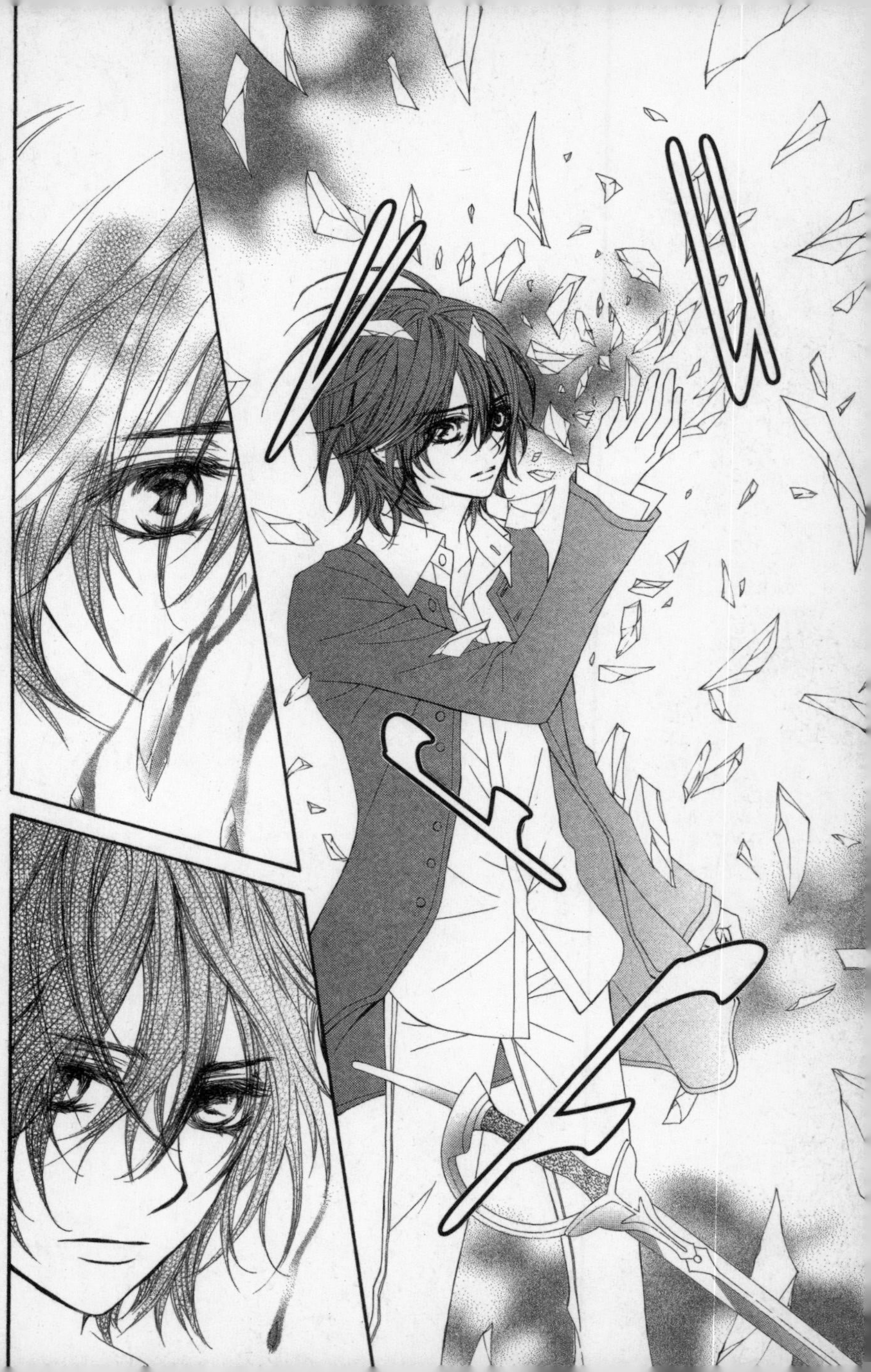

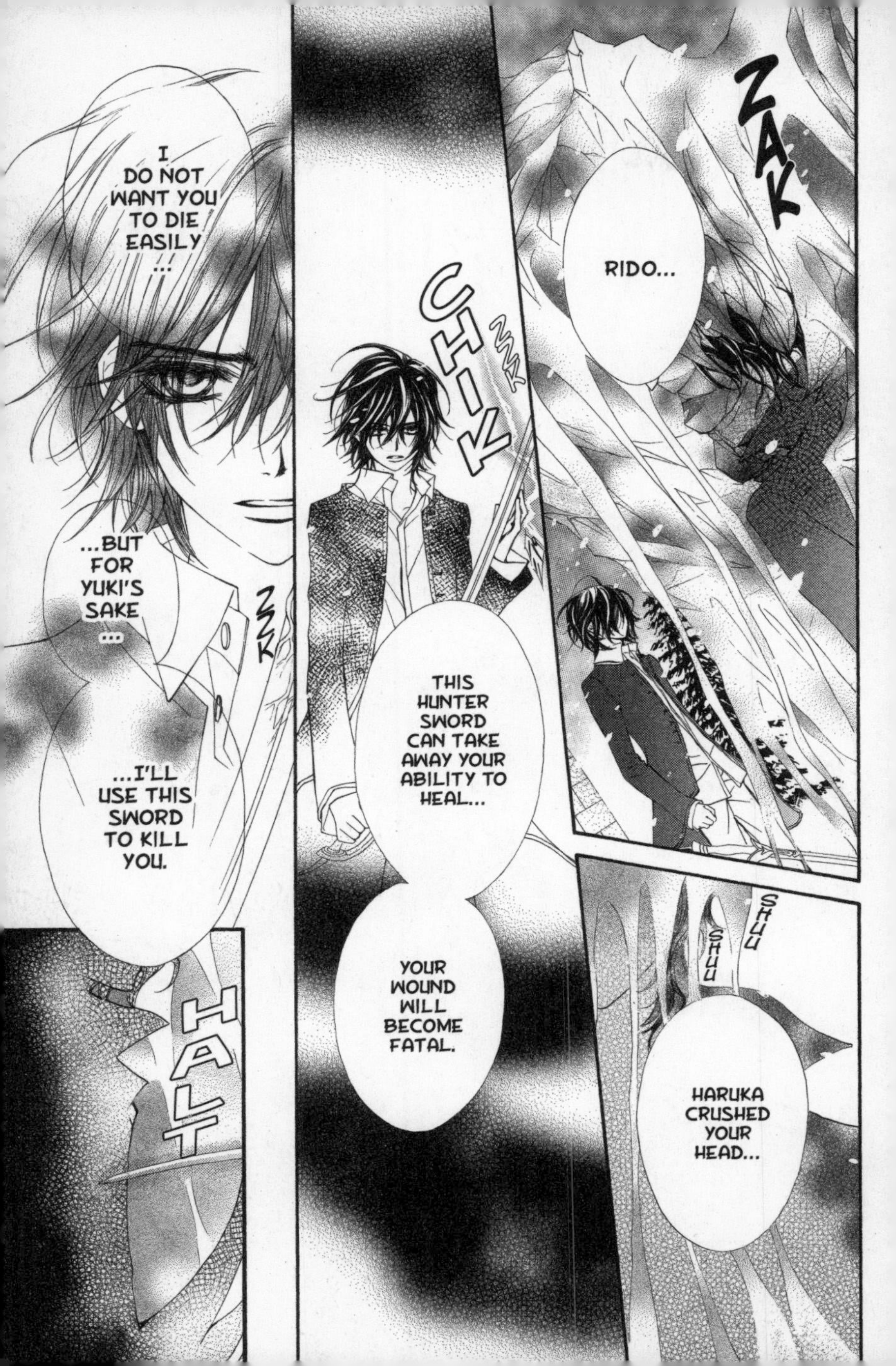
ZAK
RIDO...
SHUU
SHUU
HARUKA CRUSHED YOUR HEAD...
CHIK
ZNNK
THIS HUNTER SWORD CAN TAKE AWAY YOUR ABILITY TO HEAL...
YOUR WOUND WILL BECOME FATAL.
I DO NOT WANT YOU TO DIE EASILY...
...BUT FOR YUKI'S SAKE...
ZZK
...I'LL USE THIS SWORD TO KILL YOU.
HALT

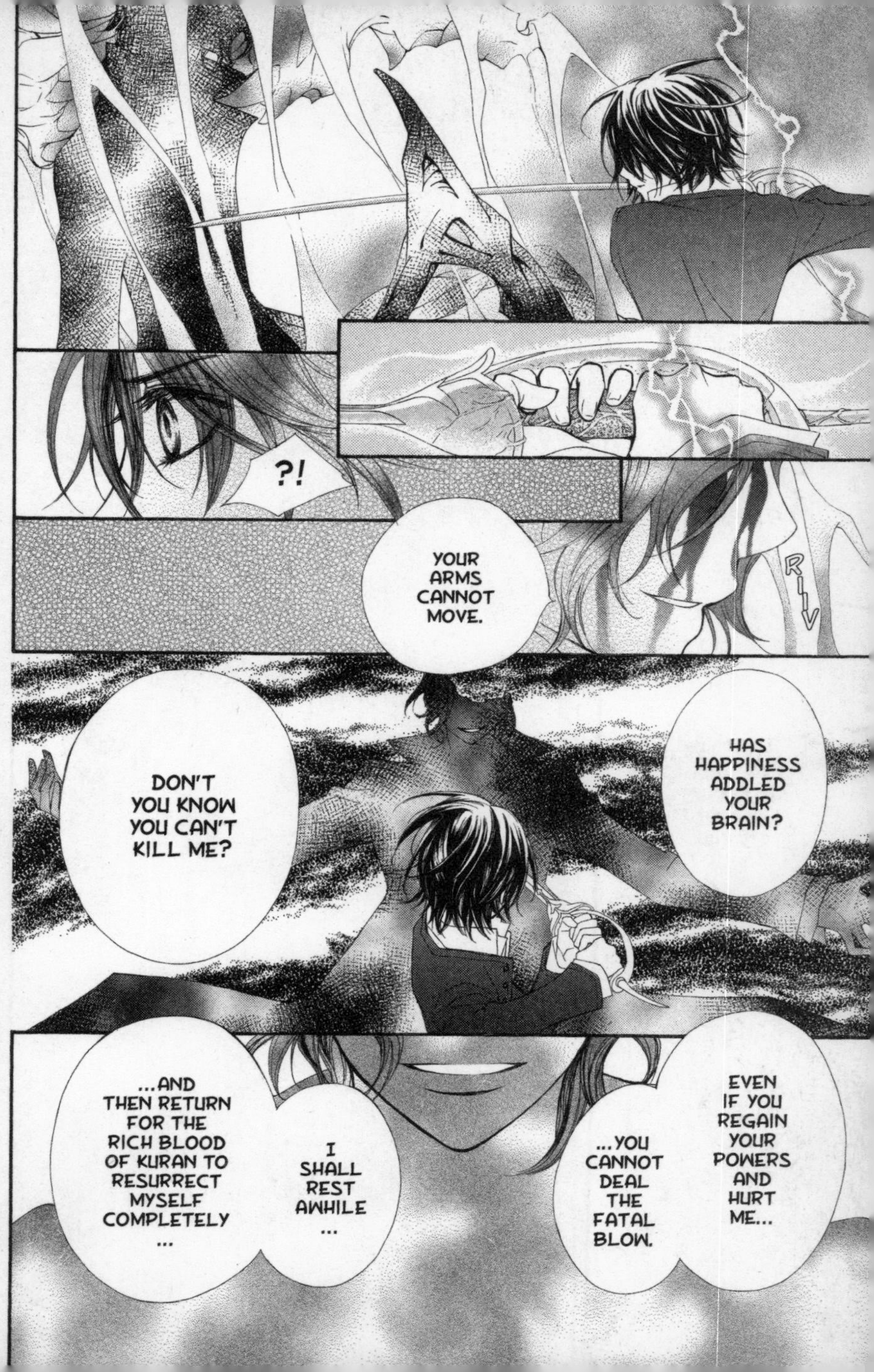
?!
RIIV
YOUR ARMS CANNOT MOVE.
HAS HAPPINESS ADDLED YOUR BRAIN?
DON'T YOU KNOW YOU CAN'T KILL ME?
EVEN IF YOU REGAIN YOUR POWERS AND HURT ME...
...YOU CANNOT DEAL THE FATAL BLOW.
I SHALL REST AWHILE ...
...AND THEN RETURN FOR THE RICH BLOOD OF KURAN TO RESURRECT MYSELF COMPLETELY ...

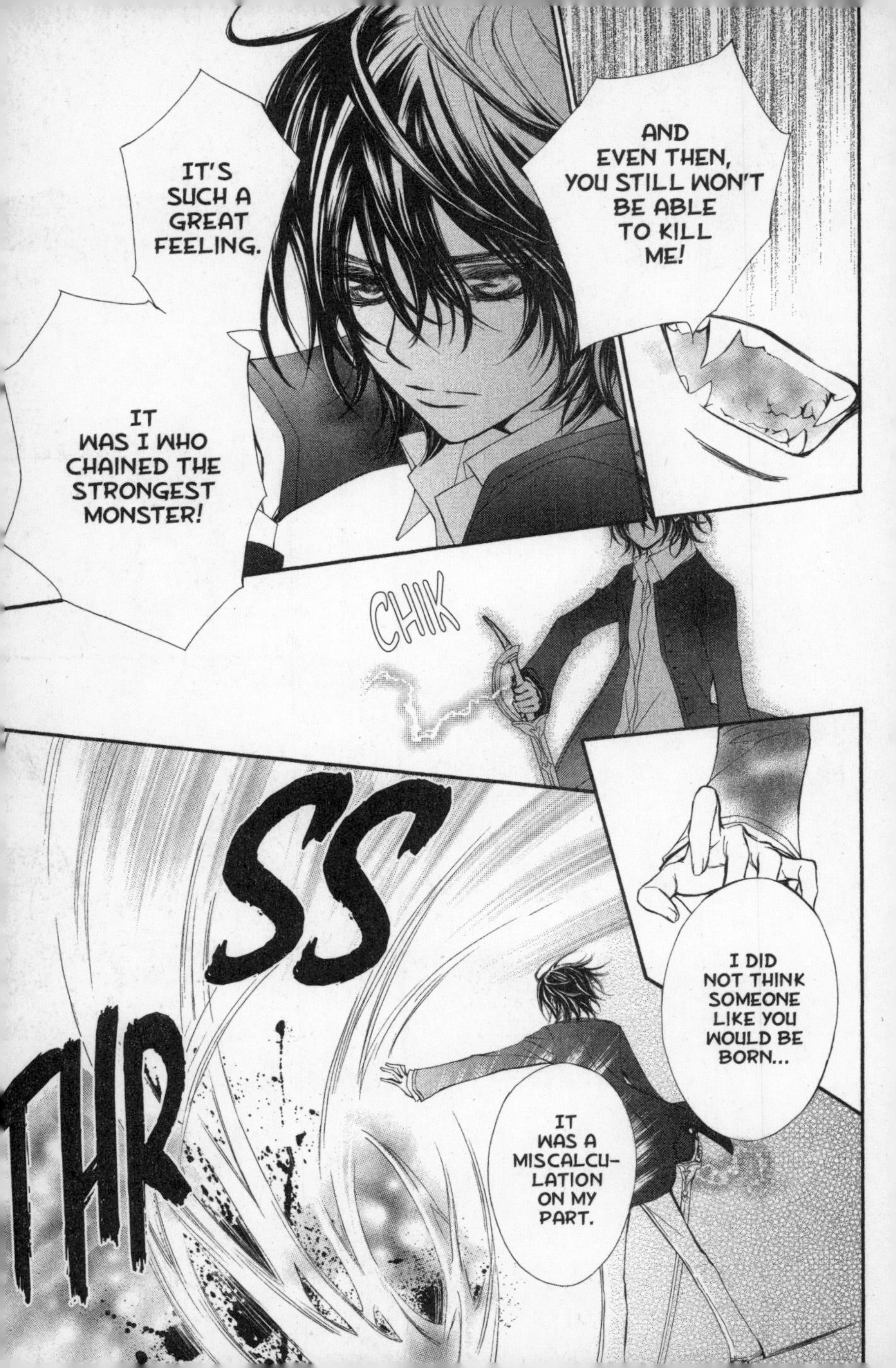
AND EVEN THEN, YOU STILL WON'T BE ABLE TO KILL ME!
IT'S SUCH A GREAT FEELING.
IT WAS I WHO CHAINED THE STRONGEST MONSTER!
CHIK
I DID NOT THINK SOMEONE LIKE YOU WOULD BE BORN...
IT WAS A MISCALCU-LATION ON MY PART.
THR
SS

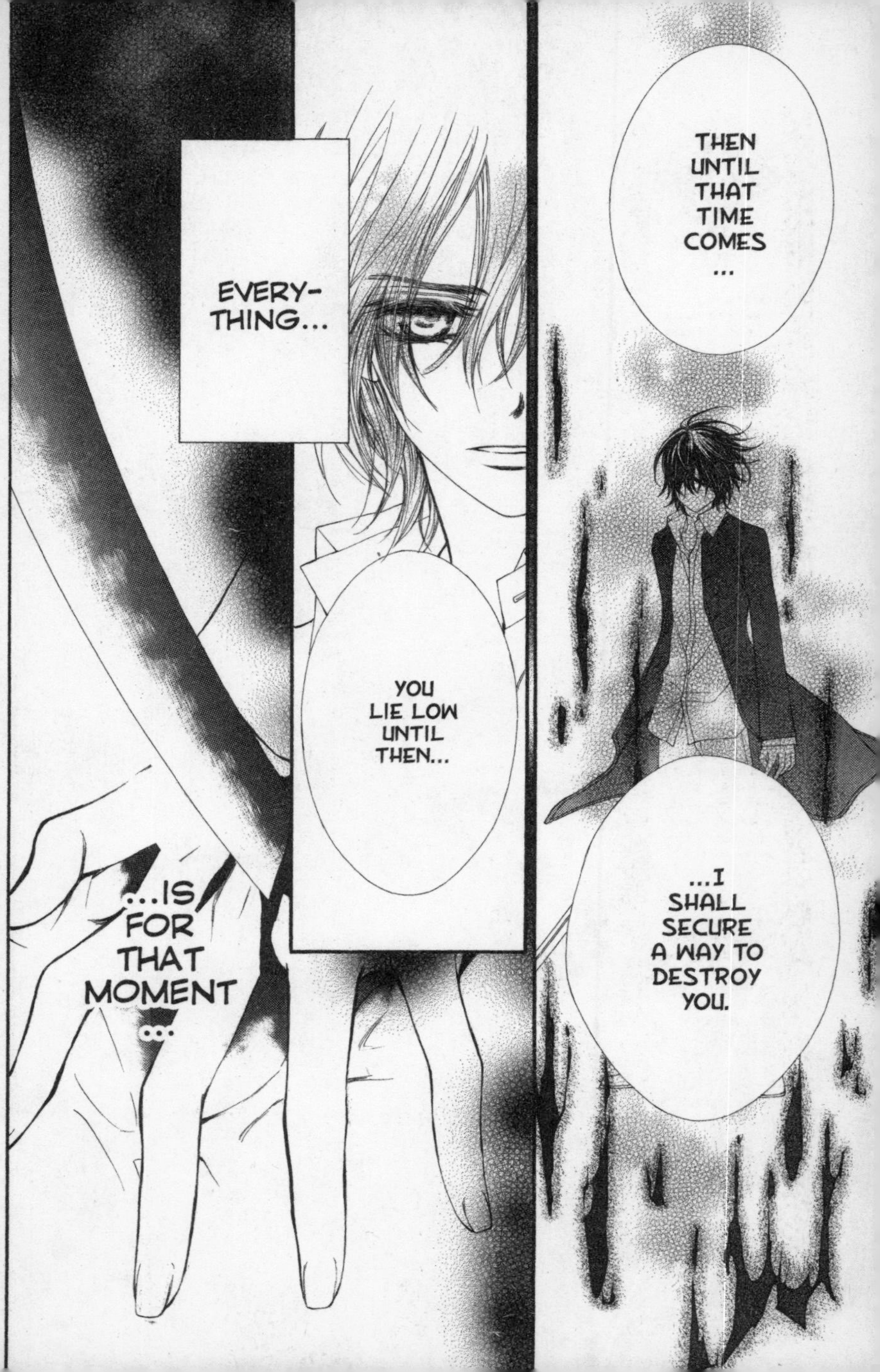
THEN UNTIL THAT TIME COMES ...
...I SHALL SECURE A WAY TO DESTROY YOU.
EVERY-THING...
YOU LIE LOW UNTIL THEN...
...IS FOR THAT MOMENT ...

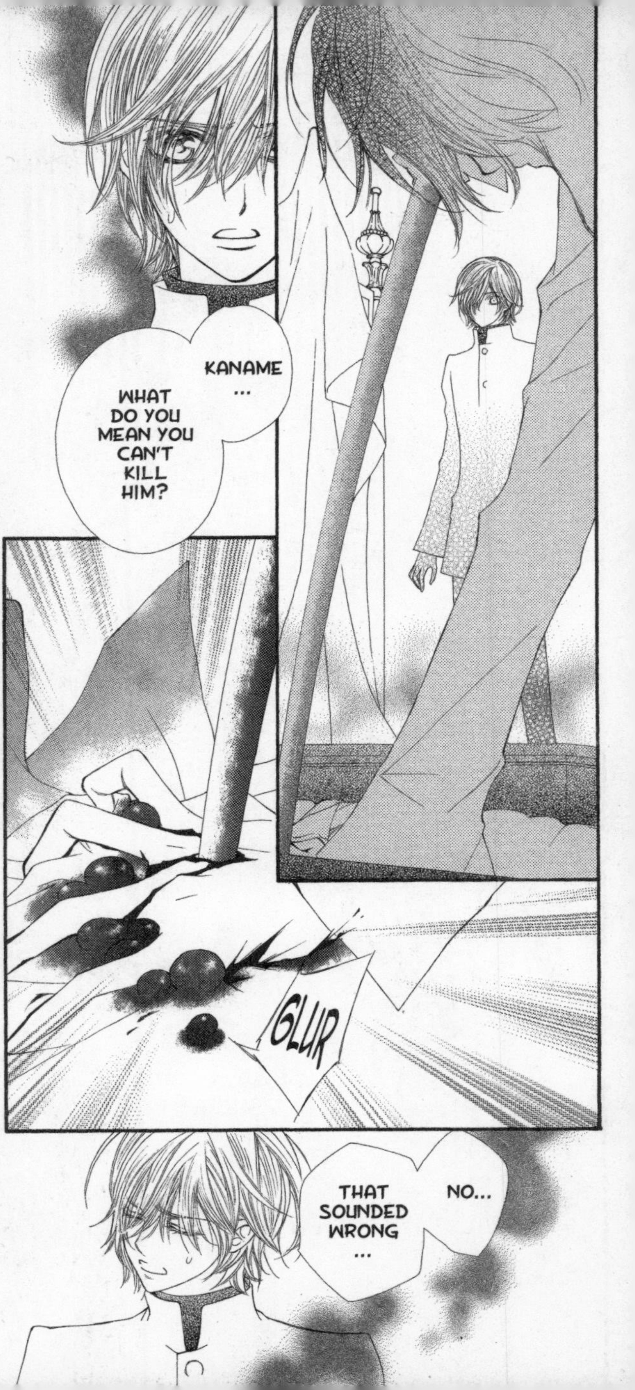
KANAME ...
WHAT DO YOU MEAN YOU CAN'T KILL HIM?
GLUR
NO...
THAT SOUNDED WRONG ...

IV

I've already answered this in interviews, but Part I of *Vampire Knight* will end around vol. 9 or 10. I will continue with Part II directly after. The editor-in-chief apparently asked this too. Recently there have been many letters asking, "Is the manga ending?" and this is my response. Actually, people were asking that same question around the time of the Third Night.

I'm making people anxious...Uh-oh. That means it's drawn so that it seems as if I'm dying to end it, although I have no intention of doing so, huh? Maybe it will happen again in the future...but I intend to continue drawing until I announce that the end is near. Definitely! I'll do my best to make the story exciting.

I'd be happy if you continued reading this manga! See you!

樋野まつり

Matsuri Hino

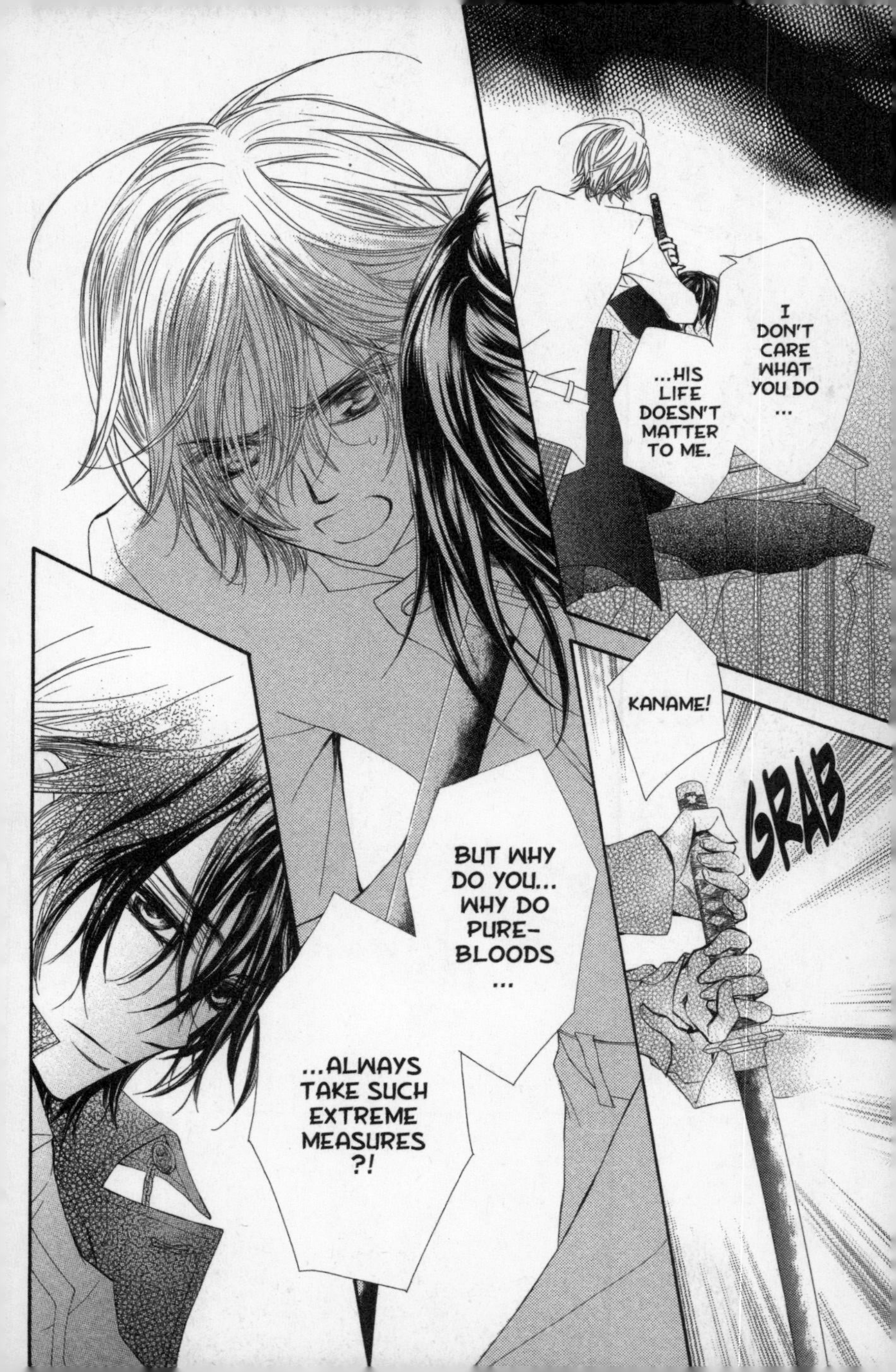
I DON'T CARE WHAT YOU DO ...
...HIS LIFE DOESN'T MATTER TO ME.
KANAME!
GRAB
BUT WHY DO YOU... WHY DO PURE-BLOODS ...
...ALWAYS TAKE SUCH EXTREME MEASURES ?!

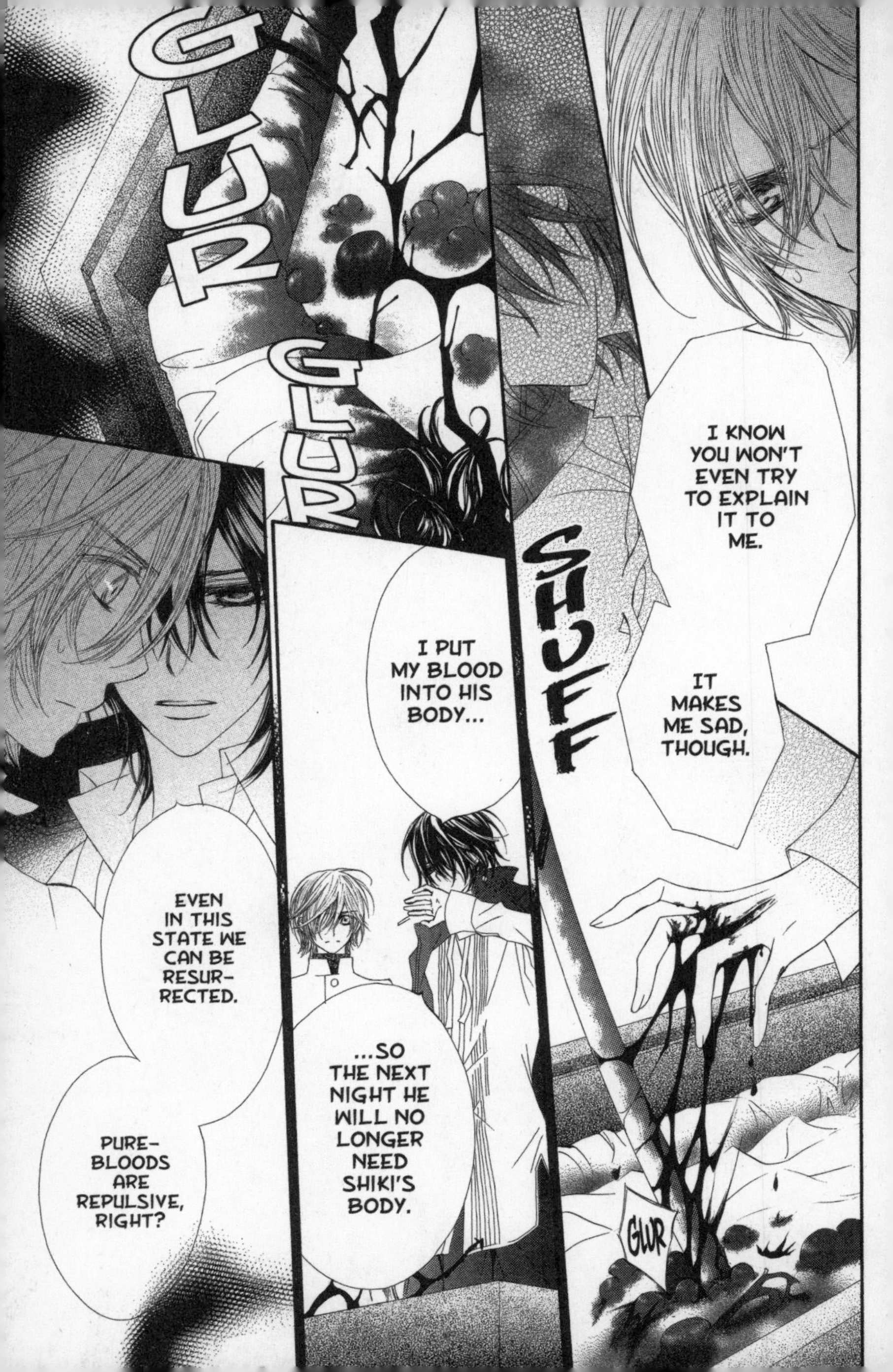
I KNOW YOU WON'T EVEN TRY TO EXPLAIN IT TO ME.
IT MAKES ME SAD, THOUGH.
SHUFF
GLUR
GLUR GLUR
I PUT MY BLOOD INTO HIS BODY...
...SO THE NEXT NIGHT HE WILL NO LONGER NEED SHIKI'S BODY.
EVEN IN THIS STATE WE CAN BE RESURRECTED.
PURE-BLOODS ARE REPULSIVE, RIGHT?

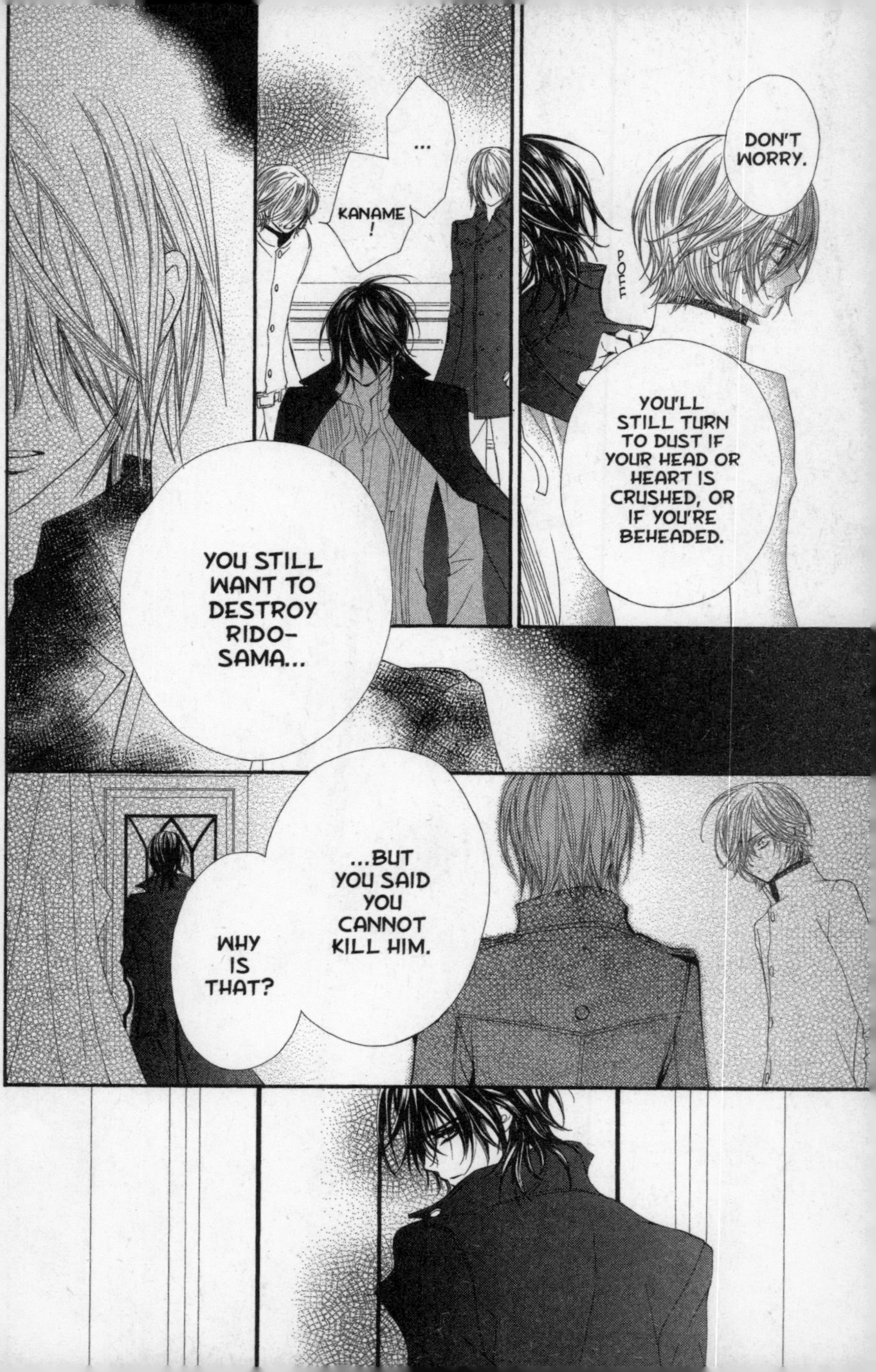
DON'T WORRY.
POFF
YOU'LL STILL TURN TO DUST IF YOUR HEAD OR HEART IS CRUSHED, OR IF YOU'RE BEHEADED.
...
KANAME!
YOU STILL WANT TO DESTROY RIDO-SAMA...
...BUT YOU SAID YOU CANNOT KILL HIM.
WHY IS THAT?

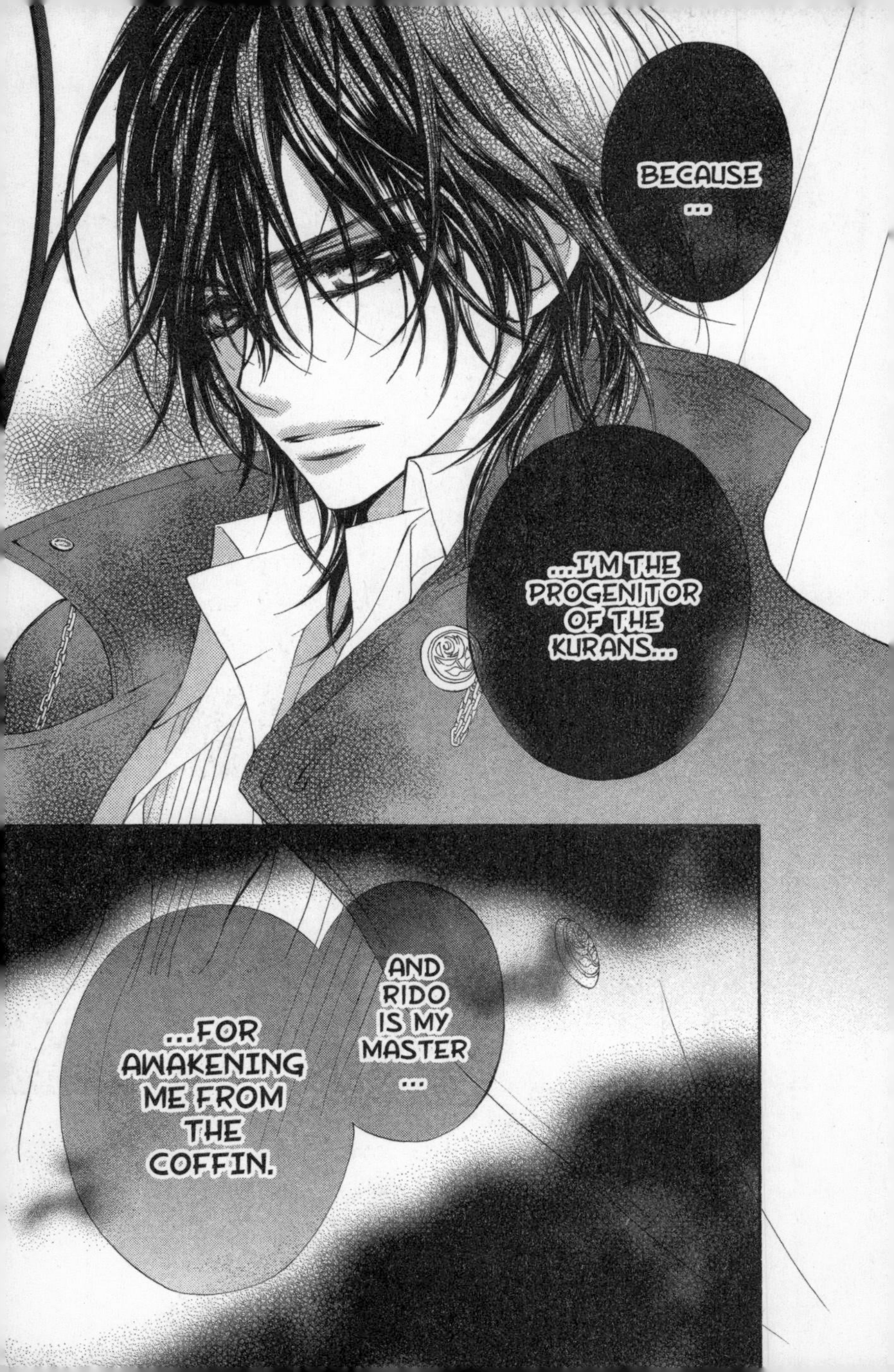
BECAUSE ...
...I'M THE PROGENITOR OF THE KURANS...
AND RIDO IS MY MASTER ...
...FOR AWAKENING ME FROM THE COFFIN.

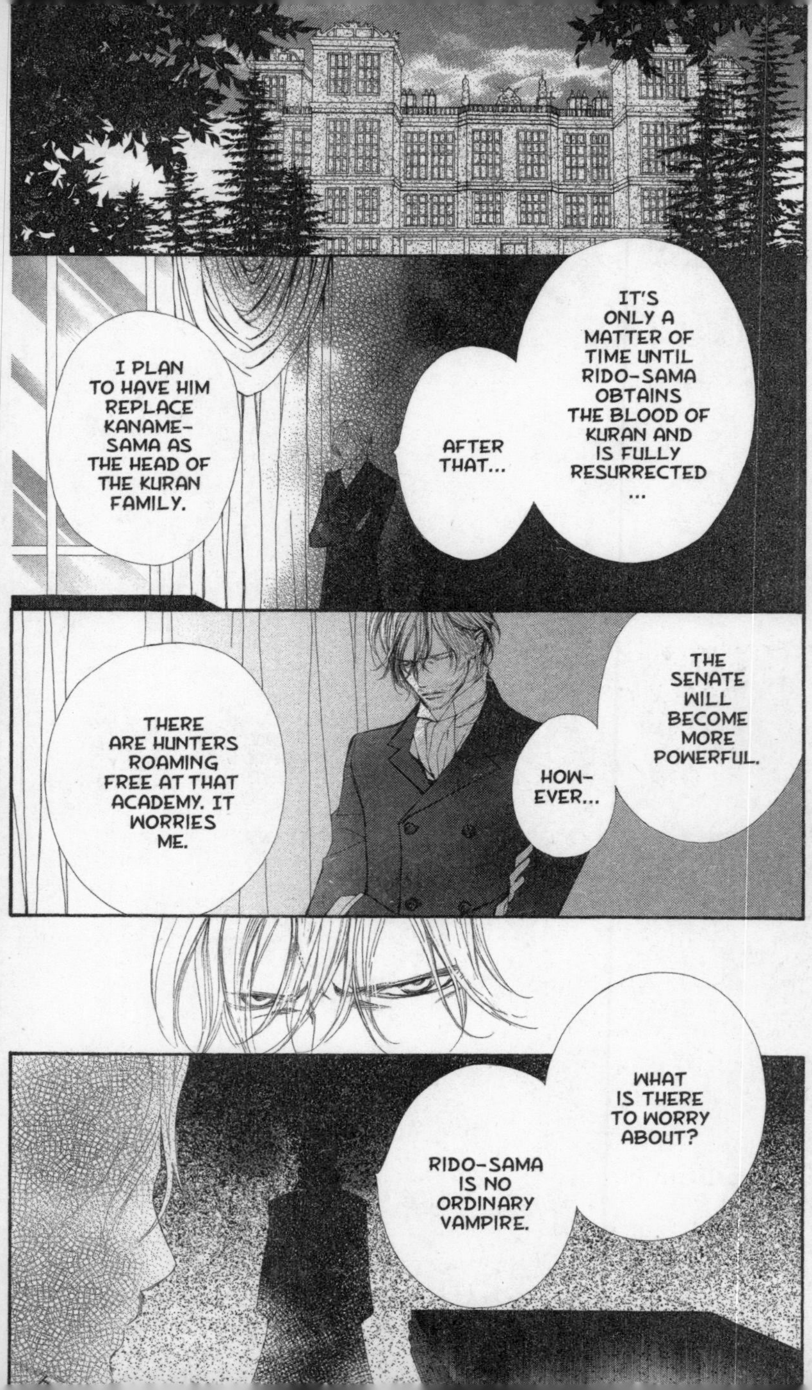
IT'S ONLY A MATTER OF TIME UNTIL RIDO-SAMA OBTAINS THE BLOOD OF KURAN AND IS FULLY RESURRECTED ...
AFTER THAT...
I PLAN TO HAVE HIM REPLACE KANAME-SAMA AS THE HEAD OF THE KURAN FAMILY.
THE SENATE WILL BECOME MORE POWERFUL.
HOW-EVER...
THERE ARE HUNTERS ROAMING FREE AT THAT ACADEMY. IT WORRIES ME.
WHAT IS THERE TO WORRY ABOUT?
RIDO-SAMA IS NO ORDINARY VAMPIRE.

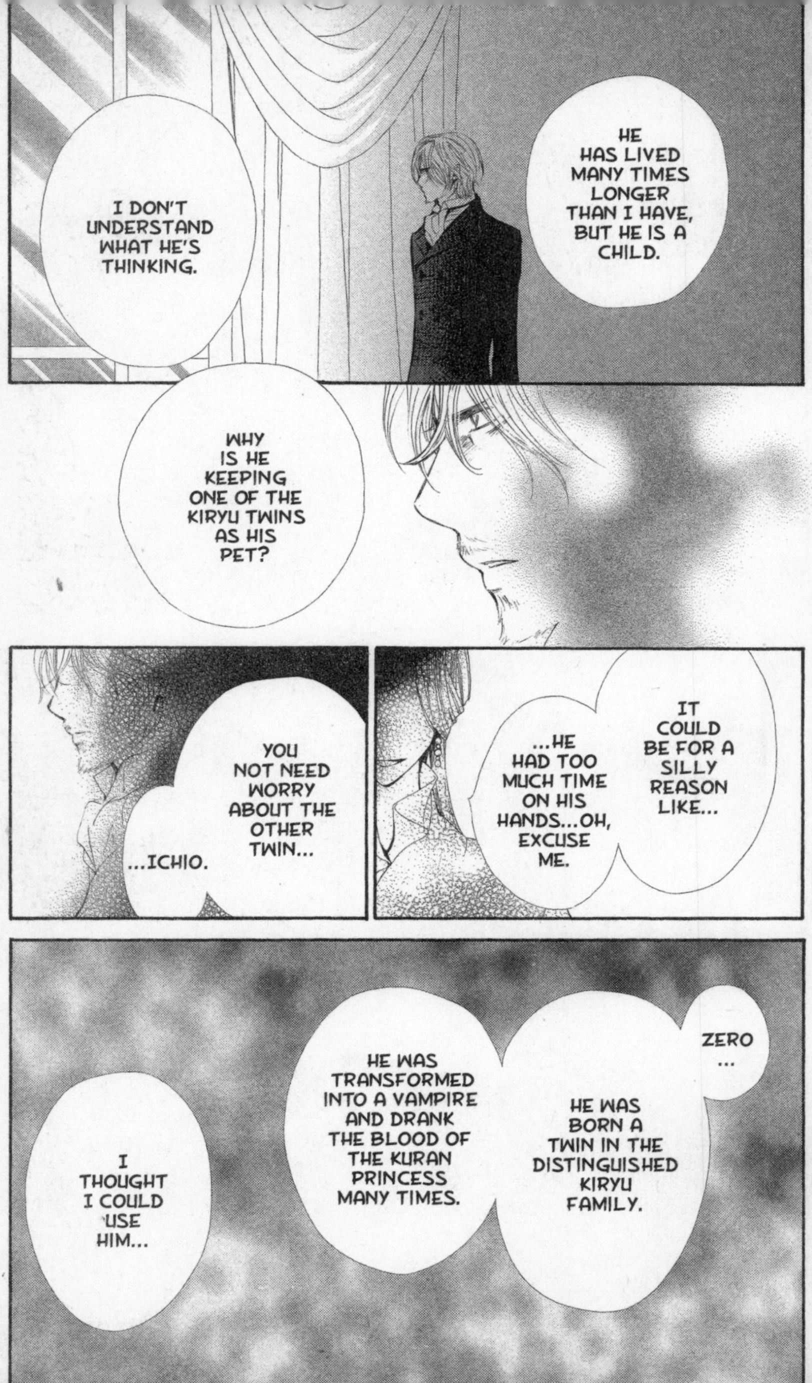
HE HAS LIVED MANY TIMES LONGER THAN I HAVE, BUT HE IS A CHILD.
I DON'T UNDERSTAND WHAT HE'S THINKING.
WHY IS HE KEEPING ONE OF THE KIRYU TWINS AS HIS PET?
IT COULD BE FOR A SILLY REASON LIKE...
...HE HAD TOO MUCH TIME ON HIS HANDS...OH, EXCUSE ME.
YOU NOT NEED WORRY ABOUT THE OTHER TWIN...
...ICHIO.
ZERO...
HE WAS BORN A TWIN IN THE DISTINGUISHED KIRYU FAMILY.
HE WAS TRANSFORMED INTO A VAMPIRE AND DRANK THE BLOOD OF THE KURAN PRINCESS MANY TIMES.
I THOUGHT I COULD USE HIM...

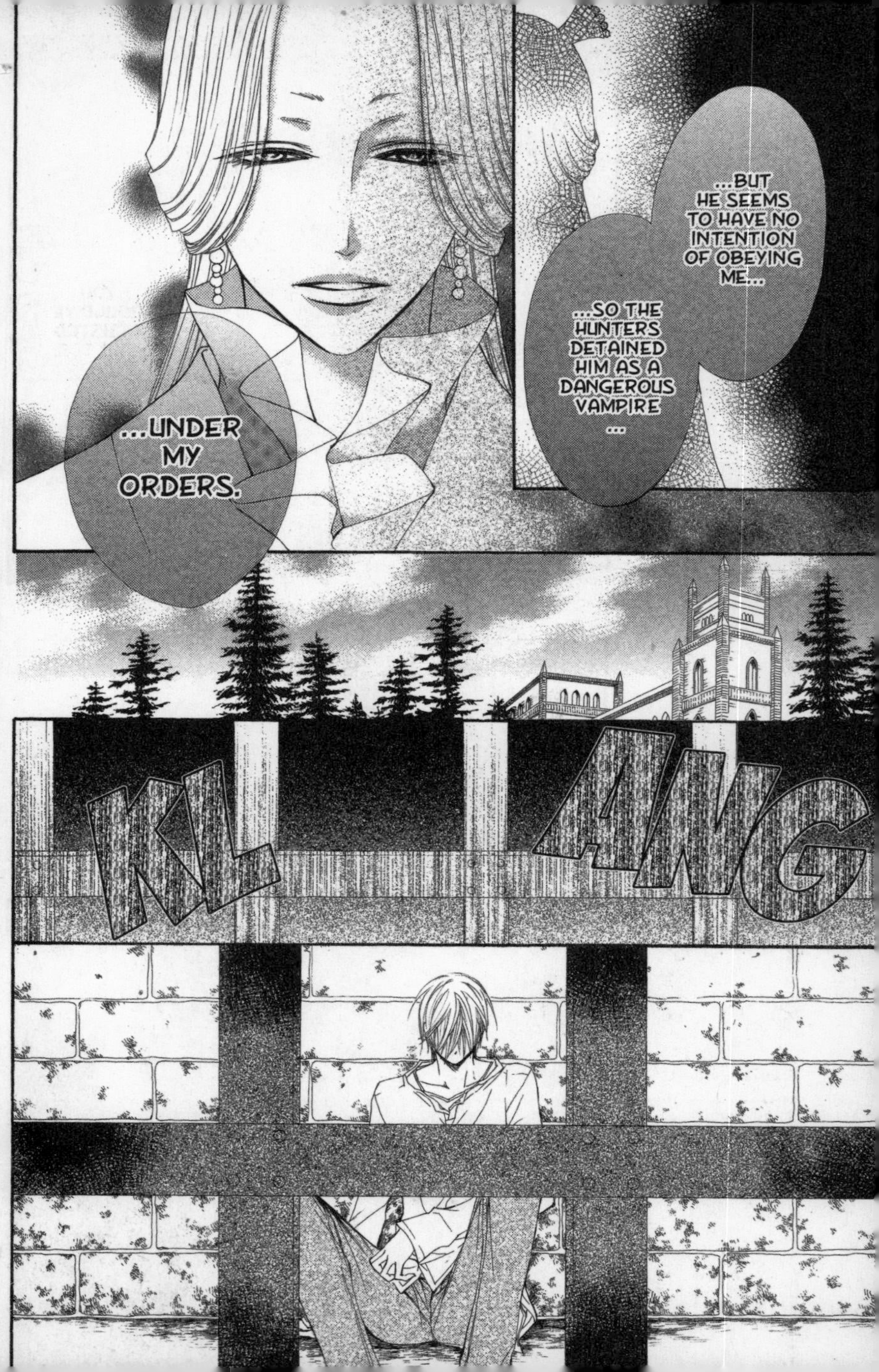
...BUT HE SEEMS TO HAVE NO INTENTION OF OBEYING ME...
...SO THE HUNTERS DETAINED HIM AS A DANGEROUS VAMPIRE ...
...UNDER MY ORDERS.
KLANG

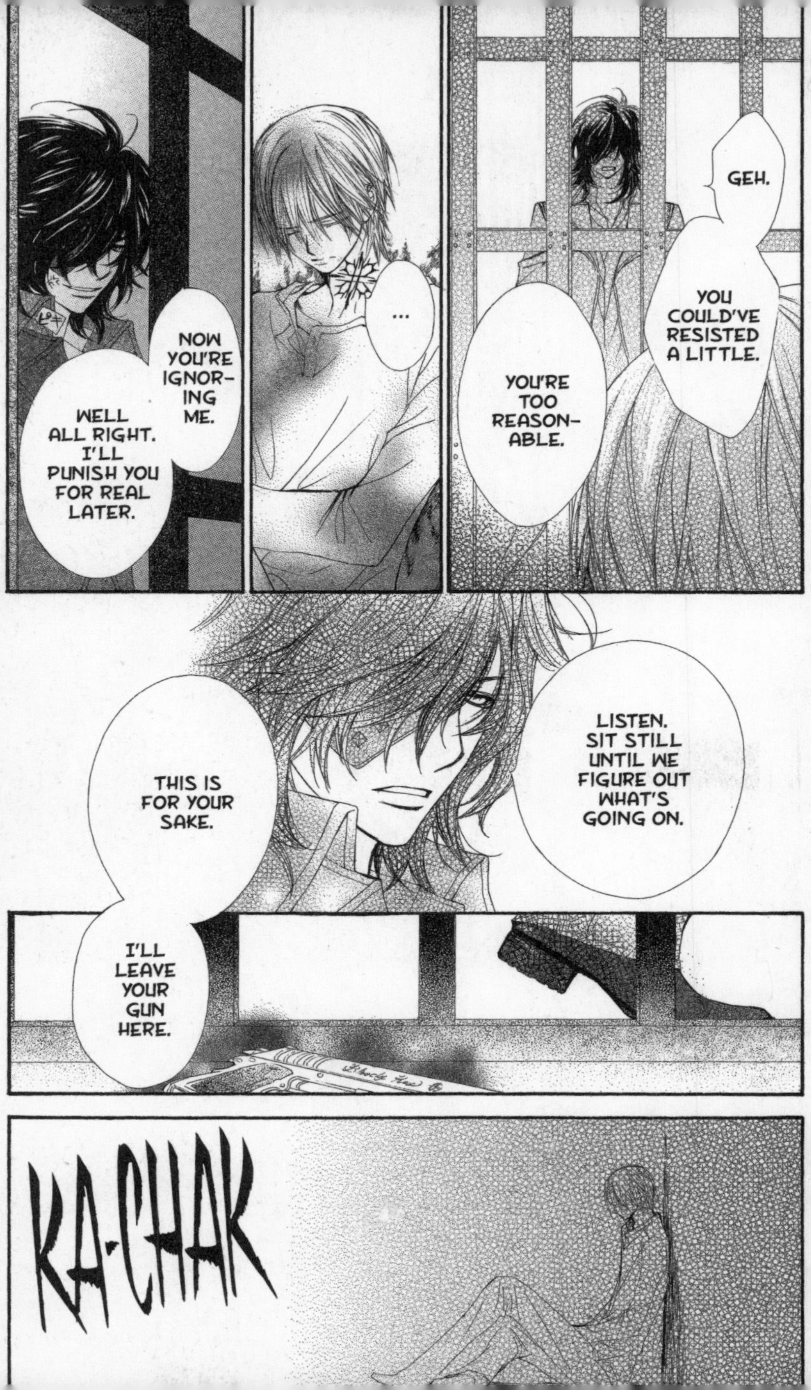
GEH.
YOU COULD'VE RESISTED A LITTLE.
YOU'RE TOO REASONABLE.
...
NOW YOU'RE IGNORING ME.
WELL ALL RIGHT. I'LL PUNISH YOU FOR REAL LATER.
LISTEN. SIT STILL UNTIL WE FIGURE OUT WHAT'S GOING ON.
THIS IS FOR YOUR SAKE.
I'LL LEAVE YOUR GUN HERE.
KA-CHAK

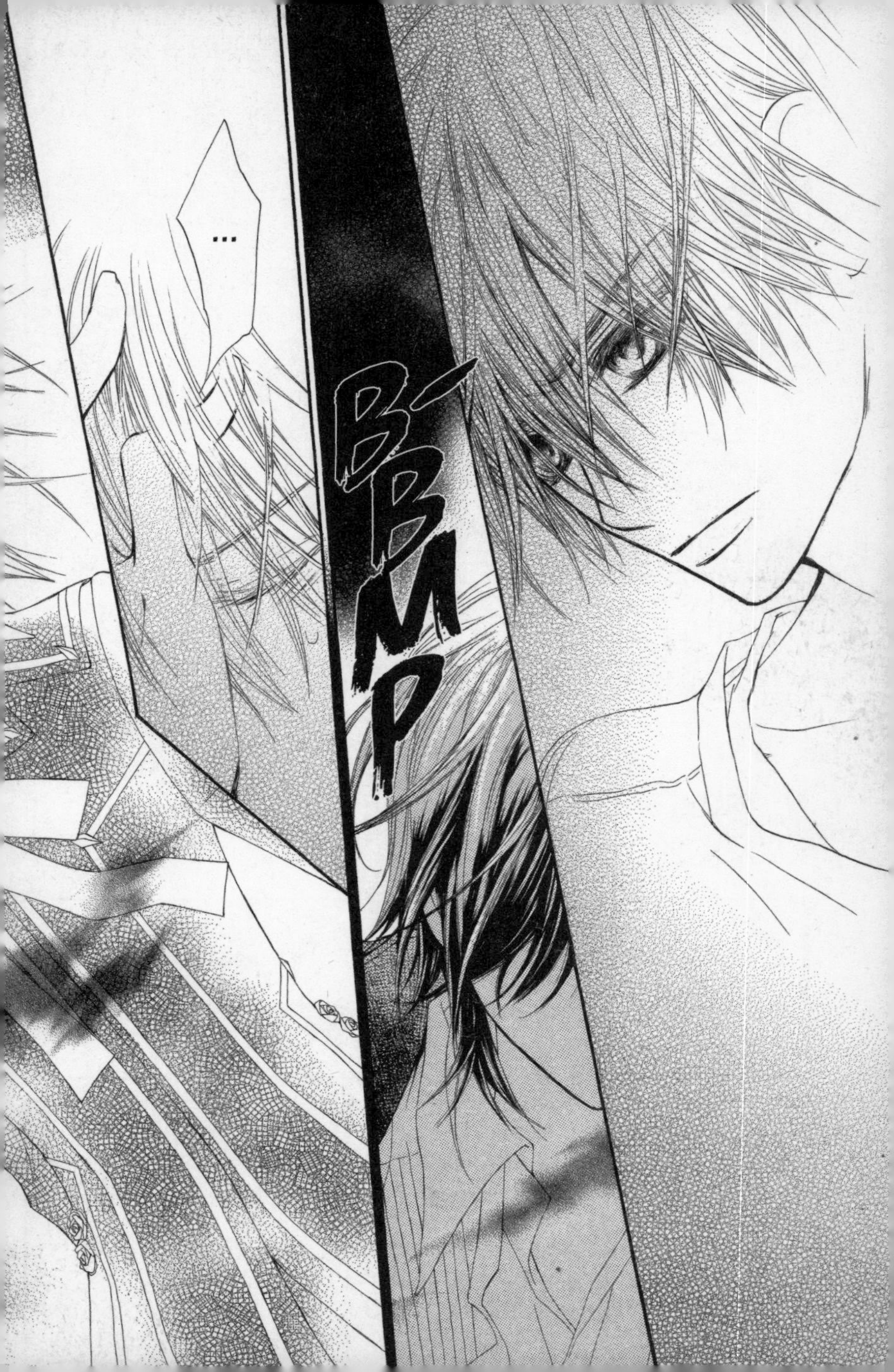
B-BMP
...

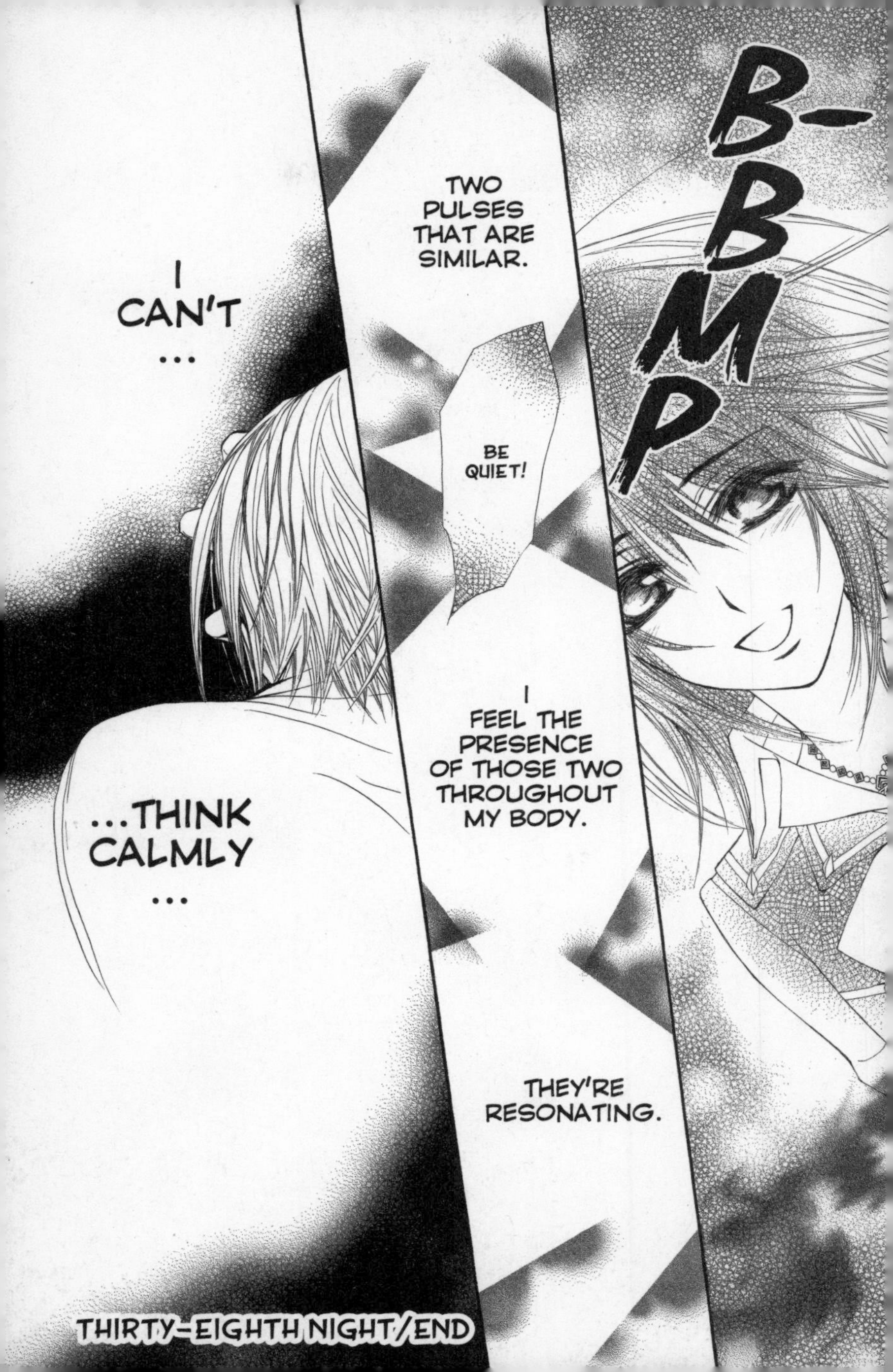

THIRTY-EIGHTH NIGHT/END

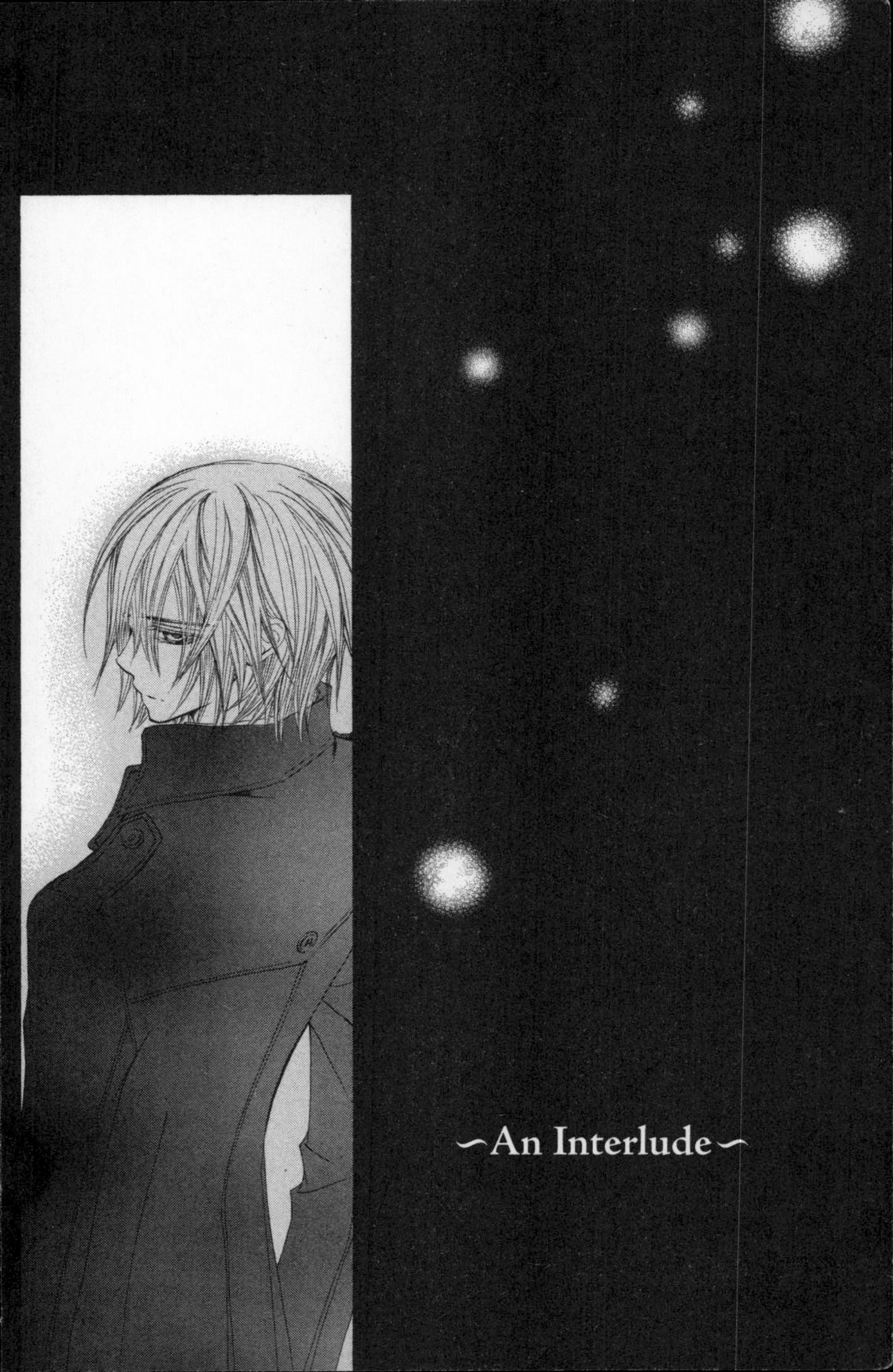
~An Interlude~

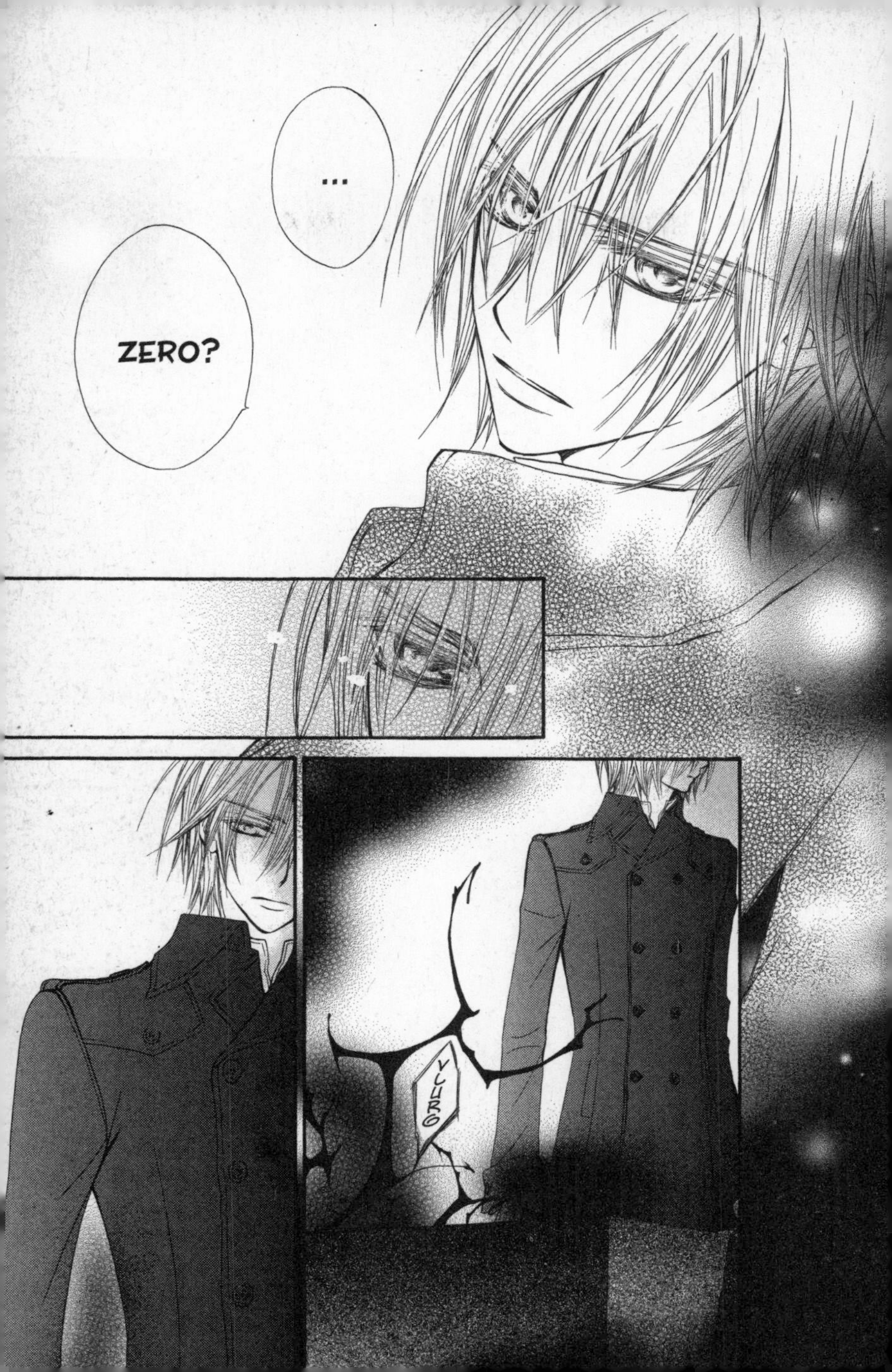
...
ZERO?
VLURG

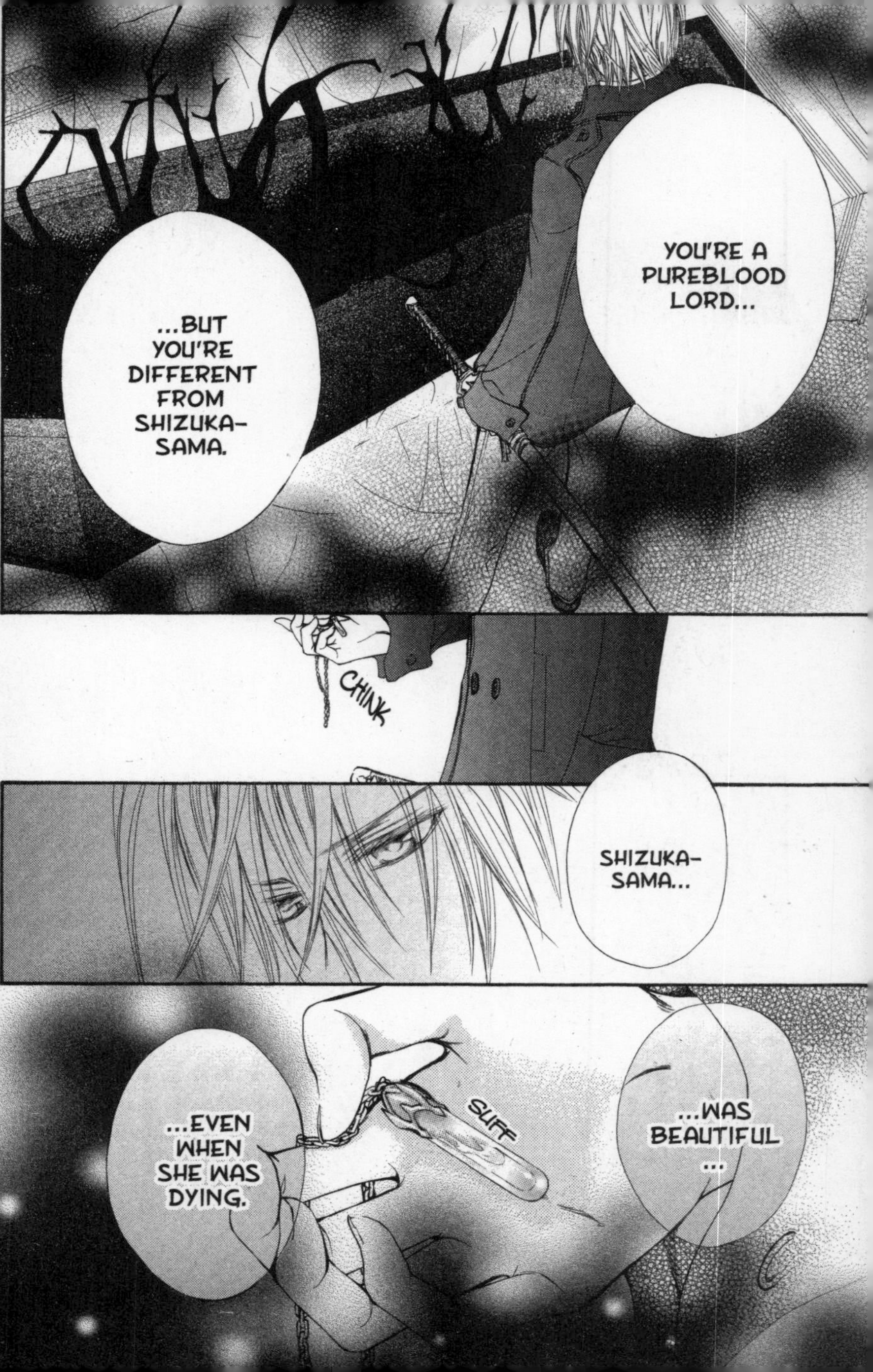
YOU'RE A PUREBLOOD LORD...
...BUT YOU'RE DIFFERENT FROM SHIZUKA-SAMA.
CHINK
SHIZUKA-SAMA...
...WAS BEAUTIFUL ...
SLIFF
...EVEN WHEN SHE WAS DYING.

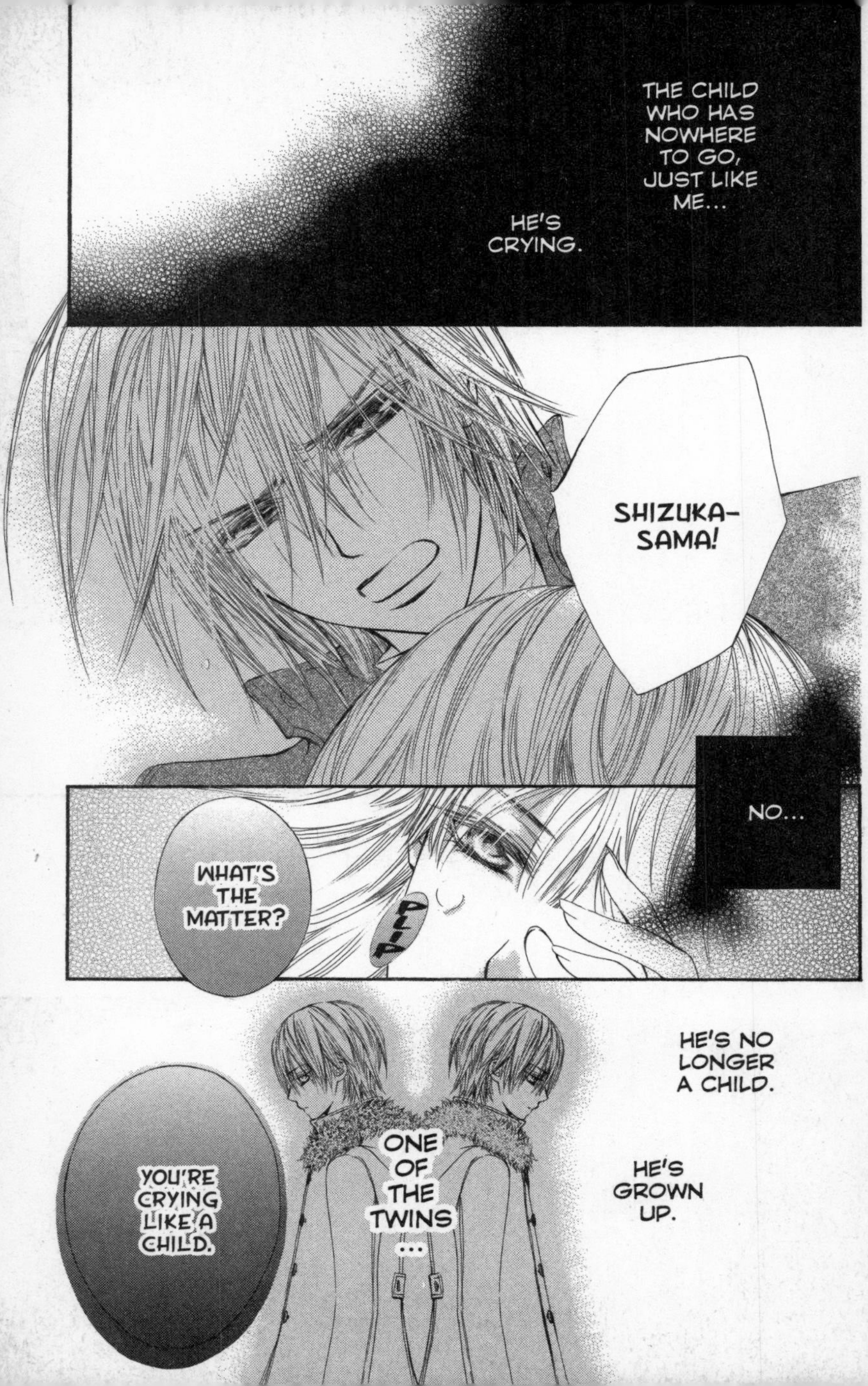
THE CHILD WHO HAS NOWHERE TO GO, JUST LIKE ME...
HE'S CRYING.
SHIZUKA-SAMA!
NO...
PLIP
WHAT'S THE MATTER?
HE'S NO LONGER A CHILD.
HE'S GROWN UP.
ONE OF THE TWINS...
YOU'RE CRYING LIKE A CHILD.

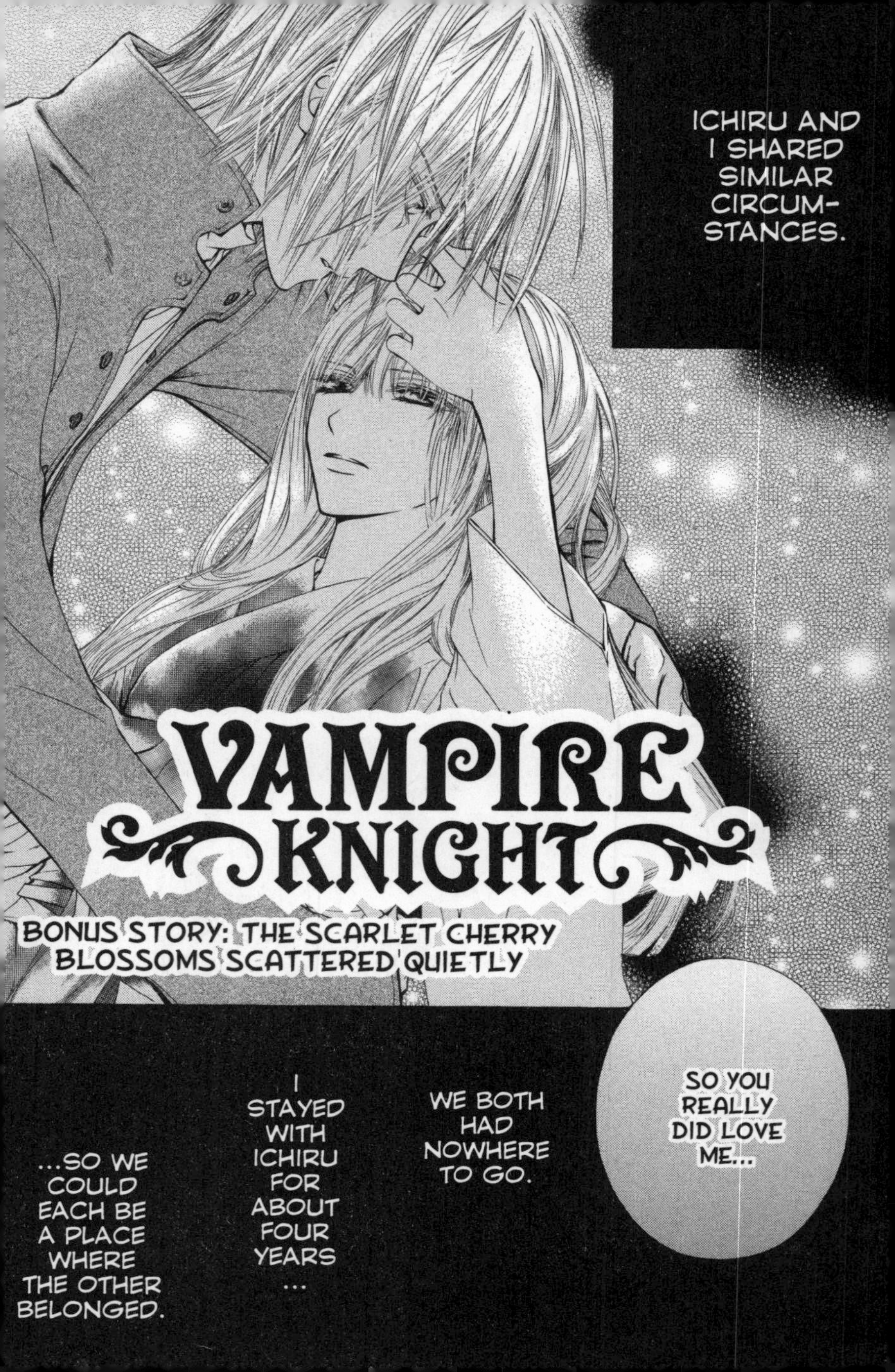
ICHIRU AND I SHARED SIMILAR CIRCUM-STANCES.
VAMPIRE KNIGHT
BONUS STORY: THE SCARLET CHERRY BLOSSOMS SCATTERED QUIETLY
SO YOU REALLY DID LOVE ME...
WE BOTH HAD NOWHERE TO GO.
I STAYED WITH ICHIRU FOR ABOUT FOUR YEARS...
...SO WE COULD EACH BE A PLACE WHERE THE OTHER BELONGED.

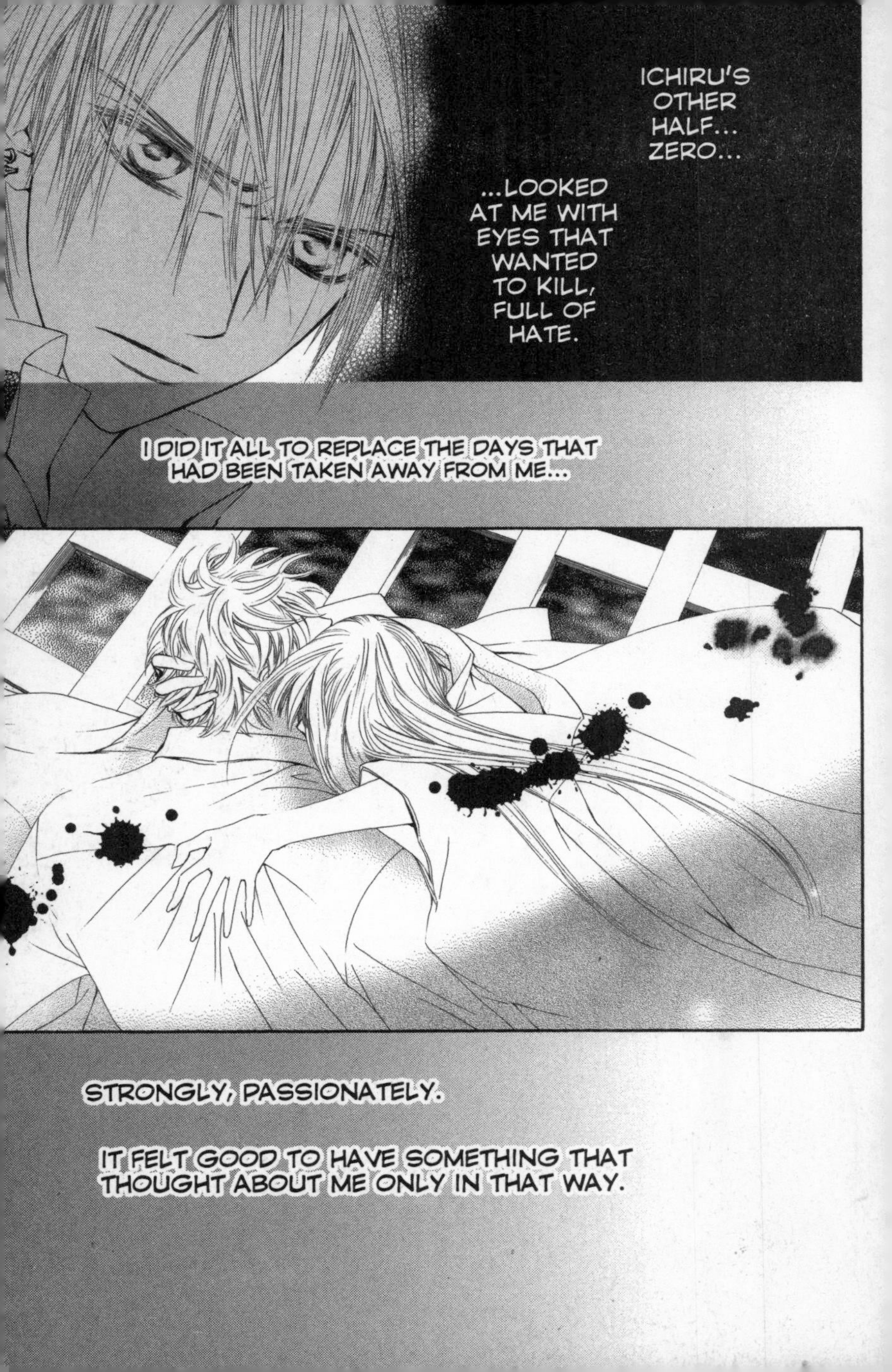
ICHIRU'S OTHER HALF... ZERO...
...LOOKED AT ME WITH EYES THAT WANTED TO KILL, FULL OF HATE.
I DID IT ALL TO REPLACE THE DAYS THAT HAD BEEN TAKEN AWAY FROM ME...
STRONGLY, PASSIONATELY.
IT FELT GOOD TO HAVE SOMETHING THAT THOUGHT ABOUT ME ONLY IN THAT WAY.

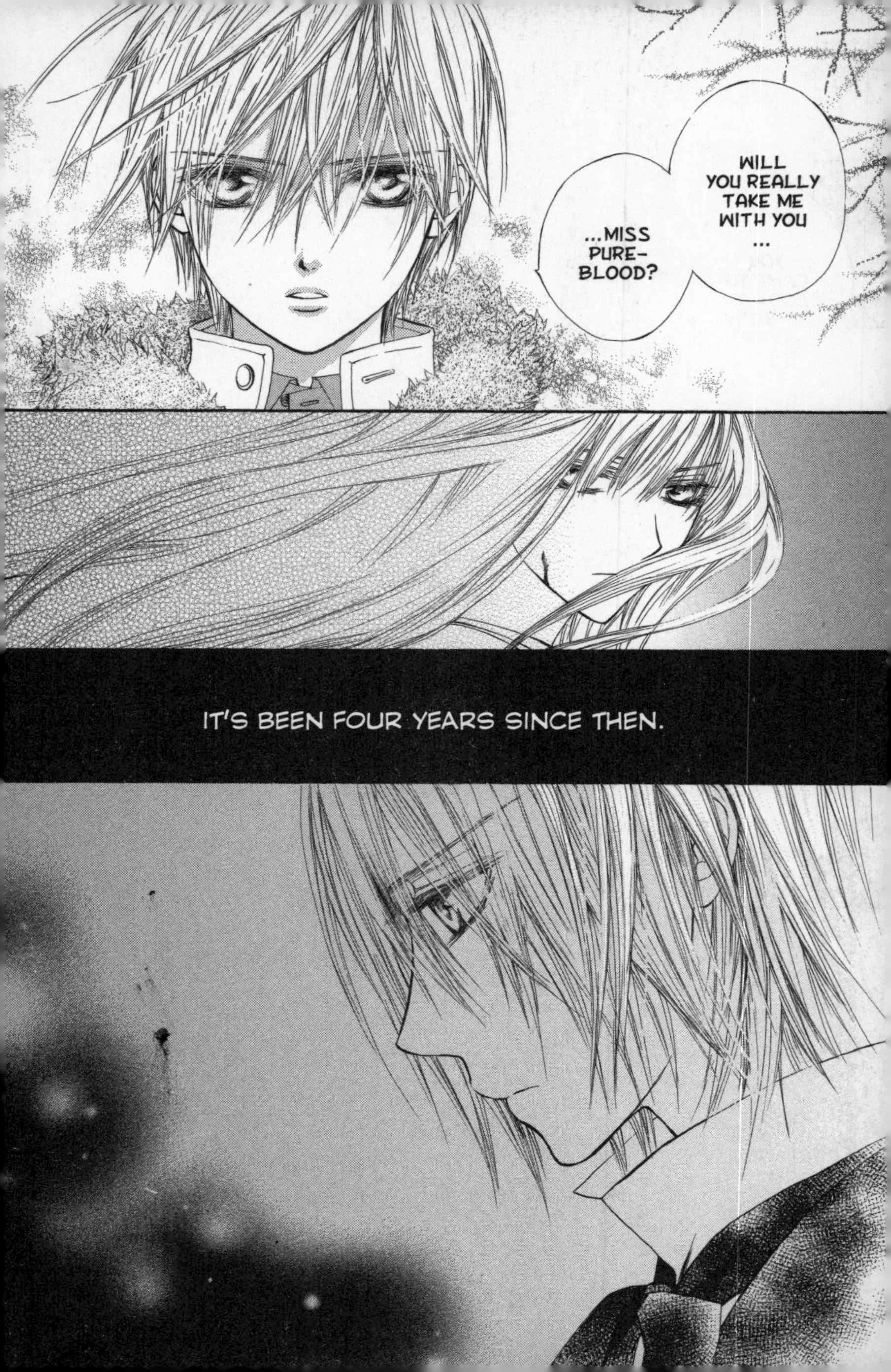
WILL YOU REALLY TAKE ME WITH YOU ...
...MISS PURE-BLOOD?
IT'S BEEN FOUR YEARS SINCE THEN.

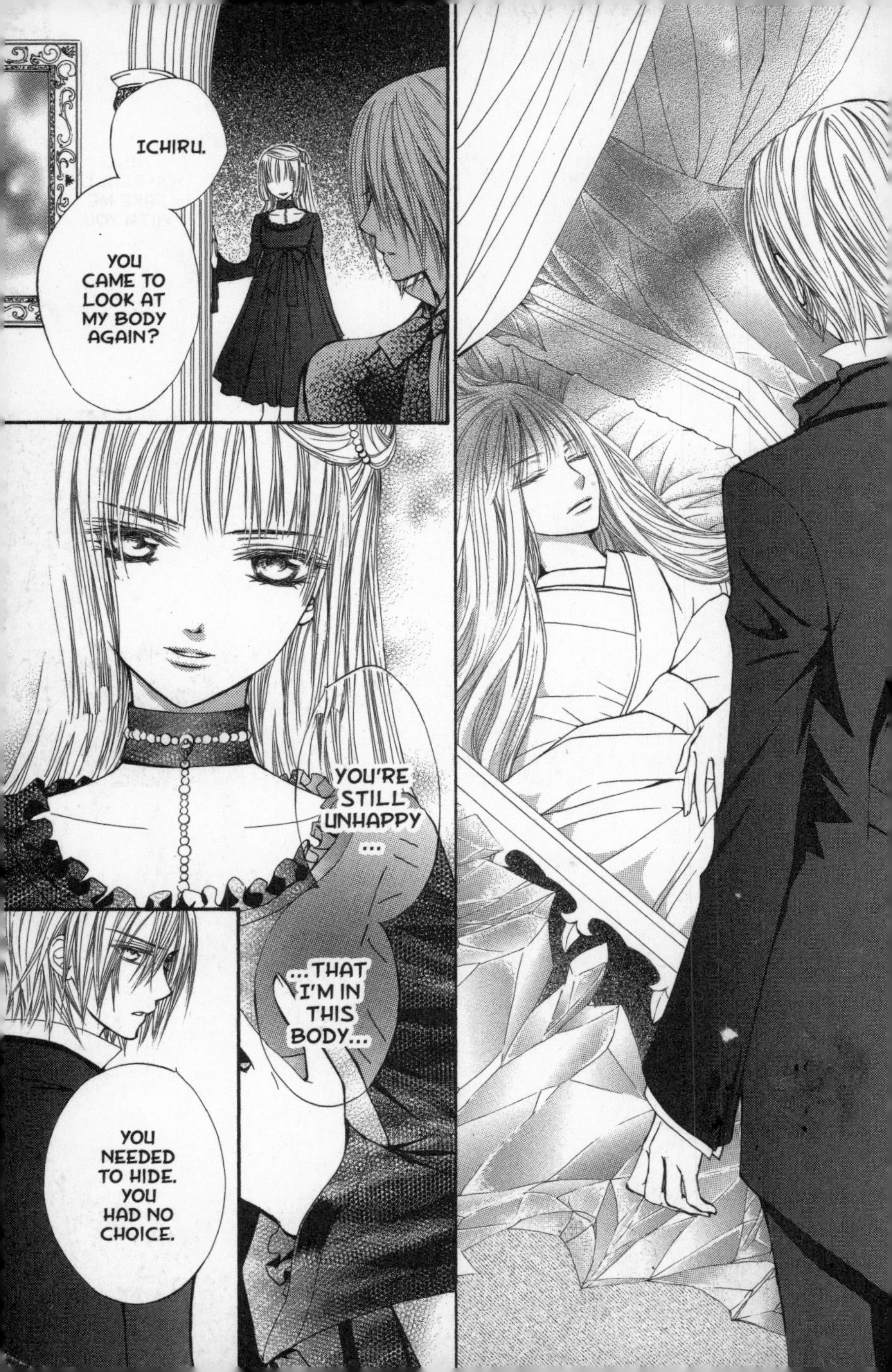
ICHIRU.
YOU CAME TO LOOK AT MY BODY AGAIN?
YOU'RE STILL UNHAPPY ...
...THAT I'M IN THIS BODY...
YOU NEEDED TO HIDE. YOU HAD NO CHOICE.

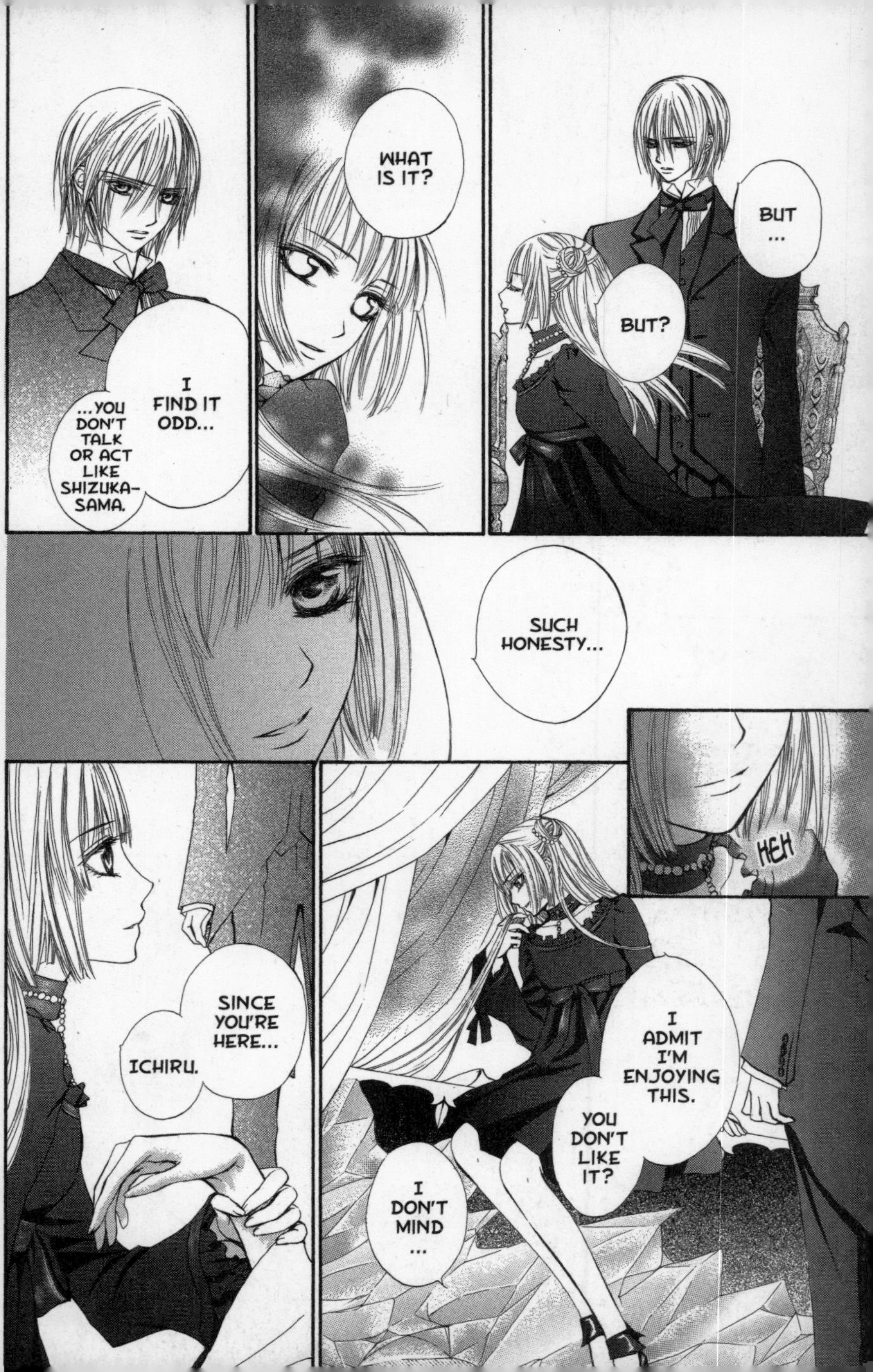

BUT ...
BUT?
WHAT IS IT?
I FIND IT ODD...
...YOU DON'T TALK OR ACT LIKE SHIZUKA-SAMA.
SUCH HONESTY...
HEH
I ADMIT I'M ENJOYING THIS.
YOU DON'T LIKE IT?
I DON'T MIND ...
SINCE YOU'RE HERE...
ICHIRU.

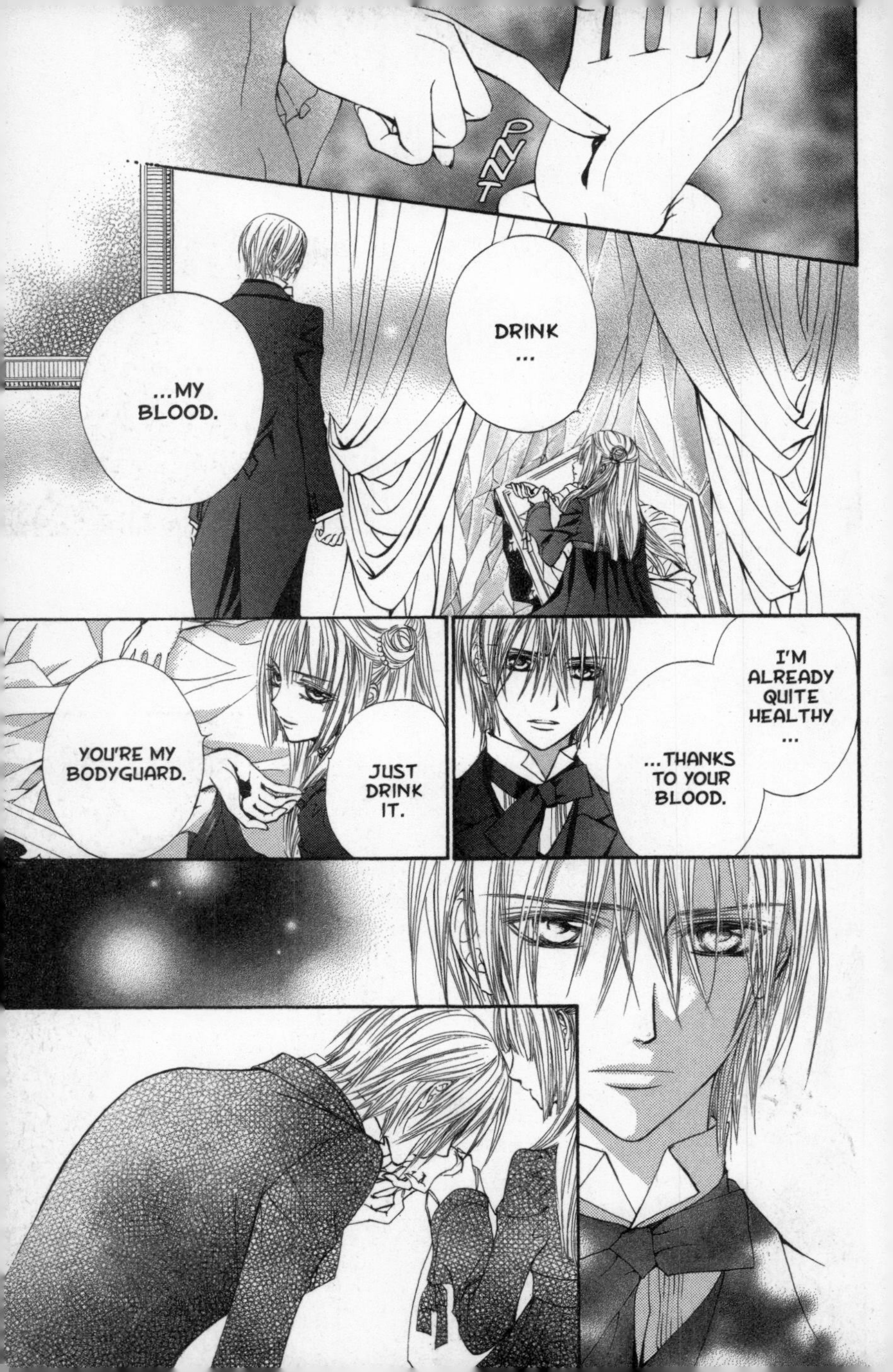
PNNT
DRINK ...
...MY BLOOD.
I'M ALREADY QUITE HEALTHY ...
...THANKS TO YOUR BLOOD.
JUST DRINK IT.
YOU'RE MY BODYGUARD.

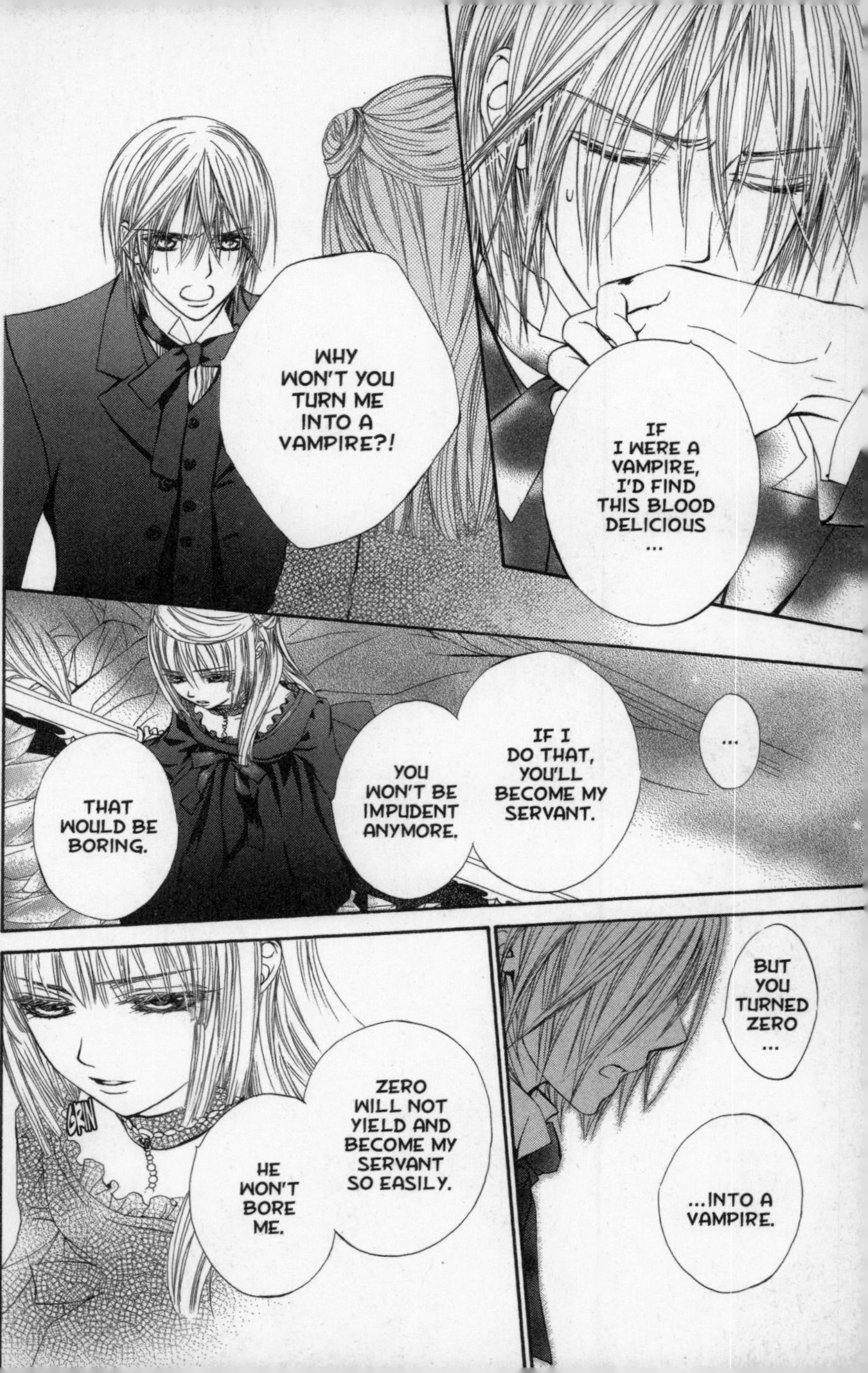
IF I WERE A VAMPIRE, I'D FIND THIS BLOOD DELICIOUS ...
WHY WON'T YOU TURN ME INTO A VAMPIRE?!
...
IF I DO THAT, YOU'LL BECOME MY SERVANT.
YOU WON'T BE IMPUDENT ANYMORE.
THAT WOULD BE BORING.
BUT YOU TURNED ZERO ...
...INTO A VAMPIRE.
ZERO WILL NOT YIELD AND BECOME MY SERVANT SO EASILY.
HE WON'T BORE ME.
GRIN

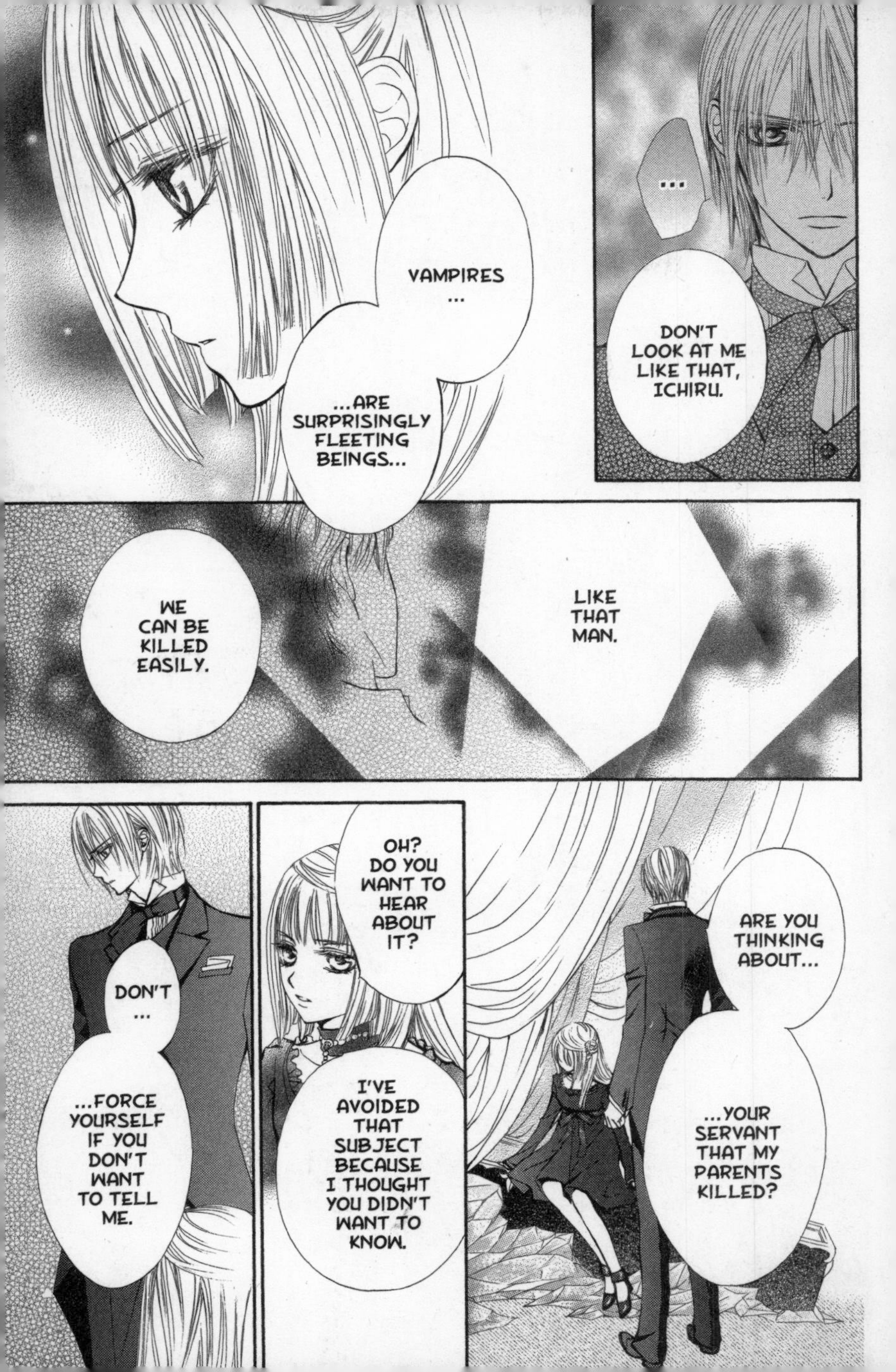
...
DON'T LOOK AT ME LIKE THAT, ICHIRU.
VAMPIRES ...
...ARE SURPRISINGLY FLEETING BEINGS...
LIKE THAT MAN.
WE CAN BE KILLED EASILY.
ARE YOU THINKING ABOUT...
...YOUR SERVANT THAT MY PARENTS KILLED?
OH? DO YOU WANT TO HEAR ABOUT IT?
I'VE AVOIDED THAT SUBJECT BECAUSE I THOUGHT YOU DIDN'T WANT TO KNOW.
DON'T ...
...FORCE YOURSELF IF YOU DON'T WANT TO TELL ME.

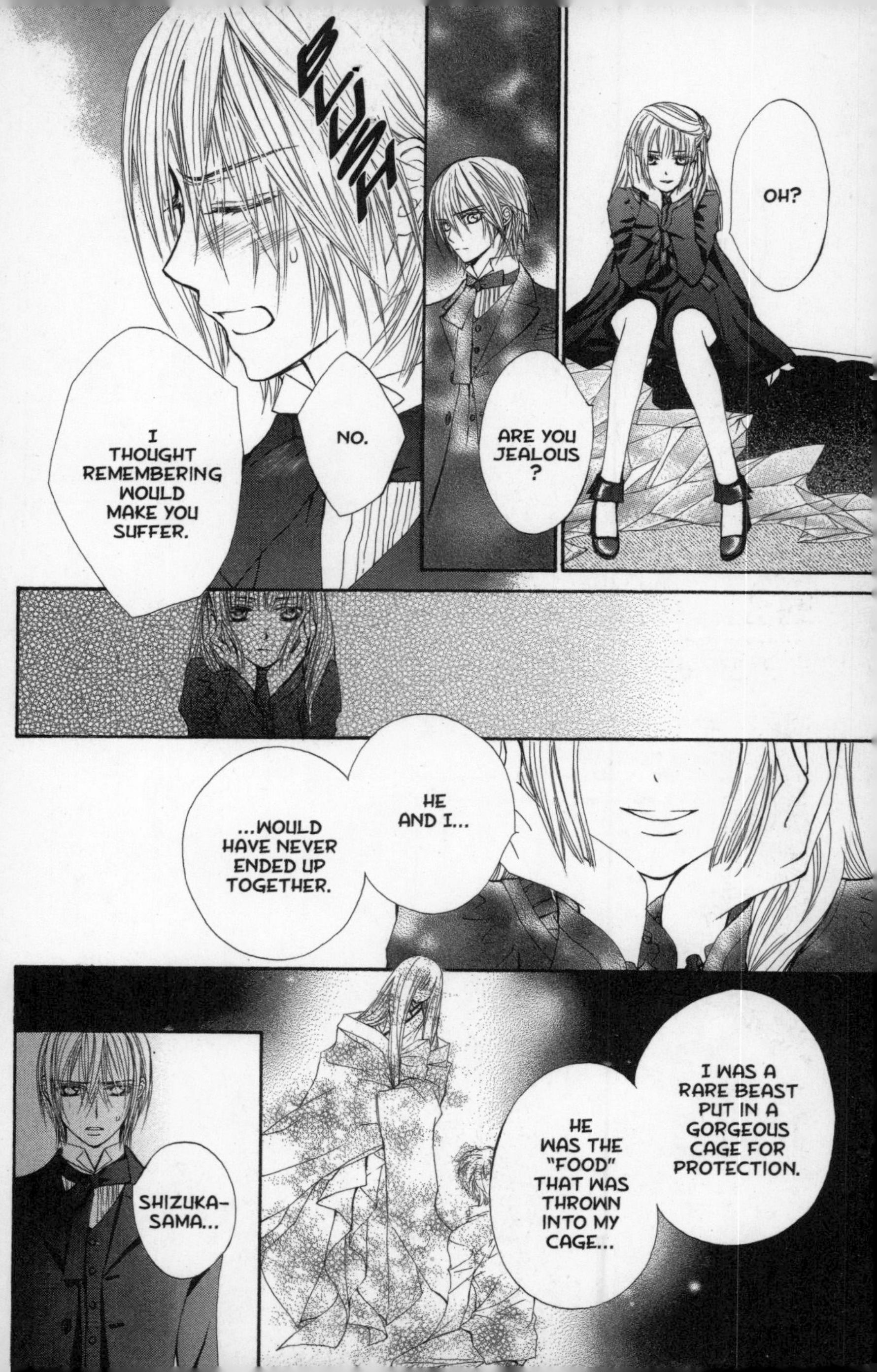
OH?
ARE YOU JEALOUS ?
NO.
I THOUGHT REMEMBERING WOULD MAKE YOU SUFFER.
HE AND I...
...WOULD HAVE NEVER ENDED UP TOGETHER.
I WAS A RARE BEAST PUT IN A GORGEOUS CAGE FOR PROTECTION.
HE WAS THE "FOOD" THAT WAS THROWN INTO MY CAGE...
SHIZUKA-SAMA...

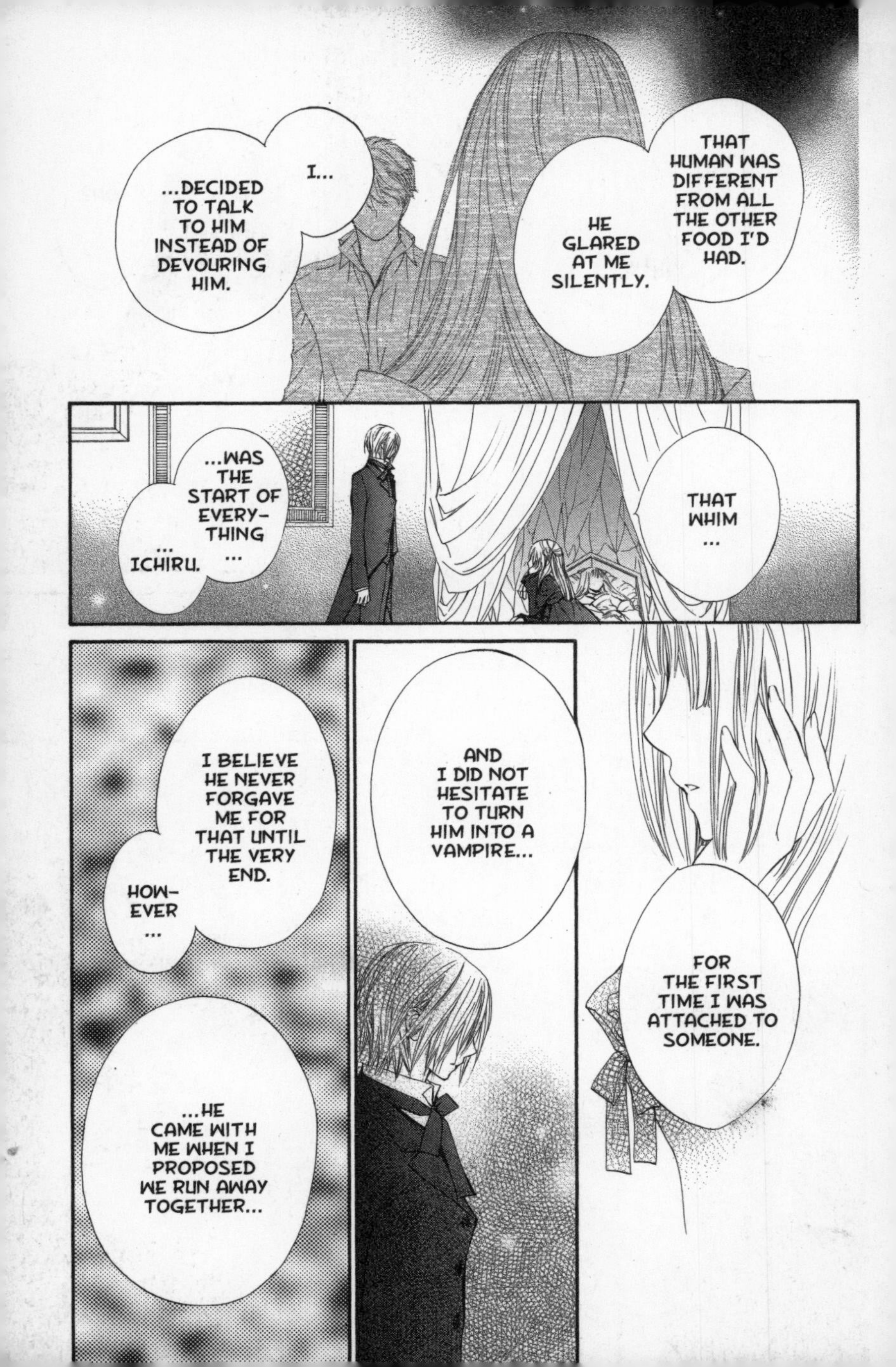
THAT HUMAN WAS DIFFERENT FROM ALL THE OTHER FOOD I'D HAD.
HE GLARED AT ME SILENTLY.
I...
...DECIDED TO TALK TO HIM INSTEAD OF DEVOURING HIM.
THAT WHIM...
...WAS THE START OF EVERYTHING...
...ICHIRU.
FOR THE FIRST TIME I WAS ATTACHED TO SOMEONE.
AND I DID NOT HESITATE TO TURN HIM INTO A VAMPIRE...
I BELIEVE HE NEVER FORGAVE ME FOR THAT UNTIL THE VERY END.
HOW-EVER...
...HE CAME WITH ME WHEN I PROPOSED WE RUN AWAY TOGETHER...

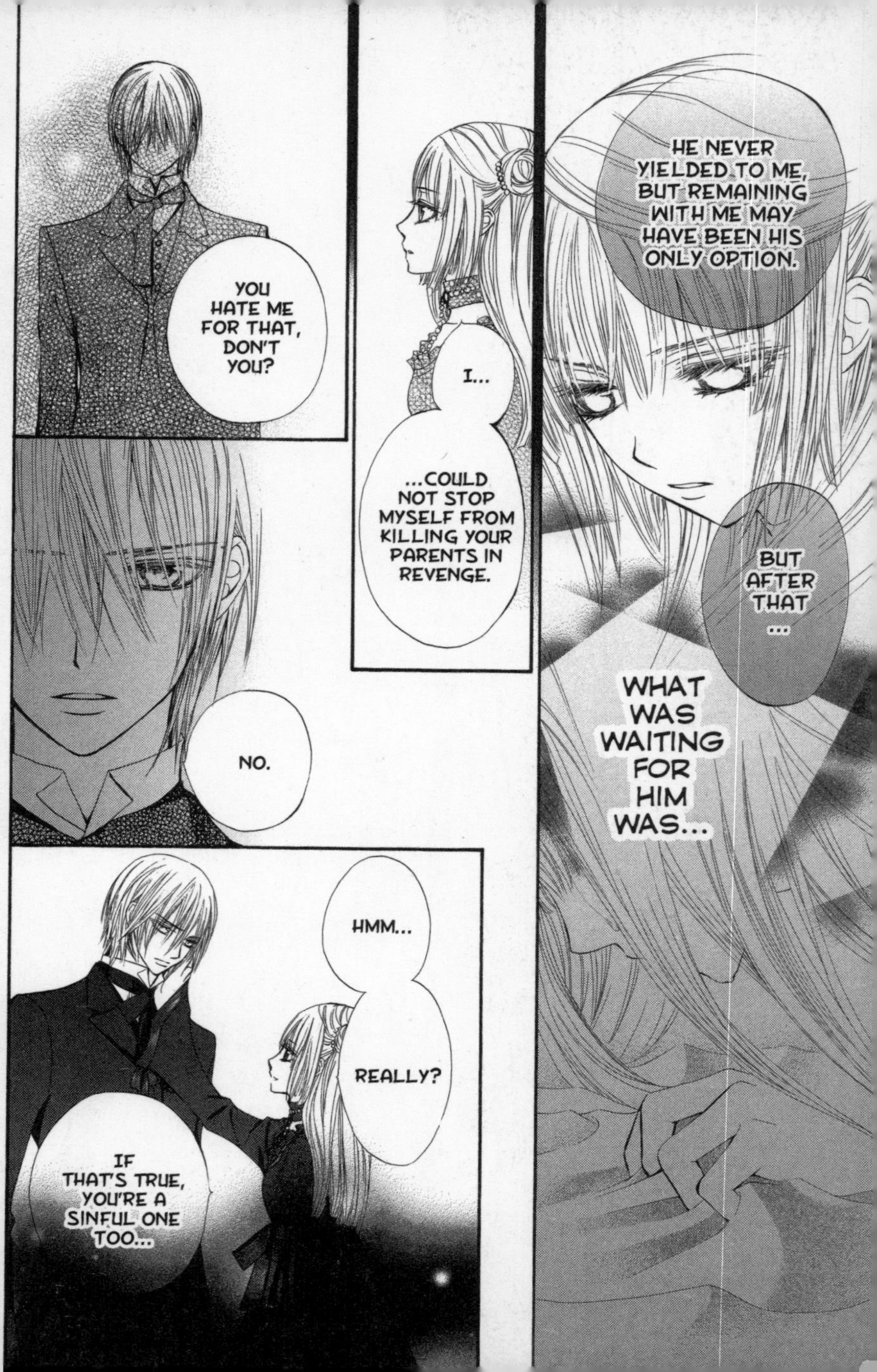
HE NEVER YIELDED TO ME, BUT REMAINING WITH ME MAY HAVE BEEN HIS ONLY OPTION.
BUT AFTER THAT ...
WHAT WAS WAITING FOR HIM WAS...
I...
...COULD NOT STOP MYSELF FROM KILLING YOUR PARENTS IN REVENGE.
YOU HATE ME FOR THAT, DON'T YOU?
NO.
HMM...
REALLY?
IF THAT'S TRUE, YOU'RE A SINFUL ONE TOO...

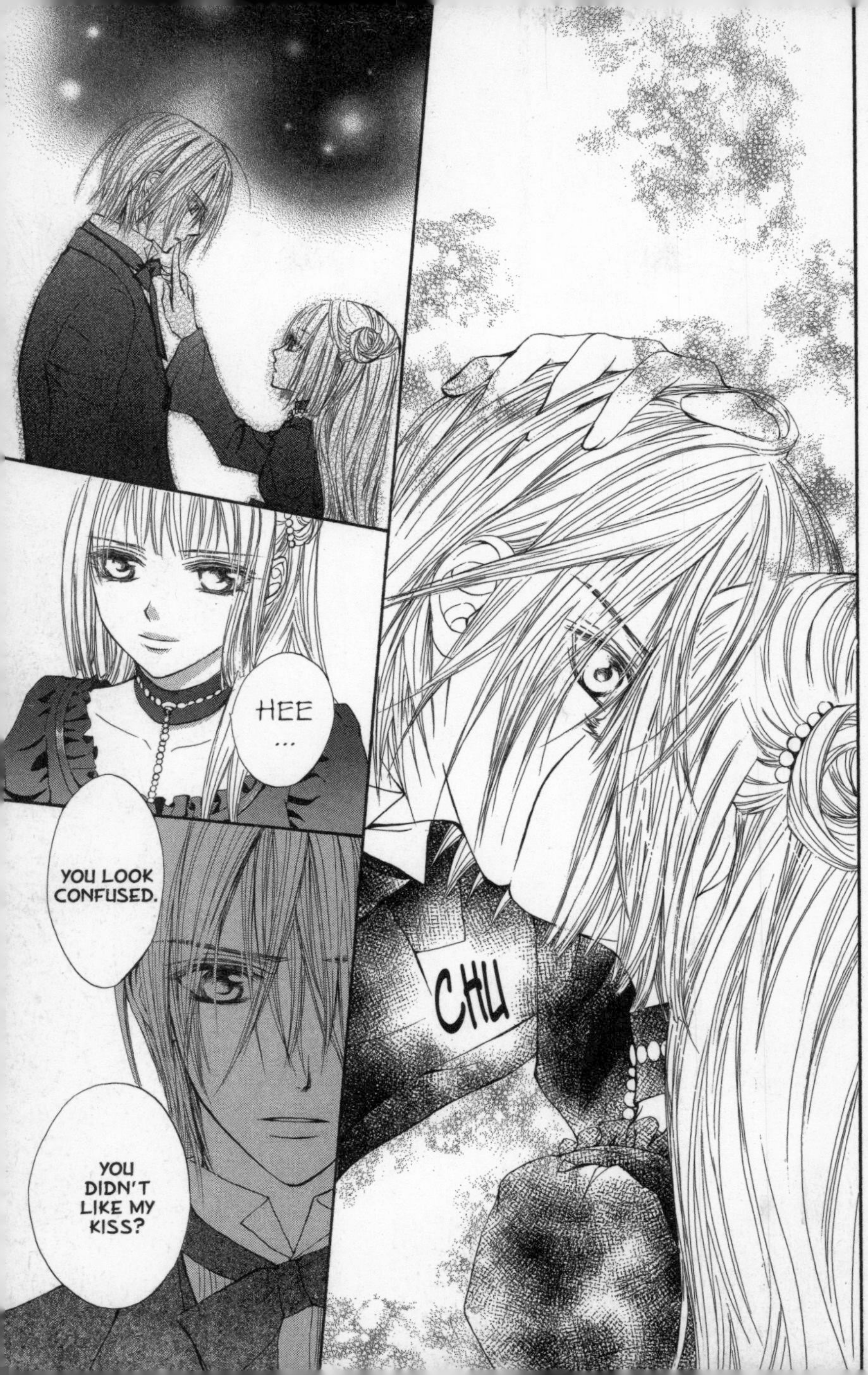
CHU
HEE ...
YOU LOOK CONFUSED.
YOU DIDN'T LIKE MY KISS?

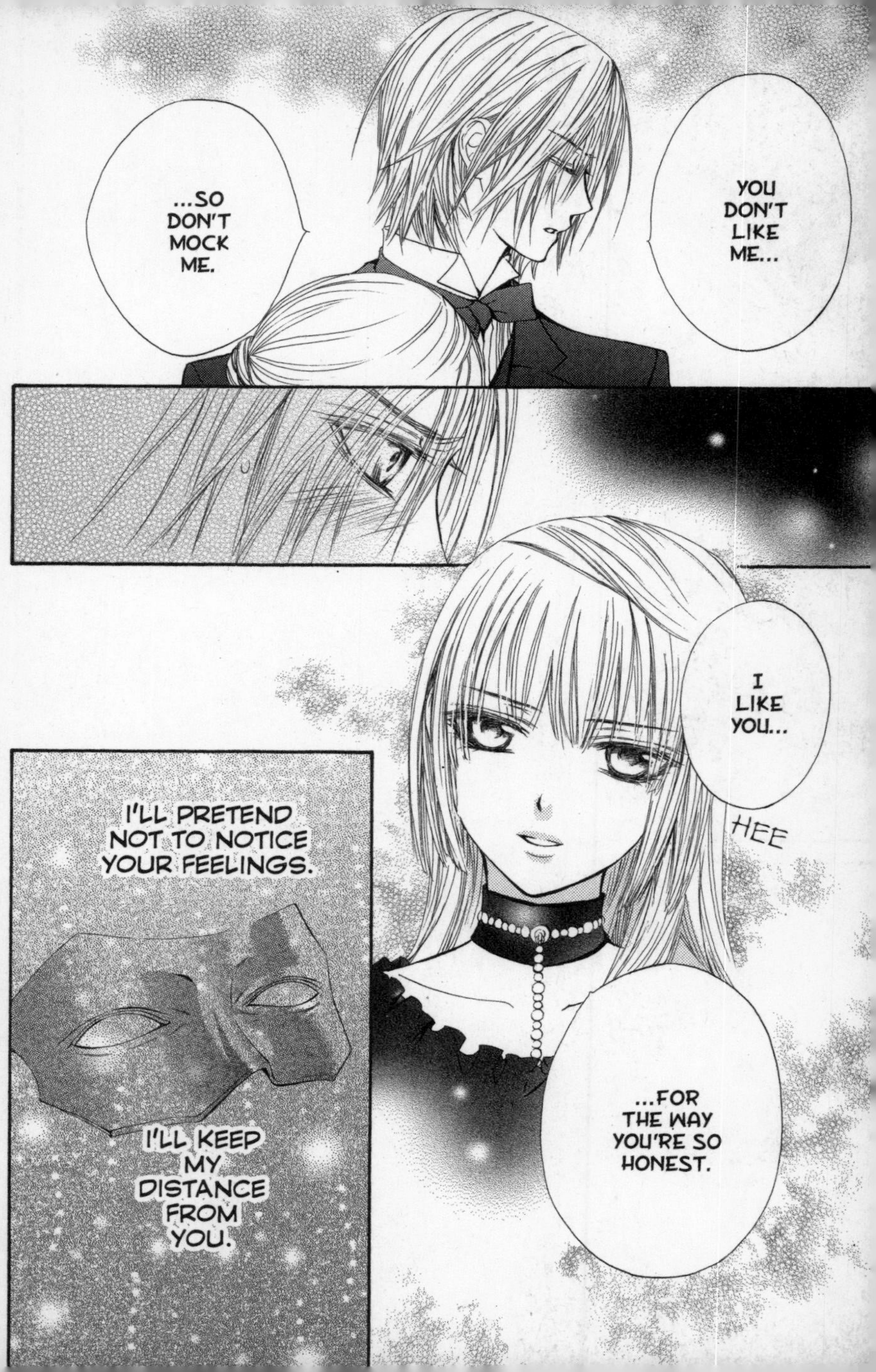
YOU DON'T LIKE ME...
...SO DON'T MOCK ME.
I LIKE YOU...
HEE
...FOR THE WAY YOU'RE SO HONEST.
I'LL PRETEND NOT TO NOTICE YOUR FEELINGS.
I'LL KEEP MY DISTANCE FROM YOU.

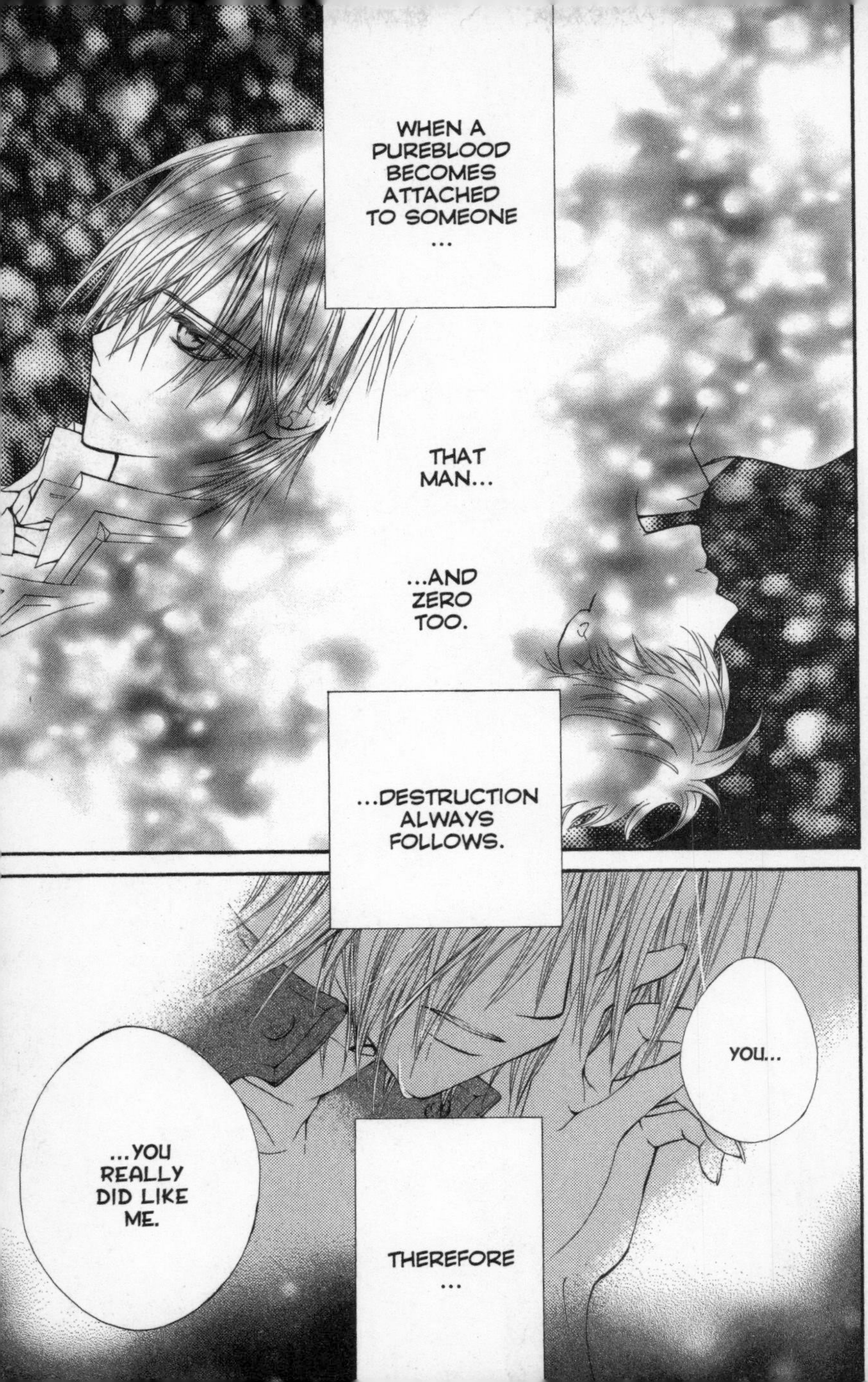
WHEN A PUREBLOOD BECOMES ATTACHED TO SOMEONE ...
THAT MAN...
...AND ZERO TOO.
...DESTRUCTION ALWAYS FOLLOWS.
YOU...
...YOU REALLY DID LIKE ME.
THEREFORE ...

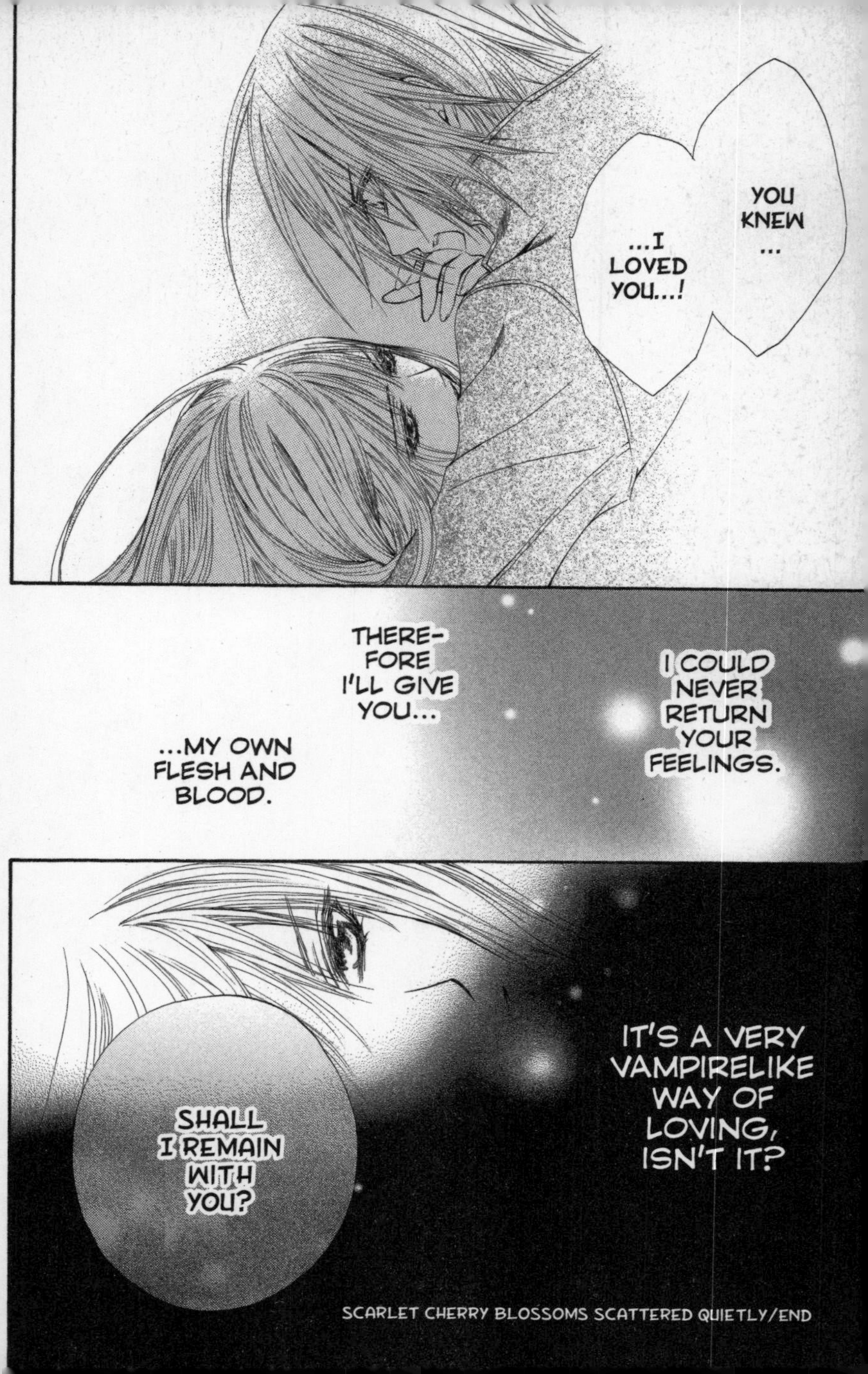
YOU KNEW ...
...I LOVED YOU...!
I COULD NEVER RETURN YOUR FEELINGS.
THERE-FORE I'LL GIVE YOU...
...MY OWN FLESH AND BLOOD.
IT'S A VERY VAMPIRELIKE WAY OF LOVING, ISN'T IT?
SHALL I REMAIN WITH YOU?
SCARLET CHERRY BLOSSOMS SCATTERED QUIETLY/END

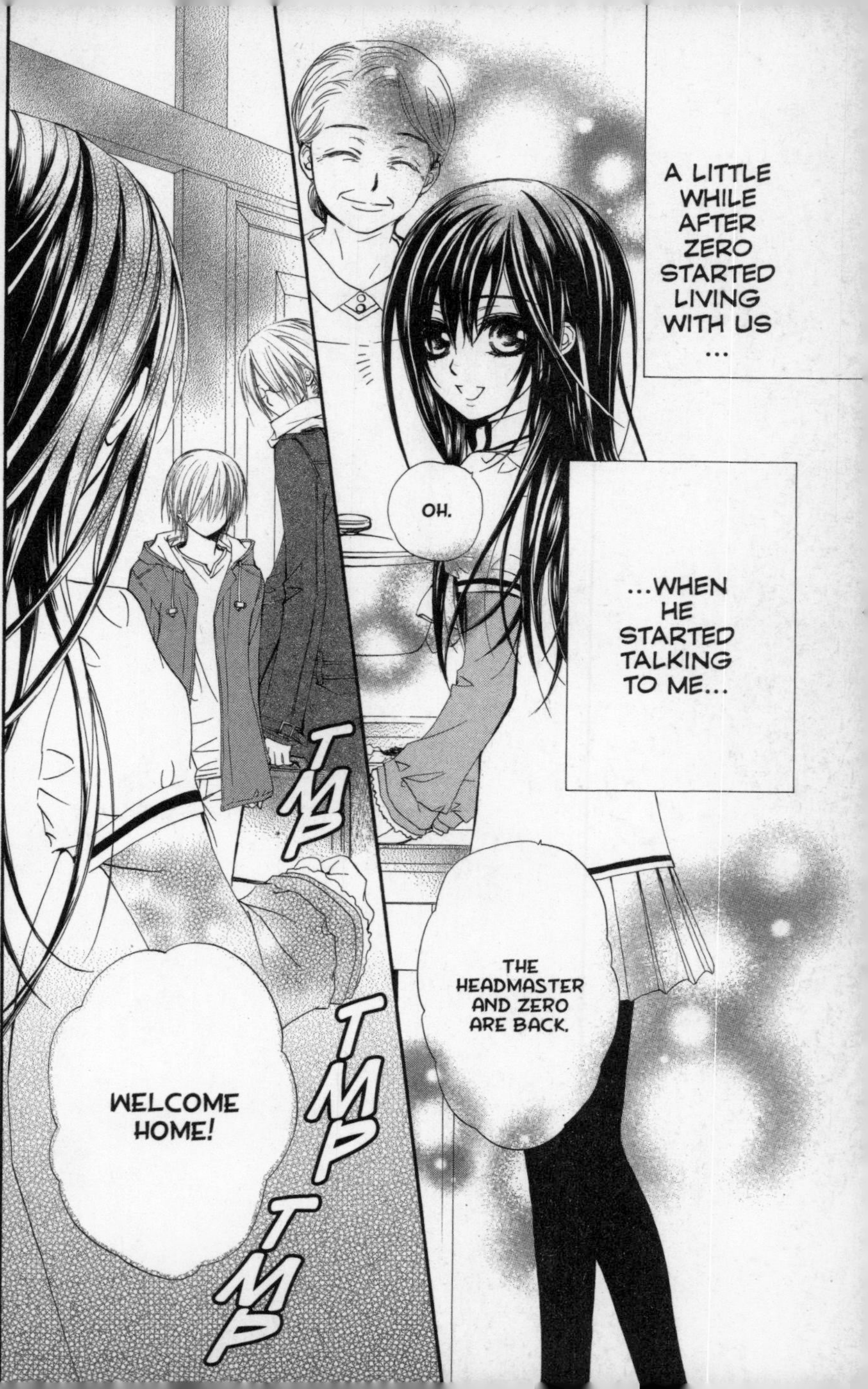
A LITTLE WHILE AFTER ZERO STARTED LIVING WITH US ...
OH.
...WHEN HE STARTED TALKING TO ME...
THE HEADMASTER AND ZERO ARE BACK.
TMP
TMP
TMP
TMP
WELCOME HOME!

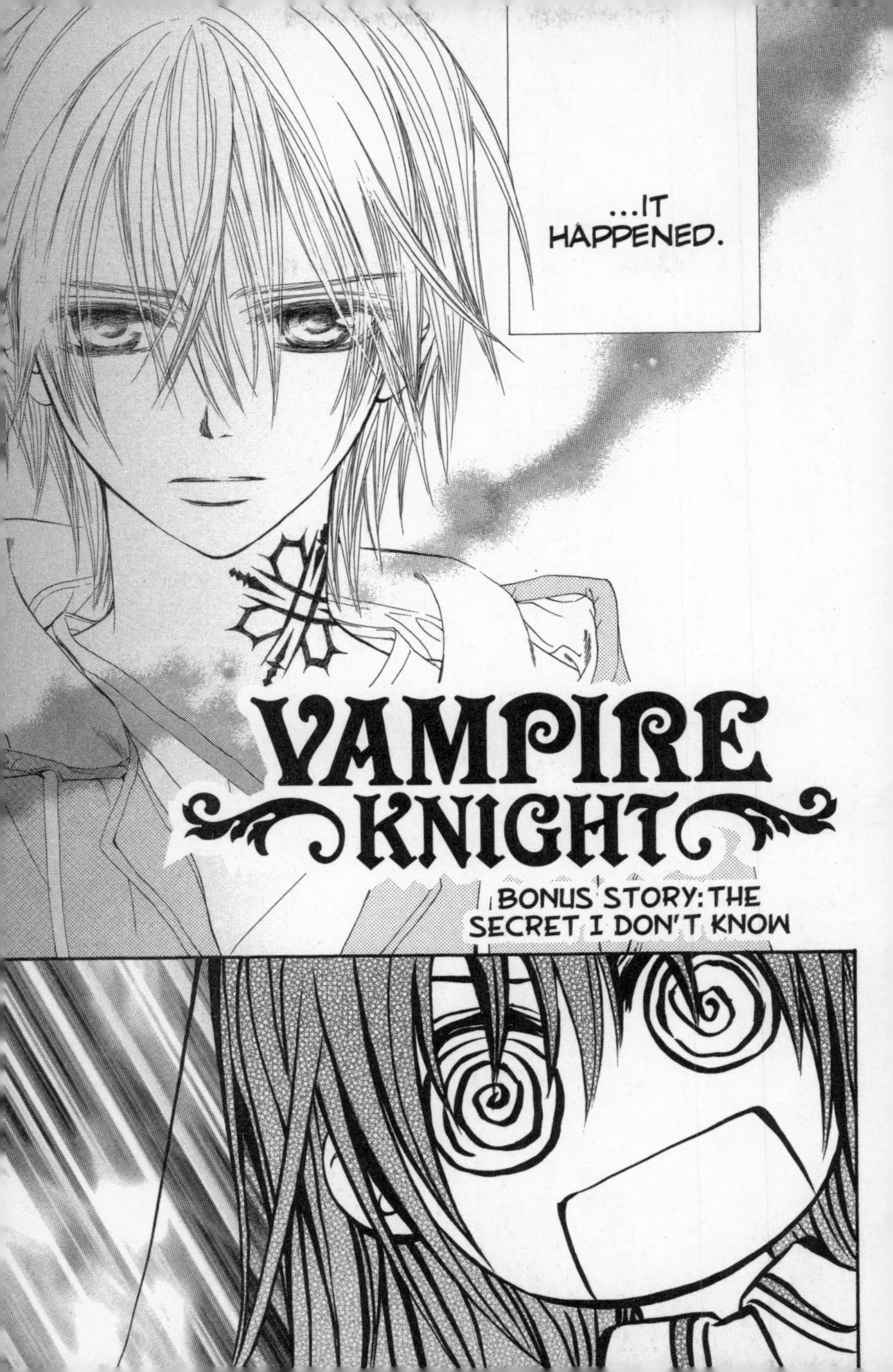
...IT HAPPENED.
VAMPIRE KNIGHT
BONUS STORY: THE SECRET I DON'T KNOW

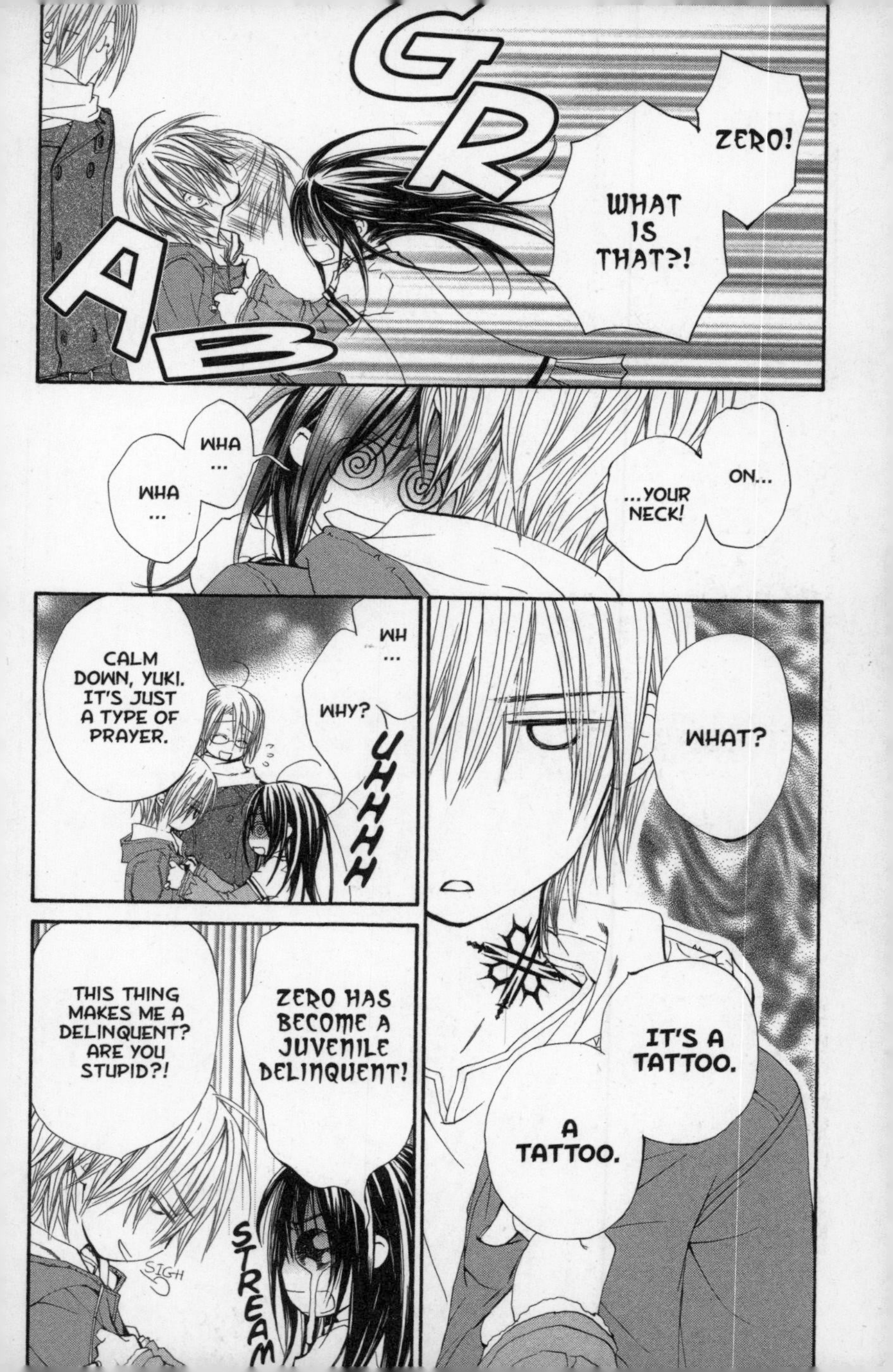
ZERO!
WHAT IS THAT?!
GRAB
ON... ...YOUR NECK!
WHA... WHA...
WHAT?
IT'S A TATTOO.
A TATTOO.
WH... WHY?
UHHHH
CALM DOWN, YUKI. IT'S JUST A TYPE OF PRAYER.
ZERO HAS BECOME A JUVENILE DELINQUENT!
STREAM
THIS THING MAKES ME A DELINQUENT? ARE YOU STUPID?!
SIGH

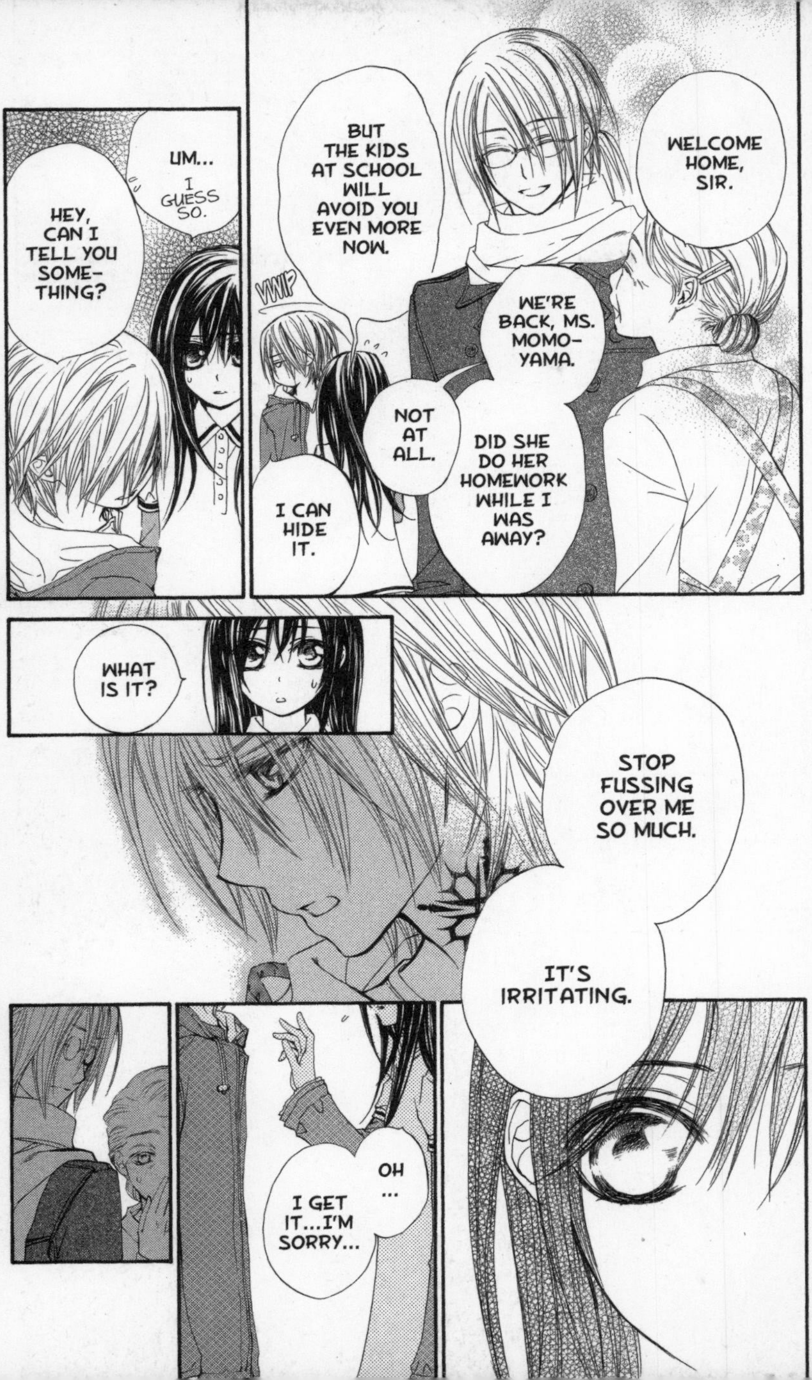
WELCOME HOME, SIR.
WE'RE BACK, MS. MOMOYAMA.
DID SHE DO HER HOMEWORK WHILE I WAS AWAY?
NOT AT ALL.
BUT THE KIDS AT SCHOOL WILL AVOID YOU EVEN MORE NOW.
VWIP
I CAN HIDE IT.
UM... I GUESS SO.
HEY, CAN I TELL YOU SOMETHING?
WHAT IS IT?
STOP FUSSING OVER ME SO MUCH.
IT'S IRRITATING.
OH...
I GET IT...I'M SORRY...

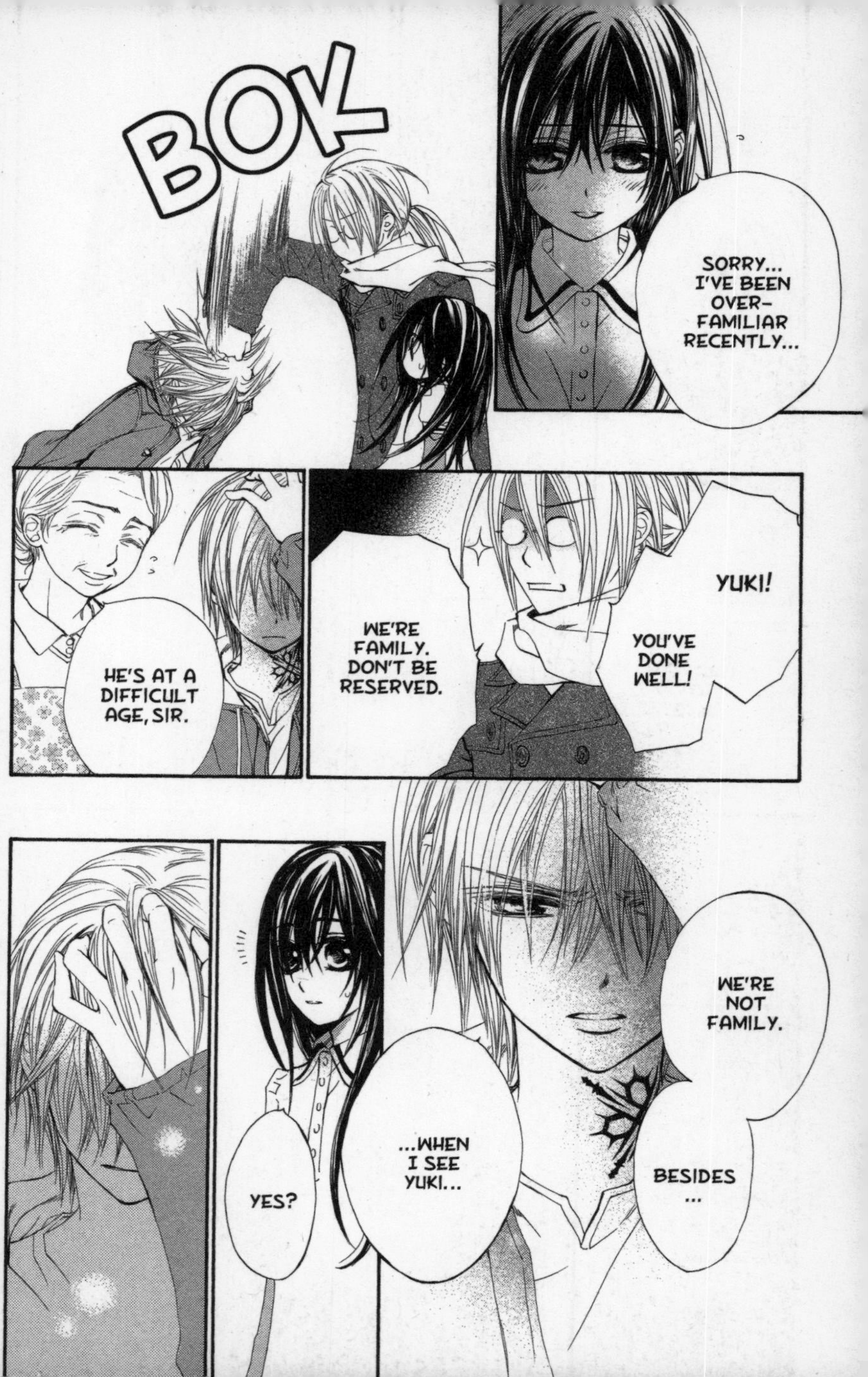
SORRY... I'VE BEEN OVER-FAMILIAR RECENTLY...
BOK
YUKI!
YOU'VE DONE WELL!
WE'RE FAMILY. DON'T BE RESERVED.
HE'S AT A DIFFICULT AGE, SIR.
WE'RE NOT FAMILY.
BESIDES ...
...WHEN I SEE YUKI...
YES?

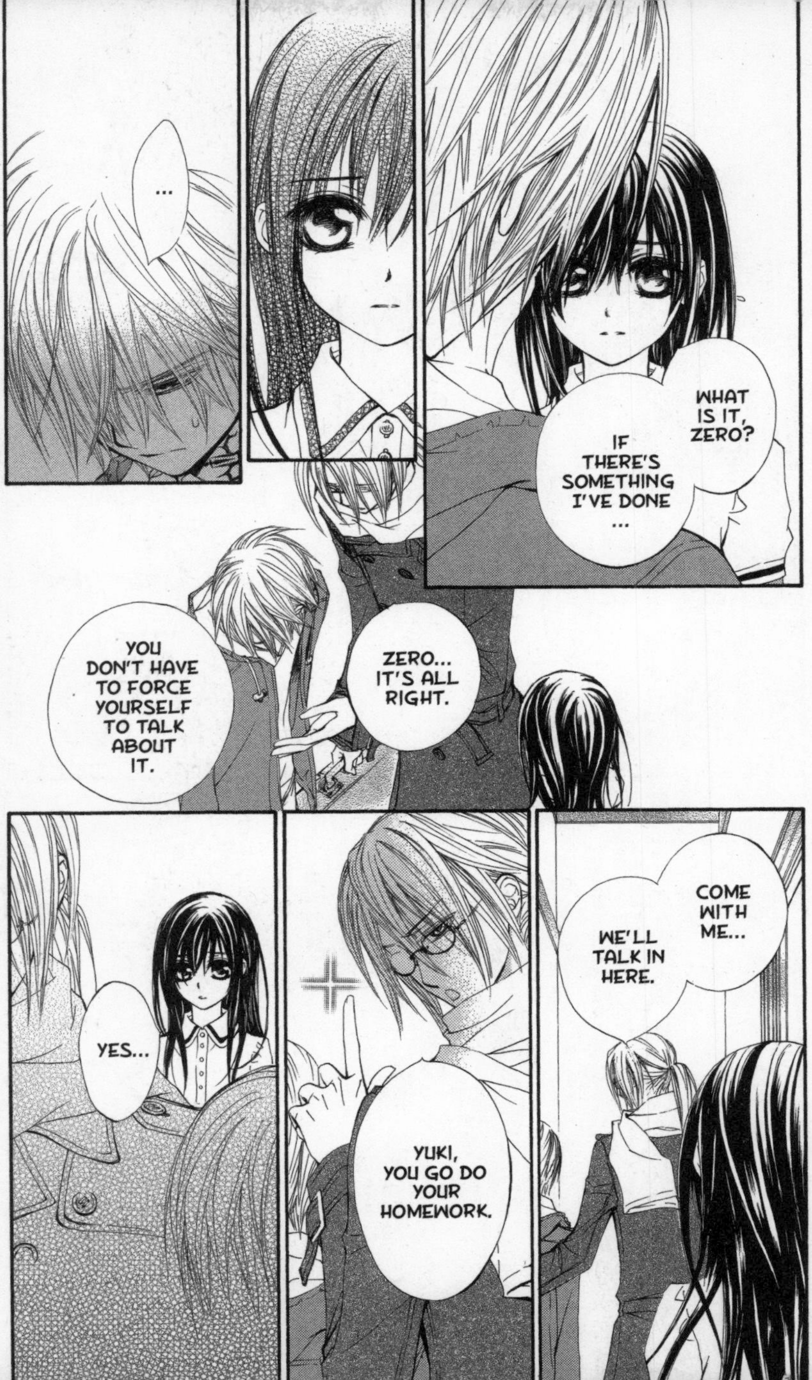
WHAT IS IT, ZERO?
IF THERE'S SOMETHING I'VE DONE ...
...
ZERO... IT'S ALL RIGHT.
YOU DON'T HAVE TO FORCE YOURSELF TO TALK ABOUT IT.
COME WITH ME...
WE'LL TALK IN HERE.
YUKI, YOU GO DO YOUR HOMEWORK.
YES...

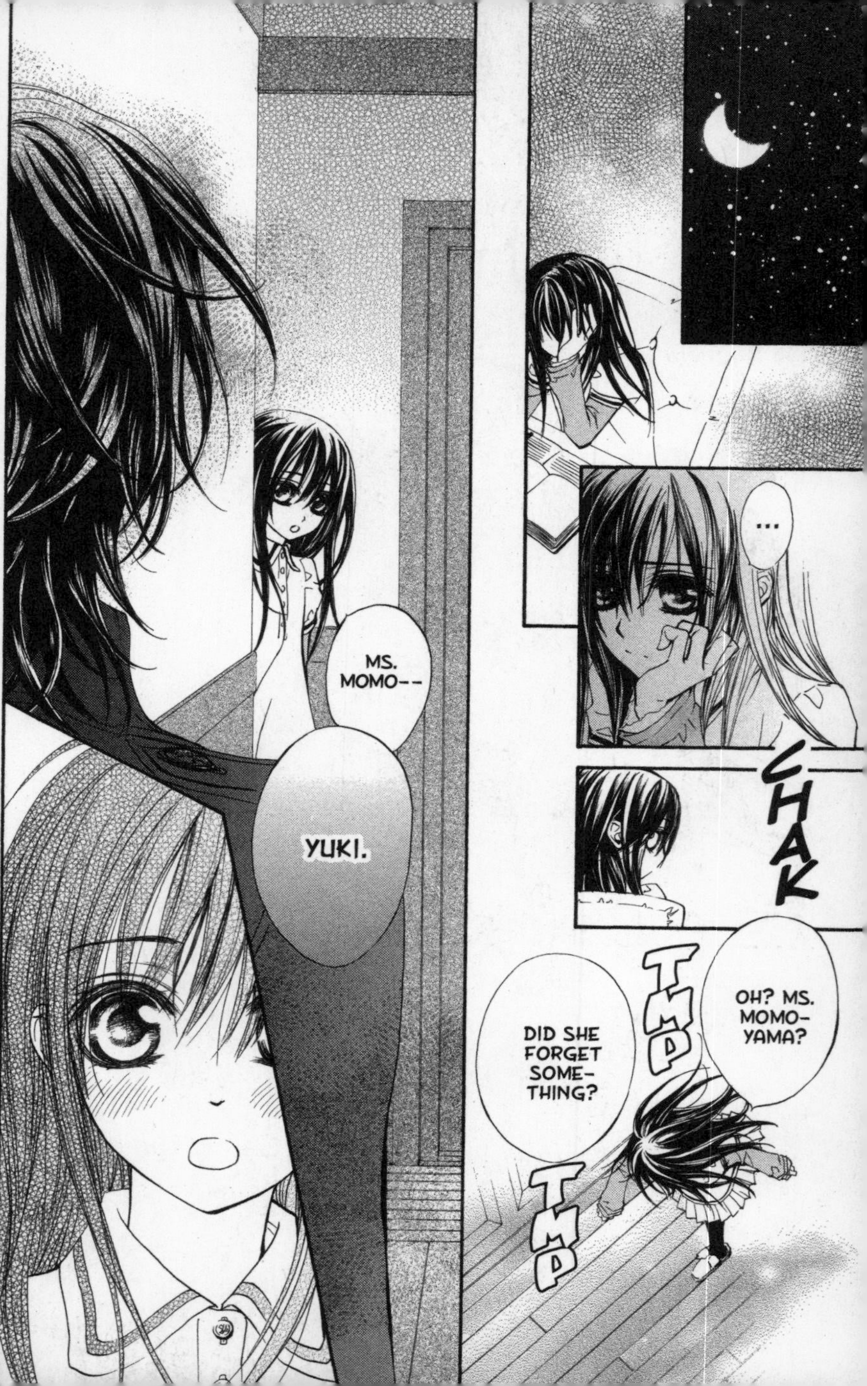
...
CHAK
OH? MS. MOMO-YAMA?
TMP
DID SHE FORGET SOME-THING?
TMP
MS. MOMO--
YUKI.

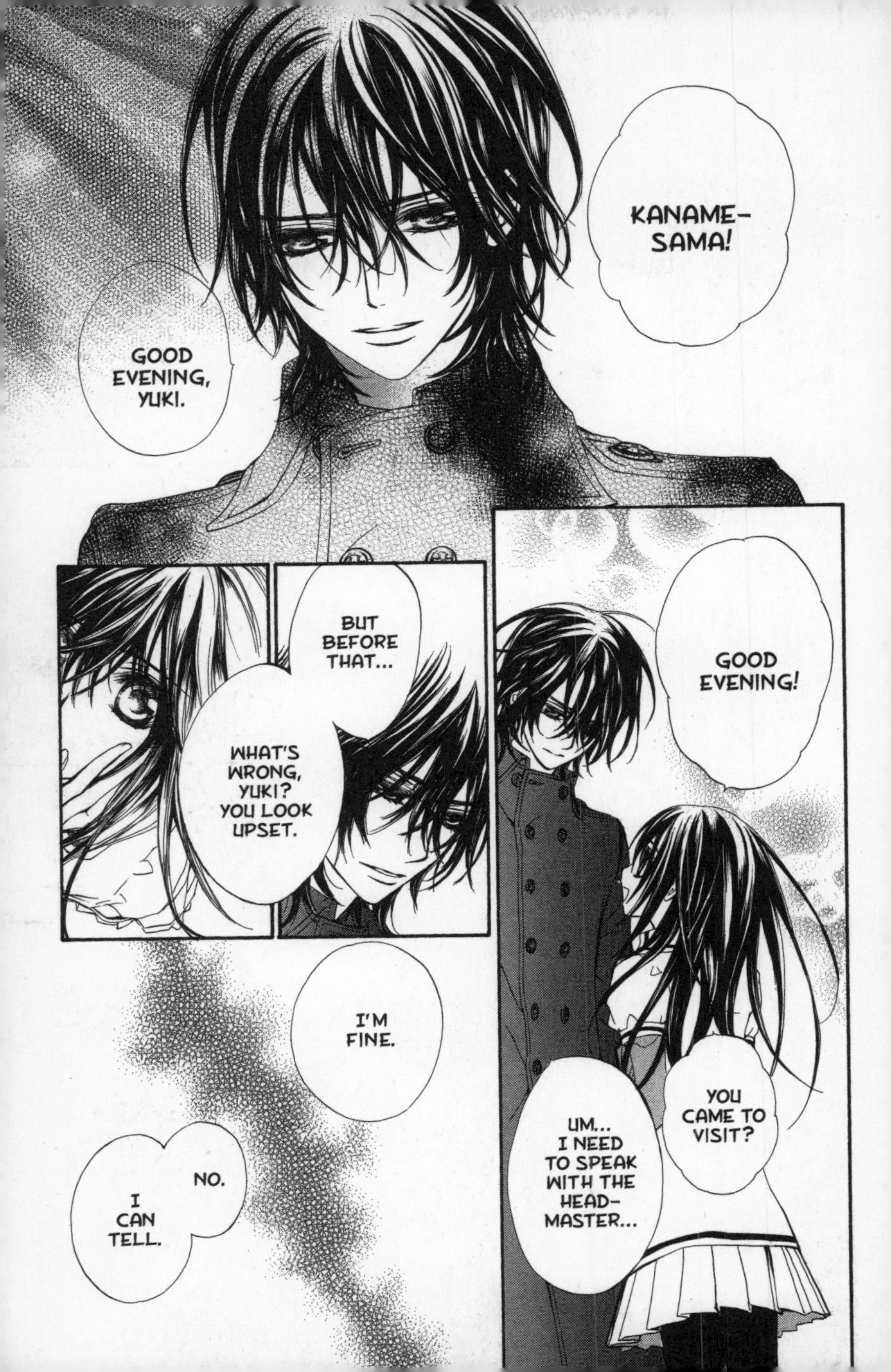
KANAME-SAMA!
GOOD EVENING, YUKI.
GOOD EVENING!
YOU CAME TO VISIT?
UM... I NEED TO SPEAK WITH THE HEAD-MASTER...
BUT BEFORE THAT...
WHAT'S WRONG, YUKI? YOU LOOK UPSET.
I'M FINE.
NO.
I CAN TELL.

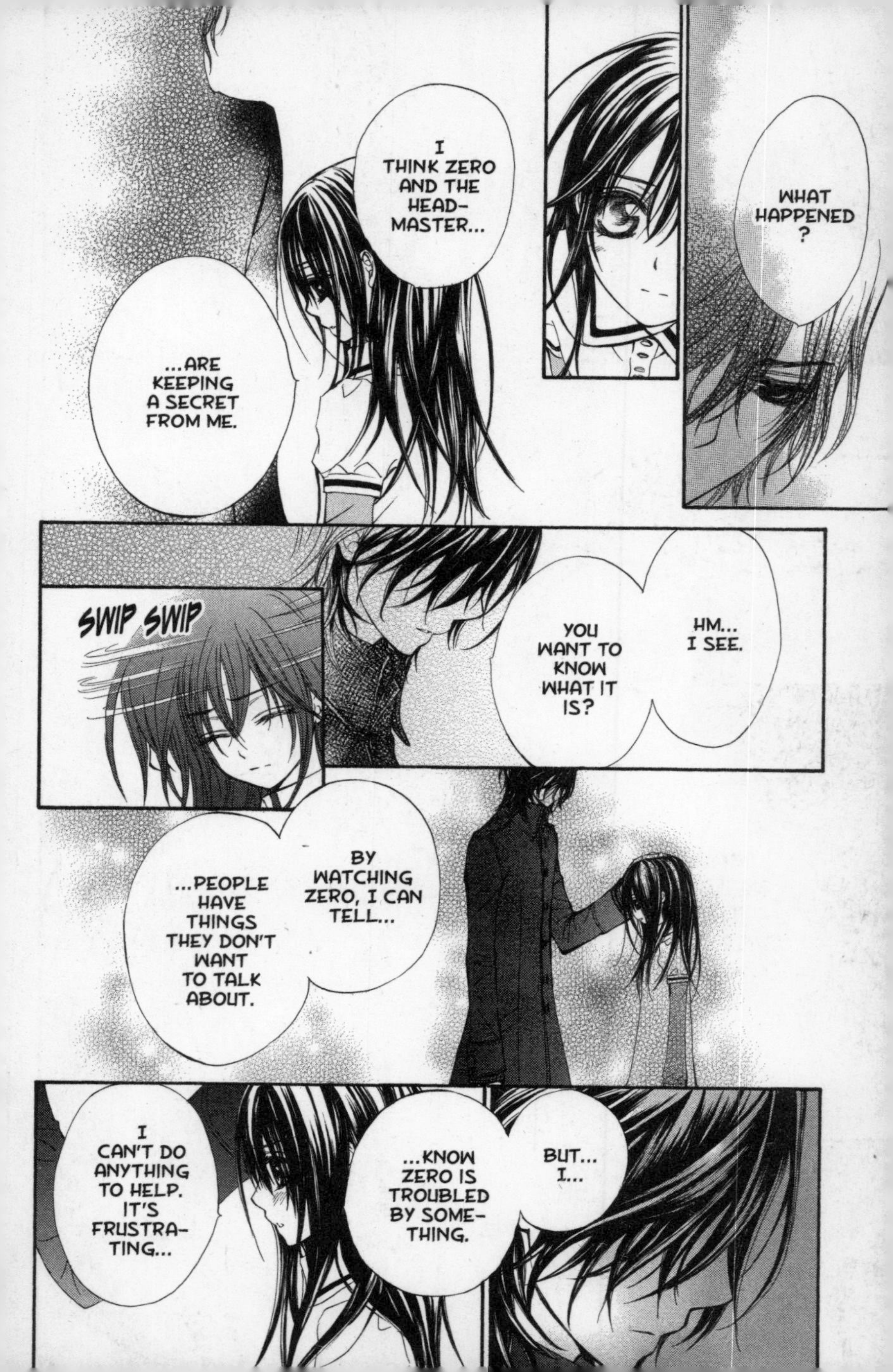
WHAT HAPPENED?
I THINK ZERO AND THE HEADMASTER...
...ARE KEEPING A SECRET FROM ME.
HM... I SEE.
YOU WANT TO KNOW WHAT IT IS?
SWIP SWIP
BY WATCHING ZERO, I CAN TELL...
...PEOPLE HAVE THINGS THEY DON'T WANT TO TALK ABOUT.
BUT... I...
...KNOW ZERO IS TROUBLED BY SOMETHING.
I CAN'T DO ANYTHING TO HELP. IT'S FRUSTRATING...

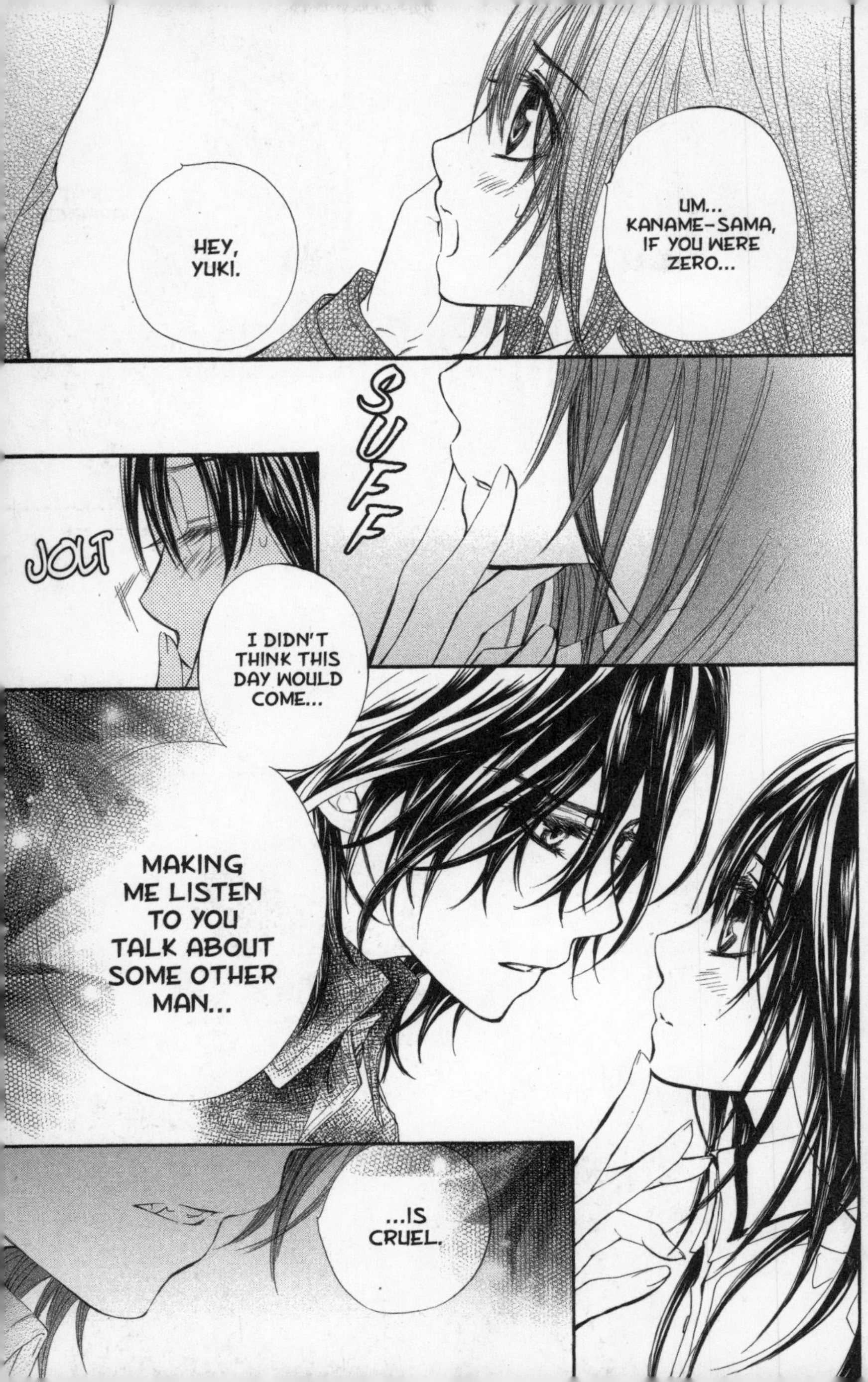
UM... KANAME-SAMA, IF YOU WERE ZERO...
HEY, YUKI.
SUFF
JOLT
I DIDN'T THINK THIS DAY WOULD COME...
MAKING ME LISTEN TO YOU TALK ABOUT SOME OTHER MAN...
...IS CRUEL.

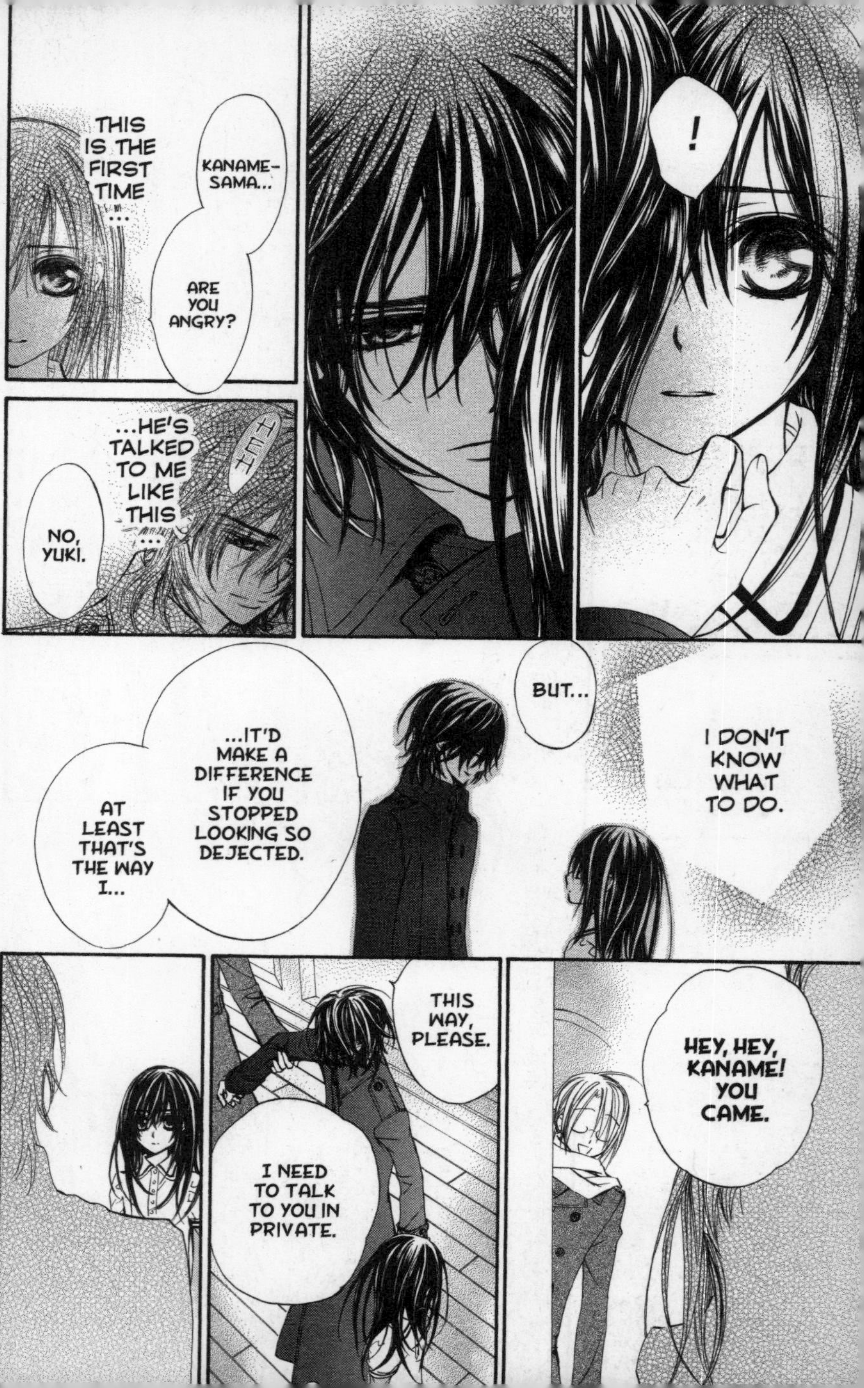
!
KANAME-SAMA...
ARE YOU ANGRY?
THIS IS THE FIRST TIME...
...HE'S TALKED TO ME LIKE THIS...
HEH
NO, YUKI.
I DON'T KNOW WHAT TO DO.
BUT...
...IT'D MAKE A DIFFERENCE IF YOU STOPPED LOOKING SO DEJECTED.
AT LEAST THAT'S THE WAY I...
HEY, HEY, KANAME! YOU CAME.
THIS WAY, PLEASE.
I NEED TO TALK TO YOU IN PRIVATE.

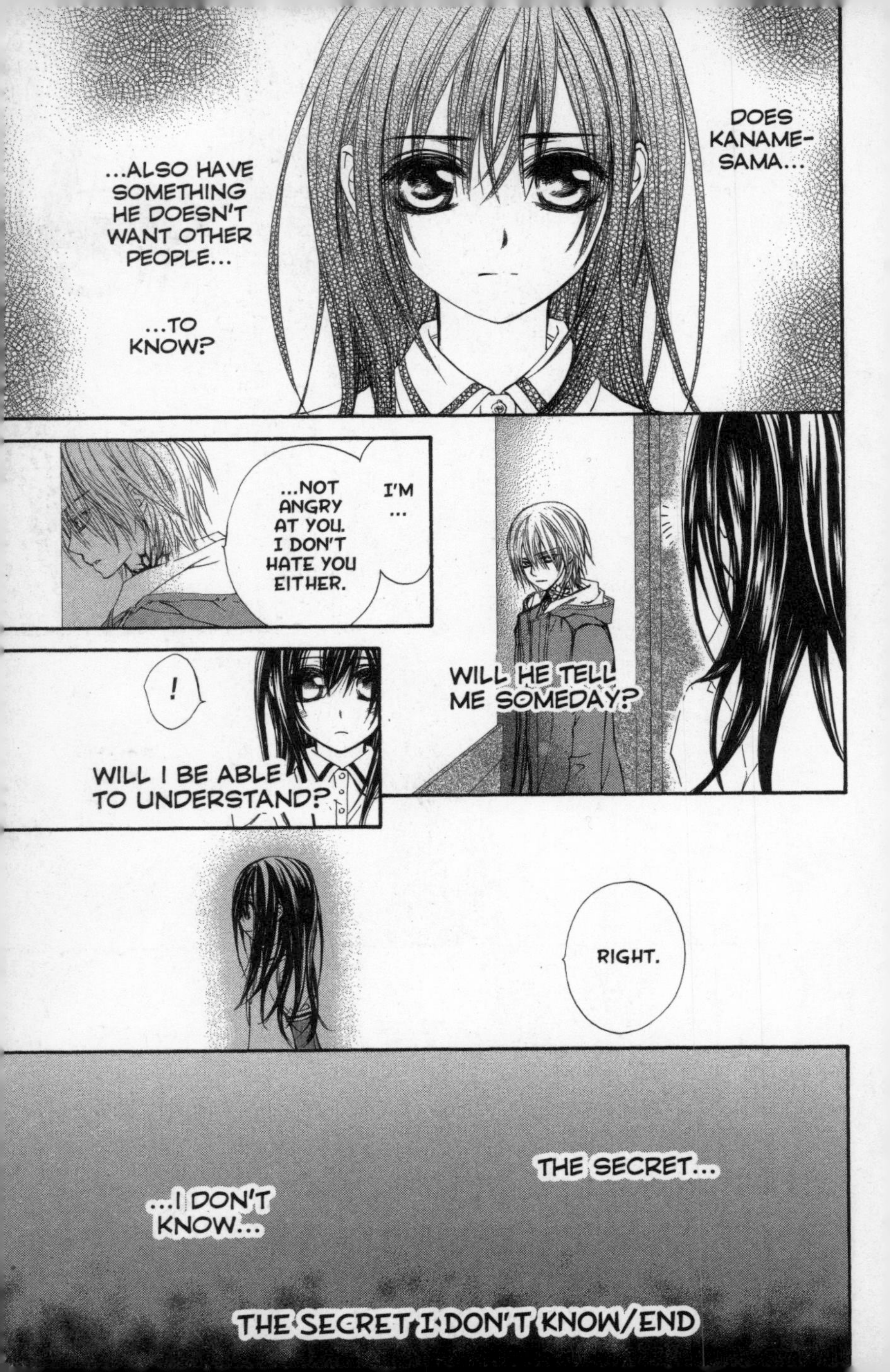
DOES KANAME-SAMA...
...ALSO HAVE SOMETHING HE DOESN'T WANT OTHER PEOPLE...
...TO KNOW?
WILL HE TELL ME SOMEDAY?
I'M...
...NOT ANGRY AT YOU. I DON'T HATE YOU EITHER.
!
WILL I BE ABLE TO UNDERSTAND?
RIGHT.
THE SECRET...
...I DON'T KNOW...
THE SECRET I DON'T KNOW/END

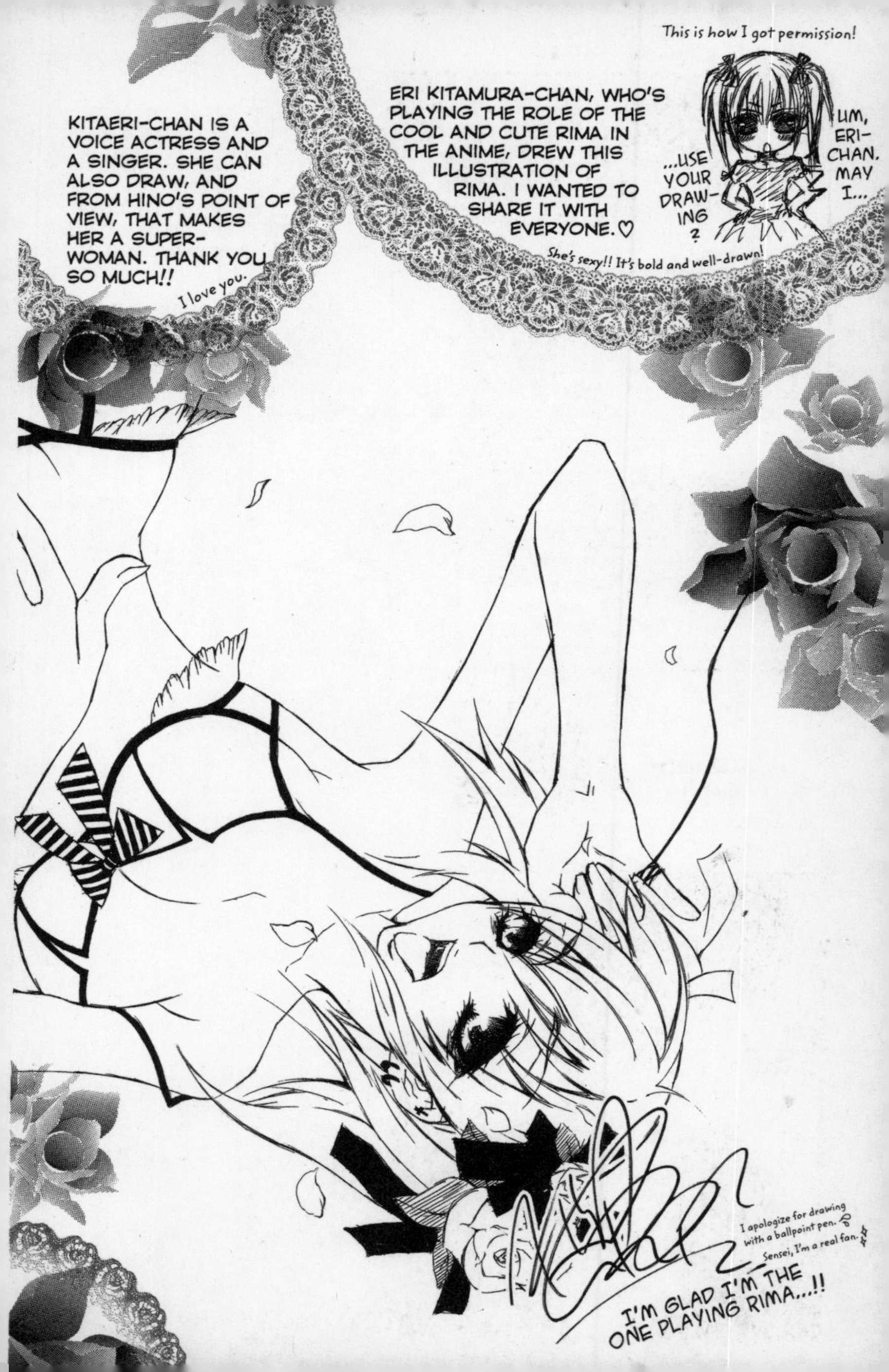
This is how I got permission!
UM, ERI-CHAN. MAY I...
...USE YOUR DRAWING?
She's sexy!! It's bold and well-drawn!
ERI KITAMURA-CHAN, WHO'S PLAYING THE ROLE OF THE COOL AND CUTE RIMA IN THE ANIME, DREW THIS ILLUSTRATION OF RIMA. I WANTED TO SHARE IT WITH EVERYONE. ♡
KITAERI-CHAN IS A VOICE ACTRESS AND A SINGER. SHE CAN ALSO DRAW, AND FROM HINO'S POINT OF VIEW, THAT MAKES HER A SUPER-WOMAN. THANK YOU SO MUCH!!
I love you.
I apologize for drawing with a ballpoint pen.
Sensei, I'm a real fan.
I'M GLAD I'M THE ONE PLAYING RIMA...!!

I'LL DO IT, ALTHOUGH IT DOESN'T QUITE FIT IN WITH THE MAIN STORY.

VAMPIRES COVERED IN BLOOD ARE PROHIBITED FROM ENTERING THIS PAGE!!

A LOOK INSIDE KANAME'S PSYCHE

KANAME?
CUTE
Kaname?
ADORABLE
HEE HEE
KANAME-SAMA!
HEE HEE
TAP TAP
BLUSH
KANAME-SAMA...
KANAME!
ICHIJO? HOW WILL SHE SAY MY NAME NEXT?
VLURG VLURG
THIS IS NOT THE TIME...

DAMAGE

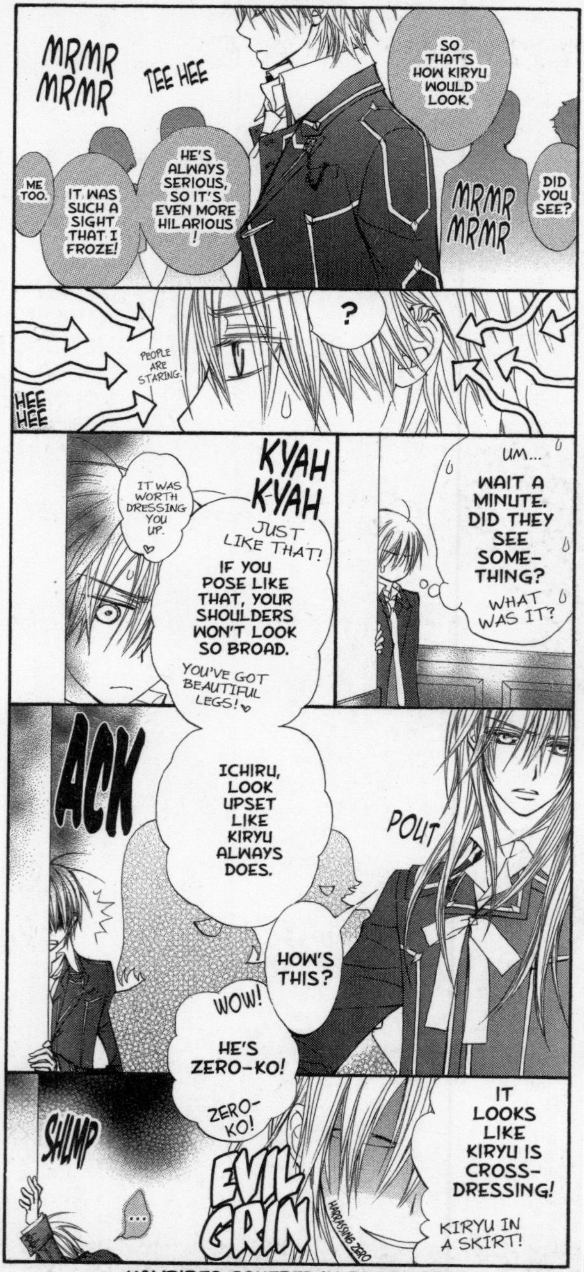
SO THAT'S HOW KIRYU WOULD LOOK.
DID YOU SEE?
MRMR MRMR
TEE HEE
MRMR MRMR
HE'S ALWAYS SERIOUS, SO IT'S EVEN MORE HILARIOUS!
IT WAS SUCH A SIGHT THAT I FROZE!
ME TOO.
?
PEOPLE ARE STARING.
HEE HEE
UM...
WAIT A MINUTE. DID THEY SEE SOME-THING?
WHAT WAS IT?
KYAH K-YAH
IT WAS WORTH DRESSING YOU UP.
JUST LIKE THAT!
IF YOU POSE LIKE THAT, YOUR SHOULDERS WON'T LOOK SO BROAD.
YOU'VE GOT BEAUTIFUL LEGS!
ICHIRU, LOOK UPSET LIKE KIRYU ALWAYS DOES.
POUT
ACK
HOW'S THIS?
WOW!
HE'S ZERO-KO!
IT LOOKS LIKE KIRYU IS CROSS-DRESSING!
KIRYU IN A SKIRT!
ZERO-KO!
HARRASSING ZERO
EVIL GRIN
SHLMP
...

VAMPIRES COVERED IN BLOOD ARE PROHIBITED FROM ENTERING THIS PAGE/END

I'm grateful to O. Mio-sama, K. Midori-sama, I. Asami-sama, H-sama, and my mother!

EDITOR'S NOTES

Characters

Matsuri Hino puts careful thought into the names of her characters in *Vampire Knight*. Below is the collection of characters through volume 8. Each character's name is presented family name first, per the kanji reading.

黒主優姫

Cross Yuki

Yuki's last name, *Kurosu*, is the Japanese pronunciation of the English word "cross." However, the kanji has a different meaning—*kuro* means "black" and *su* means "master." Her first name is a combination of *yuu*, meaning "tender" or "kind," and *ki*, meaning "princess."

錐生零

Kiryu Zero

Zero's first name is the kanji for *rei*, meaning "zero." In his last name, *Kiryu*, the *ki* means "auger" or "drill," and the *ryu* means "life."

玖蘭枢

Kuran Kaname
Kaname means "hinge" or "door."
The kanji for his last name is a
combination of the old-fashioned
way of writing *ku*, meaning "nine,"
and *ran*, meaning "orchid": "nine
orchids."

藍堂英

Aido Hanabusa
Hanabusa means "petals of a flower."
Aido means "indigo temple." In
Japanese, the pronunciation of *Aido* is
very close to the pronunciation of the
English word *idol*.

架院暁

Kain Akatsuki
Akatsuki means "dawn" or "day-
break." In *Kain*, *ka* is a base or
support, while *in* denotes a building
that has high fences around it, such
as a temple or school.

早園瑠佳

Souen Ruka

In *Ruka*, the *ru* means "lapis lazuli" while the *ka* means "good-looking" or "beautiful." The *sou* in Ruka's surname, *Souen*, means "early," but this kanji also has an obscure meaning of "strong fragrance." The *en* means "garden."

一条拓麻

Ichijo Takuma

Ichijo can mean a "ray" or "streak." The kanji for *Takuma* is a combination of *taku*, meaning "to cultivate" and *ma*, which is the kanji for *asa*, meaning "hemp" or "flax," a plant with blue flowers.

支葵千里

Shiki Senri

Shiki's last name is a combination of *shi*, meaning "to support" and *ki*, meaning "mallow"—a flowering plant with pink or white blossoms. The *ri* in *Senri* is a traditional Japanese unit of measure for distance, and one *ri* is about 2.44 miles. *Senri* means "1,000 *ri*."

夜刈十牙
Yagari Toga

Yagari is a combination of *ya*, meaning "night," and *gari*, meaning "to harvest." *Toga* means "ten fangs."

一条麻遠, 一翁
Ichijo Asato, aka "Ichio"

Ichijo can mean a "ray" or "streak." Asato's first name is comprised of *asa*, meaning "hemp" or "flax," and *tou*, meaning "far off." His nickname is *ichi*, or "one," combined with *ou*, which can be used as an honorific when referring to an older man.

若葉沙頼
Wakaba Sayori

Yori's full name is Sayori Wakaba. *Wakaba* means "young leaves." Her given name, *Sayori*, is a combination of *sa*, meaning "sand," and *yori*, meaning "trust."

星煉
Seiren

Sei means "star" and *ren* means "to smelt" or "refine." *Ren* is also the same kanji used in *rengoku*, or "purgatory."

遠矢莉磨
Toya Rima

Toya means a "far-reaching arrow." Rima's first name is a combination of *ri*, or "jasmine," and *ma*, which signifies enhancement by wearing away, such as by polishing or scouring.

紅まり亜
Kurenai Maria

Kurenai means "crimson." The kanji for the last *a* in Maria's first name is the same that is used in "Asia."

錐生壱縷
Kiryu Ichiru

Ichi is the old-fashioned way of writing "one," and *ru* means "thread."

緋桜閑, 狂咲姫
Hio Shizuka, Kuruizaki-hime

Shizuka means "calm and quiet." In Shizuka's family name, *hi* is "scarlet," and *ou* is "cherry blossoms." Shizuka Hio is also referred to as the "Kuruizaki-hime." *Kuruizaki* means "flowers blooming out of season," and *hime* means "princess."

藍堂月子
Aido Tsukiko

Aido means "indigo temple." *Tsukiko* means "moon child."

白蕗更

Shirabuki Sara

Shira is "white," and *buki* is "butterbur," a plant with white flowers. *Sara* means "renew."

黒主灰閻

Cross Kaien

Cross, or *Kurosu*, means "black master." Kaien is a combination of *kai*, meaning "ashes," and *en*, meaning "village gate." The kanji for *en* is also used for Enma, the ruler of the Underworld in Buddhist mythology.

玖蘭李土

Kuran Rido

Kuran means "nine orchids." In *Rido*, *ri* means "plum" and *do* means "earth."

玖蘭樹里

Kuran Juri

Kuran means "nine orchids." In her first name, *ju* means "tree" and a *ri* is a traditional Japanese unit of measure for distance. The kanji for *ri* is the same as in Senri's name.

玖蘭悠

Kuran Haruka

Kuran means "nine orchids." *Haruka* means "distant" or "remote."

Terms

-sama: The suffix *sama* is used in formal address for someone who ranks higher in the social hierarchy. The vampires call their leader "Kaname-sama" only when they are among their own kind.

Zero-ko: The suffix *ko* is used to make the name feminine.

Matsuri Hino burst onto the manga scene with her series *Kono Yume ga Sametara* (When This Dream Is Over), which was published in *LaLa DX* magazine. Hino was a manga artist a mere nine months after she decided to become one.

With the success of her popular series *Captive Hearts* and *MeruPuri*, Hino has established herself as a major player in the world of shojo manga. *Vampire Knight* is currently serialized in *LaLa* magazine.

Hino enjoys creative activities and has commented that she would have been either an architect or an apprentice to traditional Japanese craft masters if she had not become a manga artist.

VAMPIRE KNIGHT
Vol. 8
Shojo Beat Manga Edition

This manga contains material that was originally published in English in *Shojo Beat* magazine, January–July 2009 issues. Artwork in the magazine may have been slightly altered from that presented here.

STORY AND ART BY
MATSURI HINO

Translation & English Adaptation/Tomo Kimura
Touch-up Art & Lettering/Rina Mapa
Graphic Design/Amy Martin
Editor/Nancy Thistlethwaite

VP, Production/Alvin Lu
VP, Publishing Licensing/Rika Inouye
VP, Sales & Product Marketing/Gonzalo Ferreyra
VP, Creative/Linda Espinosa
Publisher/Hyoe Narita

Vampire Knight by Matsuri Hino © Matsuri Hino 2008. All rights reserved. First published in Japan in 2008 by HAKUSENSHA, Inc., Tokyo. English language translation rights arranged with HAKUSENSHA, Inc., Tokyo.

Printed in Canada

Published by VIZ Media, LLC
P.O. Box 77010
San Francisco, CA 94107

10 9 8 7 6 5 4 3 2 1
First printing, November 2009

PARENTAL ADVISORY
VAMPIRE KNIGHT is rated T+ for Older Teen and is recommended for ages 16 and up. This volume contains sexual themes and violence.
ratings.viz.com

www.viz.com

www.shojobeat.com